NAVAHO LEGENDS

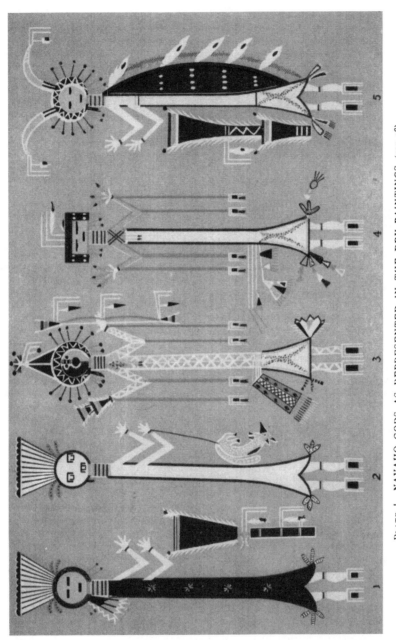

PLATE I. NAVAHO GODS AS REPRESENTED IN THE DRY-PAINTINGS (par. 98).

(1. *Hastséḥogan*[74] 2. *Hastsévalti*[78] 3. Dsaha*ḍoldzá*[209] 4. *Yébaad* (par. 78).[209] 5. *Gánaskĭḍi*[207]

NAVAHO LEGENDS

Collected and Translated by

WASHINGTON MATTHEWS

With Illustrations, Texts,
Interlinear Translations, and Melodies

Foreword by

GRACE A. McNELEY

Orthographic Note by

ROBERT W. YOUNG

University of Utah Press
Salt Lake City

Library of Congress Cataloging-in-Publication Data

Navaho legends / collected and translated by Washington Matthews,
  with illustrations, texts, interlinear translations, and melodies ;
  foreword by Grace McNeley ; orthographic note by Robert W. Young.
      p.   cm.
    Originally published: Boston : Houghton, Mifflin, 1897.
    Includes bibliographical references and index.
    ISBN 0-87480-424-8 (alk. paper)
    1. Navajo Indians—Legends.   2. Navajo Indians—Religion and
  mythology.   I. Matthews, Washington, 1843–1905.
  E99.N3N273   1994
  398.2'089'972—dc20   93-35973

CONTENTS

ILLUSTRATIONS

FOREWORD

Grace Anna McNeley

As a young Navajo student attending Western schools, I received my education from people who seemed to lack any knowledge of the Navajo way of life. These educators advanced the values of the *bilagaana,* the white man, emphasizing mastery of the English language and its use as a vehicle for communication, even with my own people. In contrast, my native tongue, *Dine bizaad,* was devalued as a language of no significance.

The alien values that were thrust upon me during those years are too numerous to enumerate here. Let the illustration of language displacement suffice to convey the magnitude of the substitution and, to the imaginative reader, the attendant anxieties we children experienced. Yet, as I trusted my elders to teach me how best to conduct my life, I also trusted the teachers of *bilagaana* culture—at least at first. As I grew to maturity, I began to observe that what the white man was teaching was not complementary to my native teachings; rather, it was an effort to assimilate me.

One factor that assisted the assimilation effort was the dearth of reading materials about native cultures, in this case material about Navajo life. I recall my attempts to find information about Navajo life in libraries for my assignments and finding none. Those I did find were often permeated with condescending or even pejorative tones. The image was not good. No wonder the white man wanted to "educate" Native Americans toward a different image—an image of himself.

I do not recall exactly how I happened to come across Washington Matthews. Here, in *Navaho Legends,* I read about Navajo

life for the first time, the mythology, the ceremonies, portrayed
as the people themselves, I know, live, tell their stories, and perform their rites. It was an account of a culture graced with honor
and dignity. The keepers of the great legends and ceremonies,
the *hatathli* or singers, were observed by Matthews as men of
intelligence and humor, with a generosity manifested in their willingness to share their knowledge with him.

At the time of its publication in 1897, *Navaho Legends* provided
an important new perspective for the reading public, which until
then had never been exposed to a positive account of Navajo culture. Matthews himself seems to have been aware of this when
he recounts in the introduction an earlier view of the Navajo
people offered by Dr. Letherman. This medical doctor at Fort
Defiance ventured that the Navajos had no religion, no knowledge of their origin or history, and that their singing was "but a
succession of grunts, and . . . anything but agreeable."

Washington Matthews provided both the foundation and stim-
ulus for much of the subsequent ethnographic work on Navajo
culture. His work may be considered the root and trunk of the
tree of knowledge about Navajo life from which later folklorists
and ethnographers have branched and from which they continue
to draw sustenance.

Who was this man, alone, it seems, in his powers of objective
description and his sensitivity to the inherent dignity and value of
Navajo culture?

WASHINGTON MATTHEWS, 1843–1905

In the following sketch, I draw heavily from Robert Marshall
Poor's unpublished thesis, "Washington Matthews: An
Intellectual Biography," completed in 1976 and available through
the University of Nevada, Reno. Those interested in further bio-
graphical information may wish to consult the references and
extensive bibliography at the end of Poor's treatise.

Washington Matthews was born 17 July 1843 in Killiney, a sub-
urb of Dublin, Ireland. Following the death of his mother,
Matthews's father, Dr. Nicholas Blaney Matthews, emigrated to
America with his two sons in 1847 and settled briefly in what was
then known as the Wisconsin Territory. Not long after, the family
returned to Ireland for three years, then crossed the Atlantic

once again, this time settling farther west in Dubuque, Iowa. Dubuque became home for Washington Matthews, where he received his schooling and then began medical studies in his father's office. He earned his medical degree from the University of Iowa in May 1864.

With the Civil War still in progress, Matthews served as assistant surgeon at a hospital for Confederate prisoners at Rock Island, Illinois. In May 1865 he was reappointed to the regular army and ordered up the Missouri to a string of military outposts. By August of that year Matthews found himself at the old trading post of Fort Berthold, where he became post surgeon for a small contingent of recruited former Confederate prisoners.

Fort Berthold held a special significance for Washington Matthews, for it was here that he came into close contact with Native Americans for the first time. These were the Arickarees, Grosventres (also known as the Minetarees and Hidatsa), and Mandans who, having been decimated by disease and war, had sought refuge from the hostile Sioux Nation. It seems that almost immediately Matthews began studying these people with a great deal of attention and commitment.

Matthews spent about two years at Fort Berthold, departing in 1867 for field expeditions under General Alfred Terry against the Sioux. During the years 1868–72, he reportedly served at Forts Stevenson, Rice, and Buford in North Dakota. His career as an army surgeon focused on attending to such general health issues as scurvy, venereal disease, diarrhea, pneumonia, and sanitary conditions at these frontier posts. He seems to have performed his duties as surgeon conscientiously.

Life at the forts demanded isolation from such social activities as one may experience in a city—invitations to dinner parties, meaningful conversation, lectures, and so forth. Matthews not only gathered ethnographic data on the Indians at Fort Berthold, but he also reportedly involved himself in marriage with a Hidatsa woman who is alleged to have borne him a son. His wife is said to have died of tuberculosis soon after giving birth. Reports of this marriage are based on records kept by one Margaret Schevill Link, who asserted to her associates an interest in writing a biography of Washington Matthews. Matthews himself apparently left no record of a marriage to "a Hidatsa chief's daughter" or a son named Berthold, as in the Link report. It is known that in 1877 he married Caroline Wortherspoon, daughter of an army doctor. This seems to have been a lifelong marriage, although, as Poor observes, Matthews does not mention her in any of his publications. Matthews had no children by Caroline.

Poor suggests that Matthews's evolution as a writer began with his accounts of daily frontier life and his encounters with people whose character gave color to these frontier posts. Poor cites a narrative about a French–Indian intepreter, Pierre Garreau, who spoke French as well as several Indian languages. Matthews apparently attended a council in which Garreau's interpretation had to pass through four languages—Cheyenne, Arickaree, French, and English—before it reached the intended party. Another Matthews description is of a man by the name of Charles Conklin, an "amusing swindler" without loyalty to anyone and who "knew it all." (A Navajo reader is reminded of Coyote in this characterization.) Matthews also left an impression of an old fur trader named John Brazeau whom he took in when the company the old man worked for was sold and Brazeau was literally turned out to die. The most notable character impression, which Matthews helped develop into book form, is that of Charles Larpenteur, a mountain man who entrusted his autobiography to Matthews to revise and publish in Larpenteur's lifetime. Unfortunately this schedule was not realized, but after extensive revisions with additional assistance Matthews had it published as *Forty Years a Fur Trader on the Upper Missouri.*

It was Matthews's work with the language of the Hidatsa Indians that secured his recognition as an ethnologist. According to Poor this work established the foundation for subsequent work on Hidatsa and related languages by such investigators as Lowie, Robinett, and Kennord. Robert Spencer, in his summary of the linguistic contributions made by Matthews, confirms that Matthews's account of Hidatsa grammar and philology is essentially correct. Two of them, *Grammar and Dictionary of the Hidatsa* and *Hidatsa–English Dictionary,* were published in Shea's Library of American Linguistics beginning in 1873. The *Ethnography and Philology of the Hidatsa Indians,* published by the U.S. Geological and Geographical Survey in 1877, is an expanded and definitive version of his Hidatsa material, which he continued to work on while stationed at Alcatraz military prison from 1875 to 1876.

Describing Matthews's work on the Hidatsa, Poor mentions

that these studies were for ethnographic "salvage," description of a native people's life as it was lived prior to the insurgence of alien ways. This work established Matthews as an authority on Indians, in the eyes of his contemporaries, and prepared him for subsequent work among the Navajo.

Several significant developments in the American Southwest set the stage for the arrival of young Matthews. Along with most of the present-day Southwest, the Navajo homeland had been secured from Mexico as a U.S. possession in 1848. Though the Navajo were then subdued militarily, culminating in 1864 in the Long Walk to detainment at Fort Sumner, they survived as a nation and on their return in 1868 regained much of their traditional land. By 1880 the Navajo had reestablished their subsistence economy and were again able to follow their lifeways in relative isolation. From an ethnographic point of view, a virgin culture lay in wait for the delight of whosoever would explore it. There were, it is true, several existing accounts of Navajo life, and contemporaries of Matthews were writing about the Navajo, but these accounts were often sketchy, ungrounded in primary ethnographic study, or perhaps even based on Matthews's work and confirming his reports.

Matthews, still in his late thirties, arrived at Fort Wingate in September 1880. He immediately began studying the Navajo language and acquainting himself with the local *hatathli*, establishing relationships with them as paid informants. He also assumed the acquaintance with such men as Frank Cushing, John Gregory Bourke, and Thomas Keam, all of whom apparently helped Matthews initiate his ethnographic work. During 1883-84 he submitted his first Navajo manuscripts, *Navajo Silversmiths* and *Navajo Weavers,* both published by the Bureau of American Ethnology in its second and third annual reports. During this time Matthews was also busy gathering materials for a grammar and dictionary of the Navajo language, data on ceremonial and related practices, and material for his next publications, *Navajo Names for Plants* and *Natural Naturalists.*

In the spring of 1884 Matthews was ordered to Washington but made arrangements for a brief return to witness an entire Mountain Chant, including the Night Chant and sandpaintings from which he made drawings. The publication that followed, *A Part of the Navajo's Mythology,* was his first substantive paper on

Navajo religion. But it was his publication of *The Mountain Chant: A Navajo Ceremony* in 1887 that brought Matthews fame as the author of the first complete description of an Indian ceremony. While assigned to the Washington office, Matthews continued his Navajo work, even bringing a medicine man, Tall Chanter, to Washington to work with him on Night Chant materials.

In 1890 Matthews began his second extended stay in the Southwest. Again based at Fort Wingate, Matthews continued gathering data on the Night Chant, the Navajo language, and music. Two years later he suffered a stroke, which forced him to retire from military life. He finally returned to Washington in 1895 at the age of fifty-two, bringing with him a great mass of material from which he shaped his major contributions, *Navaho Legends* and *The Night Chant: A Navajo Ceremony*. The latter has been described as probably the best tribal study ever published. Matthews received many honors and much praise during his retirement.

MATTHEWS IN RETROSPECT

It is somewhat ironic that Washington Matthews viewed his work as part of a salvage effort undertaken to preserve the vanishing cultures of native North America for science and posterity. For, although the Navajo Nation has indeed lost some of its ceremonies, and although there have since been major changes in Navajo life and culture, today the Navajo Nation continues to be blessed with its Tall Chanters—and the ceremonial healing system thrives. The Navajo language remains strong in homes and community gatherings and is resurgent in schools. Like Matthews a century ago, young Navajo bilingual and bicultural researchers are still able to go directly to the elders, particularly the singers, for traditional knowledge.

In retrospect, Navajo culture of a hundred years ago did not need to be salvaged by outsiders. Long before, the Navajo Nation had developed its own ways of preserving its sacred and cultural knowledge. The work of Matthews is now being utilized in ways he could scarcely have imagined, not only by *bilagaana* scholars in their continuing efforts to comprehend an "alien," living culture, but also by modern Navajos as a secondary source of knowledge to supplement that of their fathers and grandfathers.

The version of the Navajo origin legends in this book is now one of a number of such renditions, but its value persists in its richness of detail and its documentation of important aspects of Navajo knowledge from a hundred years ago. The reprinting of *Navaho Legends* is timely in providing enhanced access to a work that continues to hold interest for scholars in diverse fields of study and, increasingly, for Navajo people in our ongoing efforts to preserve and strengthen our cultural traditions.

NAVAHO LEGENDS

INTRODUCTION

PREFATORY REMARKS

1. THE legends contained in this book are those of the Navaho[1] Indians, a tribe living in the southwestern portion of the United States ; mostly in the Territories of New Mexico and Arizona, but partly in the States of Colorado and Utah. A definite reservation of over 12,000 square miles has been set apart for them ; but in every direction, beyond the borders of this reservation, isolated families and small bands may be found dwelling, either temporarily or permanently, in localities where there are springs, streams, pools, or artificial reservoirs of water. Some have taken up homesteads — or have otherwise acquired a legal title to lands beyond the borders of the reservation ; others are merely squatters. A brief description of these Indians — their arts, religion, ceremonies, etc. — is included in this introduction, in the belief that, if the reader possesses some knowledge of the Navaho before he begins to read the tales, he may have a better understanding of the latter. But much more information, of interest to the ethnographer, will be found in notes. Some items in the introduction could not properly have appeared in the notes, as there was nothing in the tales to suggest them. Other items might perhaps as well have been transferred to the notes ; the decision to put them in the introduction was often arbitrary.

2. *Title of Book.* — In selecting a title for this book, the word Legends was chosen, rather than Myths, for the reason that the tales contained herein, though mostly mythical, are not altogether such. In the Origin Legend, the last chapter, " The Growth of the Navaho Nation," is in part traditional or historical, and it is even approximately correct in many of its dates, as has been shown by Frederick Webb Hodge in his paper on the " Early Navaho and Apache." [301]

HOME OF THE NAVAHOES.

3. The land which the Navahoes occupy is arid, though not an absolute desert. The precipitation at an altitude of 7,000 feet

amounts on an average to only 14.10 inches during the year (at lower altitudes it is less, at higher altitudes greater), and this is generally confined to two short seasons of moisture separated from one another by months of absolute drought, which, except in specially favored localities, would destroy any of our ordinary field-crops. But there are small spots, far apart, where irrigation can be practised, and there are other places, apparently deserts, which no white man would think of cultivating, but where Indians raise meagre crops of corn, squashes, and melons.

4. *Soil.* — He who stands on the brow of the mesa at the Indian pueblo of Walpi, in Arizona, may unravel one secret of Indian agriculture in the arid region, and learn why ancient ruins may be found in the most desolate parts. Six hundred feet below him stretches a sandy plain which at most seasons of the year seems almost an absolute desert ; yet in summer it is green with rows of dwarf corn. Little rain falls on it and there is no irrigation ; yet the corn grows and furnishes a return which repays an Indian, at least, for his labor. Through the plain runs a gully which at certain seasons drains the water from a high table-land beyond. The water does not all flow off, but in part settles under the sandy surface, and keeps the subsoil moist throughout the year. By planting deep, the Indian farmers reach this moist subsoil, and place their seeds where the long drought cannot destroy them. On the side of the mesa, peach-trees flourish, with hidden moisture that comes out between the rocky strata at the mesa's edge. Localities similar to those described are found in the Navaho land, and similarly used by the Navaho for farms and peach orchards. The myths make frequent allusions to such farms or gardens.

5. A few fields have recently been made by white men in the high meadows of the Zuñi Mountains at altitudes above 8,000 feet, where potatoes, oats, barley, and garden vegetables are raised without irrigation ; but farming at such altitudes was never tried by the Navahoes, and they knew nothing of cultivating the crops named above. (Beside their aboriginal crops, they have for a long time raised a little wheat. Potatoes grow wild in the Navaho country.

6. *Mines.* — Fortunately for the Navahoes, no mines of precious metals have yet been discovered on their reservation ; although for years past rumors of such discoveries have from time to time been circulated, and unwelcome prospectors have frequently invaded their territory. For many years previous to 1892 the principal attraction lay in the Carrizo Mountains.[2] A legend of a mine called the Lost Adam, and of miners murdered in these mountains, had circulated long through Colorado mining camps. Troubles between intruders and Indians became so frequent and threatening in this

region that General McCook, then commanding the Department of Arizona, which included the Navaho reservation, determined to make an expedition and settle, if possible, the question of the existence of valuable mines in the Carrizo Mountains. A commission, consisting of Gen. A. McD. McCook, U. S. A., ex-Gov. John L. Barstow of Vermont, and Prof. J. G. Allyn of New Mexico, was appointed. The commission entered the mountains with a mounted escort in May, 1892, and invited prospectors who had previously visited the region to come and show where the mineral lay. They came, and then it appeared

Fig. 1.   Manuelito.

they had staked off various claims and given them felicitous names such as the western miners know how to coin, — the " Lucky Bill," the " Boggy Snoggy," etc.   Specimen ores were collected from every point where they were seen, and submitted to careful expert examination ; but all proved worthless.   Some fine gold has been found in the sands of the San Juan River,[3] within the Navaho reservation ; but it has not been found profitable to work for it.

7. *Surface — Forests.* — The surface of the country over which the Navahoes are scattered varies in altitude from 4,000 feet, or less, in the valley of the Colorado, to over 11,000 feet in the high peaks of Tsïsnadzïʹni,[52] San Mateo,[54] San Francisco,[56] and the San Juan [58] range, which traditionally border their land.   In the central and more thickly inhabited portion the highest eminence is in the Tuincha Mountains, 9,575 feet.   The average altitude is about 6,000

feet. The country consists mostly of great plains and of plateaux or mesas. While the lower levels, except in the bottom-lands of the constantly flowing rivers, are destitute of trees, the mesas, at altitudes of from 6,000 to 7,000 feet, are well covered with low forests of piñon (*Pinus edulis*), red cedar (*Juniperus virginianus*) and juniper (*Juniperus occidentalis*). At altitudes of 7,000 feet

Fig. 2. Mariano.

white pine (*Pinus ponderosa*) is sparingly found ; but at altitudes of 8,000 feet or more it grows abundantly and attains a good size. Spruce (*Pseudotsuga taxifolia*) is found in shaded valleys, and on northern hill-slopes above 7,000 feet, but it does not form an important part of the forest. It is an essential element in certain rites. Cottonwood (*Populus monolifera* and *P. wislizenii*), aspen (*Populus tremuloides*), oak (*Quercus gambellii*), oak-bark juniper (*Juniperus pachyphlœa*), and other trees grow less abundantly.

8. *Pasturage — Flocks and Herds.* — While the Navaho Indians cultivate the soil, it is evident, from what has been said, that they do not do so to any great extent. Their crops furnish but a small part of their subsistence. But their sterile country is fairly well adapted to the raising of sheep and goats. These form their chief food supply, and the former their principal source of wealth. With the money received for their wool they purchase flour and other provisions from the white traders, as well as various articles of luxury and utility. They possess many ponies and ride a great deal. They raise a few neat cattle.

9. As domesticated sheep and goats were unknown in America previous to the discovery by Columbus, and were unknown in New Mexico previous to the expedition of Coronado in A. D. 1540, it follows that the Navahoes have not been shepherds for many centuries. It would appear from their legends that it is not many years since they have become a prosperous and wealthy people (and such they now are, for savages) ; that in old days they were even poor hunters ; and that they lived largely on the seeds of wild plants and on small animals that they caught in fall-traps. How meagrely they were dressed and equipped the legends also tell us. (See pars. 382, 384, 391.)

POPULATION.

10. No exact census of the tribe has ever been taken, and it would not now be an easy task to take one, because the Navahoes are scattered so widely and over such a wild and rugged territory. Their low huts, built in tangled cedar-woods or in regions of scattered rocks, are often so obscurely hidden that one may ride through a cluster of a dozen inhabited houses thinking there is not

Fig. 3. Jake the Silversmith.

Fig. 4. *T*ánapa.

an Indian within ten miles of him. When the Navahoes were held in captivity at Fort Sumner, New Mexico, from 1863 to 1867, they depended for subsistence mostly on rations supplied by the United States, and then these captives, at least, could be accurately counted. There were in 1867 7,300 in captivity.[298] Owing to desertions on the one hand, and additional surrenders on the other, the numbers varied from time to time.

11. But while the majority of the tribe were prisoners of war, it is well known that all were not captured during General Carson's invasion in 1863, but that many still roamed at large while their brethren were prisoners. The count of the prisoners, therefore, does not show the strength of the tribe.

12. Perhaps the most accurate census ever taken was that of 1869. "In November of 1869 a count was made of the tribe, in order to distribute among them 30,000 head of sheep and 2,000 goats. Due notice was given months before, and the tribe was present. The Indians were all put in a large corral, and counted as they went in. A few herders, holding the small herds that they

Fig. 5. Hádapa (from photograph by J. K. Hillers).

had then bunched on the surrounding hills, were not in the corral. The result of this count showed that there were less than 9,000 Navahoes all told, making a fair allowance for all who had failed to come in. At that time everything favored getting a full count; rations were issued to them every four days; they had but little stock, and, in addition to the issue of the sheep and goats, there were also two years' annuities to be given out. The season of the year was favorable, the weather fine, and they were all anxious to get the sheep and goats and annuities." [268]

13. In 1890 a count of these Indians was made as a part of the Eleventh Census of the United States.[297] Before the count was begun, the writer was informed by one of the enumerators that the plan to be employed was this : The Navaho country was to be divided into a number of districts, and a special enumerator was to be sent to each district at the same time to visit each hut and take the number of each family. Whether this method was carried out, the report of the Eleventh Census does not tell us. But this plan, while probably the best that could be employed at the time with the means allotted, was very imperfect and admitted of numerous sources of error, of which two may be specified. Many huts might easily be passed unnoticed, for reasons already given, and this would make the enumeration too low. Many families might easily have been counted in more than one district, for the Navaho frequently shifts his abode, and this would make the count too high. The result of this enumeration was to give the tribe a population of 17,204 for that year. White men, living in the Navaho country at the time, generally considered the estimate excessive. If the count of 1869 be approximately correct, that of 1890 is probably not. It is not reasonable to suppose that by natural increase alone — and no other source of increment is known — the tribe should have nearly doubled in twenty-one years. It would require birth-rates much higher and death-rates much lower than those commonly found in Indian tribes to double the population in that time. The Indian mother is not prolific.

14. The Navahoes say that during their captivity they had much sickness and diminished in numbers ; but nothing has been found in official reports to corroborate such statements. All who have any intimate knowledge of the Navahoes agree that they have increased rapidly since they were restored to their ancient homes in 1869. During nearly fifteen years that the author has had opportunity to observe them, he has noticed no marked signs of physical degeneration among them. Their general health and their power of resisting disease appeared about as good in 1894 as in 1880. Consumption and scrofula, those greatest enemies of our reservation Indians, have not yet begun to trouble the Navahoes. The change from the rude hut to the close stone house, which is rapidly going on among this people, is likely to affect their health in the future, and probably not for the better. Fortunately for them, they have little fancy for stoves, but prefer open fireplaces such as the Pueblos and Mexicans use. In the year 1888, while the writer was absent from New Mexico, they had an epidemic of throat disease, the

precise character of which has not been ascertained. They say that about 800 people died that winter. During the winter of 1894–95 they suffered from scarcity of food, — an unusual experience for them, and the government had to assist them. An increased mortality ensued, which undoubtedly would have been much

Fig. 6. Navaho man (from photograph by J. K. Hillers).

greater had it not been for the prompt action of their agent, Maj. Constant Williams, U. S. A., in securing supplies for them.

RACIAL AFFINITY — APPEARANCE.

15. The Navahoes are usually regarded by ethnologists as being, by blood as well as by language, of the Dèné or Athapascan stock, and such, probably, they are in the main. But their Origin Legend represents them as a very mixed race, containing ele-

Fig. 7.   Navaho man (from photograph by Hillers).

ments of Zuñian and other Pueblo stocks, of Shoshonian and Yuman, and the appearance of the people seems to corroborate the legend.   There is no such thing as a general or prevailing Navaho type.   The people vary much in feature and stature.   Every variety of Indian face and form may be seen among them, — tall men with aquiline noses and prominent features, such as we find among the Crows and Dakotas ; dwarfish men with subdued features, such as we see among the Pueblos of New Mexico and Arizona, and every intermediate variety.

16. The countenances of the Navahoes are, as a rule, intelligent and expressive ; some are stern and angry, some pleasant and smiling, others calm and thoughtful ; but seldom are any seen that are dull and stupid.   These characteristics are to be noted among the women as well as among the men.   The social position

of the Navaho women is one of great independence; much of the wealth of the nation belongs to them; they are the managers of their own property, the owners of their own children, and their freedom lends character to their physiognomies.

17. Fig. 1 is a picture of Manuelito, who for many years was the most influential chief among the Navahoes. Latterly he lost much of his influence in consequence of his intemperate habits, though he was regarded as a sage counsellor till the time of his death, which occurred in 1893. When he was gone, an old Indian, announcing his death to the writer, said: "We are now a people without eyes, without ears, without a mind." Fig. 2 represents another chief of much influence named Mariano, who also

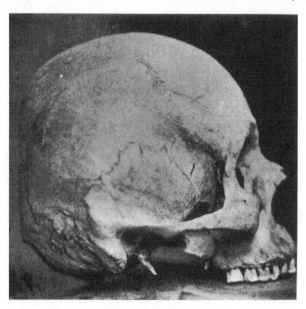

Fig. 8. Navaho skull, flattened at occiput. Hyperbrachycephalic.
Length-breadth index, 96.93.

became addicted to drink in his old age and died in 1893. Fig. 3 shows a very intelligent and trustworthy Indian, a silversmith, known as Jake among the whites, but called by the Navahoes Náltsos Nigéhani, or Paper-carrier, because in his youth he was employed as a mail-carrier between Forts Wingate and Defiance. He it was who communicated to the author version B [306] of the Origin Legend. He practised a short medicine rite, was an adept in singing sacred songs, and often led in song in the great rites. His silver-work was in great demand, and he worked hard at his trade. In 1894 he accompanied a circus through the Eastern States, with his workshop as a side-show; but the journey proved too much for him — he died of heart disease on his return to New Mexico. Fig. 4 is a portrait of a Navaho woman named *T*ánapa, who took

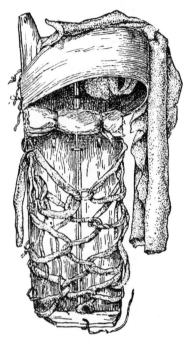

her hair out of braid preparatory to standing before the camera. Fig. 5 is a woman named Hádapa, whose smiling face is introduced as a contrast to the stern brow of *T*ánapa. Figs. 6 and 7 are Navaho men whose names have not been recorded. The expressions of their faces are in marked contrast.

CRANIA.

18. As a rule the crania of the Navahoes are brachycephalic, and very few are dolichocephalic. The shortening seems to be due to a flattening in the occipital region (fig. 8). The author is of opinion that this is caused by the use of the baby-case, with a hard, un-yielding wooden back (fig. 9), in which the Navaho women carry their infants. This flattening of the Navaho occiput has been the subject of some controversy. It

Fig 9. Navaho baby-case or cradle
(after Mason).

is true that the cradle is padded to a slight extent; but the padding consists of the bark of the cliff rose (*Cowania mexicana*), called by the Navaho awétsal, or baby-bed, which forms a rather rigid pillow. True, again, when the baby is carried on the mother's back, its head often hangs forward and does not come in contact with the back of the cradle or the pillow; but most of the time the child lies on its back, and its tender occiput is subjected to deforming pressure.

LANGUAGE.

19. The language of the Navaho undoubtedly belongs in the main to the Athapascan family. Hubert Howe Bancroft, in his "Native Races of the Pacific States" (vol. iii. p. 583),[292] tells us that the Athapascans or "Tinneh" are "a people whose diffusion is only equalled by that of the Aryan or Semitic nations of the

Old World. The dialects of the Tinneh language are by no means confined within the limits of the hyperborean division. Stretching from the northern interior of Alaska down into Sonora and Chihuahua, we have here a linguistic line of more than four thousand miles in length, extending diagonally over forty-two degrees of latitude, like a great tree whose trunk is the Rocky Mountain range, whose roots encompass the deserts of Arizona and New Mexico, and whose branches touch the borders of Hudson Bay and of the Arctic and Pacific Oceans." But the Origin Legend declares it is a mixed language (par. 395), and it is but reasonable to suppose that such a composite race cannot possess a very pure lan-

Fig. 10. Conical lodge with storm-door (from photograph by James Mooney).

guage. The various accessions to the tribe from other stocks have probably added many words of alien origin. What these additions are is not now known, and will not be known until all the languages of the Southwest have been thoroughly studied.

HOUSES.

20. The habitations of the Navahoes are usually of a very simple character. The most common form consists of a conical frame, made by setting up a number of sticks at an angle of about forty-five degrees. An opening is left on one side of the cone to

answer as a doorway. The frame is covered with weeds, bark, or grass, and earth, except at the apex, where the smoke from the fire in the centre of the floor is allowed to escape. In the door-way an old blanket hangs, like a curtain, in place of a door. But the opening of the door is not a simple hiatus, as many descriptions would lead one to suppose. A cross-piece, forming a lintel, connects the jambs at a convenient height, and the triangular space between the lintel and the smoke-hole is filled in as shown in fig. 10. A picture in Schoolcraft's extensive work [327] (vol. iii. plate 17) is intended to represent a Navaho lodge; but it appears to have been drawn by Captain Eastman from an imperfect description. In this picture the doorway is shown as extended up and continuous with the smoke-hole.

21. Some lodges are made of logs in a polygonal form, as shown in fig. 11. Again they are occasionally built partly of stone, as shown in fig. 12. In cold weather a small storm-door or portico is often erected in front of the door (fig. 10), and an outer and an inner curtain may be hung to more effectually keep out the wind.

22. *Shelters.* — Contiguous to the hut, the Navaho usually constructs a rude shelter of branches. Here, in fair weather, the family

Fig. 11. Hut of logs.

Fig. 12. Hut built partly of stone.

often cook and spend most of the day. Here, too, the women erect their looms and weave or set out their metates and grind corn, and some even choose to sleep here. Such a "corral" is shown in fig. 12.

23. *Summer Houses.* — In summer they often occupy structures more simple than even the hut described above. Fig. 13 represents a couple of summer houses in the Zuñi Mountains. A structure of this kind is built in a few hours. A couple of forked sticks are set upright in the ground ; slanting poles are laid against this in the direction of the prevailing winds, so as to form a windbreak, half wall and half roof, and this is covered with grass, weeds, and earth. The ends may be similarly inclosed, or may be merely covered in with evergreen branches. One side of the house is completely open. In fig. 13 a loom is shown set up for work in one of these rude structures, the aboriginal appearance of which is somewhat marred by having a piece of old canvas lying on top.

24. *Medicine-lodges.* — The medicine-lodges, when erected in regions where long poles may be cut, are usually built in the form of the ordinary hogáns (huts), though of much greater size (fig. 14). When these large lodges are constructed at low altitudes, where only stunted trees grow, they are built on a rude frame with walls and roof separate, somewhat on the same plan as the lodges formerly

Fig. 13. Summer houses.

used by the Arickarees, Mandans, and other tribes on the Missouri, and seeming a connecting link between the Navaho hogán and the Mandan earth-lodge.[184]

25. *Sweat-houses.* — The sweat-house or sudatory is a diminutive form of the ordinary hogán or hut as described in par. 20, except that it has no smoke-hole (for fire is never kindled in it), neither has it a storm-door.   It is sometimes sunk partly underground and is always thickly covered with earth.   Stones are heated in a fire outside and carried, with an extemporized tongs of sticks, into the sudatory.

Fig. 14.   Medicine-lodge.

Fig. 15 poorly represents one of these structures. When ceremonially used, the frame is constructed of different materials for different ceremonies, and the house is sometimes decorated with dry-paintings.[82]

26. *Modern Houses.* — During the past ten years, a few of the more progressive Navahoes have built themselves rectangular stone houses, with flat roofs, glazed windows, wooden doors, and regular chimneys, such as their neighbors, the Mexicans and Pueblo Indians, build. They have had before them, for centuries, examples of such houses, and they are an imitative and docile people. The reason they

Fig. 15. Sudatory.

have not copied at an earlier date is probably a superstitious reason. They believe a house haunted or accursed in which a human being dies.[91] They abandon it, never enter it again, and usually destroy it. With such a superstition prevailing, they hesitate to build permanent dwellings. Perhaps of late years the superstition is becoming weakened, or they have found some mystic way of averting the supposed evil.

ARTS.

27. The arts of the Navahoes are not numerous. They make a very rude and inartistic pottery, — vastly inferior to that of the neighboring Pueblo tribes, — and they make but little of it. Their bows and arrows are not equal to those of the northern Indians, and, since they have both money and opportunity to purchase modern firearms, bows and arrows are falling into disuse. They do not consider themselves very expert dressers of deerskin, and purchase their best buckskins from other tribes. The women do very little embroidery, either with beads or porcupine-quills, and this little is unskilfully done. The legends indicate that in former days they stole or purchased embroideries from the Utes.

28. *Basketry.* — They make excellent baskets, but very few of them, and have a very limited range of forms and patterns. In developing their blanket-making to the highest point of Indian art, the women of this tribe have neglected other labors. The much ruder but allied Apaches, who know nothing of weaving woollen fabrics, make more baskets than the Navahoes, and make them in much greater variety of form, color, and quality. The Navahoes buy most of their baskets and wicker water-jars from other tribes.

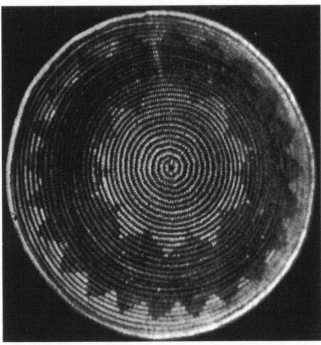

Fig. 16. Sacred basket.

Fig. 17. Sacred basket.

They would possibly lose the art of basketry altogether if they did not require certain kinds to be used in the rites, and only women of the tribe understand the special requirements of the rites. Figs. 16 and 17 show the patterns of baskets almost exclusively made. These are used in ceremonies, and are called by the author sacred baskets. A further description of them is given in a note.[5]

29. *Silver-work.* — There are a few silversmiths in the tribe, whose work, considering the rudeness of their tools and processes, is very artistic. It is much sought after by white people, who admire its rude beauty. Probably the art of the smith has not existed long among the Navahoes. In a treatise entitled " Navajo Silversmiths," [307] the author described the art as it existed in 1881 ; but the work has improved since that time with the introduction of better tools. Then the smith built his forge on the ground and squatted to do his work ; now he builds it on an elevated frame (fig. 10), and sits on a stool or chair to work. Fig. 18 represents silver ornaments made by Jake in 1881.

30. *Weaving.* — It is in the art of weaving that the Navahoes

excel all other Indians within the borders of the United States. In durability, fineness of finish, beauty of design, and variety of pattern, the Navaho blanket has no equal among the works of our aborigines. The author has written a treatise on "Navajo Weavers," [309] in which he describes their art as it existed some thirteen years ago. But since that treatise was written the art has changed. It has improved in one respect : an important new invention has been made or introduced, — a way of weaving blankets with different designs on opposite sides. It has deteriorated in another respect : fugitive aniline dyes, purchased from the traders, have taken the place of the permanent native dyes formerly used. In the finer blankets, yarn obtained from white traders has supplanted the yarn laboriously twilled on the old distaff. Navaho blankets are represented in figs. 1, 2, 5, 6, 7, and 12.

Fig. 18. Silver ornaments. Powder-chargers, hollow beads, buttons, bracelets.

31. The Navahoes weave diagonal cloth and diamond-shaped diagonals, and to do this a change is made in the mechanism of their simple looms. They weave belts or sashes, garters and saddle-girths, and these articles, too, require changes in the arrangement of the looms and in the methods of weaving. Fig. 20 represents an ordinary loom, with one set of healds. Fig. 21 represents a loom arranged for weaving diagonal cloth with two sets of healds. Fig. 4 shows a woman wearing a belt of native manufacture. The women depicted in figs. 5 and 21 wear dresses of Navaho cloth.

Fig. 19. Woman spinning.

32. It is not only for gain that the Navaho woman weaves her blanket. Having worn it for a time, until it has lost its novelty, she may sell it for a price that scarcely pays her for the yarn. One who possesses large herds, and is wealthy for an Indian, will weave as assiduously as her poorest neighbor. At best, the labor brings low wages. The work is done, to no small extent, for artistic recreation, just as the females of our own race embroider and do "fancy work" for mere pastime.

33. *Knitting.* — They knit stockings with four needles, but these stockings are devoid of heels and toes. As the needles now used are of wire and obtained from the whites, it might be thought that the art of knitting was learned from our people; but knitted leggings, made of human hair, and wooden knitting-needles, have been found in the Navaho land, in cliff-dwellings which, there is reason to believe, were abandoned before the arrival of the Spaniards.

INDUSTRY.

34. It cannot be said of the Navaho men, as it is often said of the men of other Indian tribes, that they are either too proud or too lazy to perform manual labor. They are, and apparently always have been, willing to do any remunerative work. When the Atlantic and Pacific Railroad was constructed near their reservation, in 1881, much of the grading was done by Navaho laborers. The white men who worked with them, and who had the strongest antipathy to Chinese laborers, said that they liked the Indians because they were good comrades on the work and kept up prices. A stalwart man is not ashamed to wash and iron clothes for wages, which he may want only to spend in gambling. They have been employed at Fort Wingate to dig cellars and make adobes, and at the latter work proved themselves more expert than the more experienced men of Zuñi.

35. Begging, which among other tribes is so often annoying to the white man, is little practised by the Navahoes. The few who have ever begged from the author persuaded themselves that they had some claim on him. On the whole, they are a self-supporting people, and add to the wealth of the community at large. But little government aid has been given them since they were released from captivity and supplied with stock in return for that slaughtered by our troops when their land was invaded.

POETRY AND MUSIC.

36. For many years the most trusted account of the Navaho Indians of New Mexico and Arizona was to be found in a letter written by Dr. Jonathan Letherman,[303] of the army, and published in the Smithsonian report for 1855. Dr. Letherman had lived three years at Fort Defiance, in the heart of the Navaho country, when he wrote this letter, and he acknowledges his indebtedness, for assistance in preparing it, to Major Kendrick, who long commanded Fort Defiance. Both the doctor and the major were men of unusual ability. The former (having changed the spelling of his name to Letterman) afterwards distinguished himself as medical director of the Army of the Potomac, and the latter was, for many years, professor of chemistry at the National Military Academy.

37. From this letter the following statement concerning the Navahoes is extracted: "Of their religion little or nothing is known, as, indeed, all inquiries tend to show that they have none." "The lack of tradition is a source of surprise. They have no knowledge of their origin or of the history of the tribe." "They have fre-

quent gatherings for dancing." "Their singing is but a succession of grunts, and is anything but agreeable."

38. The evidence of these gentlemen, one would think, might be taken as conclusive. Yet, fifteen years ago, when the author first found himself among the Navahoes, he was not influenced in the least by the authority of this letter. Previous experience with the Indians had taught him of how little value such negative evidence might be, and he began at once to investigate the religion,

Fig. 20. Ordinary loom.

traditions, and poetic literature, of which, he was assured, the Navahoes were devoid.

39. He had not been many weeks in New Mexico when he discovered that the dances to which Dr. Letherman refers were religious ceremonials, and later he found that these ceremonials might vie in allegory, symbolism, and intricacy of ritual with the ceremonies of any people, ancient or modern. He found, erelong, that these heathens, pronounced godless and legendless, possessed lengthy myths and traditions — so numerous that one can never hope to collect them all, a pantheon as well stocked with gods and heroes as that of the ancient Greeks, and prayers which, for length and vain repetition, might put a Pharisee to the blush.

40. But what did the study of appalling "succession of grunts" reveal? It revealed that besides improvised songs, in which the Navahoes are adepts, they have knowledge of thousands of signifi-

cant songs — or poems, as they might be called — which have been
composed with care and handed down, for centuries perhaps, from
teacher to pupil, from father to son, as a precious heritage, throughout the wide Navaho nation.   They have songs of travelling, appropriate to every stage of the journey, from the time the wanderer
leaves his home until he returns.   They have farming songs, which
refer to every stage of their simple agriculture, from the first view
of the planting ground in the spring to the "harvest home."   They
have building songs,[6] which celebrate every act in the structure of
the hut, from "thinking about it" to moving into it and lighting the
first fire.   They have songs for hunting, for war, for gambling, in
short for every important occasion in life, from birth to death, not
to speak of prenatal and *post-mortem* songs.   And these songs are
composed according to established (often rigid) rules, and abound
in poetic figures of speech.

41. *Sacred Songs.* — Perhaps the most interesting of their metrical compositions are those connected with their sacred rites, — their
religious songs.   These rites are very numerous, many of them of
nine days' duration, and with each is associated a number of appropriate songs.   Sometimes, pertaining to a single rite, there are two
hundred songs or more which may not be sung at other rites.

42. The songs must be known to the priest of the rite and his
assistants in a most exact manner, for an error made in singing a
song may be fatal to the efficacy of a ceremony.   In no case is an
important mistake tolerated, and in some cases the error of a single
syllable works an irreparable injury.   A noteworthy instance of this
rule is a song sung at the beginning of work on the last night of the
great ceremony of the night chant.   The rite is one which may cost
the patron from two hundred to three hundred dollars.   It has lasted
eight days and nights, when four singers, after long and careful
instruction by the priest, come forth painted, adorned, and masked
as gods to sing this song of the atsá'*l*ei.   Several hundred people —
many from the farthest confines of the Navaho land — have come
to sit up all night and witness the public ceremonies.   The song is
long, and is mostly made up of meaningless or obsolete expressions
which convey no idea to the mind of the singer, yet not a single
vocable may be omitted, mispronounced, or misplaced.   A score or
more of critics who know the song by heart are listening with
strained attention.   If the slightest error is made it is at once pro-
claimed, the fruitless ceremony terminates abruptly, and the disap-
pointed multitude disperses.

43. The songs all contain significant words ; but these, for poetic
requirements, are often greatly distorted, and the distortions must
be kept in mind.   In speaking thus, scant justice is done to the

Navaho poets. Similar distortions found in an Aryan tongue with a written literature are spoken of as figures of orthography and etymology, and, although there is yet no standard of spelling for the Navaho language, we would perhaps do well to apply the same terms in speaking of the Navaho compositions. The distortions are not always left to the whim of the composer. They are made systematically, as a rule. If the language were reduced to a standard spelling, we should find that the Navaho poets have as many figures of these classes as the English poets have, and perhaps more.

44. Some of the words, too, are archaic, — they mean nothing in modern Navaho ; but the priests assign traditional meanings to them, and this adds to the task of memorizing. But, in addition to the significant words, there are (as instanced above) numerous meaningless vocables in all songs, and these must be recited with a care at least equal to that bestowed on the rest of the composition.

Fig. 21. Loom for weaving diagonal cloth.

These meaningless sounds are commonly introduced in the preludes and refrains of the stanzas and in the verse endings, but they may occur anywhere in the song.

45. The preludes and refrains here referred to are found, with rare exceptions, in every stanza and in every song. Although they are all either totally meaningless or only partly significant, they are the most characteristic parts of the poems, and the singer cons the preludes over when he wishes to call to mind any particular composition, just as we often remember a poem or song by means of the first line. They are rarely or never quite alike in any

two songs, and great ingenuity is often displayed in giving them variety.

46. There is yet another burden laid on the memory of the singer of sacred songs, and this is the order of their arrangement. The songs of each ceremony are divided into groups which must follow one another in an established order, and each song has, in the group to which it belongs, a place that must not be changed under penalty of divine displeasure. To sing, during the progress of a rite, the sixth Song of the Whirling Sticks before the fifth song is sung, would be a sacrilege as great as to chant the syllables óhohohó, in place of éhehehé. To remember this exact order of sequence in a set of two hundred or three hundred songs is no easy task.[322]

47. But it may be said : "Perhaps things were different with the Navahoes in Dr. Letherman's day. May they not have learned from other tribes, or have themselves invented all this ceremony and song since he knew them?" The reply to this is, that it is absurd to suppose that such an elaborate system of rites and songs could have grown up among an illiterate people in the twenty-five years that elapsed between Dr. Letherman's departure from the Navaho country and the author's arrival there. Besides, the latter obtained his information from men of advanced age — from sixty to eighty years old — who practised these rites and sang these songs in their youth, and who in turn learned them from men of a departed generation. The shamans who conduct these ceremonies, tell these tales, and sing these songs are scattered widely over the Navaho country. Men who are scarcely acquainted with one another, and who learned from different preceptors, will sing the same sacred songs and to exactly the same tune. All the lore of the Navaho priesthood was undoubtedly extant in Dr. Letherman's time and for ages before.

48. *Songless Women.* — It is remarkable that, while the Navaho men are such fruitful composers of song and such ardent singers, the women, as a rule, do not sing. Among the wild hunting tribes of the North, as the author knew them thirty years ago, the women not only had songs of their own, but they took part in the ceremonial songs of the men. The Pueblo Indian women of New Mexico, neighbors of the Navahoes, have many fine songs, the song of the corn-grinders, often heard in Zuñi, being especially wild and musical. But usually the Navaho woman is songless. The writer tried a long time to find a woman who could sing, and offered good pecuniary inducements before he got one. She came from a distance of thirty miles. She knew no songs peculiar to her sex, but her father was a medicine-man, who frequently

repeated his songs at home in order to familiarize himself with them, and she gradually picked up several of them. She sang in a musical soprano with much spirit, and was one of the most pleasing singers heard in the tribe.

49. *Figures of Speech.* — It is probable that all rhetorical figures of speech known to our poets may be found in these simple compositions of the Navahoes. But in many cases the allusions are to such recondite matters of symbolism, or incidents in their myths, that they could be made plain, if at all, only by a tedious recital. Thus it would not be easy to make clear in a few words why, when the goddess Estsánatlehi, in one of the songs to her honor, is spoken of as climbing a wand of turquoise, we know the poet means to say she is ascending San Mateo Mountain, in New Mexico, or why, when he speaks of her as climbing a wand of haliotis shell, he is endeavoring to tell us that she is ascending the peak of San Francisco in Arizona. Yet we may gain some idea of the meaning by referring to the myth (par. 193).

50. But some of the metaphors and similes are not so hard to understand. Here is a translation of the Dove Song, one of the gambling songs sung in the game of kĕsĭtsé : —

> Wos Wos picks them up (seeds),
> Wos Wos picks them up,
> Glossy Locks picks them up,
> Red Moccasin picks them up,
> Wos Wos picks them up.[273] [316]

Here Wos Wos (Wōsh Wōsh) is an onomatope for the dove, equivalent to our " coo coo " ; but it is used as a noun. Glossy Locks and Red Moccasin are figurative expressions for the dove, of obvious significance. Metaphor and synecdoche are here combined.

51. Antithesis is not an uncommon figure with the Navaho poet. Here is an instance of it in a song belonging to the mountain chant, one of the great nine-day ceremonies of the shamans : —

> The voice that beautifies the land !
> The voice above,
> The voice of the thunder,
> Among the dark clouds
> Again and again it sounds,
> The voice that beautifies the land.
>
> The voice that beautifies the land !
> The voice below,
> The voice of the grasshopper,
> Among the flowers and grasses
> Again and again it sounds,
> The voice that beautifies the land.

Here the great voice of the thunder above is contrasted with the feeble voice of the grasshopper below, yet both are voices that make the world beautiful.

52. Many instances of climax have been noted. One here presented is from the mountain chant. It has but two steps to the ladder : —

> Maid Who Becomes a Bear
>   Sought the gods and found them,
> On the summits of the mountains
>   Sought the gods and found them,
> Truly with my sacrifice
>   Sought the gods and found them.
> Somebody doubts it, so I have heard.
>
> Holy Young Woman
>   Sought the gods and found them,
> On the summits of the clouds
>   Sought the gods and found them,
> Truly with my sacrifice
>   Sought the gods and found them.
> Somebody doubts it, so I have heard.

Maid Who Becomes a Bear (Tsĭké *Sas* Nátlehi) [90] is an important character in Navaho mythology. The last line in each stanza is an instance of irony.

53. It will be seen from the instances given that they understand the value of repetition in poetry. The refrain is a favorite form of expression ; but they know of other means of giving verbal melody to their songs, as may be seen in the following original text of the Bluebird (*Sialia arctica*) Song : —

> Tsi*h*ayilkáe *d*óla aní,
> Áya*s do*ʈlĭ′*z*i bĭza holó,
> Bĭza *h*ozónigo, bĭza holó,
> Bĭza holónigo hwíhe ĭnlí
> *D*óla aní. *D*óla aní.

To appreciate this a translation is not necessary, but it is given, as the reader may wish to know it : —

> Just at daylight *Sialia* calls.
> The bluebird has a voice,
> He has a voice, his voice melodious,
> His voice melodious that flows in gladness.
> *Sialia* calls. *Sialia* calls.

The regular Navaho name for the bluebird " *d*óli " (changed here to " *d*óla " for poetic reasons) is translated *Sialia*, to distinguish it from the descriptive term " áya*s do*ʈlĭ′*z*i," which means literally bluebird.

54. *Rhyme.* — They are not ignorant of the value of rhyme in poetry, but they more often produce this by the repetition of signifi-

cant or meaningless syllables than by selecting different words with similar endings. Still we often find this, the more difficult means, resorted to as in the above song of the bluebird.

55. *Music.* — To the casual listener it may appear that there is much sameness in the music of their songs ; but a more careful study will reveal the fact that the variety is great. It is remarkable how, with such rude instruments (an inverted basket for a drum, and a gourd rattle) to accompany them, they succeed, in a series of two hundred or more songs, in producing so many musical changes. In their sacred songs of sequence, where four or more songs of similar import follow one another, as is often the case, the music may be nearly alike (but never quite alike) in all ; but when the theme of the poetry changes, the music also takes a decided change.

56. For further information on the subject of music the reader is referred to note 272, which contains remarks by Prof. John Comfort Fillmore, formerly of Milwaukee, Wisconsin, but now of Claremont, California. Over two years ago the writer sent a number of phonographic records of Navaho songs to Professor Fillmore, who has diligently studied them and has written many of them in musical notation. Some of the musical scores are appended to the note.

TRIBAL ORGANIZATION.

57. *Gentes.* — The version of the Origin Legend by Tall Chanter, here given, accounts for only thirty-eight gentes among the Navahoes ; but this informant was able to name, in all, forty-three gentes, two of which, he said, were extinct. Lists of the Navaho gentes have been obtained from various sources, and no single authority has been found to give a greater number than this. But no two lists are quite alike ; they differ with regard to small or extinct gentes, and one list may supply a name which another has omitted. There would be at least fifty-one gentes extant and extinct in the tribe if each name so far obtained represented a different organization. But we find in the Legend instances of a gens having two names (pars. 386, 405, 428, 445).

58. On the other hand, it is possible that none of the lists may be complete. Gentes derived from women of alien races, added to the tribe since it has grown numerous and widely scattered, may exist in one part of the Navaho country unknown to the best informed persons in another part. Extinct gentes may be forgotten by one informant and remembered by another.

59. The following is a list of the forty-three gentes named by Tall Chanter : —

1. Tse‘dzĭnkĭ′ni,   House of the Black Cliffs (pars. 378–381).
2. Tse‘tláni,   Bend in a Cañon (par. 382).

3. Dsĭ'/naoĭ'/ni, Encircled Mountain (par. 385).
4. *H*askán*h*atso (*H*askan*h*atsód*h*ne'), Much Yucca (par. 386).
5. Na*h*opáni, Brown Streak; Horizontal on the Ground (par. 387).
6. Tsĭnadzĭ'ni, Black Horizontal Forest (par. 390).
7. *Th*a'nĕzá' (*Th*a'nĕzá'ni), Among the Scattered (Hills) (par. 392).
8. Dsĭ/tlá'ni, Base of the Mountain (par. 393).
9. *Th*á'paha (*Th*á'paha*d*ĭne') Among the Waters (par. 394 *et seq.*).
10. Tsa'yĭskĭ'*d*ni, Sage-brush Hill (par. 399).
11. Tse'zĭn*d*iaĭ, Trap Dyke (par. 401).
12. Klógi (Klógi*d*ĭne'), (Name of an old pueblo) (par. 403).
13. Tó'*h*ani, Beside the Water (par. 404).
14. *Th*á'tsini, Among the Red (Waters or Banks) (par. 405).

15. Kai (Kái*d*ĭne') Willows (par. 405).
16. Kĭn/ĭtsí (Kĭn/ĭtsíd*ĭ*ne', Red House (of Stone) (par. 406).
17. *D*ĕstsíni, Red Streak (par. 408).
18. Tlastsíni, Red Flat (par. 408).
19. No*t*á (No*t*ád*ĭ*ne'), Ute (par. 409).
20. Nakaí (Nakaí*d*ĭne'), White Stranger (Mexican) (par. 410).
21. *T*o'yĕtlíni, Junction of the Rivers (par. 411).
22. *H*áltso (*H*áltsod*ĭ*ne'), Yellow Bodies (par. 412).
23. *T*o'dĭtsíni, Bitter Water (par. 427).
24. Mai*t*ó' (Mai*t*ó'*d*ĭne'), Coyote Spring (par. 428).
25. *H*asĭ'zni (*H*asĭ'zd*ĭ*ne'), Mud (par. 429).
26. *T*o'dokónzi, Saline Water (par. 430, note 171).
27. Bĭ*t*á'ni, Folded Arms (par. 431).
28. Tsĭnsaká*d*ni, Lone Tree (par. 441).
29. Pi*n*bĭ*t*ó' (Pi*n*bĭ*t*ó'*d*ĭne'), Deer Spring (par. 442).
30. Tse'nahapĭ'/ni, Overhanging Rocks (par. 445).
31. *H*onagá'ni, Place of Walking (pars. 447, 448).
32. Ki*n*aá'ni, High Standing House (par. 458).
33. *T*o'ba*z*naá*z* (*T*o'ba*z*naázi), Two Come for Water (par. 449).
34. Nanas*t*ĕ'zi*n*, Black Horizontal Stripe Aliens (Zuñi) (par. 452).

35. *D*ildzéhi, (Not translated) (par. 453).
36. Á*s*ihi (Á*s*ihid*ĭ*ne'), Salt (par. 454).
37. Mai*d*ĕskĭ'*z* (Mai*d*ĕskĭ'zni), Coyote Pass (Jemez) (par. 455).
38. Tse'yana*t*ó'ni (extinct), Horizontal Water under Cliffs (par. 457).
39. *T*ó'tsoni, Great Water (par. 459).
40. Bĭ*t*áni or Dsĭ/*t*áni, Brow of Mountain.
41. Tse'yikéhe (Tse'yikéhe*d*ĭne'), Rocks Standing near One Another.
42. Tlĭzi*l*áni, Many Goats (par. 407).
43. *T*o'tsa*l*si*t*áya (extinct), Water under the Sitting Frog.

60. The following are eight names obtained from other sources, and not mentioned by Tall Chanter : —

44. Aatsósni Narrow Gorge.
45. Naa'í (Naa'í*d*ĭne'), Monocline.
46. Yóo, Beads.
47. Ka'náni, Living Arrows.
48. Tse'*th*áni, Among the Rocks.

49. *Lóka* (*Lókad´ne´*)   Reeds (*Phragmites*).
50. Tse‘*dĕ*skĭ´zni,   Rocky Pass.
51. *H*oga*n*láni,   Many Huts.

61. More than one translation of a gentile name has often been noted ; but in the above lists only one translation is given, — that which the author regards with the most favor. Often, too, different narrators account differently for the origin of the gentile names. Some of the translations are very liberal, and others, again, very brief ; but in the paragraphs and notes to which the reader is referred he will find fuller explanations. The Navahoes sometimes, but not invariably, add (as shown in the above lists) a suffix (*d´*iné‘, ni, *or* i), signifying people ; but in the above translations, to simplify the study, the word " people " is omitted.

62. There are reasons, which the author has set forth in a previous essay [318] and will not now repeat, for believing that most of the Navaho gentes were originally local exogamous groups, and not true gentes according to Morgan's definition.[325] There is little doubt that, in the majority of cases if not in all, the names of Navaho gentes, which are not the names of tribes, are simply designations of localities, even where the Legend states to the contrary ; as, for instance, when it tells us that certain gentes of the Western immigrants were named from words that women uttered when they first tasted of the magic fountains (pars. 427, 429, 430).

63. On the other hand, there are passages in the Legend which indicate that a few of the Navaho gentes were once totemic, although no evidence of clan totems is known to exist among the Navahoes at the present time, and it is not improbable that a few of the gentile names may be of totemic origin, although they are now accounted for in other ways in the Origin Legend. The passage (par. 419) which tells us that Estsánatlehi gave certain pets to the wanderers from the West, and that these pets accompanied the people on their journey, refers in all probability to the former use of totemic clan symbols, and possibly to a custom of keeping live totemic animals in captivity, — a custom prevalent among the ancient Mexicans and the modern Pueblos, though not among the modern Navahoes. Other indications of a former totemism may be found in the story of the Deer Spring People (par. 442, note 195 ; see, also, note 173).

64. In reading the fourth chapter of the Origin Legend — " Growth of the Navaho Nation " — one is impressed with the different degrees of willingness, on both sides, with which new gentes are adopted into the nation. In some instances two parties, meeting for the first time, embrace one another and become friends at once (par. 382). The clans from the Pacific coast — the Western immigrants, as they are here called — learn of the existence of kin-

dred tribes far to the east, take a long and dangerous journey to join them, and, when their march is done, they are received by the Navahoes at once as brethren. On the other hand, the legend tells us of bands that camp long in the neighborhood of the Navahoes before they become incorporated with the latter (par. 394); of other clans descended from captives (pars. 406, 454, 455); and of others that seek refuge among the Navahoes only to escape starvation or persecution at home (pars. 403, 452). On the basis of their mode of adoption, the clans may be divided into the ready and the reluctant. The cause of this is probably one of language. Bands which we know to have been allied in language to the Navahoes — such as those derived from the Apaches — will be found among the ready; while bands which we know to have spoken languages very different to the Navaho — such as those derived from the Utes, from Zuñi, and Jemez — will be found among the reluctant. It is not unreasonable to conclude that the same rule applies to clans of whose original language we know nothing.

65. *Phratries.* — The gentes of the Navahoes are divided into a number of groups, each of which may be called a phratry. Authorities in the tribe differ as to the number of the phratries, and as to the gentes that compose them. Some make but eight phratries. Captain Bourke [294] has obtained a list of eleven, with three independent gentes. Some of the Navahoes say there are twelve phratries, and suggest that they have some relation to the twelve tribes who dwelt in the first world. But the Navaho phratry seems not to be a homogeneous organization. A case is mentioned in the Legend where a gens has changed its phratral affinities (par. 451). Inquiry, too, has revealed that there are sub-groups. There may be closer bonds of alliance among some gentes in a group than there are among others in the same group. Authorities, then, may differ without invalidating each other's testimony.

66. These groups are indicated in the Legend when it says that one gens has become closely related or affiliated with another (pars. 385, 399, 403 *et al.*), or when it says that two gentes cannot intermarry (pars. 393, 401, 406). If the Navahoes have a term equivalent to "phratry," it has not been discovered. They have no special names for the different phratries; they often, but not always, speak of a phratry by the name of the most important gens in it.

67. If the Legend is to be taken as evidence, phratries have developed among the Navahoes both by segmentation of gentes and by the addition of new gentes from without; not by either method exclusively. But legendary evidence is not needed to show that gentes which bear to-day the names of alien tribes have been additions to the phratry.

68. *Forbidden Degrees of Kindred.* — A Navaho belongs to the gens of his mother and takes the name of that gens. Cases have been noted where a Navaho has been known by his gentile name and not by any other. No man may marry one of his own gens; neither may he marry one of his own phratry, though some exceptions seem to be made in the latter case where the limits of the phratry are not well defined. Where this descent in the female line exists among other tribes, it is held by some ethnographers that the man does not regard his father or his father's people as his relations, and may contract a marriage with a woman of his father's gens. Such is certainly not the case among the Navahoes. The gens and the phratry of the father are as much forbidden kindred as those of the mother.

RELIGION.

69. *Sources of Information.* — That the Navahoes have a religion — an elaborate pagan cult — has already been intimated. There is little to be gained by asking a Navaho direct questions about this. Learned controversialists and theologians, capable of analyzing and discussing their faith, have not arisen among them, or, if they have, they cannot easily communicate their philosophy to us. But the civilized scholar has abundant material from which to study their religion, and he must do the analyzing himself. In the great dry-paintings shown on the floors of the medicine-lodges, during their long ceremonies, may be seen pictures of many of the gods, with their hieratic belongings. In the ceremonies, or so-called dances, men are masked to represent gods. In the myths the acts and deeds of the divine ones are described, and we learn their thoughts and feelings, — kind, like Indians, to their kindred; usually cruel, yet often merciful and magnanimous, to their foes. In the countless songs of the rites may be found the poetic side of the divine characters, and in the long prayers we may learn their potency, and discover how man hopes to commune with them and gain their favor.

70. *No Supreme God.* — The religion of this people reflects their social condition. Their government is democratic. There is no highest chief of the tribe, and all their chiefs are men of temporary and ill-defined authority, whose power depends largely on their personal influence, their oratory, and their reputation for wisdom. It is difficult for such a people to conceive of a Supreme God. Their gods, like their men, stand much on a level of equality.

71. *Sun God.* — In the version of the Origin Legend here given, the Sun God would seem to have some precedence over the others, but in the beginning he was only one of the people; he never figures conspicuously as a Creator, and is far from omnipotent.

Other gods, less potent or less respected, lived before the time of
man, and were powerful before the sun was made.

72. *Creation.* — The Legend begins with an already created world;
there is no original creation and no Creator of all.   If the Navahoes
have a story of the beginning of all things, the author has not
learned it.   To a god called Békotsĭdi [78] is given the credit of having made all animals whose creation is not otherwise accounted
for in the myths, especially domestic animals.   Some of the Indians who have heard vaguely of our Creator are of the opinion
that Békotsĭdi is the God of the Americans.

73. *Estsánatlehi.* — But it is generally acknowledged by the Navahoes that their most revered deity is Estsánatlehi,[95] the Woman
Who Changes (or rejuvenates herself).   Much is said of her in the
legends, but something more is to be obtained by conversation
with the shamans.   The name Estsánatlehi is derived by syncopation from estsán, woman, and natléhi, to change or transform.   She
is so called because, it is supposed, she never remains in one condition, but that she grows to be an old woman, and in the course
of time becomes a young girl again, and so passes through an
endless course of lives, changing but never dying.   It is probable
that she is an apotheosis of Nature, or of the changing year.

74. The deity of fruitful Nature is properly a female and a beneficent goddess.   She is properly, too, as the legends tell us, the
wife of the Sun, to whom Nature owes her fertility.   Her home is
said to be in the west, probably for the reason that in the Navaho
country, which lies mostly on the Pacific slope, the rain comes
usually from the west, and from that direction, too, come the thaw-
ing breezes in the spring.

75. *Yolkaí Estsán.* — A divinity called Yolkaí Estsán,[96] or White
Shell Woman, created (or found, as some versions say) at the same
time as Estsánatlehi, is called the younger sister of the latter.   The
two goddesses are associated in the myths, but White Shell Woman
always acts the subordinate part, and to-day is honored with a less
degree of worship than her sister.   Estsánatlehi, made of an earthly
jewel, turquoise, is related to the land.   Yolkaí Estsán, made of
white shell from the ocean, is related to the waters.

76. *War Gods.* — Next in importance to Estsánatlehi, the sacred
brethren, Nayénĕzgani (or Nagénezgani) and To'badzĭstsíni,[127] seem
to stand.   The writer designates these as the War Gods, but the
Navahoes do not call them thus.   According to the version of the
Origin Legend here given, one of these was the child of Estsánatlehi
and the Sun; the other the child of Yolkaí Estsán and the Water, and
this is the version most consistent in all respects.   Other versions
make both the brothers children of Estsánatlehi.   Some say they

were born twins. Accepting any of these versions, they would properly be called brothers, according to the Indian system of relationship, and such they are called in the legends. Their chief mission
was to destroy the alien gods ; but they still help the warriors in battle, and aid the sick who suffer from witchcraft. The longest chapter
in the Origin Legend is devoted to recounting their genesis and
history. In reading the chapter, it will be apparent to the comparative mythologist that these characters have their counterparts, which
need not now be mentioned, in the myths of many races in both
hemispheres. From their mythic associations it would appear that
Nayénĕzgani is a god of light, with its associated heat, while *To'badʒïstsíni* is a god of darkness, with its associated moisture ; yet,
apparently in contradiction to this, the representative of the former
is painted black and wears a black mask in the ceremonies (plate
IV.), while the representative of the latter is painted red and wears
a red mask (plate VII.).

77. Nayénĕzgani, whose name signifies Slayer of the Alien
Gods,[127] is spoken of as the elder brother in the legends and always
plays the more important part. *To'badʒïstsíni*, or Child of the
Water,[127] is called the younger brother and always appears as a
subordinate character. In the ceremonies, the masquerader who
personates Nayénĕzgani always walks in front, while he who personates *To'badʒïstsíni* comes behind. The two gods are always associated in prayer and sacrifice, but here, again, Nayénĕzgani takes
precedence. In all the sacred songs where they are mentioned,
the superiority of Nayénĕzgani is indicated. Antithesis, as has
been said, is a favorite figure with the Navaho poets, and they
often employ it when speaking of these gods. The "Song of the
Approach" of the War Gods in the ceremony of klédʒi *hatál*
will serve, as well as many other compositions, to show how they
treat this subject. It may be freely translated thus : —

> He advances ! He advances !
> Now Slayer of the Alien Gods advances,
> Above, among the mountain peaks, he advances,
> In danger he advances.
>
> He advances ! He advances !
> Now Child of the Water advances
> Below, among the foothills, he advances,
> In danger he advances.

Thus both the gods come to the aid of the supplicant ; but while
the elder strides proudly on the summits of the mountains, the
younger walks humbly among the foothills.

78. *Yéi.* — There are a number of divinities in the Navaho pan-

Fig. 22. The White House. One of the houses of the yéi (from photograph by Hillers).

theon known as yéi (in compound words often pronounced ye or ge), which is translated "god" or "genius." What distinction exists between the yéi and other gods is not easy to determine definitely. The Zuñians have a class of gods called by the same name, or, more correctly, "yéyi," as Mr. Cushing pronounces it. Certain chiefs or important personages among these gods are called by names which begin with the syllables *hastsé* — as *H*astséyal*t*i [73] (Talking God), *H*astsé*h*og*an* [74] (House God). It is believed that this, if spelled etymologically, would appear as *h*astyé, but it is not so pronounced. *H*ast is a prefix denoting age, especially venerable age. We have it in the word *h*ast*í*n, which means a worthy or respected old man. *H*astyé would mean a venerable yéi or god. The yéi seem to be deities of minor importance to those previously mentioned and to be more numerous. Thus, while there is but one Estsánatlehi, but one Nayénĕzgani, and but one *T*o'bad*z*īst*s*íni there are several *H*astsé*h*ogan and several *H*astséyal*t*i, who are chiefs of the yéi. The yéi are supposed to abide in certain localities, and in prayers in their honor the home is mentioned of the yéi to whom appeal is specially made. A place called Tsé'nat*s*i, or Red Horizontal Rock, somewhere north of the San Juan River, Tse'gíhi, another place north of the San Juan, and the White House (fig. 22), in the Chelly Canyon, are important homes of the yéi.[265] Each of the sacred mountains has its group of yéi. In the myths of klédʒi *hatál,* more than a score of places are named where yéi dwell. There are some reasons for believing that the cult of the yéi is derived from the Cliff-dwellers, or from the Pueblos; but there are arguments, too, against this theory. The subject will not be further considered here. The yéi are supposed to be married and have families. The males are called yébaka; the females, yébaad.[200] *H*ast*s*é*z*ïni,[212] the god of fire, and *H*ast*s*éol*t*oi,[206] the divine huntress, or goddess of the chase, belong, as their names indicate, to the yéi; while Gá*n*askï*d*i,[207] the harvest god, and *T*ó'nenïli[98] Water Sprinkler, are associated with them in the legends.

79. *Dïgíni.* — *D*ïgï'n means sacred, divine, mysterious, or holy. It is not quite synonymous with the Dakota wakán or the Hidatsa hopá. It is not applied to the treatment of disease; it is not applied in a general way to religious ceremonial; it has not been heard applied to the aná*y*e, or other things of evil: for this reason it is often translated "holy." *D*ïgíni, derived from *d*ïgï'n, means holy people, gods, divinities. It is a name applied to the highest and lowest divinities, including the yéi (see notes 92 and 93).

80. *Alien Gods.* — Such are the gods that are friendly to the human race; but man has his enemies, too, among the mysterious powers. Chief among the latter are the aná*y*e,[7] the alien gods or inimical genii. These, being analogous to the giants and ogres of European folk-lore, are sometimes called giants in this work. They are usually represented as creatures of great size. Many of them are described in the Origin Legend. The worst have been slain, as the story relates; but others, being not unmixed evils, still remain to torment man. The legend, in accounting for their continued existence, shows the philosophic endeavor of our race to reconcile itself to the unwelcome inevitable.

81. *Water God.* — The position of Tiéholtsodi,[8] the water monster, is one of transferred allegiance. He was once the enemy of our race, but now has become friendly to it in certain ways, though it is probable that he is still thought to be responsible for cases of drowning. Other gods, who were once inimical to man but are now his friends, are mentioned in the legends (par. 354). But we are not without evidence that the Navaho fears to offend his most beneficent gods lest the latter may directly punish him, or at least withhold their succor in his hour of need.

82. *Devils.* — Besides the alien gods, there are evil spirits haunting the earth which men dread; these are the t*s*ï'ndi, whose name cannot be better translated than by calling them devils. The Navahoes frequently speak of the t*s*ï'ndi (Englished, chindee), and they often use the term as an angry exclamation, just as the profane among ourselves say, "Oh the Devil!" or "You devil!" (see pars.

257, 260), yet they dislike to discuss its character or appearance. They believe there is a devil associated with every corpse, and that it has something of the appearance of a partly decayed corpse. The spirit of the dead man goes to the lower world, which was the former home of the race, yet a demon remains with the dead body. Other Indians believe in a similar corpse spirit, yet the author has never known any who have such dread as the Navahoes of human mortuary remains. (See par. 188 and note 91.)

83. *Zoölatry.* — The legend tells us that there is a First Man and a First Woman (see pars. 160–165), who came into being in the fourth world as the result of a special act of creation : but they have not died like Adam and Eve ; they still live in some form ; they are potent ; they are immortal ; they are divine. But it is not man only that has his divine ancestral prototype : every animal on the face of the earth has its also, and many, if not all, of these are objects of worship. A share of reverence, too, in some cases, as in that of the bear, is bestowed on their mortal descendants. In the rite of the mountain chant [314] many of the sacrifices are sacred to the animals of the mountains. In short, zoölatry is an important element in Navaho worship.

84. *Local Gods.* — Some of the gods mentioned are also local divinities ; thus the War Gods are local divinities at *To'yĕ'tli* (par. 374), and the yéi are local divinities at Tsé'natṣi. But, in addition to these, there are other gods of places so numerous that a complete list of them will probably never be obtained. In the Origin Legend it is shown that each of the sacred mountains of the Navaho land (seven in number according to Tall Chanter) has its divine pair of indwelling guardians, and these seem to receive more honor than any others which are gods of places only ; but the genii of other mountains and of different rocks and canyons have their prayers and sacrifices in some of the rites.

85. Fanciful legends of places are common in all lands and among all races, but no people are more ingenious in composing such tales than our American Indians. The Navaho has unusual sources of inspiration in this direction, and he fails not to profit by them. His land abounds in wonderful geologic formations, in rocks strangely sculptured by rain and by Nature's sand-blast, in vast volcanic peaks and fields of lava ; and it abounds also, as might be expected, in myths accounting for these features, and in the genii which belong to the myths. A few of these myths are incorporated in the tales told in this work, but they are very few compared with the total of such legendary lore.

86, The strength of their belief in these local divinities may be illustrated by the following incident : The writer once made a journey, accompanied by two Navahoes, to Tsúskai[9] (Chusca Knoll), which is supposed to be the home of the Tsiké Sas Nátlehi, or Maidens who Become Bears. When the party got to the top of the ridge from which the knoll rises, and about three hundred yards from the base of the knoll, the Indians refused to go farther, saying they feared the divine ones who dwelt in the knoll. The writer proceeded alone, and had much difficulty in riding up the pathless hill, among loose rocks and fallen trees. On the summit he found a little hollow among the rocks full of sand, and, scraping into this, he discovered a number of handwrought stone and shell beads, which had been put there as sacrifices. When he descended from the knoll, he found the Indians awaiting him where he had left them, and all set out together to retrace the rough mountain trail down to Red Lake. In a little while, his horse becoming very lame, the writer was obliged to dismount. "What has made your horse lame?" asked the Indians. "He must have struck his leg against some of the fallen trees when he was climbing the knoll," was the answer. "Think not thus, foolish American," they said. "It was not the fallen trees that wounded your horse. The dígíni of the mountain have stricken him because you went where you had no right to go. You are lucky if nothing worse happens to you." Of course Indians had been up to the top of the knoll, or the beads could not have been put there; but they went only after preparatory prayer and only to deposit sacrifices.

Fig. 23. Talking kethawn.

87. *Demonolatry.* — There are writers who say that the Indians "worship the Devil" and other malevolent powers; but it is not only learned authors who speak thus. Jesus Alviso, a Mexican captive reared among the Navahoes, said to the author in 1880: "Los Indios hacen figuras de todos sus diablos, senor" ("The Indians make figures of all their devils, sir)," and it was this hint which led to the discovery of their dry-paintings. He called them devils; in this work they are called gods. Perhaps other tribes worship personifications of evil, but certainly the

Navahoes do not. The gods who are supposed to love and help men the most receive the greatest honor. The evil spirits are not worshipped except, rumor says, by the witches. It would appear, moreover, from the Origin Legend, that the worst of evil powers — the alien gods — were long ago destroyed, and that only demons of minor influence remain. The chief of witches, Estsán Na*tán*, or Woman Chief, has her home beneath the earth, in one of the lower worlds.

CEREMONIES.

88. A great number of ceremonies are practised by the Navaho priests. Many of these are of nine days' duration ; there are others that last but a single day or a few hours. To learn one of the great

Fig. 24.   Circle kethawn.

rites so as to become its *hatáli* (chanter, singer),[16] or priest, is the work of many years, and no one knows more than one such rite perfectly. The older priests know something of other rites, may assist at them and sing songs at them, but are not competent to conduct them. A priest of a great rite may know some of the lesser rites.

89. All the great ceremonies which the writer has witnessed among the Navahoes are primarily for the healing of the sick ; but the occasion is always used to ask the gods for various temporal

blessings, not only for the sick person but for all, — the shaman, the relations of the sick, and for the people in general. The invalid, for whose benefit the rite is performed, defrays all the expenses of the ceremony, which often amount in value to the sum of two hundred or three hundred dollars. The Navahoes being a scattered and to some extent a wandering people who do not build towns, they lack the organization to have rites of a more public character, such as the village Indians have.[184] Hence these healing ceremonies, in which the sick man and his relations become hosts, are used as occasions for prayer for the common weal, and as occasions in which large numbers may assemble to witness interesting exhibitions and have the social enjoyments which attend the gathering of a crowd.

90. *Minor Ceremonies.* — Among the minor ceremonies, besides those for healing the sick, are those of planting, harvesting, building, war, nubility, marriage, travel, and many other occasions in life. In addition to these, there are ceremonies for special occasions, as for bringing rain. During an unusually dry season a number of Navahoes may subscribe together and raise a good fee for a priest to sing, pray, sacrifice, and conduct a ceremony to bring rain.

91. *Origin of Ceremonies.* — The late Mr. A. M. Stephen of Arizona, who for many years studied the rites and myths of both Mokis and Navahoes, has often called the attention of the writer to the many resemblances between the cults of these two tribes, who differ so much in other respects, and he has suggested that the Navahoes may have borrowed from the Mokis. This may be the case, for the Navahoes have, probably, people of Moki descent among them, and they have had intercourse with the Mokis, both peaceful and warlike, for a long time. But, throughout all the Navaho legends so far collected, it is strongly indicated that the Navaho cultus, where borrowed, came from cliff-dwellers, from inhabitants of pueblos now deserted, and from wild tribes. The Mokis figure but little in the Navaho rite-myths. The author is inclined to believe that the Navahoes have not borrowed much directly from the Mokis, but that both tribes have taken inspiration from common sources. In radical points of symbolism, such as the sacred colors and the ceremonial circuit, the Navaho and Moki rites differ widely.

92. *Elements of Ceremonies.* — In the ceremonies there are numerous minor acts of such diverse character that they cannot be classified and are not described in this work. They can be discussed better in connection with the rites to which they belong. There are other acts of minor importance, such as the ceremonial bath [10] [82] and the administration of pollen,[11] which are considered in

the notes. But there are six elements of the worship which constitute such important parts in all the great rites that brief descriptions of them are presented in this introduction. These six are : Sacrifice, painting, masquerade, dance, prayer, and song. The last has been already discussed (par. 41 *et seq.*).

93. *Sacrifices.* — The sacrifices of the Navahoes are innocent and bloodless. Their kindly gods are easily propitiated. Like their worshippers, they are all fond of tobacco, and they prize a few feathers and beads. Even the chief war god demands no smoking hearts or blood of captives ; a little painted cigarette is all he asks in return for his favors. An extensive chapter might be written about the sacrificial cigarettes and sticks which the Navahoes call ket*á*n (Englished, kethawn), but a short description of them must suffice here. (See note 12.)

94. *Cigarettes.* — The cigarettes are usually made of the hollow joints of the common reed (*Phragmites communis*), but other plants are sometimes used. To form a cigarette, a piece of the reed is cut off with a stone knife, the node being excluded ; it is rubbed with sandstone, so that the paint may adhere ; it is painted with some symbolical device ; a wad of feathers is inserted into it to keep the tobacco from falling out ; it is filled with some kind of native tobacco,[223] usually the *Nicotiana attenuata*, or dsï*'*/na*t*o of the Navahoes ; it is sealed with moistened pollen and symbolically lighted with a rock crystal, which is held up to the sky and touched to the tip of the cigarette. After it has been prayed over it is taken out and left for — *i. e.*, sacrificed to — the god for whom it is intended. The god, they say, recognizes it by its symbolic painting and by the place where it is sacrificed. He picks it up, smells and examines it. If he is satisfied that it is properly made and that it is for him, he takes it and bestows on the supplicant the favors asked.

95. *Sacrificial Sticks.* — Besides the cigarettes, small sticks are used as sacrifices to the gods. These are made from a variety of woods, — different gods and different occasions requiring woods of different sorts, — and they are painted in a variety of ways for the same reasons. They are usually made in pairs, one for the male and the other for the female. Celibacy is not practised by the Navaho gods ; every deity has its mate, and she must be propitiated as well as he. The female is distinguished in some way from the male, and this is usually done by cutting a small facet at the tip end of the female stick (see fig. 23), to represent the square mask worn by one who masquerades as a goddess in the ceremonies. He who appears as a god wears a round cap-like mask (fig. 27), and the round cut end of the stick sufficiently represents this.

96. Often the feathers of different kinds of birds are sacrificed

Fig. 25. Kethawns (sacrificial sticks and cigarettes) in sacred
basket, ready for sacrifice.

with the kethawns, either attached to the latter or separate; also
beads of stone or shell and various kinds of powdered vegetable and
mineral substances, including pollen,[11] which is the most sacred substance employed by the Navaho priests.

97. *Disposal of Kethawns.* — The different ways in which kethawns are deposited or sacrificed are as numerous as are their forms,
materials, and decorations, and each way has its special symbolism.
Some are laid in the branches of a tree, others among rocks, others
at the base of a cliff, others, again, at the root of a tree, and others
on level ground; a few are thrown away almost at random, but most
of them are laid down with care and with rigorous ceremonial form.
All that are laid with care are placed with their tips away from the
lodge, and each is destined to go toward some particular point of the
compass. When the bearer of the sacrifice leaves the lodge, he proceeds in the direction of the place selected for the sacrifice; when
he has deposited it he turns to the right and takes a sunwise direction in returning. He does not cross his outgoing trail; he must
not walk through an ant-hill; he must run both going and coming.[12]

98. *Ceremonial Pictures.* — The pictures accompanying the Navaho
rites are among the most transitory in the history of art. In previous essays the author has called them dry-paintings. Similar

works have been observed among other tribes, both nomadic and sedentary, and the observers have designated them as " sand-paint-ings," " sand-altars," etc.   They are drawn in all the great rites, and even in some of the lesser rites — those of only one day's duration — small but handsome dry-paintings are sometimes made.   They vary in size from four to twelve feet in diameter.   Sometimes the fire in the centre of the medicine-lodge must be removed in order to accommodate them.   The groundwork is sand, which is conveyed in blankets into the medicine-lodge, and spread out over the floor to the depth of about three inches.   It is smoothed with the broad oaken battens used in weaving.

99. Before the sand is brought in, the pigments are ground to powder and put on broad pieces of pine bark, which serve as trays — or palettes, shall we say?   The pigments are five in number, — white, red, yellow, black, and gray.   The white, red, and yellow are made of sandstone.   The black is made of powdered charcoal, with which a little sandstone is mixed to facilitate the grinding and give weight to the powder.   The gray, made of black and white mixed in suitable proportions, is intended to represent blue, is called blue by the Navahoes, and, combined with the other colors, has the effect of blue in the paintings.   It will be spoken of as blue in the subsequent descriptions.   The Navahoes use indigo and a native bluish mineral pigment to paint masks, kethawns, and other small objects ; but for the dry-paintings such a large quan-tity is needed that these would be too expensive.   To apply the colored powder, a pinch of it is taken up between the thumb and first two fingers and allowed to fall slowly on the sand, while the thumb is moved over the fingers.

100. To paint one of these large pictures may require the labor of several men — a dozen sometimes — working from early morn-ing till late in the afternoon.   The picture must be finished before dark, for it is impracticable to work on it with such artificial lights as the Indians can command.   While the work is in progress the priest who conducts the ceremonies does little more than direct and criticise.   The operators have received a certain initiation. They have seen the picture painted before and are familiar with its details.   If an error is made the faulty part is not erased ; sand is spread on it to obliterate it, and the corrected drawing is made on the new deposit of sand.   The pictures are drawn according to exact and established rules.   Some parts are measured by palms and spans, and not a line of the sacred designs may be varied in them. In drawing straight lines the colored powder is poured over a tight-ened cord.   But in a few cases the artist is allowed to indulge his fancy, thus, in drawing the embroidered pouches which the gods

wear suspended at the waist (plate I.), the limner may, within certain limits, give his god as handsome a pouch as he wishes and embroider it to suit his notion. The naked forms of the mythical characters are drawn first and then the clothing and ornaments are laid on.

101. When the picture is finished a number of ceremonies (differing somewhat in different rites) are performed over it. Pollen or corn-meal may be placed on certain parts of the sacred figures, and one of these substances may be scattered over it. Water or medicinal infusions may be applied to it. At length the patient is brought in and placed sitting on the picture. Moistening his palms, the shaman or an assistant takes the colored dust from various parts of the divine figures and applies it to similar parts of the subject's body. Medicine is then usually administered in four draughts. When the patient leaves, others in the lodge who are ill, or fancy themselves ill, take dust on their palms from the picture and apply it to their own persons. He who has headache takes dust from the head in the picture and applies it to his own head. He who has sore feet takes dust from the pictured feet. When all are done the picture is badly marred ; it is then totally obliterated, — the method and ceremony of obliteration differing in different rites, — and the sand on which it was drawn is taken out of the lodge and thrown away. The floor on the lodge is swept, and the uninitiated, entering a moment later, has no evidence of what has taken place.

102. Plate I. shows pictures of five different gods as they appear separately in the dry-paintings. Figure 29 represents, in black, a complete painting (the original of which was done in five different colors) from the rite of the klédẓi *hatál,* or the night chant. It will be observed that some of the gods or yéi of plate I. are to be seen in fig. 29.

103. The medicine-men declare that these pictures have been transmitted from teacher to pupil, unchanged in all the years since they were revealed to the prophets of the rites. There are good reasons for believing that this is not strictly true : the majority of the great ceremonies may be performed only during the coldest part of the year, — the months when the snakes are dormant. No permanent copies of the pictures were ever preserved until the author painted them ; they were carried from season to season in the memories of men, and there was no final authority in the tribe to settle questions of correctness. But it is probable that changes, if they occurred, were unintentional and wrought slowly. After the writer made copies of these pictures, and it became known to the medicine-men that he had copies in his possession, it was not uncommon for the shamans, pending the performance of a ceremony, to bring young men who were to assist in the lodge, ask to see the

Fig. 26.   Mask of yucca.

paintings, and lecture on them to their pupils, pointing out the
various important points, and thus, no doubt, saving mistakes and
corrections in the medicine-lodge.   The water-color copies were
always (as the shamans knew) kept hidden at the forbidden season,
and never shown to the uninitiated of the tribe.

104. *Masquerade.* — In the rites, men appear representing gods
or other mythic characters.   Sometimes such representations are
effected by means of paint and equipment only, as in the case of
the akáninili, or messenger of the mountain chant,[314] who is dressed
to represent the prophet Dsï'lyi Neyáni as he appeared after the
Butterfly Goddess had transformed him ; but on other occasions
masks are added to the dress, as in the rites of the night chant.
In this there are twenty-one masks,[267] made of sacred buckskin,[13]
for representatives of the gods to wear, besides a mask of yucca
leaves [14] trimmed with spruce twigs (fig. 26), which the patient
wears on one occasion.   The buckskin masks, without plumes or
collars, are kept in a sack by the shaman, and he carries them on
horseback to the place where the rites are to be performed ; there

they are freshly painted, and the collars and plumes are added just
before they are to be used in the ceremony.

105. Plates IV. and VII. show the masks as they are actually
worn, and exhibit men as they are dressed and painted to represent the War Gods. In plate I. we get representations of these
masks as they are depicted in the dry-paintings. Fig. 27 shows
the mask of *H*ast*s*éyal*i*, the Talking God, as it appears when all
is ready for the dance, with plume and collar of fresh spruce twigs
applied. Fig. 28 depicts the mask of a yébaad, or female yéi. The
female masks cover only the face, leaving the hair free. The male
masks (fig. 27) cover the entire head, concealing the hair.

106. When a man is dressed in his godly costume he does not
speak ; he only makes motions and utters a peculiar cry, — each god
has his own special cry, — and he may perform acts on the patient
with his special weapon or talisman. The masquerader, they say,
is, for the time being, no longer a Navaho, but a god, and a prayer to
him is a prayer to a god. When he enters the lodge and sits down
before the sick man, the latter hands him his sacrifice and prays to
him devoutly, well knowing that it may be his own uncle or cousin,
disguised in the panoply of divinity, who receives the sacrifice.

Fig. 27. Mask of *H*ast*s*éyal*i*.

107. *Dance.* — It has been customary with travellers to speak of Indian ceremonials as dances. This is chiefly for the reason that the dance most attracts the attention of white men, and the other portions of the work are likely to pass unheeded. Dancing is rarely the most important element of an Indian ceremonial, and among the Navahoes it is always a minor element. In some of the lesser rites it does not occur at all. In the nine days' cere-

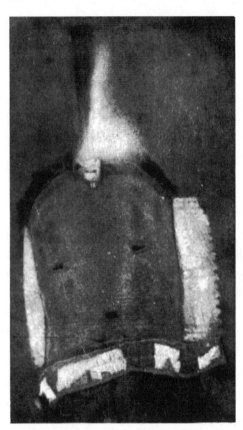

Fig. 28.   Mask of yébaad or goddess.

mony of the mountain chant it occurs only on the last night, and then forms but a part of the show, — rude dramatic performances and feats of legerdemain (see fig. 30) occupying about an equal time until the entertainment ends, soon after dawn. In the nine days' ceremony of the night chant, dancing as a part of the ceremony is confined to the last night, although undress rehearsals of the dance take place after sunset for a few days before.

108. These dances of the Navaho, although accompanied with religious symbolism, and performed often by men wearing sacred costumes, are undoubtedly intended largely to entertain the spectators. While but a few people may be present during the first eight or nine days of a great ceremony, a large crowd always gathers to witness the performances of the last night, and many people stay up all night to do this. On the last night of the mountain chant the dances are picturesque and various. Many of them are borrowed from other rites. They have been described by the author in a previous work. On the last night of the night chant the dance and song vary but little, and to the ordinary observer may seem not to vary at all. Yet the spectators who come to the mountain chant are not more wakeful and watchful than those who come to the night chant. The

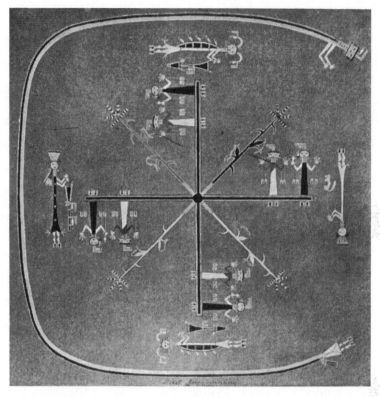

Fig. 29. Picture of *ṣi*/néole, a dry-painting of the night chant.

dancing is always rhythmical and well-timed. Figures are often introduced like those of our quadrilles; but no round dances, like our
waltz or polka, have been observed — the rough ground is not suited
for such. The dancers and the drummers practise long in private
before coming to the public exhibition.

109. *Prayer.* — In a paper entitled "The Prayer of a Navaho
Shaman," [315] the author has published a long composition, called a
prayer by the man from whom he received it, which is a simple narrative and does not contain a word of supplication. This is the only
prayer of such character obtained from a Navaho. Many other long
prayers have been recorded, all of which are formed on a common
plan. The name of a god is mentioned, and some flattering attri-
butes are given to him. If it is a god such as *H*astséyal*t*i, of which
there are more than one of the same name, his residence is mentioned. He is informed that sacrifices have been prepared for him.
He is asked to remove the spell of disease. Immediately he is
assured that it is removed. Then he is asked to bestow various
blessings on the supplicant and all his kindred and people. The

prayer is given out, one sentence at a time, by the shaman, and the patient repeats it after him, sentence by sentence.

110. These prayers, repeated by two voices, sound much like litanies, and all end with an expression (*hozóna hastlé*) analogous to the amen of Christian prayers, four times repeated; yet the Navaho prayers show in their spirit no indication of the influence of Christian teaching. They are purely pagan compositions. The only evidence of any modern influence they present is the occasional inclusion of a request for increase of wealth in the shape of horses and sheep. A typical Navaho prayer from the rites of klédɀi *hatál* is given in note 288.

111. Besides these long prayers, repeated by two persons, the shamans have many monologue prayers; there are prayers silent and vocal, formulated and extempore, used by both priest and layman; and there are short devotional sayings which may be classed as benedictions and ejaculations.

THE LEGENDS.

112. Of the many lengthy myths and legends obtained by the author from the Navahoes, three have been selected for publication in this volume. The first is the Origin Legend of the tribe; the other two are incomplete rite-myths, *i. e.*, rite-myths told by men who were not priests of the associated rites.

113. *Versions.* — As might be expected among an unlettered people, thinly scattered over a wide territory, the legends of the Navahoes have many variants. No two men will tell the same tale exactly alike, and each story-teller will probably maintain that his own version is the only reliable one. Variations of the Origin Legend, which is the property of the tribe at large, and, unlike the rite-myths, is not in the keeping of any especial order or priesthood, are particularly numerous; but even in the rite-myths, as told by priests of the rites, versions may be found. Notwithstanding these varieties, the tale-tellers agree substantially in the more important matters. Of the two rite-myths given in this work, only one version of each was procured; but several versions of the Origin Legend, complete or partial, were recorded. The one here published was selected as being the most complete, extensive, and consistent of all. Other versions often supplement it. The narrators sometimes acknowledged that they had forgotten episodes which others had remembered and detailed. The learned old shaman, *Hatáli* Něz, forgot to tell how the stars were made; while a younger and less erudite person, Jake the silversmith, related a fair version of this episode, which came also from other sources to the writer. Jake's version of the Legend, which has already been published, is desig-

nated in the notes as Version B ; [306] that of old Torlino, a priest of the *hozóni hatál,* is designated as Version A. Other versions are alluded to, but not designated by letter or number. Some fragmentary versions by other authors [291] [300] have been published, but these are not quoted in the notes.

114. *Origin Legend.* — The Origin Legend divides itself into four very distinct parts or chapters, which are named : I. The Story of the Emergence ; II. Early Events in the Fifth World ; III. The War Gods ; IV. The Growth of the Navaho Nation. The name of the first part is that given to it by the Navaho story-tellers. The names of the other parts are supplied by the author. The first part, The Story of the Emergence, ends when it is related that the people came out from the fourth world to the surface of this, the fifth world. [15]

115. *Rite-myths.* — By a rite-myth is meant a myth which accounts for the work of a ceremony, for its origin, for its introduction among the Navahoes, or for all these things combined. The Navahoes celebrate long and costly ceremonies, many of which are of nine days' duration. Each ceremony has connected with it one or more myths, or legends which may not be altogether mythical.

116. When a rite-myth is told by a priest of the rite to which the myth belongs, minute and often tedious particulars concerning the rite, its work, symbolism, and sacrifices are introduced into the tale. When such a myth is told by one who is not a priest of the rite (although he may be a priest of some other rite), these esoteric parts are altogether omitted, or only briefly alluded to. To the latter class belong the two rite-myths given in this book. They are here published because they are among the most interesting and ingenious that have been collected among the Navahoes. The attention of the reader is directed, in the notes, to a few places where esoteric or ceremonial matters are thought to be referred to. Tales containing ceremonial allusions in full are reserved for future publication, along with a description of the rites to which they pertain, as such is considered the more appropriate place for their publication.

117. In one version of the Origin Legend (Version A) a portion of this story is used as a rite-myth. It is embellished with prayers and songs, and interspersed with allusions to ceremonial work which the version of *Hatáli* Něz does not contain ; but in other respects it is inferior to the latter. Thus embellished it contributes a share to the myth of the ceremony of *hozóni hatál,* or chant of terrestrial beauty. Even in the version of *Hatáli* Něz, the songs seem introduced from some rite-myth, and scarcely to belong to the original story.

118. Whenever an opportunity has occurred of studying a rite with its associated myth, it has been found that the myth never explains all the symbolism of the rite, although it may account for all the more important acts. A primitive and underlying symbolism, which probably existed previous to the establishment of the rite, remains unexplained by the myth, as though its existence were taken as a matter of course, and required no explanation. Some explanation of this foundation symbolism may be found in the Origin Legend, or in other early legends of the tribe; but something remains which even these do not explain.

119. *Myths of the Whirling Logs.* — In the ceremony of klédzi

Fig. 30. Alili or show (" dance ") of the nahikáï in the rite of the mountain chant.

ħatál there is drawn upon the floor of the medicine-lodge a large dry-painting which is very imperfectly represented in fig. 29. The original was wrought in five colors and was about 12 feet in diameter. It depicts a vision of the prophet Béla*ħ*a*ŧ*íni, who established the rites of klédzi *ħatál*. On one occasion, says the tale, he was led, in the San Juan valley, to a lake on the borders of which grew four stalks of sacred corn, each of a different color. In the centre of the lake lay two logs crossing one another at right angles. Near both ends of each log sat a pair of yéi, or genii, male and female, making eight in all. On the shore of the lake stood four more yéi, three of whom had staves, by means of which they kept the crossed logs away from the shore and whirling in the waters. The rainbow goddess, the anthropomorphic rainbow of the Navahoes, surrounded the lake. All the circumstances of this strange scene are duly symbolized in the painting.

120. It was in his efforts to get a further explanation of this extraordinary picture that the author came upon the story of Naťí'-něsťhani. It is not the story that explains the picture, although certain passages in it (pars. 481, 488) might seem to explain it. The story to which the picture belongs is that of Béla*ha*ťíni, which may some day be published in connection with a description of the ceremony of klédʒi *hatál*, or the night chant. The prophet Béla*ha*ťíni, according to the tale, floated down the San Juan River in a hollow log, until he came to the whirling lake, where he saw the vision depicted in the dry-painting. But when the shaman had finished telling the story of Béla*ha*ťíni he said: "There is another story of a man who floated down the San Juan River in a hollow log. It is a story belonging to a different rite, the atsósidʒe *hatál*. Would you like to hear it?" It was thus that the story of Naťí'něsťhani came to be told. The narrator of the two tales was a priest of the klédʒi *hatál*, but not of the atsósidʒe *hatál*; hence one tale is crowded with allusions to acts in the ceremony, while the other, as here published, has few such allusions.

121. *The Great Shell of Kíntyél.* — The story of the Great Shell of Kíntyél, as here given, is a fragment of a rite-myth, — the myth of the yóidʒe *hatál*, or yói *hatál*[250] (bead chant), a nine days' healing ceremony. It conveys a moral often found in Navaho tales, which is, that we must not despise the poor and humble. They may be favored by the gods and prove themselves, to-morrow, more potent than those who yesterday despised and mocked them. It also signalizes the triumph of a poor Navaho over wealthy Pueblos.

122. *Translation of Legends.* — In rendering the Navaho tales into English, the author has not confined himself to a close literal translation. Such translation would often be difficult to understand, and, more often still, be uninteresting reading. He has believed it to be his duty to make a readable translation, giving the spirit of the original rather than the exact words. The tales were told in fluent Navaho, easy of comprehension, and of such literary perfection as to hold the hearer's attention. They should be translated into English of a similar character, even if words have to be added to make the sense clear. Such privileges are taken by the translators of the Bible and of the classic authors. Still the writer has taken pains never to exceed the metaphor or descriptive force of the original, and never to add a single thought of his own. If he has erred in rendering the spirit of the savage authors, it has been by diminishing rather than by exaggerating. He has erred on the side of safety. He has endeavored to "tune the sitar" rather low than high.[15a] Again, the original was often embellished with pantomime and vocal modulation which expressed more than the mere words,

and which the writer is unable to represent, and it contained extemporized onomatopes which no letters can express.

123. *Texts.* — The men who narrated to the author the tales contained in this book were not men of unlimited leisure, as many suppose the Indians to be ; they were popular shamans, or medicine-men, who had numerous engagements to conduct ceremonies during the winter months, and it was only during the winter months that they permitted themselves to tell the tales. It was usually with difficulty that arrangements were made with one of these shamans to devote a period of two or three weeks to the service of the author. Then, too, they had farms and stock which demanded their care. Neither was the author a man of unbounded leisure. Rarely could he devote more than two or three hours out of twenty-four to the work of ethnography. It has happened more than once that he has been obliged to break an engagement made with a shaman, at a cost of considerable trouble and money, in order to go on detached service away from his proper station. For these reasons it was not practicable to record the original Indian texts of all the stories. The author had to choose between copious texts and copious tales. He chose the latter. But some texts have been recorded. In order that the reader may judge how closely the liberal translation here offered follows the original, the Navaho text of the opening passages — ten paragraphs — of the Origin Legend, with interlinear translations, are given in the notes. The texts of songs, prayers, and interesting passages may also be found in the notes.

ALPHABET USED.

124. Ever since the present alphabet of the Bureau of Ethnology was established (in 1880), it has been the author's custom to use it in spelling Indian words. But heretofore he has written mostly for the scientific world, for ethnologists and philologists who either were familiar with the alphabet, or were willing to constantly refer to it in reading. As the present work is designed to reach a wider circle of readers, the propriety of using the alphabet of the Bureau becomes doubtful. Many of the author's friends have begged him not to use it in this collection of tales, believing that its unusual characters would embarrass the average reader and detract from the interest of the work. Another system has, therefore, been devised, according to which consonants printed in Roman letters have the ordinary English sounds, while those printed in Italics have sounds analogous to the English but not identical with them. The vowels, when unmarked, have the continental sounds. When these sounds are modified, diacritical marks are added in accordance with the latest edition of Webster's Dictionary. The sound of English a in

what is indicated by ạ. The only diphthong is ai, which has the sound of English i in pine. One mark not employed in Webster's orthoepy is used in this book, viz., the inverted comma after a vowel to show that it is aspirated.

125. According to this arrangement, the casual reader will find the Indian words easily legible. If he takes the trouble to consult this and the preceding paragraph he may pronounce the words almost exactly as a Navaho would ; if not he may, at least, pronounce them in a way that few Navahoes would fail to comprehend. At all events, to the majority of readers, a perfect pronunciation of the Indian words is immaterial. Many white men, living within the borders of the Navaho land, converse with these Indians in a jargon or debased language which might be spelled in English characters with their ordinary English values. For example, let us take the word for hut or house. This is properly pronounced *hog*án ; but the whites in New Mexico generally call it hogán, and the Navahoes never fail to understand the word as thus pronounced. In this form it is an adopted English word in the Southwest. The following are the values of the consonants when printed in Italics : —

d has the sound of English th in this.

g has a sound unknown in English. gh imperfectly represents it. It is the ǥ of the Dakota, or the Arabic *ghain.*

h has the sound of German ch in machen.

l is an aspirated l unknown in English. hl imperfectly represents it. It is formed with the side rather than with the tip of the tongue.

s has the sound of English sh in shot.

t has the sound of English th in thing.

z has the sound of English z in azure.

c, j, q, r, and x are not used. The sound of English ch in church is represented by t*s* ; that of English j in jug, by d*z*.

SPELLING OF NAVAHO.

126. In the many papers about the Navahoes which the author has previously written he has spelled the name of the tribe according to the Spanish system " Navajo," with the plural also in Spanish form, " Navajos." In the present work he spells it, according to English orthography, " Navaho," with an English plural, " Navahoes," and he thus intends to spell it in the future. This he does because the Spanish spelling is misleading to the majority of English readers. It may properly be asked why he should adopt an English orthography for Navaho, a name of Spanish origin, while he retains the misleading Spanish orthography of San Juan. It is not sufficient, in reply, to say that the territory of the Navaho has been in the possession of the United States since 1848, and that we have thus

acquired the right to spell this name in our own way; for a thousand other names of Spanish origin have marked our map as long, which we never ventured to change, either in spelling or pronunciation. Perhaps the best defence to be made of our course is that the name Navaho exists nowhere but within our borders. If we change the spelling here, we do not conflict with the spelling elsewhere. But there are scores of San Juans in Spanish America. We could not change the spelling of our San Juan without confusion. It were better that we should follow the example of Lord Byron and pronounce it Jew'an; but this the people of the Southwest will probably never do. They will speak of the stream as the "San Wŏn" or the "San Whŏn" for all time. Furthermore, the English spelling of Navaho is not a new thing with the writer. Many have already adopted it.

NOTES.

126. In preparing the notes the author has usually limited himself to such matters as he believes he only can explain, or such as, at least, he can explain better than any one else. In a few cases he has given information on subjects not generally known and not easily to be investigated. The temptation to wander into the seductive paths of comparative mythology, and to speculate on the more recondite significance of the myths, had to be resisted if the work were to be kept within the limits of one volume. Resemblances between the tales of the Navahoes and those of other peoples, civilized and savage, ancient and modern, are numerous and marked; but space devoted to them would be lost to more important subjects. Again, many of the readers of this book may be prepared, better than the author, to note these resemblances.

SHAMANS.[16]

127. So much has been said against the medicine-men of the Indians by various writers, who accuse them of being reactionaries, mischief-makers, and arrant deceivers, that the writer feels constrained to give some testimony in their favor, — in favor, at least, of those he has met among the Navahoes; he will not speak now for other tribes.

128. There are, among the Navahoes, charlatans and cheats who treat disease; men who pretend to suck disease out of the patient and then draw from their own mouths pebbles, pieces of charcoal, or bodies of insects, claiming that these are the disease which they have extracted. But the priests of the great rites are not to be classed with such. All of these with whom the writer is acquainted are above such trickery. They perform their ceremonies in the firm conviction that they are invoking divine aid, and their calling lends

Fig. 31. *Hatáli* Natlói.

dignity to their character. They interfere little with the political affairs of the tribe.

129. *Smiling Chanter.* — It is a source of great regret that a better likeness cannot be presented of *Hatáli* Natlói than that shown in fig. 31. It is reproduced from a painting which was copied from a dim kodak photograph. His name may be translated Smiling Chanter, or Smiling Doctor; an angry or unpleasant expression is never seen on his face. He is also called *Hatáli* Pa*h*o*z*óni, which may be translated Happy or Good-natured Chanter. He is a priest of the kled*z*i *h*at*á*l, or night chant. He would be considered a man of high character in any community. He is dignified, courteous, kind, honest, truthful, and self-respecting. But his dignity is not of the pompous kind. He has a keen sense of humor, makes an excellent joke, and is a good mimic; but, for all his fun, he is neither

vulgar nor unkind.   He never begged from the author, and never made a bargain with him in advance for his services, or named a price for them when he was done.   He always took the greatest pains to explain everything, and, after the writer had been duly initiated into the mysteries of his order, he withheld nothing.   To him we are indebted for the story of Na*tl*'nĕs*th*ani.

130. *Tall Chanter.* — Figure 32 represents an aged priest named *Hatál*i Nĕz, or Tall Chanter.   He was the first who could be persuaded to explain to the author the ceremonies or relate the rite-myths ; but when he set the example, others were found to follow. He also is a priest of the night chant.   Of late years he has become unpopular as a shaman, owing to an increasing irritability of temper ; but he exhibits no envy of his more popular rivals.   He perhaps has a better knowledge of the legends than any other man in the tribe.   Before he would confide any of his secrets to the author he said : " The chanters among the Navahoes are all brothers.   If you would learn our secrets you must be one of us.   You must forever be a brother to me.   Do you promise this ? "   He has ever since addressed the author as *S*itsĭ'li, " My younger brother," and has in turn been called *S*inái, " My elder brother."

131. *Ethics.* — Among themselves, these men have a code of ethics which is, in general, more honestly upheld than the code of our own medical profession.   They exhibit no jealousy of one another.   They boast not of the excellence of the particular rite they practise. They assist and counsel one another.   If a medicine-man, in performing a rite, finds that his supply of some sacred article is exhausted, he sends to the nearest medicine-man for it.   If the latter has it, he is obliged to give, and is not allowed to receive payment in return.

132. *Torlino.* — They are as willing as any other Indians to learn the white man's philosophy.   Old Torlino, a priest of *hozó*ni *hatál*, sent a son to school at Carlisle, and when the young man returned he no doubt imparted to his father much that he had learned there. The writer sent for the old man to get from him the myth of *hozó*ni *hatál*.   Torlino began : " I know the white men say the world is round, and that it floats in the air.   My tale says the world is flat, and that there are five worlds, one above another.   You will not believe my tale, then, and perhaps you do not want to hear it." Being assured that the tale was earnestly desired, despite of all white men's theories, he proceeded.   " I shall tell you the truth, then.   I shall tell you all that I heard from the old men who taught me, as well as I can now remember.   Why should I lie to you ? "   And then he made the interesting asseveration which is here literally translated : " I am ashamed before the earth ; I am ashamed before the heavens ; I am ashamed before the dawn ; I am ashamed before the

evening twilight; I am ashamed before the blue sky; I am ashamed before the darkness; I am ashamed before the sun; I am ashamed before that standing within me which speaks with me (my conscience!).[274] Some of these things are always looking at me. I am never out of sight. Therefore I must tell the truth. That is why I always tell the truth. I hold my word tight to my breast."

133. *Medical Practice.* — Often have the shamans come to the author for treatment for themselves and their friends, and they

Fig. 32. The Shaman *Hatáli* Něz (Tall Chanter).

never made any secret of this, but asked for medicine in the presence of the laity of their own tribe. They do not pretend to deal in panaceas. On the other hand, in cases where the author has failed to give prompt relief to a sick Indian, they have come in all sincerity and politeness and said, " I know a remedy for that difficulty. Will you let me try it?" They do not confine themselves to the practice of their shamanistic rites. They use various plants in the treatment of disease, and these, in simple, acute cases, they administer without prayer, sacrifice, or incantation.

A LAST WORD (TO POETS AND OTHERS).

134. It is possible that poets, novelists, travellers, and compilers will search this humble volume and cull from it facts and fancies,

which, clothed in fairer diction, may add interest to their pages. The author does not ask that such writers shall acknowledge the source of their inspiration. This is more than he has a right to expect. Our greatest poets have borrowed from sources as obscure and never named their creditors. The author has often, ere now, experienced the pleasure of seeing his thoughts and discoveries blazoned in print over other names. But he ventures to make a few requests of the literary borrower. He begs that the latter will not garble or distort what is here written, — that he will not put alien thoughts into the minds of these pagan heroes; that he will not arm them with the weapons nor clothe them in the habiliments of an alien race; that he will not make them act incongruous parts.

135. Stephen Powers, in his " Tribes of California "[326] (page 38), gives, in simple and direct language, the story of how fire came to the Karok nation. A few years after he wrote, some one worked his story into a "poem," which appeared, most artistically illustrated, in one of our leading magazines. In this poem the Coyote, in a quandary, is represented as "stroking his goatee." Coyotes have no goatees; Indians have no goatees. The act of stroking the goatee, in thought or perplexity, is the special mannerism of a nervous American. No allusion could be more out of place in an Indian legend. Should the poet referred to ever select any of the tales in this book to be tortured into a poem, I beg that he will not, even for the sake of making a faulty rhyme, put a beard on the chin of the Navaho Coyote God.

WASHINGTON MATTHEWS.

1262 New Hampshire Avenue, Washington, D. C.
May 1st, 1896.

LEGENDS.

PLATE II. SAN FRANCISCO MOUNTAIN (*DOKOSLÍD*), ARIZONA.[56]

(The sacred mountain of the West.)

THE NAVAHO ORIGIN LEGEND.

I. THE STORY OF THE EMERGENCE.

136. At To‘bïlʜaskï′di (in the middle of the first world), white arose in the east, and they [17] regarded it as day there, they say ; blue rose in the south, and still it was day to them, and they moved around ; yellow rose in the west and showed that evening had come ; then dark arose in the north, and they lay down and slept.[18]

137. At To‘bïlʜaskï′di water flowed out (from a central source) in different directions ; one stream flowed to the east, another to the south, and another to the west. There were dwelling-places on the border of the stream that flowed to the east, on that which flowed to the south, and on that which flowed to the west also.

138. To the east there was a place called Taʜ (Corn), to the south a place called Nahodoóla, and to the west a place called Lókatsosakád (Standing Reed). Again, to the east there was a place called Essaʟái (One Pot), to the south a place called To‘ʜádzïʜïl (They Come Often for Water), and to the west a place called Dsïllïtsíbeʜogán (House Made of the Red Mountain). Then, again, to the east there was a place called Léyaʜogán (Under-ground House), to the south a place called Tsïltsï′ntʜa (Among Aromatic Sumac), and to the west a place called Tse‘lïtsíbeʜogán (House Made of Red Rock).

139. Holatsí Dïlyï′le (dark ants) lived there. Holatsí Lïtsí (red ants) lived there. Tanïlai (dragon flies) lived there. Tsaltsá (yellow beetles) lived there. Woïntlï′zi (hard beetles) lived there. Tse‘yoáʟi (stone-carrier beetles) lived there. Kïnlï′zïn (black beetles) lived there. Maitsán (coyote-dung beetles) lived there. Tsápani (bats) lived there. Totsó‘ (white-faced beetles) lived there. Wonïstsídi (locusts) lived there. Wonïstsídikai (white locusts) lived there. These twelve people started in life there.[19]

140. To the east extended an ocean, to the south an ocean, to the west an ocean, and to the north an ocean. In the ocean to the east lay Tiéholtsodi ; he was chief of the people there. In the ocean to the south lived Tʜaltláʜale (Blue Heron), who was

chief of the people there. In the ocean to the west lay Tᴢal (Frog), who was chief of the people there. In the ocean to the north was I*d*ni'dsĭ/kaí (White Mountain Thunder), and he was chief of the people there.[20]

141. The people quarrelled among themselves, and this is the way it happened. They committed adultery, one people with another. Many of the women were guilty. They tried to stop it, but they could not. Tiéholtsodi, the chief in the east, said: "What shall we do with them? They like not the land they dwell in." In the south Blue Heron spoke to them, and in the west Frog said: "No longer shall you dwell here, I say. I am chief here." To the north White Mountain Lightning said: "Go elsewhere at once. Depart from here!"

142. When again they sinned and again they quarrelled, Tiéholtsodi, in the east, would not speak to them; Blue Heron, in the south, would not speak to them; Frog, in the west, would say nothing; and White Mountain Thunder, in the north, would not speak to them.

143. Again, at the end of four nights, the same thing happened. Those who dwelt at the south again committed crime, and again they had contentions. One woman and one man sought to enter in the east (to complain to the chief), but they were driven out. In the south they sought to go in where Blue Heron lay, but again they were driven out. In the west, where Frog was the chief, again they tried to enter; but again they were driven out. To the north again they were driven out. (The chief) said: "None of you (shall enter here). Go elsewhere and keep on going." That night at Naho*d*oóla they held a council, but they arrived at no decision. At dawn Tiéholtsodi began to talk. "You pay no attention to my words. Everywhere you disobey me; you must go to some other place. Not upon this earth shall you remain." Thus he spoke to them.

144. Among the women, for four nights they talked about it. At the end of the fourth night, in the morning, as they were rising, something white appeared in the east. It appeared also in the south, the west, and the north. It looked like a chain of mountains, without a break, stretching around them. It was water that surrounded them. Water impassable, water insurmountable, flowed all around. All at once they started.

145. They went in circles upward till they reached the sky. It was smooth. They looked down; but there the water had risen, and there was nothing else but water there. While they were flying around, one having a blue head thrust out his head from the sky and called to them, saying: "In here, to the eastward,

there is a hole." They entered the hole and went through it up to the surface (of the second world).

146. The blue one belonged to the *Hastsósidíne‘*, or Swallow People.[21] The Swallow People lived there. A great many of their houses, rough and lumpy, lay scattered all around. Each tapered toward the top, and at that part there was a hole for entrance. A great many people approached and gathered around [275] the strangers, but they said nothing.

147. The first world was red in color; the second world, into which the people had now entered, was blue.[22] They sent out two couriers, a Locust and a White Locust, to the east, to explore the land and see if there were in it any people like themselves. At the end of two days the couriers returned, and said that in one day's travel they had reached the edge of the world — the top of a great cliff that arose from an abyss whose bottom they could not see; but that they found in all their journey no people, no animals of any kind, no trees, no grass, no sage-brush, no mountains, nothing but bare, level ground. The same couriers were then dispatched in turn to the south, to the west, and to the north. They were gone on each journey two days, and when they returned related, as before, that they had reached the edge of the world, and discovered nothing but an uninhabited waste. Here, then, the strangers found themselves in the centre of a vast barren plain, where there was neither food nor a kindred people. When the couriers had returned from the north, the Swallows visited the camp of the newly arrived people, and asked them why they had sent out the couriers to the east. "We sent them out," was the reply, "to see what was in the land, and to see if there were any people like ourselves here." "And what did your couriers tell you?" asked the Swallows. "They told us that they came to the edge of the world, yet found no plant and no living thing in all the land." (The same questions were asked and the same answers given for the other points of the compass.) "They spoke the truth," said the Swallow People. "Had you asked us in the beginning what the land contained, we would have told you and saved you all your trouble. Until you came, no one has ever dwelt in all this land but ourselves." The people then said to the Swallows: "You understand our language and are much like us. You have legs, feet, bodies, heads, and wings, as we have: why cannot your people and our people become friends?" "Let it be as you wish," said the Swallows, and both parties began at once to treat each other as members of one tribe; they mingled one among the other, and addressed one another by the terms of relationship, as, my brother, my sister, my father, my son, etc.[23]

148. They all lived together pleasantly and happily for twenty-three days ; but on the twenty-fourth night one of the strangers made too free with the wife of the Swallow chief, and next morning, when the latter found out what had happened, he said to the strangers : " We have treated you as friends, and thus you return our kindness. We doubt not that for such crimes you were driven from the lower world, and now you must leave this. This is our land and we will have you here no longer. Besides, this is a bad land. People are dying here every day, and, even if we spare you, you cannot live here long." The Locusts took the lead on hearing this ; they soared upwards ; the others followed, and all soared and circled till they reached the sky.

149. When they reached the sky they found it, like the sky of the first world, smooth and hard with no opening ; but while they were circling round under it, they saw a white face peering out at them, — it was the face of Ni′ltsi, the Wind. He called to them and told them if they would fly to the south they would find a hole through which they could pass ; so off they flew, as bidden, and soon they discovered a slit in the sky which slanted upwards toward the south ; through this slit they flew, and soon entered the third world in the south.

150. The color of the third world was yellow.[22] Here they found nothing but the Grasshopper People. The latter gathered around the wanderers in great numbers, but said nothing. They lived in holes in the ground along the banks of a great river which flowed through their land to the east. The wanderers sent out the same Locust messengers that they had sent out in the second world to explore the land to the east, to the south, to the west, to the north, to find out what the land contained, and to see if there were any kindred people in it ; but the messengers returned from each journey after an absence of two days, saying they had reached the end of the world, and that they had found a barren land with no people in it save the Grasshoppers.[24]

151. When the couriers returned from their fourth journey, the two great chiefs of the Grasshoppers visited the strangers and asked them why they had sent out the explorers, and the strangers answered that they had sent them out to see what grew in the land, and to find if there were any people like themselves in it. " And what did your couriers find ? " said the Grasshopper chiefs. " They found nothing save the bare land and the river, and no people but yourselves." " There is nothing else in the land," said the chiefs. " Long we have lived here, but we have seen no other people but ourselves until you came."

152. The strangers then spoke to the Grasshoppers, as they had

spoken to the Swallows in the second world, and begged that they might join them and become one people with them. The Grasshoppers consented, and the two peoples at once mingled among one another and embraced one another, and called one another by the endearing terms of relationship, as if they were all of the same tribe.

153. As before, all went well for twenty-three days ; but on the twenty-fourth one of the strangers served a chief of the Grasshoppers as the chief of the Swallows had been served in the lower world. In the morning, when the wrong was discovered, the chief reviled the strangers and bade them depart. " For such crimes," he said, " I suppose you were chased from the world below : you shall drink no more of our water, you shall breathe no more of our air. Begone ! "

154. Up they all flew again, and circled round and round until they came to the sky above them, and they found it smooth and hard as before. When they had circled round for some time, looking in vain for an entrance, they saw a red head stuck out of the sky, and they heard a voice which told them to fly to the west. It was the head of Red Wind which they saw, and it was his voice that spoke to them. The passage which they found in the west was twisted round like the tendril of a vine; it had thus been made by the wind. They flew up in circles through it and came out in the fourth world. Four of the Grasshoppers came with them ; one was white, one blue, one yellow, and one black. We have grasshoppers of these four colors with us to this day.[25]

155. The surface of the fourth world was mixed black and white. The colors in the sky were the same as in the lower worlds, but they differed in their duration. In the first world, the white, the blue, the yellow, and the black all lasted about an equal length of time every day. In the second world the blue and the black lasted a little longer than the other two colors. In the third world they lasted still longer. In the fourth world there was but little of the white and yellow ; the blue and the black lasted most of the time. As yet there was neither sun, moon, nor star.

156. When they arrived on the surface of the fourth world they saw no living thing ; but they observed four great snow-covered peaks sticking up at the horizon, — one at the east, one at the south, one at the west, and one at the north.

157. They sent two couriers to the east. These returned at the end of two days. They related that they had not been able to reach the eastern mountain, and that, though they had travelled far, they had seen no track or trail or sign of life. Two couriers were then sent to the south. When they returned, at the end of two days, they related that they had reached a low range of mountains this

side of the great peak ; that they had seen no living creature, but
had seen two different kinds of tracks, such as they had never seen
before, and they described such as the deer and the turkey make
now. Two couriers were next sent to the west. In two days these
returned, having failed to reach the great peak in the west, and having seen no living thing and no sign of life. At last two couriers
were sent to the north. When these got back to their kindred they
said they had found a race of strange men, who cut their hair square
in front, who lived in houses in the ground and cultivated fields.
These people, who were engaged in gathering their harvest, the
couriers said, treated them very kindly and gave them food to eat.
It was now evident to the wanderers that the fourth world was
larger than any of the worlds below.

158. The day following the return of the couriers who went to the
north, two of the newly discovered race — Kisáni (Pueblos) they were
called — entered the camp of the exiles and guided the latter to a
stream of water. The water was red, and the Kisáni told the wanderers they must not walk through the stream, for if they did the
water would injure their feet. The Kisáni showed them a square
raft made of four logs, — a white pine, a blue spruce, and yellow pine,
and a black spruce, — on which they might cross ; so they went over
the stream and visited the homes of the Kisáni.

159. The Kisáni gave the wanderers corn and pumpkins to eat,
and the latter lived for some time on the food given to them daily
by their new friends. They held a council among themselves, in
which they resolved to mend their manners for the future and do
nothing to make the Kisáni angry. The land of the Kisáni had
neither rain nor snow ; the crops were raised by irrigation.

160. Late in the autumn they heard in the east the distant sound
of a great voice calling. They listened and waited, and soon heard
the voice nearer and louder. They listened still and heard the voice
a third time, nearer and louder than before. Once more they listened,
and soon they heard the voice louder still, and clear like the voice of
one near at hand. A moment later four mysterious beings appeared
to them.[26] These were : Bĭtsís *Ł*akaí, or White Body, a being like
the god of this world whom the Navahoes call *H*astséyal*ṭ*i ; Bĭtsís
*Do*ṭli′*z*, or Blue Body, who was like the present Navaho god
*Ṭ*ó‘nenĭli, or Water Sprinkler ; Bĭtsís *Ł*ĭtsói, or Yellow Body ; and
Bĭtsís *Ł*ĭzi′n, or Black Body, who was the same as the present
Navaho god of fire, *H*astsé*z*ĭni.

161. These beings, without speaking, made many signs to the
people, as if instructing them ; but the latter did not understand
them. When the gods had gone, the people long discussed the
mysterious visit, and tried to make out what the gods meant by the

signs they had made. Thus the gods visited four days in succession. On the fourth day, when the other three had departed, Black Body remained behind and spoke to the people in their own language. He said : " You do not seem to understand the signs that these gods make you, so I must tell you what they mean. They want to make more people, but in form like themselves. You have bodies like theirs ; but you have the teeth, the feet, and the claws of beasts and insects. The new creatures are to have hands and feet like ours. But you are uncleanly, you smell badly. Have yourselves well cleansed when we return ; we will come back in twelve days."

162. On the morning of the twelfth day the people washed themselves well. The women dried themselves with yellow corn-meal ; the men with white corn-meal.[27] Soon after the ablutions were completed they heard the distant call of the approaching gods. It was shouted, as before, four times, — nearer and louder at each repetition, — and, after the fourth call, the gods appeared. Blue Body and Black Body each carried a sacred buckskin. White Body carried two ears of corn, one yellow, one white, each covered at the end completely with grains.[28]

163. The gods laid one buckskin on the ground with the head to the west ; on this they placed the two ears of corn, with their tips to the east, and over the corn they spread the other buckskin with its head to the east ; under the white ear they put the feather of a white eagle, under the yellow ear the feather of a yellow eagle. Then they told the people to stand at a distance and allow the wind to enter. The white wind blew from the east, and the yellow wind blew from the west, between the skins. While the wind was blowing, eight of the Mirage People came and walked around the objects on the ground four times, and as they walked the eagle feathers, whose tips protruded from between the buckskins, were seen to move. When the Mirage People had finished their walk the upper buckskin was lifted, — the ears of corn had disappeared ; a man and a woman lay there in their stead.

164. The white ear of corn had been changed into a man, the yellow ear into a woman. It was the wind that gave them life. It is the wind that comes out of our mouths now that gives us life. When this ceases to blow we die. In the skin at the tips of our fingers we see the trail of the wind ; it shows us where the wind blew when our ancestors were created.

165. The pair thus created were First Man and First Woman (Atsé *Hastín* and Atsé Estsán). The gods directed the people to build an inclosure of brushwood for the pair. When the inclosure was finished, First Man and First Woman entered it, and the gods said to them : " Live together now as husband and wife." At the

end of four days hermaphrodite [29] twins were born, and at the end of four days more a boy and a girl were born, who in four days grew to maturity and lived with one another as husband and wife. The primal pair had in all five pairs of twins, the first of which only was barren, being hermaphrodites.

166. In four days after the last pair of twins was born, the gods came again and took First Man and First Woman away to the eastern mountain where the gods dwelt, and kept them there for four days. When they returned all their children were taken to the eastern mountain and kept there for four days. Soon after they all returned it was observed that they occasionally wore masks, such as *Hastséyalti* and *Hastséhogan* wear now, and that when they wore these masks they prayed for all good things, — for abundant rain and abundant crops. It is thought, too, that during their visit to the eastern mountain they learned the awful secrets of witchcraft, for the antíhi (witches, wizards) always keep such masks with them and marry those too nearly related to them.

167. When they returned from the eastern mountain the brothers and sisters separated ; and, keeping the fact of their former unlawful marriages secret, the brothers married women of the Mirage People and the sisters married men of the Mirage People. They kept secret, too, all the mysteries they had learned in the eastern mountain. The women thus married bore children every four days, and the children grew to maturity in four days, were married, and in their turn had children every four days. This numerous offspring married among the Kisáni, and among those who had come from the lower world, and soon there was a multitude of people in the land.

168. These descendants of First Man and First Woman made a great farm. They built a dam and dug a wide irrigating ditch. But they feared the Kisáni might injure their dam or their crops ; so they put one of the hermaphrodites to watch the dam and the other to watch the lower end of the field. The hermaphrodite who watched at the dam invented pottery. He made first a plate, a bowl, and a dipper, which were greatly admired by the people. The hermaphrodite who lived at the lower end of the farm invented the wicker water-bottle. [30] Others made, from thin split boards of cottonwood, implements which they shoved before them to clear the weeds out of the land. They made also hoes from shoulder-blades of deer and axes of stone. They got their seeds from the Kisáni.

169. Once they killed a little deer, and some one among them thought that perhaps they might make, from the skin of the head, a mask, by means of which they could approach other deer and kill them. They tried to make such a mask but failed ; they could not make it fit. They debated over the invention and considered it for

four days, but did not succeed. On the morning of the fifth day they heard the gods shouting in the distance. As on a previous occasion, they shouted four times, and after the fourth call they made their appearance. They brought with them heads of deer and of antelope. They showed the people how the masks were made and fitted, how the eye-holes were cut, how the motions of the deer were to be imitated, and explained to them all the other mysteries of the deer-hunt.[31] Next day hunters went out and several deer were killed; from these more masks were made, and with these masks more men went out to hunt; after that time the camp had abundance of meat. The people dressed the deerskins and made garments out of them.

170. The people from the third world had been in the fourth world eight years when the following incident occurred: One day they saw the sky stooping down and the earth rising up to meet it. For a moment they came in contact, and then there sprang out of the earth, at the point of contact, the Coyote and the Badger. We think now that the Coyote and the Badger are children of the sky. The Coyote rose first, and for this reason we think he is the elder brother of the Badger. At once the Coyote came over to the camp and skulked round among the people, while the Badger went down into the hole that led to the lower world.

171. First Man told the people the names of the four mountains which rose in the distance. They were named the same as the four mountains that now bound the Navaho land. There was Tsïsnadzï'ni in the east, Tsótsïʰ in the south, *D*okoslí*d* in the west, and *D*epĕ'ntsa in the north, and he told them that a different race of people lived in each mountain.

172. First Man was the chief of all these people in the fourth world, except the Kisáni. He was a great hunter, and his wife, First Woman, was very corpulent. One day he brought home from the hunt a fine fat deer. The woman boiled some of it and they had a hearty meal. When they were done the woman wiped her greasy hands on her dress, and made a remark which greatly enraged her husband; they had a quarrel about this, which First Man ended by jumping across the fire and remaining by himself in silence for the rest of the night.[32]

173. Next morning First Man went out early and called aloud to the people: "Come hither, all ye men," he said; "I wish to speak to you, but let all the women stay behind; I do not wish to see them." Soon all the males gathered, and he told them what his wife had said the night before. "They believe," he said, "that they can live without us. Let us see if they can hunt game and till the fields without our help. Let us see what sort of a living they can make

by themselves. Let us leave them and persuade the Kisáni to come with us. We will cross the stream, and when we are gone over we will keep the raft on the other side." He sent for the hermaphrodites. They came, covered with meal, for they had been grinding corn. "What have you that you have made yourselves?" he asked. "We have each two mealing-stones, and we have cups and bowls and baskets and many other things," they answered. "Then take these all along with you," he ordered, "and join us to cross the stream." Then all the men and the hermaphrodites assembled at the river and crossed to the north side on the raft, and they took over with them their stone axes and farm implements and everything they had made. When they had all crossed they sent the raft down to the Kisáni for them to cross. The latter came over, — six gentes of them, — but they took their women with them. While some of the young men were crossing the stream they cried at parting with their wives; still they went at the bidding of their chief. The men left the women everything the latter had helped to make or raise.

174. As soon as they had crossed the river some of the men went out hunting, for the young boys needed food, and some set to work to chop down willows and build huts. They had themselves all sheltered in four days.

175. That winter the women had abundance of food, and they feasted, sang, and had a merry time. They often came down to the bank of the river and called across to the men and taunted and reviled them. Next year the men prepared a few small fields and raised a little corn; but they did not have much corn to eat, and lived a good deal by hunting. The women planted all of the old farm, but they did not work it very well; so in the winter they had a small crop, and they did not sing and make merry as in the previous winter. In the second spring the women planted less, while the men planted more, cleared more land, and increased the size of their farm. Each year the fields and crops of the men increased, while those of the women diminished and they began to suffer for want of food. Some went out and gathered the seeds of wild plants to eat. In the autumn of the third year of separation many women jumped into the river and tried to swim over; but they were carried under the surface of the water and were never seen again. In the fourth year the men had more food than they could eat; corn and pumpkins lay untouched in the fields, while the women were starving.

176. First Man at length began to think what the effect of his course might be. He saw that if he continued to keep the men and the women apart the race might die out, so he called the men and spoke his thoughts to them. Some said, "Surely our race will perish," and others said, "What good is our abundance to us? We

think so much of our poor women starving in our sight that we cannot eat." Then he sent a man to the shore to call across the stream to find if First Woman were still there, and to bid her come down to the bank if she were. She came to the bank, and First Man called to her and asked if she still thought she could live alone. "No," she replied, "we cannot live without our husbands." The men and the women were then told to assemble at the shores of the stream ; the raft was sent over and the women were ferried across. They were made to bathe their bodies and dry them with meal. They were put in a corral and kept there until night, when they were let out to join the men in their feasts.[33]

177. When they were let out of the corral it was found that three were missing. After dark, voices were heard calling from the other side of the river; they were the voices of the missing ones, — a mother and her two daughters. They begged to be ferried over, but the men told them it was too dark, that they must wait until morning. Hearing this, they jumped into the stream and tried to swim over. The mother succeeded in reaching the opposite bank and finding her husband. The daughters were seized by Tiéholtsodi, the water monster, and dragged down under the water.

178. For three nights and three days the people heard nothing about the young women and supposed them lost forever. On the morning of the fourth day the call of the gods was heard, — four times as usual, — and after the fourth call White Body made his appearance, holding up two fingers and pointing to the river. The people supposed that these signs had reference to the lost girls. Some of the men crossed the stream on the raft and looked for the tracks of the lost ones ; they traced the tracks to the edge of the water, but no farther. White Body went away, but soon returned, accompanied by Blue Body. White Body carried a large bowl of white shell, and Blue Body a large bowl of blue shell. They asked for a man and a woman to accompany them, and they went down to the river. They put both the bowls on the surface of the water and caused them to spin around. Beneath the spinning bowls the water opened, for it was hollow, and gave entrance to a large house of four rooms. The room in the east was made of the dark waters, the room in the south of the blue waters, the room in the west of the yellow waters, and the room in the north of waters of all colors.[36]

179. The man and the woman descended and Coyote followed them. They went first into the east room, but there they found nothing; then they went into the south room, but there they found nothing ; next they went into the west room, where again they found nothing ; at last they went into the north room, and there they

beheld the water monster Tiéholtsodi, with the two girls he had stolen and two children of his own. The man and the woman demanded the children, and as he said nothing in reply they took them and walked away. But as they went out Coyote, unperceived by all, took the two children of Tiéholtsodi and carried them off under his robe. Coyote always wore his robe folded close around him and always slept with it thus folded, so no one was surprised to see that he still wore his robe in this way when he came up from the waters, and no one suspected that he had stolen the children of Tiéholtsodi.

180. Next day the people were surprised to see deer, turkey, and antelope running past from east to west, and to see animals of six different kinds (two kinds of Hawks, two kinds of Squirrels, the Hummingbird, and the Bat) come into their camp as if for refuge. The game animals ran past in increasing numbers during the three days following. On the morning of the fourth day, when the white light rose, the people observed in the east a strange white gleam along the horizon, and they sent out the Locust couriers to see what caused this unusual appearance. The Locusts returned before sunset, and told the people that a vast flood of waters was fast approaching from the east. On hearing this the people all assembled together, the Kisáni with the others, in a great multitude, and they wailed and wept over the approaching catastrophe. They wept and moaned all night and could not sleep.

181. When the white light arose in the east, next morning, the waters were seen high as mountains encircling the whole horizon, except in the west, and rolling on rapidly. The people packed up all their goods as fast as they could, and ran up on a high hill near by, for temporary safety. Here they held a council. Some one suggested that perhaps the two Squirrels (*H*azáitso and *H*azáistozi) might help them. "We will try what we can do," said the Squirrels. One planted a piñon seed, the other a juniper seed, and they grew so very fast that the people hoped that they would soon grow so tall that the flood could not reach their tops, and that all might find shelter there. But after the trees grew a little way they began to branch out and grew no higher. Then the frightened people called on the Weasels (Glo'ds*l̷*kái and Glo'ds*l̷zi̇*'ni). One of these planted a spruce seed and one a pine seed. The trees sprouted at once and grew fast, and again the people began to hope; but soon the trees commenced to branch, and they dwindled to slender points at the top and ceased to grow higher. Now they were in the depths of despair, for the waters were coming nearer every moment, when they saw two men approaching the hill on which they were gathered.

182. One of the approaching men was old and grayhaired; the

other, who was young, walked in advance. They ascended the hill and passed through the crowd, speaking to no one. The young man sat down on the summit, the old man sat down behind him, and the Locust sat down behind the old man, — all facing the east. The elder took out seven bags from under his robe and opened them. Each contained a small quantity of earth. He told the people that in these bags he had earth from the seven sacred mountains. There were in the fourth world seven sacred mountains, named and placed like the sacred mountains of the present Navaho land. "Ah! Perhaps our father can do something for us," said the people. "I cannot, but my son may be able to help you," said the old man. Then they bade the son to help them, and he said he would if they all moved away from where he stood, faced to the west, and looked not around until he called them ; for no one should see him at his work. They did as he desired, and in a few moments he called them to come to him. When they came, they saw that he had spread the sacred earth on the ground and planted in it thirty-two reeds, each of which had thirty-two joints. As they gazed they beheld the roots of the reeds striking out into the soil and growing rapidly downward. A moment later all the reeds joined together and became one reed of great size, with a hole in its eastern side. He bade them enter the hollow of the reed through this hole. When they were all safely inside, the opening closed, and none too soon, for scarcely had it closed when they heard the loud noise of the surging waters outside, saying, "Yi*n*, yi*n*, yi*n*."[37]

183. The waters rose fast, but the reed grew faster, and soon it grew so high that it began to sway, and the people inside were in great fear lest, with their weight, it might break and topple over into the water. White Body, Blue Body, and Black Body were along. Black Body blew a great breath out through a hole in the top of the reed ; a heavy dark cloud formed around the reed and kept it steady. But the reed grew higher and higher ; again it began to sway, and again the people within were in great fear, whereat he blew and made another cloud to steady the reed. By sunset it had grown up close to the sky, but it swayed and waved so much that they could not secure it to the sky until Black Body, who was uppermost, took the plume out of his head-band and stuck it out through the top of the cane against the sky, and this is why the reed (*Phragmites communis*) always carries a plume on its head now.[38]

184. Seeing no hole in the sky, they sent up the Great Hawk, Giní'tso, to see what he could do. He flew up and began to scratch in the sky with his claws, and he scratched and scratched till he was lost to sight. After a while he came back, and said that he

scratched to where he could see light, but that he did not get through the sky. Next they sent up a Locust.[39] He was gone a long time, and when he came back he had this story to tell: He had gotten through to the upper world, and came out on a little island in the centre of a lake. When he got out he saw approaching him from the east a black Grebe, and from the west a yellow Grebe.[40] One of them said to him: "Who are you and whence come you?" But he made no reply. The other then said: "We own half of this world, — I in the east, my brother in the west. We give you a challenge. If you can do as we do, we shall give you one half of the world; if you cannot, you must die." Each had an arrow made of the black wind. He passed the arrow from side to side through his heart and flung it down to Wonĭst*si*di, the Locust.[41] The latter picked up one of the arrows, ran it from side to side through his heart, as he had seen the Grebes do, and threw it down.[42] The Grebes swam away, one to the east and one to the west, and troubled him no more. When they had gone, two more Grebes appeared, a blue one from the south and a shining one from the north. They spoke to him as the other Grebes had spoken, and gave him the same challenge. Again he passed the arrow through his heart and the Grebes departed, leaving the land to the locust. To this day we see in every locust's sides the holes made by the arrows. But the hole the Locust made in ascending was too small for many of the people, so they sent Badger up to make it larger. When Badger came back his legs were stained black with the mud, and the legs of all badgers have been black ever since. Then First Man and First Woman led the way and all the others followed them, and they climbed up through the hole to the surface of this — the fifth — world.

II. EARLY EVENTS IN THE FIFTH WORLD.

185. The lake[43] was bounded by high cliffs, from the top of which stretched a great plain. There are mountains around it now, but these have been created since the time of the emergence. Finding no way to get out of the lake, they called on Blue Body to help them. He had brought with him from the lower world four stones; he threw one of these towards each of the four cardinal points against the cliffs, breaking holes, through which the waters flowed away in four different directions.[44] The lake did not altogether drain out by this means; but the bottom became bare in one place, connecting the island with the mainland. But the mud was so deep in this place that they still hesitated to cross, and they prayed to Nĭ′lt*si* *D*ĭlkóhi, Smooth Wind, to come to their aid.[45] Nĭ′lt*si* *D*ĭlkóhi

PLATE III. DISTANT VIEW OF SAN MATEO MOUNTAIN (TSÓTSĬL), NEW MEXICO.[54]

(The sacred mountain of the South.)

blew a strong wind, and in one day dried up the mud so that the people could easily walk over. While they were waiting for the ground to dry, the Kisáni camped on the east side of the island and built a stone wall (which stands to this day), to lean against and to shelter them from the wind.[46] The other people set up a shelter of brushwood. The women erected four poles, on which they stretched a deerskin, and under the shelter of this they played the game of three-sticks,[47] tsïn*dï*', one of the four games which they brought with them from the lower world.

186. When they reached the mainland they sought to divine their fate. To do this some one threw a hide-scraper into the water, saying: "If it sinks we perish, if it floats we live." It floated, and all rejoiced. But Coyote said: " Let me divine your fate." He picked up a stone, and saying, " If it sinks we perish ; if it floats we live," he threw it into the water. It sank, of course, and all were angry with him and reviled him; but he answered them saying : " If we all live, and continue to increase as we have done, the earth will soon be too small to hold us, and there will be no room for the cornfields. It is better that each of us should live but a time on this earth and then leave and make room for our children." They saw the wisdom of his words and were silent. The day they arrived at the shore they had two visitors, — Puma and Wolf. "We have heard," said these, "that some new people had come up out of the ground, and we have come over to see them." Puma took a bride from among the new people.

187. On the fourth day of the emergence some one went to look at the hole through which they had come out, and he noticed water welling up there ; already it was nearly on a level with the top of the hole, and every moment it rose higher. In haste he ran back to his people and told them what he had seen. A council was called at once to consider the new danger that threatened them. First Man, who rose to speak, said, pointing to Coyote : " Yonder is a rascal, and there is something wrong about him. He never takes off his robe, even when he lies down. I have watched him for a long time, and have suspected that he carries some stolen property under his robe. Let us search him." [48] They tore the robe from Coyote's shoulders, and two strange little objects dropped out that looked something like buffalo calves, but were spotted all over in various colors; they were the young of Tiéholtsodi. At once the people threw them into the hole through which the waters were pouring ; in an instant the waters subsided, and rushed away with a deafening noise to the lower world.[49]

188. On the fifth night one of the twin hermaphrodites ceased to breathe. They left her alone all that night, and, when morning

came, Coyote proposed to lay her at rest among the rocks. This they did ; but they all wondered what had become of her breath. They went in various directions to seek for its trail, but could find it nowhere. While they were hunting, two men went near the hole through which they had come from the lower world. It occurred to one of them to look down into the hole. He did so, and he saw the dead one seated by the side of the river, in the fourth world, combing her hair. He called to his companion and the latter came and looked down, too. They returned to their people and related what they had seen ; but in four days both these men died, and ever since the Navahoes have feared to look upon the dead, or to behold a ghost, lest they die themselves.[50]

189. After this it was told around that the Kisáni, who were in camp at a little distance from the others, had brought with them from the lower world an ear of corn for seed. Some of the unruly ones proposed to go to the camp of the Kisáni and take the corn away from them ; but others, of better counsel, said that this would be wrong, that the Kisáni had had as much trouble as the rest, and if they had more foresight they had a right to profit by it. In spite of these words, some of the young men went and demanded the corn of the Kisáni. The latter said, after some angry talk on both sides, "We will break the ear in two and give you whichever half you choose." The young men agreed to this bargain, and the woman who owned the ear broke it in the middle and laid the pieces down for the others to choose. The young men looked at the pieces, and were considering which they would take, when Coyote, getting impatient, picked up the tip end of the ear and made off with it. The Kisáni kept the butt, and this is the reason the Pueblo Indians have to-day better crops of corn than the Navahoes. But the Pueblos had become alarmed at the threats and angry language of their neighbors and moved away from them, and this is why the Navahoes and Pueblos now live apart from one another.

190. After the Kisáni moved away, First Man and First Woman, Black Body and Blue Body, set out to build the seven sacred mountains of the present Navaho land. They made them all of earth which they had brought from similar mountains in the fourth world. The mountains they made were Tsïsnadzï'ni in the east, Tsótsïl (Taylor, San Mateo) in the south, Dokoslíd (San Francisco) in the west, Depĕ'ntsa (San Juan) in the north, with Dsïlnáotïl, Tsolíhi, and Akïdanastáni (Hosta Butte) in the middle of the land.[51]

191. Through Tsïsnadzï'ni,[52] in the east, they ran a bolt of lightning to fasten it to the earth. They decorated it with white shells, white lightning, white corn, dark clouds, and he-rain. They set a big dish or bowl of shell on its summit, and in it they put two eggs

of the Pigeon to make feathers for the mountain. The eggs they covered with a sacred buckskin to make them hatch (there are many wild pigeons in this mountain now). All these things they covered with a sheet of daylight, and they put the Rock Crystal Boy and the Rock Crystal Girl [53] into the mountain to dwell.

192. Tsótsĭ*l*,[54] the mountain of the south, they fastened to the earth with a great stone knife, thrust through from top to bottom. They adorned it with turquoise, with dark mist, she-rain, and all different kinds of wild animals. On its summit they placed a dish of turquoise; in this they put two eggs of the Bluebird, which they covered with sacred buckskin (there are many bluebirds in Tsótsĭ*l* now), and over all they spread a covering of blue sky. The Boy who Carries One Turquoise and the Girl who Carries One Grain of Corn [55] were put into the mountain to dwell.

193. *D*okoslĭ*d*,[56] the mountain of the west, they fastened to the earth with a sunbeam. They adorned it with haliotis shell, with black clouds, he-rain, yellow corn, and all sorts of wild animals. They placed a dish of haliotis shell on the top, and laid in this two eggs of the Yellow Warbler, covering them with sacred buckskins. There are many yellow warblers now in *D*okoslĭ*d*. Over all they spread a yellow cloud, and they sent White Corn Boy and Yellow Corn Girl [57] to dwell there.

194. *D*epĕ′ntsa, the mountain in the north, they fastened with a rainbow. They adorned it with black beads (pás*z*ĭni), with the dark mist, with different kinds of plants, and many kinds of wild animals. On its top they put a dish of pás*z*ĭni; in this they placed two eggs of the Blackbird, over which they laid a sacred buckskin. Over all they spread a covering of darkness. Lastly they put the Pollen Boy and Grasshopper Girl [59] in the mountain, to dwell there.

195. Dsĭ*l*náo*t*ĭ*l*,[60] was fastened with a sunbeam. They decorated it with goods of all kinds, with the dark cloud, and the male rain. They put nothing on top of it; they left its summit free, in order that warriors might fight there; but they put Boy Who Produces Goods and Girl Who Produces Goods [61] there to live.

196. The mountain of Ts*o*líhi [62] they fastened to the earth with nĭ′ltsatlo*l* (the streak or cord of rain). They decorated it with pollen, the dark mist, and the female rain. They placed on top of it a live bird named Ts*o*zgá*l*i,[63] — such birds abound there now, — and they put in the mountain to dwell Boy Who Produces Jewels and Girl Who Produces Jewels.[64]

197. The mountain of Akĭ*d*anas*t*áni [65] they fastened to the earth with a sacred stone called tse‘*h*ad*á*h*o*nige, or mirage-stone. They decorated it with black clouds, the he-rain, and all sorts of plants. They placed a live Grasshopper on its summit, and they put the Mirage-stone Boy and the Carnelian Girl there to dwell.[66]

198. They still had the three lights and the darkness, as in the lower worlds. But First Man and First Woman thought they might form some lights which would make the world brighter. After much study and debate they planned to make the sun and moon. For the sun they made a round flat object, like a dish, out of a clear stone called tsé'tsagi. They set turquoises around the edge, and outside of these they put rays of red rain, lightning, and snakes of many kinds. At first they thought of putting four points on it, as they afterwards did on the stars, but they changed their minds and made it round. They made the moon of tsé'tson (star-rock, a kind of crystal); they bordered it with white shells and they put on its face *had*ílkï's (sheet lightning), and *tó'l*anast*s*i (all kinds of water).[67]

199. Then they counseled as to what they should do with the sun; where they should make it rise first. The Wind of the East begged that it might be brought to his land, so they dragged it off to the edge of the world where he dwelt; there they gave it to the man who planted the great cane in the lower world, and appointed him to carry it. To an old gray-haired man, who had joined them in the lower world, the moon was given to carry. These men had no names before, but now the former received the name of Tsóhanoai, or Ts*ín*hanoai, and the latter the name of Kléhanoai. When they were about to depart, in order to begin their labors, the people were sorry, for they were beloved by all. But First Man said to the sorrowing people: " Mourn not for them, for you will see them in the heavens, and all that die will be theirs in return for their labors.[68] (See notes 69 and 70 for additions to the legend.)

200. Then the people (*D*ïné', Navahoes) began to travel. They journeyed towards the east, and after one day's march they reached Ni*h*a*h*okaí (White Spot on the Earth) and camped for the night. Here a woman brought forth, but her offspring was not like a child; it was round, misshapen, and had no head. The people counselled, and determined that it should be thrown into a gully. So they threw it away; but it lived and grew up and became the monster *T*éelgĕ*t*,[181] who afterwards destroyed so many of the people.

201. Next day they wandered farther to the east, and camped at night at Tse'*t*aiská (Rock Bending Back). Here was born another misshapen creature, which had something like feathers on both its shoulders. It looked like nothing that was ever seen before, so the people concluded to throw this away also. They took it to an alkali bed close by and cast it away there. But it lived and grew and became the terrible Tse'nă'hale,[185] of whom I shall have much to tell later.

202. The next night, travelling still to the east, they camped at Tse'biná*h*otyel, a broad high cliff like a wall, and here a woman

bore another strange creature. It had no head, but had a long pointed end where the head ought to be. This object was deposited in the cliff, in a hole which was afterwards sealed up with a stone. They left it there to die, but it grew up and became the destroyer Tse'taḥotsïltá'li,[142] of whom we shall tell hereafter. Because he was closed into the rock, his hair grew into it and he could not fall.

203. The next night, when they stopped at Tse'aḥalzï'ni (Rock with Black Hole), twins were born. They were both roundish with one end tapering to a point. There were no signs of limbs or head, but there were depressions which had somewhat the appearance of eyes. The people laid them on the ground, and next day, when they moved camp, abandoned them. Tse'aḥalzï'ni is shaped like a Navaho hut, with a door in the east. It is supposed that, when they were abandoned to die, the twin monsters went into this natural hut to dwell. They grew up, however, and became the Bïnáye Aḥáni, who slew with their eyes, and of whom we shall have more to tell.

204. All these monsters were the fruit of the transgressions of the women in the fourth world, when they were separated from the men. Other monsters were born on the march, and others, again, sprang from the blood which had been shed during the birth of the first monsters,[71] and all these grew up to become enemies and destroyers of the people.

205. When they left Tse'aḥalzï'ni they turned toward the west, and journeyed until they came to a place called To'ïntsósoko (Water in a Narrow Gully), and here they remained for thirteen years, making farms and planting corn, beans, and pumpkins every spring.

206. In those days the four-footed beasts, the birds, and the snakes were people also, like ourselves, and built houses and lived near our people close to Depĕ'ntsa. They increased and became the cliff-dwellers. It must have been the flying creatures who built the dwellings high on the cliffs, for if they had not wings how could they reach their houses?

207. From To'ïntsósoko they moved to Tse'lakaíia (Standing White Rock), and here they sojourned again for thirteen years. From the latter place they moved to Tse'paḥalkaí (White on Face of Cliff), and here, once more, they remained for a period of thirteen years. During this time the monsters began to devour the people.

208. From Tse'paḥalkaí they moved to the neighborhood of Kïntyél[72] (Broad House), in the Chaco Canyon, where the ruins of the great pueblo still stand. When the wanderers arrived the pueblo was in process of building, but was not finished. The way it came to be built you shall now hear: —

209. Some time before, there had descended among the Pueblos, from the heavens, a divine gambler, or gambling - god, named No*h*oílpi, or He Who Wins Men (at play) ; his talisman was a great piece of turquoise. When he came he challenged the people to all sorts of games and contests, and in all of these he was successful. He won from them, first, their property, then their women and children, and finally some of the men themselves. Then he told them he would give them part of their property back in payment if they would build a great house ; so when the Navahoes came, the Pueblos were busy building in order that they might release their enthralled relatives and their property. They were also busy making a race-track, and preparing for all kinds of games of chance and skill.

210. When all was ready, and four days' notice had been given, twelve men came from the neighboring pueblo of Kĭ′ndo*tl*ĭz, Blue House, to compete with the great gambler. They bet their own persons, and after a brief contest they lost themselves to No*h*oílpi. Again a notice of four days was given, and again twelve men of Kĭ′ndo*tl*ĭz — relatives of the former twelve — came to play, and these also lost themselves. For the third time an announcement, four days in advance of a game, was given ; this time some women were among the twelve contestants, and they, too, lost themselves. All were put to work on the building of Kĭntyél as soon as they forfeited their liberty. At the end of another four days the children of these men and women came to try to win back their parents, but they succeeded only in adding themselves to the number of the gambler's slaves. On a fifth trial, after four days' warning, twelve leading men of Blue House were lost, among them the chief of the pueblo. On a sixth duly announced gambling day, twelve more men, all important persons, staked their liberty and lost it. Up to this time the Navahoes had kept count of the winnings of No*h*oílpi, but afterwards people from other pueblos came in such numbers to play and lose that they could keep count no longer. In addition to their own persons the later victims brought in beads, shells, turquoise, and all sorts of valuables, and gambled them away. With the labor of all these slaves it was not long until the great Kĭntyél was finished.

211. But all this time the Navahoes had been merely spectators, and had taken no part in the games. One day the voice of the beneficent god, *H*ast*s*éyal*t*i,[73] was heard faintly in the distance crying his usual call, " Wu‘hu‘hu‘hú." His voice was heard, as it is always heard, four times, each time nearer and nearer, and immediately after the last call, which was loud and clear, *H*ast*s*éyal*t*i appeared at the door of a hut where dwelt a young couple who had no children, and with them he communicated by means of signs. He told them that the people of Kĭ′ndo*tl*ĭz had lost at game with

No*h*oílpi two great shells, the greatest treasures of the pueblo ; that the Sun had coveted these shells and had begged them from the gambler ; that the latter had refused the request of the Sun and the Sun was angry. In consequence of all this, as *H*ast*s*éyal*t*i related, in twelve days from his visit certain divine personages would meet in the mountains, in a place which he designated, to hold a great ceremony. He invited the young man to be present at the ceremony and disappeared.

212. The Navaho kept count of the passing days ; on the twelfth day he repaired to the appointed place, and there he found a great assemblage of the gods. There were *H*ast*s*éyal*t*i, *H*ast*s*é*h*ogan [74] and his son, Nĭ′lt*s*i [75] (Wind), T*s*a*l*yé*l* (Darkness), T*s*ápani (Bat), *L*ĭst*s*ó (Great Snake), Tsĭlká*l*i (a little bird), Nasĭ′zi (Gopher), and many others. Besides these there were present a number of pets or domesticated animals belonging to the gambler, who were dissatisfied with their lot, were anxious to be free, and would gladly obtain their share of the spoils in case their master was ruined. Nĭ′lt*s*i (Wind) had spoken to them, and they had come to enter into the plot against No*h*oílpi. All night the gods danced and sang and performed their mystic rites for the purpose of giving to the son of *H*ast*s*é*h*ogan powers, as a gambler, equal to those of No*h*oílpi. When the morning came they washed the young neophyte all over, dried him with meal, dressed him in clothes exactly like those the gambler wore, and in every way made him look as much like the gambler as possible, and then they counselled as to what other means they should take to outwit No*h*oílpi.

213. In the first place, they desired to find out how he felt about having refused to his father, the Sun, the two great shells. " I will do this," said Nĭ′lt*s*i (Wind), "for I can penetrate everywhere, and no one can see me ;" but the others said : " No ; you can go everywhere, but you cannot travel without making a noise and disturbing people. Let T*s*a*l*yé*l* (Darkness) go on this errand, for he also goes wherever he wills, yet he makes no noise." So T*s*a*l*yé*l* went to the gambler's house, entered his room, went all through his body while he slept, and searched well his mind, and he came back saying, " No*h*oílpi is sorry for what he has done." Nĭ′lt*s*i, however, did not believe this ; so, although his services had been before refused, he repaired to the chamber where the gambler slept, and went all through his body and searched well his mind ; but he, too, came back saying No*h*oílpi was sorry that he had refused to give the great shells to his father.

214. One of the games they proposed to play is called *t*aká-*t*hadsáta, or the thirteen chips. (It is played with thirteen thin flat pieces of wood, which are colored red on one side and left white or uncolored

on the other side. Success depends on the number of chips which, being thrown upwards, fall with their white sides up.) "Leave the game to me," said the Bat; "I have made thirteen chips that are white on both sides. I will hide myself in the ceiling, and when our champion throws up his chips I will grasp them and throw down my chips instead."

215. Another game they were to play is called nánzoz.[76] (It is played with two long sticks or poles, of peculiar shape and construction, one marked with red and the other with black, and a single hoop. A long, many-tailed string, called the "turkey-claw," is secured to the end of each pole.) "Leave nánzoz to me," said Great Snake; "I will hide myself in the hoop and make it fall where I please."

216. Another game was one called tsï'nbetsiℓ, or push-on-the-wood. (In this the contestants push against a tree until it is torn from its roots and falls.) "I will see that this game is won," said Nasí'zi, the Gopher; "I will gnaw the roots of the tree, so that he who shoves it may easily make it fall."

217. In the game tsol, or ball, the object was to hit the ball so that it would fall beyond a certain line. "I will win this game for you," said the little bird Tsïlkáℓi, "for I will hide within the ball, and fly with it wherever I want to go. Do not hit the ball hard; give it only a light tap, and depend on me to carry it."

218. The pets of the gambler begged the Wind to blow hard, so that they might have an excuse to give their master for not keeping due watch when he was in danger, and in the morning the Wind blew for them a strong gale. At dawn the whole party of conspirators left the mountain, and came down to the brow of the canyon to watch until sunrise.

219. Noℓoílpi had two wives, who were the prettiest women in the whole land. Wherever she went, each carried in her hand a stick with something tied on the end of it, as a sign that she was the wife of the great gambler.

220. It was their custom for one of them to go every morning at sunrise to a neighboring spring to get water. So at sunrise the watchers on the brow of the cliff saw one of the wives coming out of the gambler's house with a water-jar on her head, whereupon the son of *Hastséℓogan* descended into the canyon and followed her to the spring. She was not aware of his presence until she had filled her water-jar; then she supposed it to be her own husband, whom the youth was dressed and adorned to represent, and she allowed him to approach her. She soon discovered her error, however, but, deeming it prudent to say nothing, she suffered him to follow her into the house. As he entered, he observed that many of the slaves

had already assembled; perhaps they were aware that some trouble was in store for their master. The latter looked up with an angry face; he felt jealous when he saw the stranger entering immediately after his wife. He said nothing of this, however, but asked at once the important question, "Have you come to gamble with me?" This he repeated four times, and each time the young *Hastséhogan* said "No." Thinking the stranger feared to play with him, No*h*oílpi went on challenging him recklessly. "I 'll bet myself against yourself;" "I 'll bet my feet against your feet;" "I 'll bet my legs against your legs;" and so on he offered to bet every and any part of his body against the same part of his adversary, ending by mentioning his hair.

221. In the mean time the party of divine ones, who had been watching from above, came down, and people from the neighboring pueblos came in, and among these were two boys, who were dressed in costumes similar to those worn by the wives of the gambler. The young *Hastséhogan* pointed to these and said, "I will bet my wives against your wives." The great gambler accepted the wager, and the four persons, two women and two mock-women, were placed sitting in a row near the wall. First they played the game of thirteen chips. The Bat assisted, as he had promised the son of *Hastséhogan*, and the latter soon won the game, and with it the wives of No*h*oílpi.

222. This was the only game played inside the house; then all went out of doors, and games of various kinds were played. First they tried nán*z*o*z*. The track already prepared lay east and west, but, prompted by the Wind God, the stranger insisted on having a track made from north to south, and again, at the bidding of Wind, he chose the red stick. The son of *Hastséhogan* threw the wheel; at first it seemed about to fall on the gambler's pole, in the "turkey-claw" of which it was entangled; but to the great surprise of the gambler it extricated itself, rolled farther on, and fell on the pole of his opponent. The latter ran to pick up the ring, lest No*h*oílpi in doing so might hurt the snake inside; but the gambler was so angry that he threw his stick away and gave up the game, hoping to do better in the next contest, which was that of pushing down trees.

223. For this the great gambler pointed out two small trees, but his opponent insisted that larger trees must be found. After some search they agreed upon two of good size, which grew close together, and of these the Wind told the youth which one he must select. The gambler strained with all his might at his tree, but could not move it, while his opponent, when his turn came, shoved the other tree prostrate with little effort, for its roots had all been severed by Gopher.

224. Then followed a variety of games, on which No*h*oílpi staked his wealth in shells and precious stones, his houses, and many of his slaves, and lost all.

225. The last game was that of the ball.   On the line over which the ball was to be knocked all the people were assembled ; on one side were those who still remained slaves ; on the other side were the freedmen and those who had come to wager themselves, hoping to rescue their kinsmen.   No*h*oílpi bet on this game the last of his slaves and his own person.   The gambler struck his ball a heavy blow, but it did not reach the line ; the stranger gave his but a light tap, and the bird within it flew with it far beyond the line, whereat the released captives jumped over the line and joined their people.

226. The victor ordered all the shells, beads, and precious stones, and the great shells, to be brought forth.   He gave the beads and shells to *H*astséyal*t*i, that they might be distributed among the gods ; the two great shells were given to the Sun.[77]

227. In the mean time No*h*oílpi sat to one side saying bitter things, bemoaning his fate, and cursing and threatening his enemies.   " I will kill you all with the lightning.   I will send war and disease among you.   May the cold freeze you!   May the fire burn you! May the waters drown you ! " he cried.   " He has cursed enough," whispered Nï′lt*s*i to the son of *H*astsé*h*og*a*n.   " Put an end to his angry words."   So the young victor called No*h*oílpi to him and said : " You have bet yourself and have lost ; you are now my slave and must do my bidding.   You are not a god, for my power has prevailed against yours."   The victor had a bow of magic power named E*t*i′n *D*i*l*yï′*l*, or the Bow of Darkness ; he bent this upwards, and placing the string on the ground he bade his slave stand on the string ; then he shot No*h*oílpi up into the sky as if he had been an arrow. Up and up he went, growing smaller and smaller to the sight till he faded to a mere speck and finally disappeared altogether.   As he flew upwards he was heard to mutter in the angry tones of abuse and imprecation, until he was too far away to be heard ; but no one could distinguish anything he said as he ascended.

228. He flew up in the sky until he came to the home of Béko-ts*ï*d*i*,[78] the god who carries the moon, and who is supposed by the Navahoes to be identical with the God of the Americans.   He is very old, and dwells in a long row of stone houses.   When No*h*oílpi arrived at the house of Békots*ï*d*i* he related to the latter all his mis-adventures in the lower world and said, " Now I am poor, and this is why I have come to see you."   " You need be poor no longer," said Békots*ï*d*i* ; " I will provide for you."   So he made for the gambler pets or domestic animals of new kinds, different to those which he had in the Chaco valley ; he made for him sheep, asses, horses,

swine, goats, and fowls. He also gave him *bayeta*,[79] and other cloths of bright colors, more beautiful than those woven by his slaves at Kĭntyél. He made, too, a new people, the Mexicans, for the gambler to rule over, and then he sent him back to this world again, but he descended far to the south of his former abode, and reached the earth in old Mexico.

229. No*h*oílpi's people increased greatly in Mexico, and after a while they began to move towards the north, and build towns along the Rio Grande. No*h*oílpi came with them until they arrived at a place north of Santa Fé. There they ceased building, and he returned to old Mexico, where he still lives, and where he is now the Nakaí *D*ĭgíni, or God of the Mexicans.

230. The Navaho who went at the bidding of the Sun to the tryst of the gods stayed with them till the gambler was shot into the sky. Then he returned to his people and told all he had seen. The young stranger went back to Tse'gíhi, the home of the yéi.

231. The wanderers were not long at Kĭntyél, but while they were they met some of the Daylight People. From Kĭntyél they moved to *To*'í'*nd*otsos, and here Mai,[80] the Coyote, married a Navaho woman. He remained in the Navaho camp nine days, and then he went to visit *D*asáni, the Porcupine. The latter took a piece of bark, scratched his nose with it till the blood flowed freely out over it, put it on the fire, and there roasted it slowly until it turned into a piece of fine meat. Porcupine then spread some clean herbs on the ground, laid the roasted meat on these, and invited his visitor to partake. Coyote was delighted; he had never had a nicer meal, and when he was leaving he invited his host to return the visit in two days. At the appointed time Porcupine presented himself at the hut of Coyote. The latter greeted his guest, bade him be seated, and rushed out of the house. In a few minutes he returned with a piece of bark. With this he scratched his nose, as he had seen Porcupine doing, and allowed the blood to flow. He placed the bloody bark over the fire, where in a moment it burst into flames and was soon reduced to ashes. Coyote hung his head in shame and Porcupine went home hungry.

232. Soon after this Coyote visited Maítso,[80] the Wolf. The latter took down, from among the rafters of his hut, two of the old-fashioned reed arrows with wooden heads, such as the Navahoes used in the ancient days; he pulled out the wooden points, rolled them on his thigh, moistened them in his mouth, and buried them in the hot ashes beside the fire. After waiting a little while and talking to his guest, he raked out from the ashes, where he had buried the arrow points, two fine cooked puddings of minced meat; these he laid on a mat of fresh herbs and told Coyote to help him-

self.   Coyote again enjoyed his meal greatly, and soon after, when
he rose to leave, he invited Wolf to pay him a visit in two days.
Wolf went in due time to the house of Coyote, and when he had
seated himself the host took two arrow-heads, as Wolf had done,
rolled them on his thigh, put them in his mouth, and buried them in
the hot ashes.   After waiting a while, he raked the ashes and found
nothing but two pieces of charred wood where he had placed the
arrow-heads.   This time he gave no evidence of his disappointment,
but sat and talked with his guest just as if nothing had happened,
until Wolf, seeing no sign of dinner and becoming very hungry, got
up and went home.

233. In those days the Chicken-hawks and the Hummingbirds
were known as great hunters.   They were friendly to one another
and dwelt together in one camp.

234. Coyote went to pay them a visit, and when he arrived at the
camp he entered one of the huts of the Hummingbirds.   He found
therein two beautiful Hummingbird maidens, gayly dressed, with
rows of deer-hoof pendants on their skirts and shoulders.   He lay
down in the lodge and said to the maidens : " Where is everybody
to-day ?   I heard there were many people camped here, but the
camp seems deserted."   The maidens replied : "There are many
people camped here, but to-day the men are all out hunting."

235. Now, Coyote was a dandy ; he was always beautifully dressed ;
he had a nice otter-skin quiver and his face was painted in spots.
The maidens, when they had looked well at him, bent their heads
together and whispered to one another, "He is a handsome young
man.   He is beautifully dressed.   He must be a person of some
importance."   He spent the day gossipping with the maidens and
telling them wonderful tales about himself.   "Would you know who
I am ? " he said.   " I am the God of Tsïsnadz̆ïʼni Mountain.   I have
no need to hunt.   All I have to do is to will the death of an animal
and it dies.   Your people have no need to wear themselves out
hunting for game.   I can kill all they want without labor."

236. At nightfall, when the hunters returned, the maidens left the
lodge, went to where their friends were assembled, and told them all
about the visitor.   When the maidens had finished their story, the
chief directed one of the young men to go over to the hut, peep in
over the curtain in the doorway, and see what the stranger looked
like.   The young man did as he was bidden, making no noise, and
looked into the lodge unobserved by Coyote.   When he returned to
the chief he said : " The stranger is a fine-looking man and is beautifully dressed.   Perhaps he is indeed a god."   The chief then said :
" It may be that all is true which he has told the maidens.   We have
to travel far in all sorts of weather and to work hard to secure food.

He may know some way to save us from labor, so let us be kind to him. Go, one of you maidens, back to the lodge to serve him." Hearing these words, the younger of the two young women returned to the lodge. Her clothing was ornamented with many pendants of bone and hoof that rattled with every movement she made, and for this reason Coyote named her Tsiké Nazí'li, or Young Woman Who Rattles.

237. In the morning she went to the lodge where her people were, and where a good breakfast was already prepared, and she brought a large dishful of the food for Coyote to eat. As she was about to depart with the food her people charged her to tell Coyote nothing of certain bad neighbors of theirs, lest he might visit them and work wonders for their benefit. But their injunctions came too late. Already Tsiké Nazí'li had told him all about these bad neighbors, and he had made up his mind to visit them.

238. When breakfast was over she said: " Now the hunters are going out." He replied : " I will go with them." So he joined the party, and they travelled together till they got to the brow of a high hill which overlooked an extensive country. Here Coyote told his companions to remain concealed while he went into the plain and drove the game toward them. When he got out of sight, he tied to his tail a long fagot of shredded cedar-bark, which he set on fire, and then he ran over the country in a wide circle as fast as he could go. Everywhere the fagot touched it set fire to the grass, and raised a long line of flame and smoke which drove the antelope up to where the hunters were concealed. A great quantity of game was killed ; the hunters returned laden with meat, and their faith in Coyote was unbounded.

239. Next morning they all went out once more to hunt. Again the hunters concealed themselves on the brow of a hill, and again Coyote tied the blazing fagot to his tail and ran. The people on the hilltop watched the line of fire advancing over the plain ; but when it turned around as if to come back to the place from which it started, it suddenly ceased. Much game was driven toward the party in ambush ; but Coyote did not return, and the hunters went to work cutting up the meat and cooking food for themselves.

240. Coyote, in the mean time, had gone to seek the bad neighbors. He untied his brand at the place where the hunters had seen the line of fire cease, and wandered off in a different direction. After a while he came to two great trees, a spruce and a pine, growing close together, and filled with chattering birds of two kinds. The spruce-tree was filled with birds called Tsí'di Béze, and the pine-tree with birds called Tsí'di Sási. They were all busily engaged in playing a game which Coyote had never seen before. They would

pull out their eyes, toss these up to the top of the tree, cry "Drop back, my eyes! Drop back!" and catch the eyes as they descended in their proper sockets. Coyote watched their play for a long time, and at length, becoming fascinated with the game, he cried out to the Tsĭ'di *Sási* in the pine-tree, "Pull out my eyes for me. I want to play, too." "No," they replied, "we will have nothing to do with you." Again and again he begged to be allowed to join in the sport, and again and again they refused him. But when he had pleaded for the fourth time, they flew down to where Coyote sat, and, taking sharp sticks, they gouged his eyes out. The eyes were thrown up to the top of the pine-tree, and when they fell down Coyote caught them in his orbits and could see again as well as ever. Coyote was delighted with the result of his first venture, and he begged them to pull his eyes out again, but they said angrily: "We do not want to play with you. We have done enough for you now. Go and leave us." But he continued to whine and beg until again they pulled out his eyes and tossed them up with the same happy result as before. Thus four times were his eyes pulled out, thrown upward, and caught back again in the head. But when he begged them to pull out his eyes for the fifth time, they went to a distance and held a council among themselves. When they returned they pulled his eyes out once more ; but this time they took pains to pull out the strings of the eyes (optic nerves) at the same time ; these they tied together, and, when the eyes were again flung up in the tree, they caught on one of the branches and there they stayed. Now Coyote was in mortal distress. "Drop back, my eyes! Drop back!" he cried. But back they never came, and he sat there with his nose pointed up toward the top of the tree, and he howled and prayed and wept. At last the birds took pity on him and said: "Let us make other eyes for him." So they took a couple of partly dried pieces of pine gum and rolled them into two balls ; these were stuck into the empty sockets, and, although they were not good eyes, they gave him sight enough to see his way home. The gum was yellow, and for this reason coyotes have had yellow eyes ever since.

241. He crept back, as best he could, to the place where he had left the hunters, and where he found them cutting and cooking meat. He sat down facing the fire, but he soon found that his gum eyes were getting soft with the heat, so he turned his side to the fire. The hunters gave him a piece of raw liver, supposing he would cook it himself. Not daring to turn towards the fire, lest his eyes should melt altogether, he threw the liver on the coals without looking, and when he tried afterwards to take it up he thrust his hand at random into the fire and caught nothing but hot coals that burned him. Fearing that his strange action was observed, he tried to pass it off

as a joke, and every time he picked up a hot coal he cried: "Don't burn me, liver! Don't burn me, liver!" After a while the hunters seated around the fire began to notice his singular motions and words, and one said to another: "He does not act as usual. Go and see what is the matter with him." The hunter who was thus bidden went over in front of Coyote, looked at him closely, and saw melted gum pouring out from between his eyelids.

242. It happened that during the day, while Coyote was absent, a messenger had come to the camp of the hunters from another camp to tell them that an individual named Mai, or Coyote, had left his home, and had been seen going toward the camp of the Hummingbirds, and to warn them against him. "He is an idler and a trickster, — beware of him," said the messenger. So when they found out the condition of their visitor they said: "This must be Coyote of whom we have heard. He has been playing with the Tsĭ'di *Sási* and has lost his eyes."

243. When they had arrived at this conclusion they started for camp and led the blind Coyote along. In the mean time they devised a plan for getting rid of him. When they got home they took the rattling dress of Tsiké Nazĭ'li and gave her an ordinary garment to wear. Then a Chicken-hawk took the dress in his beak, and, flying a little distance above the ground, shook the dress in front of Coyote. The latter, thinking the maiden was there, approached the sound, and as he did so the Chicken-hawk flew farther away, still shaking the dress. Coyote followed the rattling sound, and was thus led on to the brink of a deep canyon. Here the hawk shook the dress beyond the edge of the precipice. Coyote jumped toward where he heard the sound, fell to the bottom of the canyon, and was dashed to pieces.

244. But for all this he did not die. He did not, like other beings, keep his vital principle in his chest, where it might easily be destroyed; he kept it in the tip of his nose and in the end of his tail, where no one would expect to find it; so after a while he came to life again, went back to the camp of the birds, and asked for Tsiké Nazĭ'li. They told him she was gone away, and ordered him angrily to leave, telling him they knew who he was, and that he was a worthless fellow.

245. Coyote left the camp of the birds, and wandered around till he came to the house of one of the anáye, or alien gods, named Yé*l*apahi,[71] or Brown Giant. He was half as tall as the tallest pine-tree, and he was evil and cruel. Coyote said to the Brown Giant, "Yé*l*apahi, I want to be your servant; I can be of great help to you. The reason that you often fail to catch your enemies is that you cannot run fast enough. I can run fast and jump far; I can jump over

four bushes at one bound. I can run after your enemies and help
you to catch them." "My cousin," responded Brown Giant, "you
can do me service if you will." Coyote then directed the giant to
build a sweat-house for himself, and, while the latter was building it,
Coyote set out on another errand.

246. In those days there was a maiden of renowned beauty in the
land. She was the only sister of eleven divine brothers.[81] She had
been sought in marriage by the Sun and by many potent gods, but
she had refused them all because they could not comply with certain
conditions which she imposed on all suitors. It was to visit her
that Coyote went when he left Yé/apahi at work on the sweat-house.

247. "Why have you refused so many beautiful gods who want
you for a wife?" said Coyote to the maiden after he had greeted her.
"It would profit you nothing to know," she replied, "for you could
not comply with any one of my demands." Four times he asked
her this question, and three times he got the same reply. When he
asked her the fourth time she answered: "In the first place, I will
not marry any one who has not killed one of the anáye." When he
heard this Coyote arose and returned to the place where he had left
Yé/apahi.

248. On his way back he looked carefully for the bone of some
big animal which Great Wolf had slain and eaten. At length he
found a long thigh-bone which suited his purpose. He took this
home with him, concealing it under his shirt. When Coyote got
back, Yé/apahi had finished the sweat-house.[82] Together they built
the fire, heated the stones, and spread the carpet of leaves. Coyote
hung over the doorway four blankets of sky, — one white, one blue,
one yellow, and one black, and put the hot stones into the lodge.
Then they hung their arms and clothes on a neighboring tree,
entered the sudatory, and sat down.[83]

249. "Now," said Coyote, "if you want to become a fast runner,
I will show you what to do. You must cut the flesh of your thigh
down to the bone and then break the bone. It will heal again in a
moment, and when it heals you will be stronger and swifter than
ever. I often do this myself, and every time I do it I am fleeter of
foot than I was before. I will do it now, so that you may observe
how it is done." Coyote then produced a great stone knife and pretended to cut his own thigh, wailing and crying in the mean time,
and acting as if he suffered great pain. After a while of this pre-
tence he put the old femur on top of his thigh, held it by both ends,
and said to the giant: "I have now reached the bone. Feel it."
When the giant had put forth his hand, in the absolute darkness of
the sweat-house, and felt the bare bone, Coyote shoved the hand
away and struck the bone hard with the edge of his knife several

times until he broke the bone, and he made the giant feel the fractured ends. Then he threw away the old bone, rubbed spittle on his thigh, prayed and sang, and in a little while presented his sound thigh to the giant for his examination, saying: "See! my limb is healed again. It is as well as ever." When he had thus spoken Coyote handed his knife to Yé*l*apahi, and the latter with many tears and loud howls slowly amputated his own thigh. When the work was done he put the two severed ends together, spat upon them, sang and prayed, as Coyote had done. "*T*óhe! *T*óhe! *T*óhe!"[84] he cried, "Heal together! Grow together!" he commanded; but the severed ends would not unite. "Cousin," he called to Coyote, "help me to heal this leg." Coyote thought it was now time to finish his work. He ran from the sweat-house, seized his bow, and discharged his arrows into the helpless Yé*l*apahi, who soon expired with many wounds.

250. Coyote scalped his victim, and tied the scalp to the top of a branch which he broke from a cedar-tree; as further evidence of his victory, he took the quiver and weapons of the slain and set out for the lodge of the maiden. He knew she could not mistake the scalp, for the yéi, in those days, had yellow hair,[85] such as no other people had. When he reached the lodge he said to the maiden: "Here is the scalp and here are the weapons of one of the anáye. Now you must marry me." "No," said the maiden, "not yet; I have not told you all that one must do in order to win me. He must be killed four times and come to life again four times." "Do you speak the truth? Have you told me all?" said Coyote. "Yes; I speak only the truth," she replied. Four times he asked this question, and four times he received the same answer. When she had spoken for the fourth time Coyote said: "Here I am. Do with me as you will." The maiden took him a little distance from the lodge, laid him on the ground, beat him with a great club until she thought she had smashed every bone in his body, and left him for dead. But the point of his nose and the end of his tail she did not smash. She hurried back to her hut, for she had much work to do. She was the only woman in a family of twelve. She cooked the food and tanned the skins, and besides she made baskets. At this particular time she was engaged in making four baskets. When she returned to the lodge she sat down and went on with her basket-work; but she had not worked long before she became aware that some one was standing in the doorway, and, looking up, she beheld Coyote. "Here I am," he said; "I have won one game; there are only three more to win."

251. She made no reply, but took him off farther than she had taken him before, and pounded him to pieces with a club. She threw

the pieces away in different directions and returned to her work again; but she had not taken many stitches in her basket when again the resurrected Coyote appeared in the doorway, saying: "I have won two games; there are only two more to win."

252. Again she led him forth, but took him still farther away from the lodge than she had taken him before, and with a heavy club pounded him into a shapeless mass, until she thought he must certainly be dead. She stood a long time gazing at the pounded flesh, and studying what she would do with it to make her work sure. She carried the mass to a great rock, and there she beat it into still finer pieces. These she scattered farther than she had scattered the pieces before, and went back to the house. But she had still failed to injure the two vital spots. It took the Coyote a longer time on this occasion than on the previous occasions to pull himself together; still she had not wrought much on her basket when he again presented himself and said: "I have won three games; there is but one more game to win."

253. The fourth time she led him farther away than ever. She not only mashed him to pieces, but she mixed the pieces with earth, ground the mixture, like corn, between two stones, until it was ground to a fine powder, and scattered this powder far and wide. But again she neglected to crush the point of the nose and the tip of the tail. She went back to the lodge and worked a long time undisturbed. She had just begun to entertain hopes that she had seen the last of her unwelcome suitor when again he entered the door. Now, at last, she could not refuse him. He had fulfilled all her conditions, and she consented to become his wife. He remained all the afternoon. At sunset they heard the sound of approaching footsteps, and she said: "My brothers are coming. Some of them are evil of mind and may do you harm. You must hide yourself." She hid him behind a pile of skins, and told him to be quiet.

254. When the brothers entered the lodge they said to their sister: "Here is some fat young venison which we bring you. Put it down to boil and put some of the fat into the pot, for our faces are burned by the wind and we want to grease them." The woman slept on the north side of the lodge and kept there her household utensils. She had about half of the lodge to herself. The men slept on the south side, the eldest next to the door.

255. The pot was put on and the fire replenished, and when it began to burn well an odor denoting the presence of some beast filled the lodge. One of the brothers said: "It smells as if some animal had been in the wood-pile. Let us throw out this wood and get fresh sticks from the bottom of the pile." They did as he desired; but the unpleasant odors continued to annoy them, and

again the wood was taken from the fire and thrown away. Thinking the whole pile of wood was tainted with the smell, they went out, broke fresh branches from trees, and built the fire up again; but this did not abate the rank odor in the least. Then one said: "Perhaps the smell is in the water. Tell us, little sister, where did you get the water in the pot?" "I got it at the spring where I always get it," she replied. But they got her to throw out the water and fill the pot with snow, and to put the meat down to boil again. In spite of all their pains the stench was as bad as ever. At length one of the brothers turned to his sister and said: "What is the cause of this odor? It is not in the wood. It is not in the water. Whence comes it?" She was silent. He repeated the question three times, yet she made no answer. But when the question had been asked for the fourth time, Coyote jumped out of his hiding-place into the middle of the lodge and cried: "It is I, my brothers-in-law!" "Run out there!" the brothers commanded, and turning to their sister they said: "Run out you with him!"

256. They both departed from the lodge. As Coyote went out he took a brand from the fire, and with this he lighted a new fire. Then he broke boughs from the neighboring trees and built a shelter for himself and his wife to live in. When this was completed she went back to the lodge of her brothers, took out her pots, skins, four awls, baskets, and all her property, and carried them to her new home.

257. One of the elder brothers said to the youngest: "Go out to-night and watch the couple, and see what sort of a man this is that we have for a brother-in-law. Do not enter the shelter, but lie hidden outside and observe them." So the youngest brother went forth and hid himself near the shelter, where he could peep in and see by the light of the fire what took place and hear what was said. The pair sat side by side near the fire. Presently the woman laid her hand in a friendly manner on Coyote's knee, but Coyote threw it away. These motions were repeated four times, and when he had thrown her hand away for the fourth time he said: "I have sworn never to take a woman for a wife until I have killed her four times." For a while the woman remained silent and gazed at the fire. At length she said: "Here I am. Do with me as you will." (The myth then relates four deaths and resurrections of the woman, similar to those of the Coyote, but it does not state how or where she preserved her vital principle.) When she returned for the fourth time she lay down, and Coyote soon followed her to her couch. From time to time during the night they held long, low conversations, of which the listener could hear but little. At dawn the watcher went home. In reply to the questions of his brothers he said: "I cannot

tell you all that I saw and heard, and they said much that I could not hear ; but all that I did hear and behold was tsïndás" (devilish, evil).

258. Next morning the brothers proposed to go out hunting. While they were getting ready Coyote came and asked leave to join them, but they said to him tauntingly : "No ; stay at home with your wife ; she may be lonely and may need some one to talk to her," and they chased him out of the lodge. Just as they were about to leave he came back again and begged them to take him with them. "No," they replied, "the woman will want you to carry wood ; you must stay at home with her." They bade him begone and set out on their journey. They had not gone far on their way when he overtook them, and for the third time asked to be allowed to join the party ; but again they. drove him back with scornful words. They travelled on till they came to the edge of a deep canyon bordered with very steep cliffs, and here Coyote was seen again, skulking behind them. For the fourth time he pleaded with them ; but now the youngest brother took his part, and suggested that Coyote might assist in driving game towards them. So, after some deliberation, they consented to take Coyote along. At the edge of the canyon they made a bridge of rainbow,[86] on which they proceeded to cross the chasm. Before the brothers reached the opposite bluff Coyote jumped on it from the bridge, with a great bound, and began to frolic around, saying : " This is a nice place to play."

259. They travelled farther on, and after a while came to a mesa, or table-land, which projected into a lower plain, and was connected with the plateau on which they stood by a narrow neck of level land. It was a mesa much like that on which the three eastern towns of the Mokis stand, with high, precipitous sides and a narrow entrance. On the neck of land they observed the tracks of four Rocky Mountain sheep, which had gone in on the mesa but had not returned. They had reason, therefore, to believe that the sheep were still on the mesa. At the neck they built a fire, sat down near it, and sent Coyote in on the mesa to drive the sheep out. Their plans were successful ; soon the four sheep came running out over the neck, within easy range of the hunters' weapons, and were all killed. Presently Coyote returned and lay down on the sand.

260. In those days the horns of the Rocky Mountain sheep were flat and fleshy and could be eaten. The eldest brother said : " I will take the horns for my share." "No," said Coyote, "the horns shall be mine : give them to me." Three times each repeated the same declaration. When both had spoken for the fourth time, the eldest brother, to end the controversy, drew out his knife and began to cut one of the horns ; as he did so Coyote cried out, " Tsïnántlehi !

Tsĭnántlehi! Tsĭnántlehi! Tsĭnántlehi!" (Turn to bone! Turn to bone! Turn to bone! Turn to bone!) Each time he cried, the horn grew harder and harder, and the knife slipped as it cut, hacking but not severing the horn. This is why the horns of the Rocky Mountain sheep are now hard, not fleshy, and to this day they bear the marks of the hunter's knife. "Tsĭ'ndi! Tsĭndás biɬnáalɫi!" (You devil! You evil companion in travel!) said the hunter to Coyote.

261. The hunters gathered all the meat into one pile, and by means of the mystic power which they possessed they reduced it to a very small compass. They tied it in a small bundle which one person might easily carry, and they gave it to Coyote to take home, saying to him, "Travel round by the head of the canyon over which we crossed and go not through it, for they are evil people who dwell there, and open not your bundle until you get home."

262. The bundle was lifted to his back and he started for home, promising to heed all that had been told him. But as soon as he was well out of sight of his companions he slipped his bundle to the ground and opened it. At once the meat expanded and became again a heap of formidable size, such that he could not bind it up again or carry it; so he hung some of it up on the trees and bushes; he stuck part of it into crevices in the rocks; a portion he left scattered on the ground; he tied up as much as he could carry in a new bundle, and with this he continued on his journey.

263. When he came to the edge of the forbidden canyon he looked down and saw some birds playing a game he had never witnessed before. They rolled great stones down the slope, which extended from the foot of the cliff to the bottom of the valley, and stood on the stones while they were rolling; yet the birds were not upset or crushed or hurt in the least by this diversion. The sight so pleased Coyote that he descended into the canyon and begged to be allowed to join in the sport. The birds rolled a stone gently for him; he got on it and handled himself so nimbly that he reached the bottom of the slope without injury. Again and again he begged them to give him a trial until he thus three times descended without hurting himself. When he asked the birds for the fourth time to roll a stone for him they became angry and hurled it with such force that Coyote lost his footing, and he and the stone rolled over one another to the bottom of the slope, and he screamed and yelped all the way down.

264. After this experience he left the birds and travelled on until he observed some Otters at play by the stream at the bottom of the canyon. They were playing the Navaho game of nánzoz. They bet their skins against one another on the results of the game. But when one lost his skin at play he jumped into the water and came

out with a new skin. Coyote approached the Otters and asked to be allowed to take part in the game, but the Otters had heard about him and knew what a rascal he was. They refused him and told him to begone; but still he remained and pleaded. After a while they went apart and talked among themselves, and when they returned they invited Coyote to join them in their game. Coyote bet his skin and lost it. The moment he lost, the Otters all rushed at him, and, notwithstanding his piteous cries, they tore the hide from his back, beginning at the root of his tail and tearing forward. When they came to the vital spot at the end of his nose his wails were terrible. When he found himself denuded of his skin he jumped into the water, as he had seen the Otters doing; but, alas! his skin did not come back to him. He jumped again and again into the water; but came out every time as bare as he went in. At length he became thoroughly exhausted, and lay down in the water until the Otters took pity on him and pulled him out. They dragged him to a badger hole, threw him in there, and covered him up with earth. Previous to this adventure Coyote had a beautiful, smooth fur like that of the otter. When he dug his way out of the badger hole he was again covered with hair, but it was no longer the glossy fur which he once wore; it was coarse and rough, much like that of the badger, and such a pelt the coyotes have worn ever since.

265. But this sad experience did not make him mend his ways. He again went round challenging the Otters to further play, and betting his new skin on the game. "Your skin is of no value; no one would play for it. Begone!" they said. Being often refused and insolently treated, he at length became angry, retired to a safe distance, and began to revile the Otters shamefully. "You are braggarts," he cried; "you pretend to be brave, but you are cowards. Your women are like yourselves: their heads are flat; their eyes are little; their teeth stick out; they are ugly; while I have a bride as beautiful as the sun." He shook his foot at them as if to say, "I am fleeter than you." He would approach them, and when they made motion as if to pursue him, he would take a big jump and soon place himself beyond their reach. When they quieted down, he would approach them again and continue to taunt and revile them. After a while he went to the cliff, to a place of safety, and shouted from there his words of derision. The Otters talked together, and said they could suffer his abuse no longer, that something must be done, and they sent word to the chiefs of the Spiders, who lived farther down the stream, telling them what had occurred, and asking for their aid.

266. The Spiders crept up the bluff, went round behind where Coyote sat cursing and scolding, and wove strong webs in the trees

and bushes. When their work was finished they told the Otters what they had done, and the latter started to climb the bluff and attack Coyote. Conscious of his superior swiftness, he acted as if indifferent to them, and allowed them to come quite close before he turned to run; but he did not run far until he was caught in the webs of the Spiders. Then the Otters seized him and dragged him, howling, to the foot of the hill. He clung so hard to the grasses and shrubs as he passed that they were torn out by the roots. When the Otters got him to the bottom of the hill they killed him, or seemed to kill him. The Cliff Swallows (*Hastsósi*) [21] flew down from the walls of the canyon and tore him in pieces; they carried off the fragments to their nests, leaving only a few drops of blood on the ground; they tore his skin into strips and made of these bands which they put around their heads, and this accounts for the band which the cliff swallow wears upon his brow to-day.

267. It was nightfall when the brothers came home. They saw that Coyote had not yet returned, and they marvelled what had become of him. When they entered the lodge and sat down, the sister came and peeped in over the portière, scanned the inside of the lodge, and looked inquiringly at them. They did not speak to her until she had done this four times, then the eldest brother said: " Go back and sleep, and don't worry about that worthless man of yours. He is not with us, and we know not what has become of him. We suppose he has gone into the canyon, where we warned him not to go, and has been killed." She only said, "What have you done with him?" and went away in anger.

268. Before they lay down to sleep they sent the youngest brother out to hide where he had hidden the night before to watch their sister, and this is what he saw: At first she pretended to go to sleep. After a while she rose and sat facing the east. Then she faced in turn the south, the west, and the north, moving sunwise. When this was done she pulled out her right eye-tooth, broke a large piece from one of her four bone awls and inserted it in the place of the tooth, making a great tusk where the little tooth had once been. As she did this she said aloud: " He who shall hereafter dream of losing a right eye-tooth shall lose a brother." After this she opened her mouth to the four points of the compass in the order in which she had faced them before, tore out her left eye-tooth and inserted in its place the pointed end of another awl. As she made this tusk she said: " He who dreams of losing his left eye-tooth shall lose a sister."

269. The watcher then returned to his brothers and told them what he had seen and heard. " Go back," said they, "and watch her again, for you have not seen all her deeds." When he went

back he saw her make, as she had done before, two tusks in her lower jaw. When she had made that on the right she said : "He who dreams of losing this tooth (right lower canine) shall lose a child;" and when she made that on the left she said : "He who dreams of losing this tooth (left lower canine) shall lose a parent."

270. When she first began to pull out her teeth, hair began to grow on her hands ; as she went on with her mystic work the hair spread up her arms and her legs, leaving only her breasts bare. The young man now crept back to the lodge where his brethren waited and told them what he had seen. "Go back," they said, "and hide again. There is more for you to see."

271. When he got back to his hiding-place the hair had grown over her breasts, and she was covered with a coat of shaggy hair like that of a bear. She continued to move around in the direction of the sun's apparent course, pausing and opening her mouth at the east, the south, the west, and the north as she went. After a while her ears began to wag, her snout grew long, her teeth were heard to gnash, her nails turned into claws. He watched her until dawn, when, fearing he might be discovered, he returned to his lodge and told his brothers all that had happened. They said : "These must be the mysteries that Coyote explained to her the first night."

272. In a moment after the young man had told his story they heard the whistling of a bear, and soon a she-bear rushed past the door of the lodge, cracking the branches as she went. She followed the trail which Coyote had taken the day before and disappeared in the woods.

273. At night she came back groaning. She had been in the fatal canyon all day, fighting the slayers of Coyote, and she had been wounded in many places. Her brothers saw a light in her hut, and from time to time one of their number would go and peep in through an aperture to observe what was happening within. All night she walked around the fire. At intervals she would, by means of her magic, draw arrow-heads out of her body and heal the wounds.

274. Next morning the bear-woman again rushed past the lodge of her brethren, and again went off toward the fatal canyon. At night she returned, as before, groaning and bleeding, and again spent the long night in drawing forth missiles and healing her wounds by means of her magic rites.

275. Thus she continued to do for four days and four nights; but at the end of the fourth day she had conquered all her enemies ; she had slain many, and those she had not killed she had dispersed. The swallows flew up into the high cliffs to escape her vengeance ; the otters hid themselves in the water; the spiders retreated into holes in the ground,[87] and in such places these creatures have been obliged to dwell ever since.

276. During these four days, the brothers remained in their camp ; but at the end of that time, feeling that trouble was in store for them, they decided to go away. They left the youngest brother at home, and the remaining ten divided themselves into four different parties ; one of which travelled to the east, another to the south, another to the west, and another to the north.

277. When they were gone, the Whirlwind, Níyol, and the Knife Boy, Pésasike, came to the lodge to help the younger brother who had remained behind. They dug for him a hole under the centre of the *hogán* ; and from this they dug four branching tunnels, running east, south, west, and north, and over the end of each tunnel they put a window of gypsum to let in light from above. They gave him four weapons, — atsĭniklĭ'ska, the chain-lightning arrow ; *h*atsoil*h*álka (an old-fashioned stone knife as big as the open hand) ; natsilĭ'*t*ka, the rainbow arrow ; and *h*atsĭlkĭ'ska, the sheet-lightning arrow. They roofed his hiding-place with four flat stones, one white, one blue, one yellow, and one black. They put earth over all these, smoothing the earth and tramping it down so that it should look like the natural floor of the lodge. They gave him two monitors, Nĭ'ltsi, the Wind, at his right ear, to warn him by day of the approach of danger ; and Tsa*l*yél, darkness, at his left ear, to warn him by night.

278. When morning came and the bear-woman went forth she discovered that her brothers had departed. She poured water on the ground (*h*alĭ'z) to see which way they had gone. The water flowed to the east ; she rushed on in that direction and soon overtook three of the fugitives, whom she succeeded in killing. Then she went back to her hut to see what had become of her other brothers. Again she poured water on the level ground and it flowed off to the south ; she followed in that direction and soon overtook three others, whom she likewise slew. Returning to the lodge she again performed her divination by means of water. This time she was directed to the west, and, going that way, she overtook and killed three more of the men. Again she sought the old camp and poured on the ground water, which flowed to the north ; going on in this direction she encountered but one man, and him she slew. Once more she went back to discover what had become of her last brother. She poured water for the fifth time on the level ground ; it sank directly into the earth.

279. The brothers had always been very successful hunters and their home was always well supplied with meat. In consequence of this they had had many visitors who built in their neighborhood temporary shelters, such as the Navahoes build now when they come to remain only a short time at a place, and the remains of these shelters surrounded the deserted hut. She scratched in all these

places to find traces of the fugitive, without success, and in doing so she gradually approached the deserted hut. She scratched all around outside the hut and then went inside. She scratched around the edge of the hut and then worked toward the centre, until at length she came to the fireplace. Here she found the earth was soft as if recently disturbed, and she dug rapidly downward with her paws. She soon came to the stones, and, removing these, saw her last remaining brother hidden beneath them. "I greet you, my younger brother! Come up, I want to see you," she said in a coaxing voice. Then she held out one finger to him and said: "Grasp my finger and I will help you up." But Wind told him not to grasp her finger; that if he did she would throw him upwards, that he would fall half dead at her feet and be at her mercy. "Get up without her help," whispered Nĭ'ltsi.

280. He climbed out of the hole on the east side and walked toward the east. She ran toward him in a threatening manner, but he looked at her calmly and said: "It is I, your younger brother." Then she approached him in a coaxing way, as a dog approaches one with whom he wishes to make friends, and she led him back toward the deserted *hogán*. But as he approached it the Wind whispered: "We have had sorrow there, let us not enter," so he would not go in, and this is the origin of the custom now among the Navahoes never to enter a house in which death had occurred.[91]

281. "Come," she then said, "and sit with your face to the west, and let me comb your hair." (It was now late in the afternoon.) "Heed her not," whispered Wind; "sit facing the north, that you watch her shadow and see what she does. It is thus that she has killed your brothers." They both sat down, she behind him, and she untied his queue and proceeded to arrange his hair, while he watched her out of the corner of his eye. Soon he observed her snout growing longer and approaching his head, and he noticed that her ears were wagging. "What does it mean that your snout grows longer and that your ears move so?" he asked. She did not reply, but drew her snout in and kept her ears still. When these occurrences had taken place for the fourth time, Wind whispered in his ear: "Let not this happen again. If she puts out her snout the fifth time she will bite your head off. Yonder, where you see that chattering squirrel, are her vital parts. He guards them for her. Now run and destroy them." He rose and ran toward the vital parts and she ran after him. Suddenly, between them a large yucca[88] sprang up to retard her steps, and then a cane cactus,[89] and then another yucca, and then another cactus of a different kind. She ran faster than he, but was so delayed in running around the plants that he reached the vitals before her, and heard the lungs breathing

under the weeds that covered them. He drew forth his chain-lightning arrow, shot it into the weeds, and saw a bright stream of blood spurting up. At the same instant the bear-woman fell with the blood streaming from her side.

282. "See!" whispered Nĭ'ltsi, the Wind, "the stream of blood from her body and the stream from her vitals flow fast and approach one another. If they meet she will revive, and then your danger will be greater than ever. Draw, with your stone knife, a mark on the ground between the approaching streams." The young man did as he was bidden, when instantly the blood coagulated and ceased to flow.

283. Then the young man said: "You shall live again, but no longer as the mischievous Tsiké Sas Náḍlehi.[90] You shall live in other forms, where you may be of service to your kind and not a thing of evil." He cut off the head and said to it: "Let us see if in another life you will do better. When you come to life again, act well, or again I will slay you." He threw the head at the foot of a piñon-tree and it changed into a bear, which started at once to walk off. But presently it stopped, shaded its eyes with one paw, and looked back at the man, saying: "You have bidden me to act well; but what shall I do if others attack me?" "Then you may defend yourself," said the young man; "but begin no quarrel, and be ever a friend to your people, the *Dĭné*. Go yonder to Black Mountain (Dsĭḷḷĭzĭ n) and dwell there." There are now in Black Mountain many bears which are descended from this bear.

284. The hero cut off the nipples and said to them: "Had you belonged to a good woman and not to a foolish witch, it might have been your luck to suckle men. You were of no use to your kind; but now I shall make you of use in another form." He threw the nipples up into a piñon-tree, heretofore fruitless, and they became edible pine nuts.

285. Next he sought the homes of his friends, the holy ones, Níyol and Pésasike. They led him to the east, to the south, to the west, and to the north, where the corpses of his brothers lay, and these they restored to life for him. They went back to the place where the brothers had dwelt before and built a new house; but they did not return to the old home, for that was now a tsĭ'ndi *hogán* and accursed.[91]

286. The holy ones then gave to the young hero the name of Léyaneyani, or Reared Under the Ground, because they had hidden him in the earth when his brethren fled from the wrath of his sister. They bade him go and dwell at a place called Aḍáhyĭtsoi (Big Point on the Edge), which is in the shape of a *hogán*, or Navaho hut, and here we think he still dwells.

III. THE WAR GODS.

287. The *Dïné*ʻ now removed to Tseʻʟakaíia (White Standing Rock), where, a few days after they arrived, they found on the ground a small turquoise image of a woman; this they preserved. Of late the monsters (anáye, alien gods) had been actively pursuing and devouring the people, and at the time this image was found there were only four persons remaining alive;[92] these were an old man and woman and their two children, a young man and a young woman. Two days after the finding of the image, early in the morning, before they rose, they heard the voice of *H*astséyal*t*i, the Talking God, crying his call of "Wuʻhuʻhuʻhú" so faint and far that they could scarcely hear it. After a while the call was repeated a second time, nearer and louder than at first. Again, after a brief silence, the call was heard for the third time, still nearer and still louder. The fourth call was loud and clear, as if sounded near at hand;[26] as soon as it ceased, the shuffling tread of moccasined feet was heard, and a moment later the god *H*astséyal*t*i stood before them.

288. He told the four people to come up to the top of T*s*olíhi after twelve nights had passed, bringing with them the turquoise image they had found, and at once he departed. They pondered deeply on his words, and every day they talked among themselves, wondering why *H*astséyal*t*i had summoned them to the mountain.

289. On the morning of the appointed day they ascended the mountain by a holy trail,[93] and on a level spot, near the summit, they met a party that awaited them there. They found there *H*astséyal*t*i, *H*astsé*h*ogan (the Home God), White Body (who came up from the lower world with the *Dïné*ʻ), the eleven brothers (of Maid Who Becomes a Bear), the Mirage Stone People, the Daylight People standing in the east, the Blue Sky People standing in the south, the Yellow Light People standing in the west, and the Darkness People standing in the north. White Body stood in the east among the Daylight People, bearing in his hand a small image of a woman wrought in white shell, about the same size and shape as the blue image which the Navahoes bore.

290. *H*astséyal*t*i laid down a sacred buckskin with its head toward the west. The Mirage Stone People laid on the buckskin, heads west, the two little images, — of turquoise and white shell, — a white and a yellow ear of corn, the Pollen Boy, and the Grasshopper Girl. On top of all these *H*astséyal*t*i laid another sacred buckskin with its head to the east, and under this they now put Nïʻltsi (Wind).

291. Then the assembled crowd stood so as to form a circle, leaving in the east an opening through which *H*astséyal*t*i and *H*astsé*h*ogan

might pass in and out, and they sang the sacred song of *Hozóngisïn.*
Four times the gods entered and raised the cover. When they
raised it for the fourth time, the images and the ears of corn were
found changed to living beings in human form : the turquoise image
had become Estsánatlehi, the Woman Who Changes (or rejuvenates
herself) ; the white shell image had become Yo*l*kaí Estsán, the
White Shell Woman ; the white ear of corn had become Na*tá.l*kai
A*s*iké ; the White Corn Boy and the yellow ear of corn, Na*tá.l*tsoi
A*té.t*, the Yellow Corn Girl.[94] After the ceremony, White Body
took Pollen Boy, Grasshopper Girl, White Corn Boy, and Yellow
Corn Girl with him into T*s*olíhi ; the rest of the assembly departed,
and the two divine sisters, Estsánatlehi[95] and Yo*l*kaí Estsán,[96] were
left on the mountain alone.

292. The women remained here four nights ; on the fourth morning Estsánatlehi said : "*Sitě'z*i (younger sister), why should we
remain here ? Let us go to yonder high point and look around us."
They went to the highest point of the mountain, and when they had
been there several days Estsánatlehi said : "It is lonely here ; we
have no one to speak to but ourselves ; we see nothing but that
which rolls over our heads (the sun), and that which drops below us
(a small dripping waterfall). I wonder if they can be people. I shall
stay here and wait for the one in the morning, while you go down
among the rocks and seek the other."

293. In the morning Estsánatlehi found a bare, flat rock and lay
on it with her feet to the east, and the rising sun shone upon her.
Yo*l*kaí Estsán went down where the dripping waters descended and
allowed them to fall upon her. At noon the women met again on
the mountain top and Estsánatlehi said to her sister : "It is sad to
be so lonesome. How can we make people so that we may have
others of our kind to talk to ?" Yo*l*kaí Estsán answered : "Think,
Elder Sister ; perhaps after some days you may plan how this is to
be done."

294. Four days after this conversation Yo*l*kaí Estsán said : "Elder
Sister, I feel something strange moving within me ; what can it be ?"
and Estsánatlehi answered : "It is a child. It was for this that you
lay under the waterfall. I feel, too, the motions of a child within
me. It was for this that I let the sun shine upon me." Soon after
the voice of *H*ast*s*eyal*t*i was heard four times, as usual, and after the
last call he and *T*ó'nenïli[98] appeared. They came to prepare the
women for their approaching delivery.[99]

295. In four days more they felt the commencing throes of labor,
and one said to the other : "I think my child is coming." She had
scarcely spoken when the voice of the approaching god was heard,
and soon *H*ast*s*éyal*t*i and *T*ó'nenïli (Water Sprinkler) were seen

approaching. The former was the accoucheur of Estsánatlehi, and the latter of Yo*l*kái Estsán.[100] To one woman a drag-rope of rainbow was given, to the other a drag-rope of sunbeam, and on these they pulled when in pain, as the Navaho woman now pulls on the rope. Estsánatlehi's child was born first.[101] *H*ast*s*éyal*t*i took it aside and washed it. He was glad, and laughed and made ironical motions, as if he were cutting the baby in slices and throwing the slices away. They made for the children two baby-baskets, both alike; the foot-rests and the back battens were made of sunbeam, the hoods of rainbow, the side-strings of sheet lightning, and the lacing strings of zigzag lightning. One child they covered with the black cloud, and the other with the female rain.[102] They called the children *S*ïnáli (grandchildren), and they left, promising to return at the end of four days.

296. When the gods (yéi) returned at the end of four days, the boys had grown to be the size of ordinary boys of twelve years of age. The gods said to them: "Boys, we have come to have a race with you." So a race was arranged that should go all around a neighboring mountain, and the four started, — two boys and two yéi. Before the long race was half done the boys, who ran fast, began to flag, and the gods, who were still fresh, got behind them and scourged the lads with twigs of mountain mahogany.[103] *H*ast*s*éyal*t*i won the race, and the boys came home rubbing their sore backs. When the gods left they promised to return at the end of another period of four days.

297. As soon as the gods were gone, Nï'lt*s*i, the Wind, whispered to the boys and told them that the old ones were not such fast runners, after all, and that if the boys would practice during the next four days they might win the coming race. So for four days they ran hard, many times daily around the neighboring mountain, and when the gods came back again the youths had grown to the full stature of manhood. In the second contest the gods began to flag and fall behind when half way round the mountain, where the others had fallen behind in the first race, and here the boys got behind their elders and scourged the latter to increase their speed. The elder of the boys won this race, and when it was over the gods laughed and clapped their hands, for they were pleased with the spirit and prowess they witnessed.

298. The night after the race the boys lay down as usual to sleep; but hearing the women whispering together, they lay awake and listened. They strained their attention, but could not hear a word of what was uttered. At length they rose, approached the women, and said: "Mothers, of what do you speak?" and the women answered: "We speak of nothing." The boys then said: "Grand-

mothers, of what do you speak?" but the women again replied:
"We speak of nothing." The boys then questioned: "Who are our
fathers?" "You have no fathers," responded the women; "you are
yutáski (illegitimate)." "Who are our fathers?" again demanded the
boys, and the women answered: "The round cactus and the sitting
cactus [104] are your fathers."

299. Next day the women made rude bows of juniper wood, and
arrows, such as children play with, and they said to the boys: "Go
and play around with these, but do not go out of sight from our hut,
and do not go to the east." Notwithstanding these warnings the boys
went to the east the first day, and when they had travelled a good
distance they saw an animal with brownish hair and a sharp nose.
They drew their arrows and pointed them toward the sharp-nosed
stranger; but before they could shoot he jumped down into a canyon
and disappeared. When they returned home they told the women —
addressing them as "Mother" and "Grandmother" — what they
had seen. The women said: "That is Coyote which you saw. He
is a spy for the anáye *T*eelgĕ*t*."

300. On the following day, although again strictly warned not to
go far from the lodge, the boys wandered far to the south, and there
they saw a great black bird seated on a tree. They aimed their
arrows at it; but just as they were about to shoot the bird rose and
flew away. The boys returned to the *h*ogán and said to the women:
"Mothers, we have been to the south to-day, and there we saw a
great black bird which we tried to shoot; but before we could let
loose our arrows it flew off. "Alas!" said the women. "This was
Raven that you saw. He is the spy of the Tse‘nă'hale, the great
winged creatures that devour men."

301. On the third day the boys slipped off unknown to the anxious women, who would fain keep them at home, and walked a long
way toward the west. The only living thing they saw was a great
dark bird with a red skinny head that had no feathers on it. This
bird they tried to shoot also; but before they could do so it spread
its wings and flew a long way off. They went home and said to the
women: "Mothers, we have been to the west, and we have seen a
great dark bird whose head was red and bare. We tried to shoot it,
but it flew away before we could discharge our arrows." "It was
D*z*éso, the Buzzard, that you saw," said the women. "He is the
spy for Tse‘*ta*hotsílt*á*‘*l*i, he who kicks men down the cliffs."

302. On the fourth day the boys stole off as usual, and went
toward the north. When they had travelled a long way in that
direction, they saw a bird of black plumage perched on a tree on the
edge of a canyon. It was talking to itself, saying "a‘a‘i‘." They
aimed at it, but before they could let fly their arrows it spread its

wings and tail and disappeared down the canyon. As it flew, the boys noticed that its plumes were edged with white. When they got home they told their mothers, as before, what they had seen. "This bird that you saw," said the women, "is the Magpie. He is the spy for the Bïnáye A*h*áni, who slay people with their eyes. Alas, our children! What shall we do to make you hear us? What shall we do to save you? You would not listen to us. Now the spies of the anáye (the alien gods) in all quarters of the world have seen you. They will tell their chiefs, and soon the monsters will come here to devour you, as they have devoured all your kind before you."

303. The next morning the women made a corncake and laid it on the ashes to bake. Then Yo*l*kái Estsán went out of the *h*ogán, and, as she did so, she saw Yéitso,[105] the tallest and fiercest of the alien gods, approaching. She ran quickly back and gave the warning, and the women hid the boys under bundles and sticks. Yéitso came and sat down at the door, just as the women were taking the cake out of the ashes. "That cake is for me," said Yéitso. "How nice it smells!" "No," said Estsánatlehi, "it was not meant for your great maw." "I don't care," said Yéitso. "I would rather eat boys. Where are your boys? I have been told you have some here, and I have come to get them." "We have none," said Estsánatlehi. "All the boys have gone into the paunches of your people long ago." "No boys?" said the giant. "What, then, has made all the tracks around here?" "Oh! these tracks I have made for fun," replied the woman. "I am lonely here, and I make tracks so that I may fancy there are many people around me." She showed Yéitso how she could make similar tracks with her fist. He compared the two sets of tracks, seemed to be satisfied, and went away.

304. When he was gone, Yo*l*kaí Estsán, the White Shell Woman, went up to the top of a neighboring hill to look around, and she beheld many of the anáye hastening in the direction of her lodge. She returned speedily, and told her sister what she had seen. Estsánatlehi took four colored hoops, and threw one toward each of the cardinal points, — a white one to the east, a blue one to the south, a yellow one to the west, and a black one to the north. At once a great gale arose, blowing so fiercely in all directions from the *h*ogán that none of the enemies could advance against it.

305. Next morning the boys got up before daybreak and stole away. Soon the women missed them, but could not trace them in the dark. When it was light enough to examine the ground the women went out to look for fresh tracks. They found four footprints of each of the boys, pointing in the direction of the mountain of Dsï*l*náo*t*í*l*, but more than four tracks they could not find. They came to the conclusion that the boys had taken a holy trail, so they gave up further search and returned to the lodge.

306. The boys travelled rapidly in the holy trail,[93] and soon after sunrise, near Dsĭ/náoŭ/, they saw smoke arising from the ground. They went to the place where the smoke rose, and they found it came from the smoke-hole of a subterranean chamber. A ladder, black from smoke, projected through the hole. Looking down into the chamber they saw an old woman, the Spider Woman,[106] who glanced up at them and said : " Welcome, children. Enter. Who are you, and whence do you two come together walking ? " They made no answer, but descended the ladder. When they reached the floor she again spoke to them, asking : "Whither do you two go walking together ? " " Nowhere in particular," they answered ; " we came here because we had nowhere else to go." She asked this question four times, and each time she received a similar answer. Then she said : " Perhaps you would seek your father ? " " Yes," they answered, "if we only knew the way to his dwelling." " Ah ! " said the woman, " it is a long and dangerous way to the house of your father, the Sun. There are many of the anáye dwelling between here and there, and perhaps, when you get there, your father may not be glad to see you, and may punish you for coming. You must pass four places of danger, — the rocks that crush the traveller, the reeds that cut him to pieces, the cane cactuses that tear him to pieces, and the boiling sands that overwhelm him. But I shall give you something to subdue your enemies and preserve your lives." She gave them a charm called nayéatsos, or feather of the alien gods, which consisted of a hoop with two life-feathers (feathers plucked from a living eagle) attached, and another life-feather, hyĭná bĭltsós,[107] to preserve their existence. She taught them also this magic formula, which, if repeated to their enemies, would subdue their anger : " Put your feet down with pollen.[108] Put your hands down with pollen. Put your head down with pollen. Then your feet are pollen ; your hands are pollen ; your body is pollen ; your mind is pollen ; your voice is pollen. The trail is beautiful (bĭké hozóni). Be still." [109]

307. Soon after leaving the house of Spider Woman, the boys came to Tse'yeintĭ'li (the rocks that crush). There was here a narrow chasm between two high cliffs. When a traveller approached, the rocks would open wide apart, apparently to give him easy passage and invite him to enter ; but as soon as he was within the cleft they would close like hands clapping and crush him to death. These rocks were really people ; they thought like men ; they were anáye. When the boys got to the rocks they lifted their feet as if about to enter the chasm, and the rocks opened to let them in. Then the boys put down their feet, but withdrew them quickly. The rocks closed with a snap to crush them ; but the boys remained safe on

the outside. Thus four times did they deceive the rocks. When they had closed for the fourth time the rocks said: "Who are ye; whence come ye two together, and whither go ye?" "We are children of the Sun," answered the boys. "We come from Dsĭlnáotĭl, and we go to seek the house of our father." Then they repeated the words the Spider Woman had taught them, and the rocks said: "Pass on to the house of your father." When next they ventured to step into the chasm the rocks did not close, and they passed safely on.

308. The boys kept on their way and soon came to a great plain covered with reeds that had great leaves on them as sharp as knives. When the boys came to the edge of the field of reeds (*L*okáadikĭsi), the latter opened, showing a clear passage through to the other side. The boys pretended to enter, but retreated, and as they did so the walls of reeds rushed together to kill them. Thus four times did they deceive the reeds. Then the reeds spoke to them, as the rocks had done; they answered and repeated the sacred words. "Pass on to the house of your father," said the reeds, and the boys passed on in safety.

309. The next danger they encountered was in the country covered with cane cactuses.[89] These cactuses rushed at and tore to pieces whoever attempted to pass through them. When the boys came to the cactuses the latter opened their ranks to let the travellers pass on, as the reeds had done before. But the boys deceived them as they had deceived the reeds, and subdued them as they had subdued the reeds, and passed on in safety.

310. After they had passed the country of the cactus they came, in time, to *S*aitád, the land of the rising sands. Here was a great desert of sands that rose and whirled and boiled like water in a pot, and overwhelmed the traveller who ventured among them. As the boys approached, the sands became still more agitated and the boys did not dare venture among them. "Who are ye?" said the sands, "and whence come ye?" "We are children of the Sun, we came from Dsĭlnáotĭl, and we go to seek the house of our father." These words were four times said. Then the elder of the boys repeated his sacred formula; the sands subsided, saying: "Pass on to the house of your father," and the boys continued on their journey over the desert of sands.[110]

311. Soon after this adventure they approached the house of the Sun. As they came near the door they found the way guarded by two bears that crouched, one to the right and one to the left, their noses pointing toward one another. As the boys drew near, the bears rose, growled angrily, and acted as if about to attack the intruders; but the elder boy repeated the sacred words the Spider

Woman had taught him, and when he came to the last words, "Be still," the bears crouched down again and lay still. The boys walked on. After passing the bears they encountered a pair of sentinel serpents, then a pair of sentinel winds, and, lastly, a pair of sentinel lightnings. As the boys advanced, all these guardians acted as if they would destroy them ; but all were appeased with the words of prayer.[111]

312. The house of the Sun God was built of turquoise ; it was square like a pueblo house, and stood on the shore of a great water. When the boys entered they saw, sitting in the west, a woman ; in the south, two handsome young men ;[112] and in the north, two handsome young women. The women gave a glance at the strangers and then looked down. The young men gazed at them more closely, and then, without speaking, they rose, wrapped the strangers in four coverings of the sky, and laid them on a shelf.[113]

313. The boys had lain there quietly for some time when a rattle that hung over the door shook and one of the young women said : "Our father is coming." The rattle shook four times, and soon after it shook the fourth time, Tsóhanoai, the bearer of the sun, entered his house. He took the sun off his back and hung it up on a peg on the west wall of the room, where it shook and clanged for some time, going "tla, tla, tla, tla," till at last it hung still.

314. Then Tsóhanoai turned to the woman and said, in an angry tone : "Who are those two who entered here to-day ?" The woman made no answer and the young people looked at one another, but each feared to speak. Four times he asked this question, and at length the woman said : "It would be well for you not to say too much. Two young men came hither to-day, seeking their father. When you go abroad, you always tell me that you visit nowhere, and that you have met no woman but me. Whose sons, then, are these ? " She pointed to the bundle on the shelf, and the children smiled significantly at one another.

315. He took the bundle from the shelf. He first unrolled the robe of dawn with which they were covered, then the robe of blue sky, next the robe of yellow evening light, and lastly the robe of darkness. When he unrolled this the boys fell out on the floor. He seized them, and threw them first upon great, sharp spikes of white shell that stood in the east ; but they bounded back, unhurt, from these spikes, for they held their life-feathers tightly all the while. He then threw them in turn on spikes of turquoise in the south, on spikes of haliotis in the west, and spikes of black rock in the north ; but they came uninjured from all these trials and Tsóhanoai said : "I wish it were indeed true that they were my children."

316. He said then to the elder children, — those who lived with

him, — "Go out and prepare the sweat-house and heat for it four of the hardest boulders you can find. Heat a white, a blue, a yellow, and a black boulder." When the Winds heard this they said : "He still seeks to kill his children. How shall we avert the danger?" The sweat-house was built against a bank. Wind dug into the bank a hole behind the sudatory, and concealed the opening with a flat stone. Wind then whispered into the ears of the boys the secret of the hole and said : "Do not hide in the hole until you have answered the questions of your father." The boys went into the sweat-house, the great hot boulders were put in, and the opening of the lodge was covered with the four sky-blankets. Then Tsóhanoai called out to the boys : "Are you hot?" and they answered : "Yes, very hot." Then they crept into the hiding-place and lay there. After a while Tsóhanoai came and poured water through the top of the sweat-house on the stones, making them burst with a loud noise, and a great heat and steam was raised. But in time the stones cooled and the boys crept out of their hiding-place into the sweat-house. Tsóhanoai came and asked again : "Are you hot?" hoping to get no reply ; but the boys still answered : "Yes, very hot." Then he took the coverings off the sweat-house and let the boys come out. He greeted them in a friendly way and said : "Yes, these are my children," and yet he was thinking of other ways by which he might destroy them if they were not.

317. The four sky-blankets were spread on the ground one over another, and the four young men were made to sit on them, one behind another, facing the east. "My daughters, make these boys to look like my other sons," said Tsóhanoai. The young women went to the strangers, pulled their hair out long, and moulded their faces and forms so that they looked just like their brethren. Then Sun bade them all rise and enter the house. They rose and all went, in a procession, the two strangers last.

318. As they were about to enter the door they heard a voice whispering in their ears : "St! Look at the ground." They looked down and beheld a spiny caterpillar called Wasekede, who, as they looked, spat out two blue spits on the ground. "Take each of you one of these," said Wind, "and put it in your mouth, but do not swallow it. There is one more trial for you, — a trial by smoking." When they entered the house Tsóhanoai took down a pipe of turquoise that hung on the eastern wall and filled it with tobacco. "This is the tobacco he kills with," whispered Nḯltsi to the boys. Tsóhanoai held the pipe up to the sun that hung on the wall, lit it, and gave it to the boys to smoke. They smoked it, and passed it from one to another till it was finished. They said it tasted sweet, but it did them no harm.

319. When the pipe was smoked out and Tsóhanoai saw the boys were not killed by it, he was satisfied and said : " Now, my children, what do you want from me ? Why do you seek me ? " " Oh, father ! " they replied, "the land where we dwell is filled with the anáye, who devour the people. There are Yéitso and *T*éelgĕ*t*, the Tse'náhale, the Bĭnáye A*h*áni, and many others. They have eaten nearly all of our kind ; there are few left ; already they have sought our lives, and we have run away to escape them. Give us, we beg, the weapons with which we may slay our enemies. Help us to destroy them."

320. "Know," said Tsóhanoai, "that Yéitso who dwells at Tsó-tsi*l* is also my son, yet I will help you to kill him. I shall hurl the first bolt at him, and I will give you those things that will help you in war." He took from pegs where they hung around the room and gave to each a hat, a shirt, leggings, moccasins, all made of pe*s* (iron or knives),[114] a chain-lightning arrow, a sheet-lightning arrow, a sunbeam arrow, a rainbow arrow, and a great stone knife or knife club (pe*sh*ál).[115] "These are what we want," said the boys. They put on the clothes of pe*s*, and streaks of lightning shot from every joint.[116]

321. Next morning Tsóhanoai led the boys out to the edge of the world, where the sky and the earth came close together, and beyond which there was no world. Here sixteen wands or poles leaned from the earth to the sky ; four of these were of white shell, four of turquoise, four of haliotis shell, and four of red stone.[117] A deep stream flowed between them and the wands. As they approached the stream, Nĭ'lt*s*i, the Wind, whispered: "This is another trial ;" but he blew a great breath and formed a bridge of rainbow,[86] over which the brothers passed in safety. Nĭ'lt*s*i whispered again : " The red wands are for war, the others are for peace ; " so when Tsóhanoai asked his sons : "On which wands will ye ascend ?" they answered : " On the wands of red stone," for they sought war with their enemies. They climbed up to the sky on the wands of red stone, and their father went with them.[118]

322. They journeyed on till they came to Yága*h*oka, the sky-hole, which is in the centre of the sky.[119] The hole is edged with four smooth, shining cliffs that slope steeply downwards, — cliffs of the same materials as the wands by which they had climbed from the earth to the sky. They sat down on the smooth declivities, — Tsóhanoai on the west side of the hole, the brothers on the east side. The latter would have slipped down had not the Wind blown up and helped them to hold on. Tsóhanoai pointed down and said : "Where do you belong in the world below ? Show me your home." The brothers looked down and scanned the land ; but they could distin-

guish nothing; all the land seemed flat; the wooded mountains looked like dark spots on the surface; the lakes gleamed like stars, and the rivers like streaks of lightning. The elder brother said : "I do not recognize the land, I know not where our home is." Now Nĭ'ltsi prompted the younger brother, and showed him which were the sacred mountains and which the great rivers, and the younger exclaimed, pointing downwards : "There is the Male Water (San Juan River), and there is the Female Water (Rio Grande) ; yonder is the mountain of Tsĭsnadᴢĭ'ni ; below us is Tsótsĭ*l*; there in the west is *D*okoslí*d*; that white spot beyond the Male Water is *D*epĕ'ntsa ; and there between these mountains is Dsĭ*l*náo*t*í*l*, near which our home is." "You are right, my child, it is thus that the land lies," said Tsóhanoai. Then, renewing his promises, he spread a streak of lightning; he made his children stand on it, — one on each end, — and he shot them down to the top of Tsótsĭ*l* (Mt. San Mateo, Mt. Taylor).

323. They descended the mountain on its south side and walked toward the warm spring at *T*ó'sa*t*o.[120] As they were walking along under a high bluff, where there is now a white circle, they heard voices hailing them. "Whither are you going? Come hither a while." They went in the direction in which they heard the voices calling and found four holy people, — Holy Man, Holy Young Man, Holy Boy, and Holy Girl. The brothers remained all night in a cave with these people, and the latter told them all about Yéitso.[121] They said that he showed himself every day three times on the mountains before he came down, and when he showed himself for the fourth time he descended from Tsótsĭ*l* to *T*ó'sa*t*o to drink ; that, when he stooped down to drink, one hand rested on Tsótsĭ*l* and the other on the high hills on the opposite side of the valley, while his feet stretched as far away as a man could walk between sunrise and noon.

324. They left the cave at daybreak and went on to *T*ó'sa*t*o, where in ancient days there was a much larger lake than there is now. There was a high, rocky wall in the narrow part of the valley, and the lake stretched back to where Blue Water is to-day. When they came to the edge of the lake, one brother said to the other: "Let us try one of our father's weapons and see what it can do." They shot one of the lightning arrows at Tsótsĭ*l*; it made a great cleft in the mountain, which remains to this day, and one said to the other : "We cannot suffer in combat while we have such weapons as these."

325. Soon they heard the sound of thunderous footsteps, and they beheld the head of Yéitso peering over a high hill in the east; it was withdrawn in a moment. Soon after, the monster raised his head

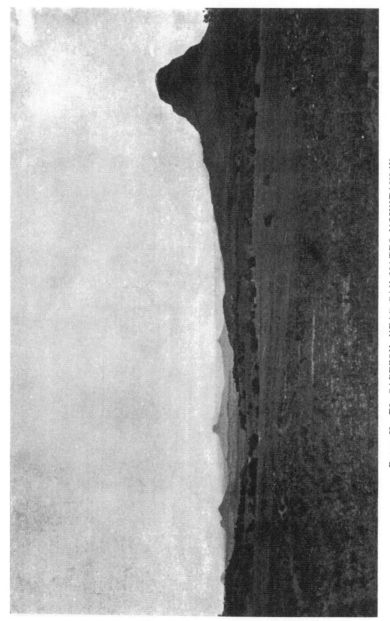

PLATE V. EL CABEZON, NEAR SAN MATEO MOUNTAIN.[128]

(Heads of Yéitso and other giants slain by the Navaho War Gods.)

and chest over a hill in the south, and remained a little longer in sight than when he was in the east. Later he displayed his body to the waist over a hill in the west; and lastly he showed himself, down to the knees, over Tsótsi*l* in the north.[122] Then he descended the mountain, came to the edge of the lake, and laid down a basket which he was accustomed to carry.

326. Yéitso stooped four times to the lake to drink, and, each time he drank, the waters perceptibly diminished; when he had done drinking, the lake was nearly drained.[123] The brothers lost their presence of mind at sight of the giant drinking, and did nothing while he was stooping down. As he took his last drink they advanced to the edge of the lake, and Yéitso saw their reflection in the water. He raised his head, and, looking at them, roared: "What a pretty pair have come in sight! Where have I been hunting?" (*i. e.*, that I never saw them before). Yinike*t*óko! Yinike*t*óko!"[124] "Throw (his words) back in his mouth," said the younger to the elder brother. "What a great thing has come in sight! Where have we been hunting?" shouted the elder brother to the giant. Four times these taunts were repeated by each party. The brothers then heard Ni'lts*i* whispering quickly, "Akó'! Akó'! Beware! Beware!" They were standing on a bent rainbow just then; they straightened the rainbow out, descending to the ground, and at the same instant a lightning bolt, hurled by Yéitso, passed thundering over their heads. He hurled four bolts rapidly; as he hurled the second, they bent their rainbow and rose, while the bolt passed under their feet; as he discharged the third they descended, and let the lightning pass over them. When he threw the fourth bolt they bent the rainbow very high, for this time he aimed higher than before; but his weapon still passed under their feet and did them no harm. He drew a fifth bolt to throw at them; but at this moment the lightning descended from the sky on the head of the giant and he reeled beneath it, but did not fall.[125] Then the elder brother sped a chain-lightning arrow; his enemy tottered toward the east, but straightened himself up again. The second arrow caused him to stumble toward the south (he fell lower and lower each time), but again he stood up and prepared himself to renew the conflict. The third lightning arrow made him topple toward the west, and the fourth to the north. Then he fell to his knees, raised himself partly again, fell flat on his face, stretched out his limbs, and moved no more.

327. When the arrows struck him, his armor was shivered in pieces and the scales flew in every direction. The elder brother said: "They may be useful to the people in the future."[126] The brothers then approached their fallen enemy and the younger

scalped him. Heretofore the younger brother bore only the name
of *To‘bad͡zĭsts͓íni*, or Child of the Water; but now his brother gave
him also the warrior name of Naídik͓ĭsi (He Who Cuts Around).
What the elder brother's name was before this we do not know;
but ever after he was called Nayénĕzg͓ani (Slayer of the Alien
Gods).[127]

328. They cut off his head and threw it away to the other side of
Tsótsĭ*l*, where it may be seen to-day on the eastern side of the
mountain.[128] The blood from the body now flowed in a great stream
down the valley, so great that it broke down the rocky wall that
bounded the old lake and flowed on. Nĭ́lts͓i whispered to the
brothers: "The blood flows toward the dwelling of the Bĭnáye
A*h*áni; if it reaches them, Yéitso will come to life again." Then
Nayénĕzg͓ani took his pe*sh*ál, or knife club, and drew with it across
the valley a line. Here the blood stopped flowing and piled itself
up in a high wall. But when it had piled up here very high it began
to flow off in another direction, and Nĭ́lts͓i again whispered: "It now
flows toward the dwelling of *Sa*snalkáhi, the Bear that Pursues;
if it reaches him, Yéitso will come to life again." Hearing this,
Nayénĕzg͓ani again drew a line with his knife on the ground, and
again the blood piled up and stopped flowing. The blood of Yéitso
fills all the valley to-day, and the high cliffs in the black rock that
we see there now are the places where Nayénĕzg͓ani stopped the flow
with his pe*sh*ál.[129]

329. They then put the broken arrows of Yéitso and his scalp
into his basket and set out for their home near Dsĭ*l*náo*t*í*l*. When
they got near the house, they took off their own suits of armor and
hid these, with the basket and its contents, in the bushes. The
mothers were rejoiced to see them, for they feared their sons were
lost, and they said: "Where have you been since you left here yesterday, and what have you done?" Nayénĕzg͓ani replied: "We have
been to the house of our father, the Sun. We have been to Tsótsĭ*l*
and we have slain Yéitso." "Ah, my child," said Estsánatlehi, "do
not speak thus. It is wrong to make fun of such an awful subject."
"Do you not believe us?" said Nayénĕzg͓ani; "come out, then, and
see what we have brought back with us." He led the women out
to where he had hidden the basket and showed them the trophies of
Yéitso. Then they were convinced and they rejoiced, and had a
dance to celebrate the victory.[130]

330. When their rejoicings were done, Nayénĕzg͓ani said to his
mother: "Where does *T*éelgĕ*t*[131] dwell?" "Seek not to know," she
answered, "you have done enough. Rest contented. The land of
the anáye is a dangerous place. The anáye are hard to kill." "Yes,
and it was hard for you to bear your child," the son replied (meaning

that she triumphed notwithstanding). "He lives at Bike*h*al*z*ï'n," she said. Then the brothers held a long council to determine what they should do. They made two cigarette kethawns of a plant called aze*l*a*d*ï*l*téhe,[132] one black and one blue, each three finger-widths long; to these they attached a sunbeam and laid them in a turquoise dish. "I shall go alone to fight *T*éelgě*t*," said Nayénĕzgạni, "while you, younger brother, remain at home and watch these kethawns. If they take fire from the sunbeam, you may know that I am in great danger; as long as they do not take fire, you may know that I am safe." This work was finished at sundown.[133]

331. Nayénĕzgạni arose early next morning and set out alone to find *T*éelgě*t*. He came, in time, to the edge of a great plain, and from one of the hills that bordered it he saw the monster lying down a long way off. He paused to think how he could approach nearer to him without attracting his attention, and in the mean time he poised one of his lightning arrows in his hand, thinking how he should throw it. While he stood thus in thought, Nasï'zi, the Gopher, came up to him and said: "I greet you, my friend! Why have you come hither?" "Oh, I am just wandering around," said Nayénĕzgạni. Four times this question was asked and this answer was given. Then Nasï'zi said: "I wonder that you come here; no one but I ever ventures in these parts, for all fear *T*éelgě*t*. There he lies on the plain yonder." "It is him I seek," said Nayénĕzgạni; "but I know not how to approach him." "Ah, if that is all you want, I can help you," said Gopher; "and if you slay him, all I ask is his hide. I often go up to him, and I will go now to show you." Having said this, Nasï'zi disappeared in a hole in the ground.

332. While he was gone Nayénĕzgạni watched *T*éelgě*t*. After a while he saw the great creature rise, walk from the centre in four different directions, as if watching, and lie down again in the spot where he was first seen. He was a great, four-footed beast, with horns like those of a deer. Soon Nasï'zi returned and said: "I have dug a tunnel up to *T*éelgě*t*, and at the end I have bored four tunnels for you to hide in, one to the east, one to the south, one to the west, and one to the north. I have made a hole upwards from the tunnel to his heart, and I have gnawed the hair off near his heart. When I was gnawing the hair he spoke to me and said: 'Why do you take my hair?' and I answered, 'I want it to make a bed for my children.' Then it was that he rose and walked around; but he came back and lay down where he lay before, over the hole that leads up to his heart."

333. Nayénĕzgạni entered the tunnel and crawled to the end. When he looked up through the ascending shaft of which Nasï'zi had told him, he saw the great heart of *T*éelgě*t* beating there. He sped

his arrow of chain-lightning and fled into the eastern tunnel. The
monster rose, stuck one of his horns into the ground, and ripped the
tunnel open. Nayénĕzgạni fled into the south tunnel; *T*éelgĕ*t* then
tore the south tunnel open with his horns, and the hero fled into the
west tunnel. When the west tunnel was torn up he fled into the
north tunnel. The anáye put his horn into the north tunnel to
tear it up, but before he had half uncovered it he fell and lay still.
Nayénĕzgạni, not knowing that his enemy was dead, and still fearing
him, crept back through the long tunnel to the place where he first
met Nasĭ′zi, and there he stood gazing at the distant form of *T*éelgĕ*t*.

334. While he was standing there in thought, he observed approaching him a little old man dressed in tight leggings and a tight
shirt, with a cap and feather on his head; this was *H*azaí, the
Ground Squirrel. "What do you want here, my grandchild?" said
*H*azaí. "Nothing; I am only walking around," replied the warrior.
Four times this question was asked and four times a similar answer
given, when Ground Squirrel spoke again and inquired: "Do you
not fear the anáye that dwells on yonder plain?" "I do not know,"
replied Nayénĕzgạni; "I think I have killed him, but I am not certain." "Then I can find out for you," said *H*azaí. "He never
minds me. I can approach him any time without danger. If he is
dead I will climb up on his horns and dance and sing." Nayénĕzgạni
had not watched long when he saw *H*azaí climbing one of the horns
and dancing on it. When he approached his dead enemy he found
that *H*azaí had streaked his own face with the blood of the slain (the
streaks remain on the ground squirrel's face to this day), and that
Nasĭ′zi had already begun to remove the skin by gnawing on the
insides of the fore-legs. When Gopher had removed the skin, he
put it on his own back and said: "I shall wear this in order that, in
the days to come, when the people increase, they may know what
sort of a skin *T*éelgĕ*t* wore." He had a skin like that which covers
the Gopher to-day. *H*azaí cut out a piece of the bowel, filled it with
blood, and tied the ends; he cut out also a piece of one of the
lungs, and he gave these to Nayénĕzgạni for his trophies.[134]

335. When Nayénĕzgạni came home again, he was received with
great rejoicing, for his mother had again begun to fear he would
never more return. "Where have you been, my son, and what have
you done since you have been gone?" she queried. "I have been
to Bike*h*alzĭ′n and I have slain *T*éelgĕ*t*," he replied. "Ah, speak
not thus, my son," she said; "he is too powerful for you to talk thus
lightly about him. If he knew what you said he might seek you out
and kill you." "I have no fear of him," said her son. "Here is his
blood, and here is a piece of his liver. Do you not now believe I
have slain him?" Then he said: "Mother, grandmother, tell me,

PLATE VI. LAVA FLOW IN THE VALLEY OF THE SAN JOSÉ, NEW MEXICO.[129]

(The blood of Yéitso.)

where do the Tse'nă'hale [135] dwell?" "They dwell at *Tsé'bĭ/aï* (Winged Rock)," [136] she answered, "but do not venture near them; they are fierce and strong."

336. Next morning early he stole away, taking with him the piece of bowel filled with blood. He climbed the range of mountains where the hill of Tsúskai rises, and travelled on till he came to a place where two great snakes lay. Since that day these snakes have been changed into stone. He walked along the back of one of the snakes, and then he stepped from one snake to the other and went out on the plain that stretched to the east of the mountains, until he came close to Tsé'bĭ/aï, which is a great black rock that looks like a bird. While he was walking along he heard a tremendous rushing sound overhead, like the sound of a whirlwind, and, looking up, he saw a creature of great size, something like an eagle in form, flying toward him from the east. It was the male Tse'nă'hale. The warrior had barely time to cast himself prone on the ground when Tse'nă'hale swooped over him. Thus four times did the monster swoop at him, coming each time from a different direction. Three times Nayénĕzgạni escaped; but the fourth time, flying from the north, the monster seized him in his talons and bore him off to Tsé'bĭ/aï.

337. There is a broad, level ledge on one side of Tsé'bĭ/aï, where the monster reared his young; he let the hero drop on this ledge, as was his custom to do with his victims, and perched on a pinnacle above. This fall had killed all others who had dropped there; but Nayénĕzgạni was preserved by the life-feather, the gift of Spider Woman, which he still kept. When the warrior fell he cut open the bag of bowel that he carried and allowed the blood of *Téelgĕt* to flow out over the rock, so that the anáye might think he was killed. The two young approached to devour the body of the warrior, but he said " Sh!" at them. They stopped and cried up to their father : " This thing is not dead ; it says 'Sh!' at us." "That is only air escaping from the body," said the father ; "Never mind, but eat it." Then he flew away in search of other prey. When the old bird was gone, Nayénĕzgạni hid himself behind the young ones and asked them, "When will your father come back, and where will he sit when he comes?" They answered : "He will return when we have a he-rain, [137] and he will perch on yonder point" (indicating a rock close by on the right). Then he inquired : "When will your mother return, and where will she sit?" "She will come when we have a she-rain, [137] and will sit on yonder point" (indicating a crag on the left). He had not waited long when drops of rain began to fall, the thunder rolled, lightning flashed, the male Tse'nă'hale returned and perched on the rock which the young had pointed out. Then

Nayénĕzgạni hurled a lightning arrow and the monster tumbled to the foot of Winged Rock dead. After a while rain fell again, but there was neither thunder nor lightning with it. While it still poured, there fell upon the ledge the body of a Pueblo woman, covered with fine clothes and ornamented with ear pendants and necklaces of beautiful shells and turquoise. Nayénĕzgạni looked up and beheld the female Tse'nǎ'hale soaring overhead (she preyed only on women, the male only on men). A moment later she glided down, and was just about to light on her favorite crag, when Nayénĕzgạni hurled another lightning arrow and sent her body down to the plain to join that of her mate.

338. The young ones now began to cry, and they said to the warrior: "Will you slay us, too?" "Cease your wailing," he cried. "Had you grown up here you would have been things of evil; you would have lived only to destroy my people; but I shall now make of you something that will be of use in the days to come when men increase in the land." He seized the elder and said to it, "You shall furnish plumes for men to use in their rites, and bones for whistles." He swung the fledgling back and forth four times; as he did so it began to change into a beautiful bird with strong wings, and it said: "Sŭk, sŭk, sŭk, sŭk." Then he threw it high in the air. It spread its pinions and soared out of sight, an eagle. To the younger he said: "In the days to come men will listen to your voice to know what will be their future: sometimes you will tell the truth; sometimes you will lie." He swung it back and forth, and as he did so its head grew large and round; its eyes grew big; it began to say, "Uwú, uwú, uwú, uwú," and it became an owl. Then he threw it into a hole in the side of the cliff and said: "This shall be your home." [138]

339. As he had nothing more to do at Tsé'bị/aï, he determined to go home, but he soon found that there was no way for him to descend the rock; nothing but a winged creature could reach or leave the ledge on which he stood. The sun was about half way down to the horizon when he observed the Bat Woman walking along near the base of the cliff. "Grandmother," he called aloud, "come hither and take me down." "Tsĕ'dăni," [139] she answered, and hid behind a point of rock. Again she came in view, and again he called her; but she gave him the same reply and hid herself again. Three times were these acts performed and these words said. When she appeared for the fourth time and he begged her to carry him down, he added: "I will give you the feathers of the Tse'nǎ'hale if you will take me off this rock." When she heard this she approached the base of the rock, and soon disappeared under the ledge where he stood. Presently he heard a strange flapping sound,[140] and a voice

calling to him : " Shut your eyes and go back, for you must not see how I ascend." He did as he was bidden, and soon after the Bat Woman stood beside him. "Get into this basket, and I will carry you down," she demanded. He looked at the large carrying-basket which she bore on her back, and observed that it hung on strings as thin as the strings of a spider's web. "Grandmother," he said, " I fear to enter your basket ; the strings are too thin." " Have no fear," she replied ; " I often carry a whole deer in this basket : the strings are strong enough to bear you." Still he hesitated, and still she assured him. The fourth time that he expressed his fear she said : " Fill the basket with stones and you will see that I speak the truth." He did as he was bidden, and she danced around with the loaded basket on her back ; but the strings did not break, though they twanged like bowstrings. When he entered the basket she bade him keep his eyes shut till they reached the bottom of the cliff, as he must not see how she managed to descend. He shut his eyes, and soon felt himself gradually going down ; but he heard again the strange flapping against the rock, which so excited his curiosity that he opened his eyes. Instantly he began to fall with dangerous rapidity, and the flapping stopped ; she struck him with her stick and bade him shut his eyes. Again he felt himself slowly descending, and the flapping against the rock began. Three times more he disobeyed her, but the last time they were near the bottom of the cliff, and both fell to the ground unhurt.

340. Together they plucked the two Tse'nă'hale, put the feathers in her basket, and got the basket on her back. He reserved only the largest feather from one wing of each bird for his trophies. As she was starting to leave he warned her not to pass through either of two neighboring localities, which were the dry beds of temporary lakes ; one was overgrown with weeds, the other with sunflowers. Despite his warning she walked toward the sunflowers. As she was about to enter them he called after her again, and begged her not to go that way, but she heeded him not and went on. She had not taken many steps among the sunflowers when she heard a fluttering sound behind her, and a little bird of strange appearance flew past her close to her ear. As she stepped farther on she heard more fluttering and saw more birds of varying plumage, such as she had never seen before, flying over her shoulders and going off in every direction. She looked around, and was astonished to behold that the birds were swarming out of her own basket. She tried to hold them in, to catch them as they flew out, but all in vain. She laid down her basket and watched, helplessly, her feathers changing into little birds of all kinds, — wrens, warblers, titmice, and the like, — and flying away, until her basket was empty. Thus it was that the little birds were created.[141]

341. When he got home *To'badzĭstsíni* said to him : " Elder brother, I have watched the kethawns all the time you were gone.   About midday the black cigarette took fire, and I was troubled, for I knew you were in danger ; but when it had burned half way the fire went out and then I was glad, for I thought you were safe again."   " Ah, that must have been the time when Tse'nă'hale carried me up and threw me on the rocks," said Nayénĕzgạni.   He hung his trophies on the east side of the lodge, and then he asked his mother where Tse'*ta*hotsĭl*tá'li* [142] dwelt.   She told him he lived at Tse'*dezá* ; but, as on previous occasions, she warned him of the power of the enemy, and tried to dissuade him from seeking further dangers. Next morning he set out to find Tse'*ta*hotsĭl*tá'li*, He Who Kicks (People) Down the Cliff.   This anáye lived on the side of a high cliff, a trail passed at his feet, and when travellers went that way he kicked them down to the bottom of the precipice.   Nayénĕzgạni had not travelled long when he discovered a well-beaten trail ; following this, he found that it led him along the face of a high precipice, and soon he came in sight of his enemy, who had a form much like that of a man.   The monster reclined quietly against the rock, as if he meditated no harm, and Nayénĕzgạni advanced as if he feared no danger, yet watching his adversary closely.   As he passed, the latter kicked at him, but he dodged the kick and asked : " Why did you kick at me ? "   " Oh, my grandchild," said the anáye, " I was weary lying thus, and I only stretched out my leg to rest myself."   Four times did Nayénĕzgạni pass him, and four times did the monster kick at him in vain.   Then the hero struck his enemy with his great stone knife over the eyes, and struck him again and again till he felt sure that he had slain him ; but he was surprised to find that the body did not fall down the cliff.   He cut with his knife under the corpse in different places, but found nothing that held it to the rock until he came to the head, and then he discovered that the long hair grew, like the roots of a cedar, into a cleft in the rock. When he cut the hair,[143] the body tumbled down out of sight.   The moment it fell a great clamor of voices came up from below.   " I want the eyes," screamed one ; " Give me an arm," cried another ; " I want the liver," said a third ; " No, the liver shall be mine," yelled a fourth ; and thus the quarrelling went on.   " Ah ! " thought Nayénĕzgạni, " these are the children quarrelling over the father's corpse.   Thus, perhaps, they would have been quarrelling over mine had I not dodged his kicks."

342. He tried to descend along the trail he was on, but found it led no farther.   Then he retraced his steps till he saw another trail that seemed to lead to the bottom of the cliff.   He followed it and soon came to the young of the anáye, twelve in number, who had

just devoured their father's corpse; the blood was still streaming from their mouths. He ran among them, and hacked at them in every direction with his great stone knife. They fled; but he pursued them, and in a little while he had killed all but one. This one ran faster than the rest, and climbed among some high rocks; but Nayénĕzgạni followed him and caught him. He stopped to take breath; as he did so he looked at the child and saw that he was disgustingly ugly and filthy. "You ugly thing," said Nayénĕzgạni; "when you ran from me so fleetly I thought you might be something handsome and worth killing; but now that I behold your face I shall let you live. Go to yonder mountain of Natsïsaán [144] and dwell there. It is a barren land, where you will have to work hard for your living, and will wander ever naked and hungry." The boy went to Natsïsaán, as he was told, and there he became the progenitor of the Pahutes, a people ugly, starved, and ragged, who never wash themselves and live on the vermin of the desert. [145]

343. He went to where he had first found the children of Tse'taḥotsïltá'li. Nothing was left of the father's corpse but the bones and scalp. (This anáye used to wear his hair after the manner of a Pueblo Indian.) The hero cut a piece of the hair from one side of the head and carried it home as a trophy. When he got home there were the usual questions and answers and rejoicings, and when he asked his mother, "Where is the home of the Bïnáye Aḥáni, the people who slay with their eyes," she begged him, as before, to rest contented and run no more risks; but she added: "They live at Tse'aḥalzï'ni, Rock with Black Hole." [146] This place stands to this day, but is changed since the anáye dwelt there. It has still a hole, on one side, that looks like a door, and another on the top that looks like a smoke-hole.

344. On this occasion, in addition to his other weapons, he took a bag of salt with him on his journey. [147] When he came to Tse'aḥalzï'ni he entered the rock house and sat down on the north side. In other parts of the lodge sat the old couple of the Bïnáye Aḥáni and many of their children. They all stared with their great eyes at the intruder, and flashes of lightning streamed from their eyes toward him, but glanced harmless off his armor. Seeing that they did not kill him, they stared harder and harder at him, until their eyes protruded far from their sockets. Then into the fire in the centre of the lodge he threw the salt, which spluttered and flew in every direction, striking the eyes of the anáye and blinding them. While they held down their heads in pain, he struck with his great stone knife and killed all except the two youngest.

345. Thus he spoke to the two which he spared: "Had you grown up here, you would have lived only to be things of evil and to destroy

men ; but now I shall make you of use to my kind in the days to come when men increase on the earth." To the elder he said : " You will ever speak to men and tell them what happens beyond their sight ; you will warn them of the approach of enemies," and he changed it into a bird called Tsĭdĭ*ltó*i [148] (shooting or exploring bird). He addressed the younger, saying : " It will be your task to make things beautiful, to make the earth happy." And he changed it into a bird called *Ho*stódi,[149] which is sleepy in the daytime and comes out at night.

346. When he reached home with his trophies, which were the eyes [150] of the first Bĭnáye A*h*áni he had killed, and told what he had done, Estsánatlehi took a piece of the lung of *T*éelge*t* (which he had previously brought home), put it in her mouth, and, dancing sang this song : —

> Nayénĕzgani brings for me,
> Of *T*éelge*t* he brings for me,
> Truly a lung he brings for me,
> The people are restored.
>
> *T*o‘badzĭstsíni brings for me,
> Of Tse‘nă'hale he brings for me,
> Truly a wing he brings for me,
> The people are restored.
>
> *L*éyaneyani brings for me,
> Of Tse‘*ta*hotsĭ*ltá*‘*l*i he brings for me,
> Truly a side-lock he brings for me,
> The people are restored.
>
> Tsówenatlehi [151] brings for me,
> Of Bĭnáye A*h*áni he brings for me,
> Truly an eye he brings for me,
> The people are restored.[276]

347. When she had finished her rejoicings he asked, " Where shall I find *S*asnalkáhi (Bear that Pursues) ? " " He lives at Tse‘bahástsĭt (Rock that Frightens)," she replied ; but again she plead with him, pictured to him the power of the enemy he sought, and begged him to venture no more.

348. Next morning he went off to Rock that Frightens and walked all around it, without meeting the bear or finding his trail. At length, looking up to the top of the rock, he saw the bear's head sticking out of a hole, and he climbed up. The bear's den was in the shape of a cross, and had four entrances. Nayénĕzgani looked into the east entrance, the south entrance, and the west entrance without getting sight of his enemy. As he approached the north entrance he saw the head of the watching bear again ; but it was

instantly withdrawn, and the bear went toward the south entrance. The hero ran round fast and lay in wait. In a little while the bear thrust forth his head to look, and Nayénĕzgạni cut it off with his great stone knife.

349. He addressed the head, saying : " You were a bad thing in your old life, and tried only to do mischief ; but in new shapes I shall make you of use to the people ; in the future, when they increase upon the earth, you will furnish them with sweet food to eat, with foam to cleanse their bodies, and with threads for their clothing." He cut the head into three pieces : he threw one to the east, where it became tsási, or *h*askán (*Yucca baccata*) ; he threw another to the west, where it became tsásitsoz (*Yucca angustifolia*) ; and he threw the third to the south, where it became nó*t*a (mescal). He cut off the left forepaw to take home as a trophy.

350. " Where shall I find Tsé'nagahi (Travelling Stone) ? " he said after he had returned from his encounter with Pursuing Bear and shown his trophy to his people. " You will find him in a lake near where Tsé'espai points up," answered Estsánatlehi ; but she implored him not to go near the lake. He did not heed her, and next morning he went off to seek the Travelling Stone.

351. He approached the lake on the north side, while the wind was blowing from the south, but he saw nothing of the stone. Thence he went around to the south side of the lake. When he got here the stone scented him, rose to the surface, poised itself a moment, and flew toward Nayénĕzgạni as if hurled by a giant hand. Raising his lightning arrow, he held it in the course of the stone and knocked a piece off the latter. When the stone fell he struck another piece off with his knife. Tsé'nagahi now saw it had a powerful foe to contend against ; so, instead of hurling itself at him again, it fled and Nayénĕzgạni went in pursuit. He chased it all over the present Navaho land, knocking pieces off it in many places [152] as he followed, until at length he chased it into the San Juan River at Tsĭn*tá*hokata, where a point of forest runs down toward the river.

352. Travelling Stone sped down with the current and Nayénĕzgạni ran along the bank after it. Four times he got ahead of the stone, but three times it escaped him by dipping deep into the river. When he headed it off for the fourth time, he saw it gleaming like fire under the water, and he stopped to gaze at it. Then the stone spoke and said : "*S*awé (my baby, my darling), take pity on me, and I shall no longer harm your people, but do good to them instead. I shall keep the springs in the mountains open and cause your rivers to flow ; kill me and your lands will become barren." Nayénĕzgạni answered : " If you keep this promise I shall spare you ; but if you

ever more do evil as you have done before, I shall seek you again, and then I shall not spare you." Tsé'nagahi has kept his promise ever since, and has become the Tiéholtsodi of the upper world.

353. He brought home no trophy from the contest with Tsé'nagahi. It had now been eight days since he left the house of the Sun.[153] He was weary from his battles with the anáye, and he determined to rest four days. During this time he gave his relatives a full account of his journeys and his adventures from first to last, and as he began he sang a song : —

> Nayénĕzgạni to Atsé Estsán began to tell,
> About Bĭ*t*éelgĕ*t*i he began to tell,
> From homes of giants coming, he began to tell.

> *T*o'bad*z*ĭsts*í*ni to Estsánatlehi began to tell,
> About the Tse'nă'hale he began to tell,
> From homes of giants coming, he began to tell.

> *L*éyaneyani to Atsé Estsán began to tell,
> Of Tse'*ta*hots*í*l*t*á'*l*i he began to tell,
> From homes of giants coming, he began to tell.

> Tsówenatlehi to Estsánatlehi began to tell,
> About Bĭnáye A*h*áni he began to tell,
> From homes of giants coming, he began to tell.[277]

354. There were still many of the anáye to kill ; there was White under the Rock, Blue under the Rock, Yellow under the Rock, Black under the Rock, and many yé*l*apahi, or brown giants. Besides these there were a number of stone pueblos, now in ruins, that were inhabited by various animals (crows, eagles, etc.),[154] who filled the land and left no room for the people. During the four days of rest, the brothers consulted as to how they might slay all these enemies, and they determined to visit again the house of the Sun. On the morning of the fourth night they started for the east. They encountered no enemies on the way and had a pleasant journey. When they entered the house of the Sun no one greeted them ; no one offered them a seat. They sat down together on the floor, and as soon as they were seated lightning began to shoot into the lodge. It struck the ground near them four times. Immediately after the last flash Ts*á*pani, Bat, and *T*ó'nenĭli, Water Sprinkler, entered. " Do not be angry with us," said the intruders ; " we flung the lightning only because we feel happy and want to play with you :" still the brothers kept wrathful looks on their faces, until Nĭ'lts*i* whispered into their ears : " Be not angry with the strangers. They were once friends of the anáye and did not wish them to die ; but now they are friends of yours, since you have conquered the greatest of the anáye." Then, at last, Tsóhanoai spoke to his children, saying :

"These people are rude; they respect no one. Heed them not. Here are seats for you. Be seated." Saying this, he offered the brothers a seat of shell and a seat of turquoise; but Nïʻltsi told the brothers not to take them. "These are seats of peace," he said; "you still want help in war. Nayénĕzgạni, take the seat of red stone, which is the warrior's seat; and you, Toʻbadẕïstsíni, stand." They did as the Wind bade them.

355. "My children, why do you come to me again?" asked Tsóhanoai, the bearer of the sun. "We come for no special purpose; we come only to pass away the time," Nayénĕzgạni answered. Three times he asked this question and got the same reply. When he asked for the fourth time, he added, "Speak the truth. When you came to me before I gave you all you asked for." Now it was Toʻbadẕïstsíni who replied: "Oh, father! there are still many of the anáye left, and they are increasing. We wish to destroy them." "My children," said Tsóhanoai, "when I helped you before, I asked you for nothing in return. I am willing to help you again; but I wish to know, first, if you are willing to do something for me. I have a long way to travel every day, and often, in the long summer days, I do not get through in time, and then I have no place to rest or eat till I get back to my home in the east. I wish you to send your mother to the west that she may make a new home for me." "I will do it," said Nayénĕzgạni; "I will send her there." But Toʻbadẕïstsíni said: "No, Estsánatlehi is under the power of none; we cannot make promises for her, she must speak for herself, she is her own mistress; but I shall tell her your wishes and plead for you." The room they were in had four curtains which closed the ways leading into other apartments. Tsóhanoai lifted the curtain in the east, which was black, and took out of the room in the east five hoops: one of these was colored black, another blue, a third yellow, and a fourth white, the fifth was many-colored and shining. Each hoop had attached to it a knife of the same color as itself. He took out also four great hailstones, colored like the four first hoops. He gave all these to his sons and said: "Your mother will know what to do with these things."

356. When they got their gifts they set out on their homeward journey. As they went on their way they beheld a wonderful vision. The gods spread before them the country of the Navahoes as it was to be in the future when men increased in the land and became rich and happy. They spoke to one another of their father, of what he had said to them, of what they had seen in his house, and of all the strange things that had happened. When they got near their journey's end they sang this song : —

Nayénĕzgạni, he is holy,
Thus speaks the Sun,
Holy he stands.

*To*ʻbadzĭstsɪ́ni, he is holy,
Thus speaks the Moon,
Holy he moves.

*Lé*yaneyani, he is holy,
Thus speaks the Sun,
Holy he stands.

Tsówenatlehi, he is holy,
Thus speaks the Moon,
Holy he moves.[278]

357. When they got within sight of their home they sang this song : —

Slayer of Giants,
Through the sky I hear him.
His voice sounds everywhere,
His voice divine.

Child of the Water,
Through the floods I hear him.
His voice sounds everywhere,
His voice divine.

Reared 'neath the Earth,
Through the earth I hear him.
His voice sounds everywhere,
His voice divine.

The Changing Grandchild,
Through the clouds I hear him.
His voice sounds everywhere,
His voice divine.[279]

358. When the brothers got home they said to Estsánatlehi: "Here are the hoops which our father has given us, and he told us you knew all about them. Show us, then, how to use them." She replied : "I have no knowledge of them." Three times she thus answered their questions. When they spoke to her for the fourth time and Nayénĕzgạni was becoming angry and impatient, she said : "I have never seen the Sun God except from afar. He has never been down to the earth to visit me. I know nothing of these talismans of his, but I will try what I can do." She took the black hoop to the east, set it up so that it might roll, and spat through it the black hail, which was four-cornered ; at once the hoop rolled off to the east and rolled out of sight. She took the blue hoop to the south, set it up, and spat through it the blue hail, which was six-cornered. Then the hoop rolled away to the south and disappeared. She car-

ried the yellow hoop to the west, set it up, and spat through it the eight-cornered yellow hail; the hoop rolled off to the west and was lost to sight. She bore the white hoop to the north; spat through it the white hail, which had eleven corners, and the hoop sped to the north until it was seen no more. She threw the shining hoop up toward the zenith, threw the four colored knives in the same direction, and blew a powerful breath after them. Up they all went until they were lost to sight in the sky. As each hoop went away thunder was heard.[155]

359. During four days after this nothing of importance happened, and no change came in the weather. At the end of four days they heard thunder high up in the sky, and after this there were four days more of good weather. Then the sky grew dark, and something like a great white cloud descended from above. Estsánatlehi went abroad; she saw in all directions great whirlwinds which uprooted tall trees as if they had been weeds, and tossed great rocks around as if they had been pebbles. "My son, I fear for our house," she said when she came back. "It is high among the mountains, and the great winds may destroy it." When he heard this, Nayénĕzgani went out. He covered the house first with a black cloud, which he fastened to the ground with rainbows; second, with a black fog, which he fastened down with sunbeams; third, with a black cloud, which he secured with sheet-lightning; and fourth, with a black fog, which he secured with chain-lightning. At sunset that evening they caught a little glimpse of the sun; but after that, continuously for four days and four nights, it was dark; a storm of wind and hail prevailed, such as had never been seen before, and the air was filled with sharp stones carried before the wind. The people stayed safe in the lodge, but they could hear the noise of the great storm without. On the morning of the fifth day the tumult ceased, and Nayénĕzgani, going out, found that all was calm, though it was still dark. He now proceeded to remove the coverings from the lodge and threw them upwards toward the heavens. As the first covering, a sheet of fog, ascended, chain-lightning shot out of it (with chain-lightning it had been fastened down). As the second covering, a cloud, ascended, sheet-lightning came forth from it. As the third covering, a fog, went up, sunbeams streamed from it; and as the fourth cover, a robe of cloud, floated up, it became adorned with rainbows. The air was yet dark, and full of dust raised by the high wind; but a gentle shower of rain came later, laying the dust, and all was clear again. All the inmates of the lodge now came out, and they marvelled to see what changes the storm had wrought: near their house a great canyon had been formed; the shape of the bluffs around had been changed, and solitary pillars of rock [156] had been hewn by the winds.

360. "Surely all the anáye are now killed," said Estsánatlehi. "This storm must have destroyed them." But Nĭ'ltsi whispered into Nayénĕzgạni's ear, "San (Old Age) still lives." The hero said then to his mother: "Where used Old Age to dwell?" His mother would not answer him, though he repeated his question four times. At last Nĭ'ltsi again whispered in his ear and said: "She lives in the mountains of *D*epĕ'ntsa."

361. Next morning he set out for the north, and when, after a long journey, he reached *D*epĕ'ntsa, he saw an old woman who came slowly toward him leaning on a staff. Her back was bent, her hair was white, and her face was deeply wrinkled. He knew this must be Sa*n*. When they met he said: "Grandmother, I have come on a cruel errand. I have come to slay you." "Why would you slay me?" she said in a feeble voice, "I have never harmed any one. I hear that you have done great deeds in order that men might increase on the earth, but if you kill me there will be no increase of men; the boys will not grow up to become fathers; the worthless old men will not die; the people will stand still. It is well that people should grow old and pass away and give their places to the young. Let me live, and I shall help you to increase the people." "Grandmother, if you keep this promise I shall spare your life," said Nayénĕzgạni, and he returned to his mother without a trophy.

362. When he got home Nĭ'ltsi whispered to him: "*H*akáz Estsán (Cold Woman) still lives." Nayénĕzgạni said to Estsánatlehi: "Mother, grandmother, where does Cold Woman dwell?" His mother would not answer him; but Nĭ'ltsi again whispered, saying: "Cold Woman lives high on the summits of *D*epĕ'ntsa, where the snow never melts."

363. Next day he went again to the north and climbed high among the peaks of *D*epĕ'ntsa, where no trees grow and where the snow lies white through all the summer. Here he found a lean old woman, sitting on the bare snow, without clothing, food, fire, or shelter. She shivered from head to foot, her teeth chattered, and her eyes streamed water. Among the drifting snows which whirled around her, a multitude of snow-buntings were playing; these were the couriers she sent out to announce the coming of a storm. "Grandmother," he said, "a cruel man I shall be. I am going to kill you, so that men may no more suffer and die by your hand," and he raised his knife-club to smite her. "You may kill me or let me live, as you will. I care not," she said to the hero; "but if you kill me it will always be hot, the land will dry up, the springs will cease to flow, the people will perish. You will do well to let me live. It will be better for your people." He paused and thought upon her words. He lowered the hand he had raised to strike her, saying: "You speak wisely,

grandmother; I shall let you live." He turned around and went home.

364. When Nayénĕzgạni got home from this journey, bearing no trophy, Wind again whispered in his ear and said : "Tie*in* (Poverty) still lives." He asked his mother where Poverty used to live, but she would not answer him. It was Wind who again informed him. "There are two, and they dwell at Dsĭ*ld*asdzĭ'ni."

365. He went to Dsĭ*ld*asdzĭ'ni next day and found there an old man and an old woman, who were filthy, clad in tattered garments, and had no goods in their house. "Grandmother, grandfather," he said, "a cruel man I shall be. I have come to kill you." "Do not kill us, my grandchild," said the old man : "it would not be well for the people, in days to come, if we were dead ; then they would always wear the same clothes and never get anything new. If we live, the clothing will wear out and the people will make new and beautiful garments ; they will gather goods and look handsome. Let us live and we will pull their old clothes to pieces for them." So he spared them and went home without a trophy.

366. The next journey was to seek *D*ĭtsĭ'n, Hunger, who lived, as Nĭ'ltsi told him, at Tló*had*askaí, White Spot of Grass. At this place he found twelve of the Hunger People. Their chief was a big, fat man, although he had no food to eat but the little brown cactus. "I am going to be cruel," said Nayénĕzgạni, "so that men may suffer no more the pangs of hunger and die no more of hunger." "Do not kill us," said the chief, "if you wish your people to increase and be happy in the days to come. We are your friends. If we die, the people will not care for food ; they will never know the pleasure of cooking and eating nice things, and they will never care for the pleasures of the chase." So he spared also the *D*ĭtsĭ'n, and went home without a trophy.

367. When Nayénĕzgạni came back from the home of Hunger, Nĭ'ltsi spoke to him no more of enemies that lived. The Slayer of the Alien Gods said to his mother : "I think all the anáye must be dead, for every one I meet now speaks to me as a relation ; they say to me, 'my grandson,' 'my son,' 'my brother.' "[157] Then he took off his armor — his knife, moccasins, leggings, shirt, and cap — and laid them in a pile ; he put with them the various weapons which the Sun had given him, and he sang this song : —

> Now Slayer of the Alien Gods arrives
> Here from the house made of the dark stone knives.
> From where the dark stone knives dangle on high,
> You have the treasures, holy one, not I.
>
> The Offspring of the Water now arrives,
> Here from the house made of the serrate knives.

From where the serrate knives dangle on high,
You have the treasures, holy one, not I.

He who was Reared beneath the Earth arrives,
Here from the house made of all kinds of knives.
From where all kinds of knives dangle on high,
You have the treasures, holy one, not I.

The hero, Changing Grandchild, now arrives,
Here from the house made of the yellow knives.
From where the yellow knives dangle on high,
You have the treasures, holy one, not I.[280]

368. His song had scarcely ceased when they heard, in the far east, a loud voice singing this song : —

With Slayer of the Alien Gods I come,
From the house made of dark stone knives I come,
From where dark knives dangle on high I come,
With implement of sacred rites I come,
        Dreadful to you.

With Offspring of the Waters now I come,
From the house made of serrate knives I come,
From where the serrate knives hang high I come,
With implement of sacred rites I come,
        Divine to you.

With Reared beneath the Earth now do I come,
From house of knives of every kind I come,
Where knives of every kind hang high I come,
With implement of sacred rites I come,
        Dreadful to you.

Now with the Changing Grandchild here I come,
From the house made of yellow knives I come,
From where the yellow knives hang high I come,
With implement of sacred rites I come,
        Dreadful to you.[281]

369. As the voice came nearer and the song continued, Estsánatlehi said to the youths : "Put on quickly the clothes you usually wear, Tsóhanoai is coming to see us; be ready to receive him," and she left the lodge, that she might not hear them talk about the anáye.

370. When the god had greeted his children and taken a seat, he said to the elder brother : "My son, do you think you have slain all the anáye?" "Yes, father," replied the son, "I think I have killed all that should die." "Have you brought home trophies from the slain?" the father questioned again. "Yes, my father," was the reply; "I have brought back wing-feathers, and lights and hair and

eyes, and other trophies of my enemies." "It is not well," said Tsóhanoai, "that the bodies of these great creatures should lie where they fell; I shall have them buried near the corpse of Yéitso. (He got the holy ones to carry the corpses to San Mateo and hide them under the blood of Yéitso, and this is the reason we do not see them lying all over the land now, but sometimes see them sticking out of the rocks.)[159] He took the trophies and the armor and said : " These I shall carry back to my house in the east and keep them safe. If you ever need them again, come and get them." Promising to come back again in four days, and meet Estsánatlehi on the top of Tsolíhi, he departed.

371. At the end of four days Estsánatlehi went to the top of Tsolíhi and sat down on a rock. Tsóhanoai came, sat beside her, and sought to embrace her; but she avoided him, saying : "What do you mean by this ? I want none of your embraces." ' It means that I want you for my own," said the bearer of the Sun. " I want you to come to the west and make a home for me there." " But I do not wish to do so," said she. "What right have you to ask me ? " " Have I not given your boys the weapons to slay the alien gods ? " he inquired, and added : " I have done much for you : now you must reward me." She replied, " I never besought you to do this. You did not do it on my account ; you did it of your own good will, and because your sons asked you." He urged another reason : "When Nayénězgani visited me in the east, he promised to give you to me." "What care I for his promise ? " she exclaimed ; " I am not bound by it. He has no right to speak for me." Thus four times she repulsed him. When he pleaded for the fifth time, saying : "Come to the west and make a home for me," she said : "Let me hear first all you have to promise me. You have a beautiful house in the east. I have never seen it, but I have heard how beautiful it is. I want a house just the same built for me in the west ; I want to have it built floating on the water, away from the shore, so that in the future, when people increase, they will not annoy me with too many visits. I want all sorts of gems — white shell, turquoise, haliotis, jet, soapstone, agate, and redstone — planted around my house, so that they will grow and increase. Then I shall be lonely over there and shall want something to do, for my sons and my sister will not go with me. Give me animals to take along. Do all this for me and I shall go with you to the west." He promised all these things to her, and he made elk, buffalo, deer, long-tail deer, mountain sheep, jack-rabbits, and prairie-dogs to go with her.

372. When she started for her new home the *Hadáhonestiddíne'* and the *Hadáhonigedíne'*, two tribes of divine people,[160] went with

her and helped her to drive the animals, which were already numerous. They passed over the *T*uïntsá range at Pés*l*ïts*i* (Red Knife or Red Metal), and there they tramped the mountain down so that they formed a pass. They halted in Ts*ï*nlí valley to have a ceremony [161] and a foot-race, and here the animals had become vastly more numerous. When they crossed Dsï*ll*ïz*ï*'n (Black Mountain),[162] the herd was so great that it tramped a deep pass whose bottom is almost on a level with the surrounding plain; at Black Mountain all the buffaloes broke from the herd and ran to the east; they never returned to Estsánatlehi and are in the east still. At *H*os*t*ódi*t*o' the elks went to the east and they never returned. From time to time a few, but not all, of the antelope, deer, and other animals left the herd and wandered east. Four days after leaving Ts*ï*nlí valley they arrived at *D*okos*l*íd (San Francisco Mountain), and here they stopped to perform another ceremony. What happened on the way from this mountain to the great water in the west, we do not know, but after a while Estsánatlehi arrived at the great water and went to dwell in her floating house beyond the shore. Here she still lives, and here the Sun visits her, when his journey is done, every day that he crosses the sky. But he does not go every day; on dark, stormy days he stays at home in the east and sends in his stead the serpents of lightning, who do mischief.

373. As he journeys toward the west, this is the song he sings: —

> In my thoughts I approach,
> The Sun God approaches,
> Earth's end he approaches,
> Estsánatlehi's hearth approaches,
> In old age walking
> The beautiful trail.

> In my thoughts I approach,
> The Moon God approaches,
> Earth's end he approaches,
> Yo*l*kái Estsán's hearth approaches,
> In old age walking
> The beautiful trail.[282]

374. When Estsánatlehi had departed, Nayénĕzg̣ani and *T*o'badz*ï*sts*i*ni went, as their father had bidden them, to *T*o'yĕ'tli,[163] where two rivers join, in the valley of the San Juan; there they made their dwelling, there they are to this day, and there we sometimes still see their forms in the San Juan River.[164] The Navahoes still go there to pray, but not for rain, or good crops, or increase of stock; only for success in war, and only the warriors go.

IV. GROWTH OF THE NAVAHO NATION.

375. Before Estsánatlehi left, she said to Yo/kaí Estsán: "Now, younger sister, I must leave you. Think well what you would most like to do after I am gone." The younger sister replied: "I would most like to go back to Depĕ'ntsa, where our people came from." "Alas! you will be lonely there," said the elder sister. "You will want for some one around you to make a noise and keep you company." Still, when Estsánatlehi left, Yolkaí Estsán turned her face toward Depĕ'ntsa. She went with the two brothers as far as To'yĕ'tli, and, when these stopped there, she set out alone for the mountains.

376. When she got to Depĕ'ntsa (the San Juan Mountains), she went first to a place lying east of Hadzinaí (the Place of Emergence), named Dsĭ/ladĭ/téhi; in an old ruined pueblo on its side she rested during the day, and at night she went to the top of the mountain to sleep. On the second day she went to a mountain south of the Place of Emergence, called Dsĭlí'ndĭ/téhi; rested on the side of the mountain during the day, and on its top at night. She began now to feel lonely, and at night she thought of how men might be made to keep her company. She wandered round in thought during the third day, and on the third night she slept on top of Dsĭ/tagĭ/téhi, a mountain west of Hadzinaí. On the fourth day she walked around the Place of Emergence, and wandered into the old ruins she found there. On the fourth night she went to the top of Dsĭ/ĭnĭ/téz, the mountain which lies to the north of the Place of Emergence, and there she rested, but did not sleep; for she thought all the time about her loneliness, and of how people might be made. On the fifth day she came down to the shores of the lake which surrounded the Place of Emergence, and built a shelter of brush. "I may as well stay here," she said to herself; "what does it avail that I wander round?" She sat up late that night thinking of her lonely condition. She felt that she could not stay there longer without companionship. She thought of her sister in the far west, of the Twelve People, of the gods that dwelt in the different mountains, and she thought she might do well to go and live with some of them.

377. The next morning she heard faintly, in the early dawn, the voice of Hastséyal/i shouting his usual "Wu'hu'hu'hú," in the far east. Four times the cry was uttered, each time louder and nearer. Immediately after the last call the god appeared. "Where did you save yourself?" he asked the White Shell Woman, meaning, "Where were you, that you escaped the anáye when they ravaged

the land?" "I was at Dsĭ*l*náo*tĭl* with my sister," she said; "but for five nights I have been all alone in these mountains. I have been hoping that something might happen to relieve my great loneliness, —that I might meet some one. *Sĭtsaí* (Grandfather), whence do you come?" He replied: "I come from Tse'gíhi,[165] the home of the gods. I pity your loneliness and wish to help you. If you remain where you are, I shall return in four days and bring Estsánatlehi, the divine ones of all the great mountains, and other gods, with me." When he left, she built for herself a good hut with a storm door. She swept the floor clean, and made a comfortable bed of soft grass and leaves.

378. At dawn on the fourth day after the god departed, Yo*l*kaí Estsán heard two voices calling,—the voice of *H*ast*s*éyal*t*i, the Talking God, and the voice of *H*ast*s*é*h*ogan, the House God. The voices were heard, as usual, four times, and immediately after the last call the gods appeared. It was dark and misty that day; the sun did not rise. Soon after the arrival of the first two, the other promised visitors came, and they all formed themselves in a circle east of the lodge, each in the place where he or she belonged. Thus the divine ones of Tsĭsnadzĭ'ni stood in the east; those of Tsótsĭ*l* (San Mateo Mountain) in the south; those of *D*okoslĭ*d* (San Francisco Mountain) in the west; those of *D*epĕ'ntsa (San Juan Mountain) in the north. Each one present had his appropriate place in the group. At first Yo*l*kaí Estsán stood in the west; but her sister, Estsánatlehi, said to her: "No, my young sister; go you and stand in the east. My place is in the west," and thus they stood during the ceremony. Estsánatlehi brought with her two sacred blankets called *D*ĭ*l*pĭ'*l*-naská, the Dark Embroidered, and *L*akaí-naská, the White Embroidered. *H*ast*s*é*h*ogan brought with him two sacred buckskins, and the Nalkénaa*z* (a divine couple who came together walking arm in arm) brought two ears of corn,—one yellow, one white,—which the female carried in a dish of turquoise.

379. *H*ast*s*éyal*t*i laid the sacred blankets on the ground, and spread on top of these one of the sacred buckskins with its head to the west. He took from the dish of the female Nalkénaa*z* the two ears of corn, handing the white ear to Tse'gá*d*ĭna*r*ĭni A*s*iké, the Rock Crystal Boy of the eastern mountain, and the yellow ear to Na*t*á*l*tsoi A*t*é*t*, the Yellow Corn Girl of San Francisco Mountain. These divine ones laid the ears on the buckskin,—the yellow with its tip toward the west, the white with its tip toward the east. *H*ast*s*éyal*t*i picked up the ears, and nearly laid them down on the buckskin with their tips to the east, but he did not let them touch the buckskin; as he did this he uttered his own cry of "Wu'hu'hu'hú." Then he nearly laid them down with their tips to the south, giving

as he did so *Hastséhogan's* cry of " *Ha*-wa-u-ú." With similar motions he pointed the ears to the west and the north. Next he raised them toward the sky, and at length laid them down on the buckskin, with their tips to the east. He accompanied each act with a cry of his own or of *Hastséhogan*, alternating as in the beginning. So the ears were turned in every direction, and this is the reason the Navahoes never abide in one home like the Pueblos, but wander ever from place to place. Over the ears of corn he laid the other sacred buckskin with its head to the east, and then Nĭ'ltsi, the Wind, entered between the skins. Four times, at intervals, *Hastséyalti* raised the buckskins a little and peeped in. When he looked the fourth time, he saw that the white ear of corn was changed to a man, and the yellow ear to a woman. It was Nĭ'ltsi who gave them the breath of life. He entered at the heads and came out at the ends of the fingers and toes, and to this day we see his trail in the tip of every human finger. The Rock Crystal Boy furnished them with mind, and the Grasshopper Girl gave them voices. When *Hastséyalti* at last threw off the top buckskin, a dark cloud descended and covered like a blanket the forms of the new pair. Yo/kaí Estsán led them into her *hogán*, and the assembled gods dispersed. Before he left, *Hastséyalti* promised to return in four days.

380. No songs were sung and no prayers uttered during their rites, and the work was done in one day. The *hogán* near which all these things happened still stands; but since that time it has been transformed into a little hill. To-day (A. D. 1884) seven times old age has killed since this pair was made by the holy ones from the ears of corn. The next very old man who dies will make the eighth time.[166]

381. Early on the fourth morning after his departure *Hastséyalti* came again as he had promised, announcing his approach by calling four times as usual. When White Shell Woman heard the first call, she aroused the young people and said: " Get up, my children, and make a fire. *Hastséyalti* is coming." He brought with him another couple, *Hadáhonige Asiké* (Mirage Boy) and *Hadáhonestid Atét* (Ground-heat Girl). He gave Yo/kaí Estsán two ears of corn, saying, " Grind only one grain at a time," and departed. Yo/kaí Estsán said to the newly-arrived couple : " This boy and girl of corn cannot marry one another, for they are brother and sister; neither can you marry one another, for you are also brother and sister, yet I must do something for you all." So she married the boy made of corn to the Ground-heat Girl, and the Mirage Boy to the girl made of corn. After a time each couple had two children, — a boy and a girl. When these were large enough to run around, this family all moved away from *Hadzinaí*, where they had lived four years, to Tse'/akaíia

(White Standing Rock). The two men were busy every day hunting rabbits, rats, and other such animals, for on such game they chiefly lived. From these people are descended the gens of Tse'-dzïnkï′ni,[167] House of the Dark Cliffs ; so named because the gods who created the first pair came from the cliff houses of Tse'gíhi, and brought from there the ears of corn from which this first pair was made.

382. After they had lived thirteen years at Tse'ʌakaíia, during which time they had seen no sign of the existence of any people but themselves, they beheld one night the gleam of a distant fire. They sought for the fire all that night and the next day, but could not find it. The next night they saw it again in the same place, and the next day they searched with greater vigilance, but in vain. On the third night, when the distant gleam shqne again through the darkness, they determined to adopt some means, better than they had previously taken, to locate it. They drove a forked stick firmly into the ground ; one of the men got down on his hands and knees, spreading them as wide apart as possible, and sighted the fire through the fork of the stick. Next morning he carefully placed his hands and knees in the tracks which they had made the night before, and once more looked through the fork. His sight was thus guided to a little wooded hollow on the side of a far-off mountain. One of the men walked over to the mountain and entered the little hollow, which was small and could be explored in a few moments ; but he discovered no fire, no ashes, no human tracks, no evidence of the presence of man. On the fourth night all the adults of the party took sight over the forked stick at the far twinkle, and in the morning when they looked again they found they had all sighted the same little grove on the distant mountain-side. " Strange !" said the man who had hunted there the day before ; "the place is small. I went all through it again and again. There was no sign of life there, and not a drop of water that could reflect a ray from a star or from the moon." Then all the males of the family, men and boys, went to explore the little wood. Just as they were about to return, having found nothing, Wind whispered into the ear of one : " You are deceived. That light shines through a crack in the mountain at night. Cross the ridge and you will find the fire." [168] They had not gone far over the ridge when they saw the footprints of men, then the footprints of children, and soon they came to the camp. One party was as much rejoiced as the other to find people like themselves in the wilderness. They embraced one another, and shouted mutual greetings and questions. "Whence do you come ?" said the strangers. " From Tse'ʌakaíia," was the response. " And whence come you ?" asked the men of

the White Standing Rock. " We tarried last," replied the strangers,
" at *To'ï'nd*otsos, a poor country, where we lived on ducks and
snakes.[169] We have been here only a few days, and now we live on
ground-rats, prairie-dogs, and wild seeds." The new party consisted
of twelve persons, — five men, three women, one grown girl, one
grown boy, and two small children. The Tse'd*z*ïnkï'ni people took
the strangers home with them, and Yo*l*kaí Estsán welcomed them,
saying : " A*h*aláni *s*a*s*tsíni ! " (Greeting, my children !) The place
where the Tse'd*z*ïnkï'ni found the strangers encamped was called
Tsé'tlana (Bend in a Canyon) ; so they gave them the name of
Tse'tláni, or Tse'tláni*d*íne', and from them is descended the present gens of Tse'tláni in the Navaho nation.

383. The next morning after the arrival of the Tse'tláni, *H*ast*s*é-
yal*t*i came once more to the lodge of the White Shell Woman ; but
he talked with her apart from the others, and when he was gone she
told no one what he said. In three days he came back again ; again
they talked apart, and when *H*ast*s*éyal*t*i was gone she remained
silent. It was her custom to sleep with one of the little girls, who
was her favorite and companion. In the morning after the second
visit of *H*ast*s*éyal*t*i she said to this little girl : " I am going to
leave you. The gods of Tse'gíhi have sent for me ; but I shall
not forget your people, and shall come often to watch over them and
be near them. Tell them this when they waken." When she had
spoken she disappeared from the sight of the little girl, and when
the people woke they searched, but could find her nowhere. They
supposed she had gone to Tse'gíhi and tarried there a while before
she went to *D*epĕ'ntsa to dwell forever in the house of White Shell,
which had been prepared for her there. The fourth night after the
departure of Yo*l*kaí Estsán the little girl had a dream, which she
related to her people in the morning. In the vision she saw Yo*l*kaí
Estsán, who said to her : " My grandchild, I am going to *D*epĕ'ntsa
to dwell. I would take you with me, for I love you, were it not
that your parents would mourn for you. But look always for the
she-rain when it comes near your dwelling, for I shall ever be in the
she-rain."

384. While at White Standing Rock the men wandered much
around the country in search of food. Some who had been to
To'dokónzi (Saline Water) said the latter was a better place than
than that in which they lived ; that there were some porcupines
there, an abundance of rats, prairie-dogs, and seed-bearing plants ;
and that there were steep-sided mesa points in the neighborhood
where they might surround large game.[170] After the departure of
Yo*l*kaí Estsán the people all moved to *To*'dokónzi ; [171] but they
remained here only a few days, and then went to T*s*a'olgá*h*as*z*e.

Here they planted some grains of corn from the two ears that *H*ast*s*éyal*t*i had given them long ago. This was a very prolific kind of corn ; when planted, several stalks sprouted from each grain, and a single grain, when ground, produced a large quantity of meal, which lasted them many days.

385. When they had been fourteen years at T*s*a'olgá*h*as*z*e they were joined by another people, who came from the sacred mountain of Dsĭ*l*náo*t*í*l*, and were therefore called Dsĭ*l*nao*t*ĭ'*l*ni, or Dsĭ*l*nao*t*ĭ'*l*-*d*ĭne'. These were regarded as *d*ĭné' *d*ĭgíni, or holy people, because they had no tradition of their recent creation, and were supposed to have escaped the fury of the alien gods by means of some miraculous protection. They did not camp at first with the older settlers, but dwelt a little apart, and sent often to the latter to borrow pots and metates. After a while all joined together as one people, and for a long time these three gentes have been as one gens and have become close relations to one another. The new-comers dug among old ruins and found pots and stone axes ; with the latter they built themselves huts.

386. Seven years after the arrival of the Dsĭ*l*nao*t*ĭ'*l*ni a fourth gens joined the Navahoes. The new arrivals said they had been seeking for the Dsĭ*l*nao*t*ĭ'*l*ni all over the land for many years. Sometimes they would come upon the dead bushes of old camps. Sometimes they would find deserted brush shelters, partly green, or, again, quite green and fresh. Occasionally they would observe faint footprints, and think they were just about to meet another people like themselves in the desolate land ; but again all traces of humanity would be lost. They were rejoiced to meet at last the people they so long had sought. The new-comers camped close to the Dsĭ*l*nao*t*ĭ'*l*ni, and discovered that they and the latter carried similar red arrow-holders,[172] such as the other gentes did not have, and this led them to believe that they were related to the Dsĭ*l*nao-*t*ĭ'*l*ni. The Navahoes did not then make large skin quivers such as they have in these days ; they carried their arrows in simpler contrivances. The strangers said that they came from a place called *H*a*s*kán*h*atso (much *Yucca baccata*), and that they were the *H*a*s*kán*d*ĭne', or Yucca People ; but the older gentes called them *H*a*s*kán*h*atso, or *H*a*s*kan*h*atsó*d*ĭne', from the place whence they came.[173]

387. Fourteen years after the accession of the fourth gens, the Navahoes moved to Kĭntyél (which was then a ruin), in the Chaco Canyon. They camped there at night in a scattering fashion, and made so many fires that they attracted the attention of some strangers camped on a distant mountain, and these strangers came down next day to find out who the numerous people were that kin-

dled so many fires. As the strangers, who were also *d*íné' *d*ïgíni, or holy people, said they came from Na*h*opá (Place of the Brown Horizontal Streak), the Navahoes called them Na*h*opáni. They joined the tribe, camping near the *H*askán*h*atso and Dsĭ*l*naot*ï*'*l*ni.

388. It was autumn when the fifth gens was received. Then the whole tribe moved to the banks of the San Juan River and settled at a place called Tsïn*t*ó'betlo [174] (Tree Sweeping Water), where a peculiar white tree hangs over the stream and sweeps the surface of the water with its long branches : there is no other tree of its kind near by. Here they determined to remain some time and raise crops; so they built warm huts for the winter, and all the fall and winter, when the days were fair, they worked in the bottom-lands grubbing up roots and getting the soil ready for gardens to be planted in the spring. The elder gentes camped farther down the stream than those more newly arrived.

389. In those days the language which the Navahoes spoke was not the same they speak now. It was a poor language then ; it is better in these days.

390. When the tribe had been living six years on the banks of the San Juan, a band joined them who came from Tsĭ'nad*z*ĭn [175] (Black Horizontal Forest), and were named as a gens from the place whence they came. The Navahoes observed that in this band there was a man who talked a great deal to the people almost every morning and evening. The Navahoes did not at first understand what this meant ; but after a while they learned he spoke to his people because he was their chief. His name was Nabĭnĭl*t*áhi.

391. While living at the San Juan the people amused themselves much with games. They played mostly nán*zoz* [76] in the daytime and kĕsĭt*s*é [176] at night. They had as yet no horses, domestic sheep, or goats. They rarely succeeded in killing deer or Rocky Mountain sheep. When they secured deer it was sometimes by still-hunting them, sometimes by surrounding one and making it run till it was exhausted, and sometimes by driving them over precipices. When a man got two skins of these larger animals he made a garment of them by tying the fore-legs together over his shoulders. The woman wore a garment consisting of two webs of woven cedar bark, one hanging in front and one behind ; all wore sandals of yucca fibre or cedar bark. They had headdresses made of weasel-skins and rat-skins, with the tails hanging down behind. These headdresses were often ornamented with colored artificial horns, made out of wood, or with the horns of the female mountain sheep shaved thin. Their blankets were made of cedar bark, of yucca fibre, or of skins sewed together.[177] Each house had, in front of the door, a long passageway, in which hung two curtains, — one at the

outer, the other at the inner end, — made usually of woven cedar bark.   In winter they brought in plenty of wood at night, closed both curtains, and made the house warm before they went to sleep. Their bows were of plain wood then ; the Navahoes had not yet learned to put animal fibre on the backs of the bows.[178]   Their arrows were mostly of reeds tipped with wood ; but some made wooden arrows.[180]   The bottom-land which they farmed was sur- rounded by high bluffs, and hemmed in up-stream and down-stream by jutting bluffs which came close to the river.   After a time the tribe became too numerous for all to dwell and farm on this spot, so some went up in the bluffs to live and built stone storehouses in the cliffs,[179] while others — the Tsĭnadₐĭ′ni — went below the lower promontory to make gardens.   Later yet, some moved across the San Juan and raised crops on the other side of the stream.[180]

392.   Eight years after the coming of the Tsĭnadₐĭ′ni, some fires were observed at night on a distant eminence north of the river, and spies were sent out to see who made them.   The spies brought back word that they had found a party of strangers encamped at a place called *Tha*‘nĕzá‘, Among the Scattered (Hills).   Soon after, this party came in and joined the Navahoes, making a new gens, which was called *Tha*‘nĕzá‘ni.   The strangers said they were de- scended from the *Hadáh*onige*dí*ne‘, or Mirage People.   The remains of their old huts are still to be seen at *Tha*‘nezá‘.

393.   Five years after the *Tha*‘nĕzá‘ni were added, another people joined the tribe ; but what gods sent them none could tell.   They came from a place called Dsĭ*l*tlá‘ (Base of Mountain), and were given the name of Dsĭ*l*tlá‘ni.   As they had headdresses, bows, ar- rows, and arrow-holders similar to those of the *Tha*‘nĕzá‘ni they concluded they must be related to the latter.   Ever since, these two gentes have been very close friends, — so close that a member of one cannot marry a member of the other.   The Dsĭ*l*tlá‘ni knew how to make wicker water-bottles, carrying-baskets, and earthen pots, and they taught their arts to the rest of the people.

394.   Five years later, they were joined on the San Juan by a numerous band who came originally from a place called *T*há‘paha- *h*alkaí, White Valley among the Waters, which is near where the city of Santa Fé now stands.   These people had long viewed in the western distance the mountains where the Navahoes dwelt, wonder- ing if any one lived there, and at length decided to go thither. They journeyed westward twelve days till they reached the moun- tains, and they spent eight days travelling among them before they encountered the Navahoes.   Then they settled at *To*ʻi′nd*o*tsos and lived there twelve years, subsisting on ducks and fish,[169] but making no farms.   All this time they were friendly to the Navahoes and

exchanged visits; but, finding no special evidences of relationship with the latter, they dwelt apart. When at length they came to the San Juan to live, marriages had taken place between members of the two tribes, and the people from Among the Waters became a part of the Navaho nation, forming the gens of *Thá*'paha. They settled at a place called Hyíĕ*t*yĭn (Trails Leading Upward), close to the Navahoes. Here was a smooth, sandy plain, which they thought would be good for farming, and the chief, whose name was Góntso, or Big Knee, had stakes set around the plain to show that his people claimed it. The people of the new gens were good hunters, skilled in making weapons and beautiful buckskin shirts, and they taught their arts to the other gentes.

395. The *Thá*'paha then spoke a language more like the modern Navaho than that which the other gentes spoke. The languages were not alike. The chief of the Tsĭnad*z*ĭ'ni and Góntso often visited one another at night, year after year, for the purpose of uniting the two languages and picking out the words in each that were best. But the words of the *Thá*'paha were usually the best and plainest; [182] so the new language resembles the *Thá*'paha more than it resembles the old Navaho.

396. While the *Thá*'paha lived at Hyíĕ*t*yĭn they had always abundant crops,—better crops than their neighbors had. Sometimes they could not harvest all they raised, and let food lie ungathered in the field. They built stone storehouses, something like pueblo houses, among the cliffs, and in these stored their corn. The storehouses stand there yet. The *Thá*'paha remained at Hyíĕ*t*yĭn thirteen years, during which time many important events occurred, as will be told, and then they moved to Az*d*elts*i*gi.

397. Góntso had twelve wives; four of these were from the gens of Tsĭnad*z*ĭ'ni, four from the gens of Dsĭ*l*tlá'ni, and four from the gens of *Tha*'nĕzá'ni. He used to give much grain from his abundant harvests to the gentes to which his wives belonged; but, in spite of his generosity, his wives were unfaithful to him. He complained to their relations and to their chiefs; these remonstrated with the wives, but failed to improve their ways. At last they lost patience with the women and said to Góntso: "Do with them as you will. We shall not interfere." So the next wife whom he detected in crime he mutilated in a shameful way, and she died in consequence. He cut off the ears of the next transgressor, and she, too, died. He amputated the breasts of the third wife who offended him, and she died also. He cut off the nose of the fourth; she did not die. He determined then that cutting the nose should, in future, be the greatest punishment imposed on the faithless wife,—something that would disfigure but not kill,—and the rest of the

people agreed with him.[183]   But this had no effect on the remaining wives; they continued to lapse from virtue till all were noseless. Then they got together and began to plot mischief against their husband, Big Knee.   They spoke so openly of their evil intentions that he feared to let any of them stay in his lodge at night and he slept alone.

398. About this time the people determined to have a great cere- mony for the benefit of Big Knee; so they made great preparations and held a rite of nine days' duration.[184]   During its progress the mutilated women remained in a hut by themselves, and talked about the unkindness of their people and the vengeance due to their hus- band.   They said one to another: " We should leave our people and go elsewhere."   On the last night of the ceremony there was a series of public exhibitions in a corral, or circle of branches, such as the Navahoes have now on the last night of the ceremony of the mountain chant,[185] and among the different alíli, or entertainments of the night, was a dance by the mutilated women.   When their time came they entered the circle, each bearing a knife in her hand, and danced around the central fire, peering among the spectators as if searching for their husband; but he was hidden in the wall of branches that formed the circle.   As they danced they sang a song the burden of which was " Pésla aṣilá."   (It was the knife that did it to me.)   When they had finished their dance they left the corral, and, in the darkness without, screamed maledictions at their peo- ple, saying : " May the waters drown ye!   May the winters freeze ye!   May the fires burn ye!   May the lightnings strike ye!" and much more.   Having cursed till they were tired, they departed for the far north, where they still dwell, and now, whenever they turn their faces to the south, we have cold winds and storms and lightning.

399. Not long after this memorable ceremony a number of Utes visited the Navahoes.   They came when the corn-ears were small, and remained till the corn was harvested.   They worked for the Navahoes, and when their stomachs were filled all left except one family, which consisted of an old couple, two girls, and a boy. These at first intended to stay but a short time after their friends had gone; but they tarried longer and longer, and postponed their going from time to time, till they ended by staying with the Nava- hoes till they died.   They made particular friends with the *Tháʻpaha*, and got into the way of speaking to the latter people as they would to relations.   One of the girls, whose name was Tsáʻyĭskĭ*d* (Sage- Brush Hill), lived to be an old woman and the mother of many chil- dren.   From her is descended the gens of Tsaʻyĭskĭ*d*ni, which is so closely allied to the *Tháʻpaha* that a member of one of these gentes may not marry a member of the other.

400. Soon after the departure of the Utes the Navahoes were joined by a group of people who, when they came to tell their story, were found to have come from *Thá'paha-halkaí*, and to have made wanderings similar to those of the people who first came from that place. The new people spoke, also, the same language as the *Thá'paha*. For these reasons they were not formed into a new gens, but were joined to the gens of *Thá'paha*.

401. Some years later a large band came from the south to the settlement on the San Juan. It consisted of Apaches, who told the Navahoes that they had left their old tribe forever and desired to become Navahoes. They had not come to visit, they said, but to stay. They all belonged to one gens among the Apaches, — the gens of Tse'*zĭndiaí* (Trap-dyke),[186] and they were admitted into the tribe as a new gens with their old name. From the beginning they showed a desire to associate with *Thá'paha*, and now they are closely related to the latter and must not marry with them. Another band of Apaches, which came a little later, was added to the same gens.

402. About this time there was a great famine in Zuñi, and some people from this pueblo came to the San Juan to dwell with the Navahoes. They came first to the *Thá'paha*, and, although they had women in the party, they were not formed into a new gens, but added to *Thá'paha*. The gens of Zuñi was formed later.

403. The famine prevailed also at other pueblos, and some starving people came to the Navahoes from an old pueblo named Klógi, which was near where the pueblo of Jemez now stands. These formed the gens of Klógi, and made special friends of the *Thá'paha*.

404. The next accession was a family of seven adults, who came from a place called *Tó'hani* (Near the Water). They first visited the Dsĭ́ltlá'ni and remained, forming the gens of Tó'hani, affiliated now with Dsĭ́ltlá'ni.

405. The people who joined the Navahoes next after the Tó'hani came from a place called *Tha'tsí*, Among the Red (Waters or Banks), which was west of the San Juan settlement. From their traditions it appeared that they were not a newly created people; they had escaped in some way from the alien gods, and were for these reasons regarded as *díné' dígíni*, or holy people. They were divided into two gentes, *Thá'tsini* and Kaí*díne'*, or Willow People, and for a while they formed two gentes among the Navahoes; but in these days all traces of this division have been lost, and all their descendants are now called, without distinction, sometimes *Thá'tsini* and sometimes Kai or Kaí*díne'*.

406. Before this time the Navahoes had been a weak and peaceable tribe; but now they found themselves becoming a numerous

people and they began to talk of going to war. Of late years they
had heard much of the great pueblos along the Rio Grande, but
how their people had saved themselves from the anáye the Navahoes did not know. A man named Napaílĭn*t*a got up a war party
and made a raid on a pueblo named Kĭn*l*ĭt*s*í (Red House), and
returned with some captives, among whom was a girl captured by
Napaílĭn*t*a. From her is descended the gens of Kĭn*l*ĭt*s*í, whose
members are now close relations to Tsĭnad*z*í'ni (the gens of Napaílĭn*t*a), and cannot intermarry with the latter.

407. The captives from Kĭn*l*ĭt*s*í were, at first, slaves among the
Navahoes;[187] but their descendants became free and increased
greatly, and from them came another gens, Tlĭzi*l*áni, Many Goats,
also closely related to Tsĭnad*z*í'ni.

408. Next in order came a band of Apaches from the south representing two gentes, — *D*ĕst*s*íni (Red Streak People), and Tlast*s*íni
(Red Flat Ground People). These were adopted by the Navahoes
as two separate gentes and became close relations to the Tsĭnad*z*í'ni.

409. Not long after the arrival of these Apaches some Utes came
into the neighborhood of the Navahoes, camping at a place called
Tsé'di'yikáni (a ridge or promontory projecting into the river), not
far from Hyíĕ*t*yĭn. They had good arms of all kinds, and two varieties of shields, — one round and one with a crescentic cut in the top.
They lived for a while by themselves, and were at first unruly and
impertinent; but in the course of time they merged into the Navahoes, forming the gens of No*t*á or No*t*ád*ĭ*ne', Ute People.

410. About the time they were incorporated by the Navahoes,
or soon after, a war party of the Utes made a raid on a Mexican
settlement, somewhere near where Socorro now is, and captured
a Spanish woman. She was their slave; but her descendants became free among the Navahoes and formed the Nakaíd*ĭ*ne' (White
Stranger People), or Mexican gens, who cannot now intermarry with
No*t*ád*ĭ*ne'.

411. Góntso, or Big Knee, chief of the *T*há'paha, was still alive
and was a famous old man; but he had become feeble and had many
ailments. There was a great ceremony practised in those days called
nats*i*'d, which lasted all winter,[184] from harvest-time to planting-time;
but the Navahoes have long ceased to celebrate it. This ceremony
was held one winter for the benefit of Big Knee at the sacred place
of *T*o'yĕ'tli, the home of the War Gods. One night, while the rites
were being performed, some strangers joined the Navahoes coming
from the direction of the river. Adopted by the Navahoes, they
formed the gens of *T*o'yĕtlíni, and became closely allied to No*t*ád*ĭ*ne'
and Nakaíd*ĭ*ne'.

412. On another occasion during the same winter some Apaches

came from their country in the south to witness the ceremony of natsi'd. Among the women of the *Thá*'paha was one who visited the Apache camp and remained all night there. She became attached to an Apache youth, with whom she secretly absconded when the visitors left. For a long time her people did not know what had become of her; but many years after, learning where she was, some of her relations went to the Apache country to persuade her to return. She came back an old woman, bringing her husband and a family of three girls. The girls were handsome, had light skins and fair hair. Their grandmother, who admired them very much, insisted that a new gens should be made of them. So they were called *H*áltso, Yellow Bodies,[188] and originated the gens of that name. Their father died an old man among the Navahoes.

413. On another night of the same winter, while the ceremony for Big Knee was going on, two strange men, speaking the Navaho language, entered the camp. They said they were the advanced couriers of a multitude of wanderers who had left the shores of the great waters in the west to join the Navahoes. You shall now hear the story of the people who came from the western ocean : —

414. Surrounding Estsánatlehi's home were four mountains, located like those at the Place of Emergence — one in the east, one in the south, one in the west, and one in the north. She was in the habit of dancing on these mountains, — on the mountain in the east to bring clouds; on the mountain in the south, to bring all kinds of goods, — jewels, clothing, etc. ; on the mountain in the west, to bring plants of all kinds ; and on the mountain in the north, to bring corn and animals. On these journeys for dancing she passed from the east mountain to the south, the west, and the north mountain, the way the sun goes ; and when she was done dancing on the north mountain she retraced her course (without crossing it) to the east ; but she never completed the circle, *i. e.*, she never passed from the north directly to the east. Over the space between the north and the east mountains she never travelled. This is the way her trail lay : —

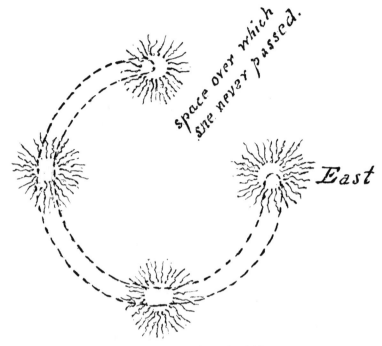

Fig. 33.   Trail of Estsánatlehi.

415. Estsánatlehi had not been long in her western home when she began to feel lonely. She had no companions there. The people who had accompanied her thither did not stay with her. She thought she might make people to keep her company, so one day, when she had completed one of her dancing journeys, she sat down on the eastern mountain. Here she rubbed epidermis from under her left arm with her right hand; she held this in her palm and it changed into four persons, — two men and two women, — from whom descended a gens to which no name was then given, but which after-terwards (as will be told) received the name of *H*onagá‘ni. She rubbed the epidermis with her left hand from under her right arm, held it in her palm as before, and it became two men and two women, from whom descended the gens afterwards known as Kin-aá‘ni. In a similar way, of epidermis rubbed from under her left breast she created four people, from whom descended the gens later known as *T*o‘dĭtsíni; of epidermis from under her right breast, four persons, from whom descended the gens called Bĭ*t*áni; of epidermis from the middle of her chest, the four whose descendants were called *Hasl*í‘zni; and of epidermis from her back between her shoulders, the four whose descendants were called Bĭ*t*á‘ni in later times.

416. She said to these: "I wish you to dwell near me, where I can always see you; but if you choose to go to the east, where your kindred dwell, you may go." She took them from her floating home to the mainland; here they lived for thirty years, during which time they married and had many children. At the end of this time the Twelve People (*Dïné‘* Naki*dáta*), or rather what was left of them, appeared among Estsánatlehi's people and said to them: "We have lost our sister who kept our house for us; we have no home; we know not where else to go; so we have come here to behold our mother, our grandmother. You have kindred in the far east who have increased until they are now a great people. We do not visit them, but we stand on the mountains and look at them from afar. We know they would welcome you if you went to them." And many more things they told about the people in the far east.

417. Now all crossed on a bridge of rainbow to the house of Estsánatlehi on the sea, where she welcomed them and embraced them. Of the *Dïné‘* Naki*dáta* but ten were left, for, as has been told, they lost their sister and their younger brother; but when they came to the home of Estsánatlehi she made for them two more people out of turquoise, and this completed their original number of twelve. She knew with what thoughts her children had come. She opened four doors leading from the central chamber of her house into four other rooms, and showed them her various treasures, saying: "Stay with me always, my children; these things shall be yours, and we shall be always happy together."

418. When the people went back from the house of Estsánatlehi to the mainland, all was gossip and excitement in their camp about what they had heard of the people in the east. Each one had a different part or version of the tale to tell, — of how the people in the east lived, of what they ate, of the way in which they were divided into gentes, of how the gentes were named, and of other things about them they had heard. "The people are few where we live," they said; "we would be better off where there are so many." They talked thus for twelve days. At the end of that time they concluded to depart, and they fixed the fourteenth day after that as the day they should leave.

419. Before they left, the *Dïné‘* Naki*dáta* and Estsánatlehi came to see them. She said: "It is a long and dangerous journey to where you are going. It is well that you should be cared for and protected on the way. I shall give you five of my pets,[189] — a bear, a great snake, a deer, a porcupine, and a puma, — to watch over you. They will not desert you. Speak of no evil deeds in the presence of the bear or the snake, for they may do the evil they hear you speak of; but the deer and the porcupine are good, — say whatever you please to say in their presence."

420. Besides these pets she gave them five magic wands. To those who were afterwards named *H*onagá'ni she gave a wand of turquoise; to those who later were called Ki*n*aá'ni, a wand of white shell; to those who became *T*o'dǐts*í*ni, a wand of haliotis shell; to those who became Bǐtá'ni, a wand of black stone; and to those who in later days became *H*as*l*ǐ'*z*ni, a wand of red stone. "I give you these for your protection," she said, "but I shall watch over you myself while you are on your journey."

421. On the appointed day they set out on their journey. On the twelfth day of their march they crossed a high ridge and came in sight of a great treeless plain, in the centre of which they observed some dark objects in motion. They could not determine what they were, but suspected they were men. They continued their journey, but did not directly approach the dark objects; they moved among the foothills that surrounded the plain, and kept under cover of the timber. As they went along they discerned the dark objects more plainly, and discovered that these were indeed human beings. They got among the foothills to one side of where the strangers were, and camped in the woods at night.

422. In spite of all the precautions taken by the travellers, they had been observed by the people of the plain, and at night two of the latter visited their camp. The visitors said they were Kǐ*l*tsói, or Kǐ*l*tsóid*í*ne' (People of the *Bigelovia graveolens*); that their tribe was numerous; that the plain in which they dwelt was extensive; and that they had watermelons getting ripe, with corn and other food, in their gardens. The people of the west concluded to remain here a while. The second night they had two more visitors, one of whom became enamored of a maiden among the wanderers, and asked for her in marriage. Her people refused him at first; but when he came the second night and begged for her again, they gave her to him. He stayed with her in the camp of her people as long as they remained in the valley, except the last two nights, when she went and stayed with his people. These gave an abundance of the produce of their fields to the wanderers, and the latter fared well. When the travellers were prepared to move, they implored the young husband to go with them, while he begged to have his wife remain with him in the valley. They argued long; but in the end the woman's relations prevailed, and the Kǐ*l*tsói man joined them on their journey. In the mean time four other men of Kǐ*l*tsói had fallen in love with maidens of the wanderers, and asked for them in marriage. The migrating band refused to leave the girls behind, so the enamored young men left their kindred and joined the travellers. The Kǐ*l*tsói tried to persuade the others to dwell in their land forever, but without avail.

423. They broke camp at last early in the morning, and travelled all day. At night a great wind arose, and the bear would not rest, but ran around the camp all night, uneasy and watchful. The men looked out and saw some of the Kĭ*l*tsói trying to approach ; but the bear warded them off and they disappeared without doing harm. In the morning it was found that the men of the Kĭ*l*tsói who had joined them on their journey had now deserted them, and it was supposed that in some way they were in league with their brethren outside.

424. The second day they journeyed far, and did not make camp until after dark. As on the previous night, the bear was awake, watchful, and uneasy all night. They supposed he was still looking out for lurking Kĭ*l*tsói. Not until daybreak did he lie down and take a little sleep while the people were preparing for the day's march.

425. On the third night the bear was again wakeful and on guard, and only lay down in the morning while the people were breaking camp. "My pet, why are you troubled thus every night?" said one of the men to the bear. The latter only grunted in reply, and made a motion with his nose in the direction whence they had come.

426. On the fourth night they camped, for mutual protection, closer together than they had camped before. The bear sat on a neighboring hill, from which he could watch the sleepers, but slept not himself all night. As before, he took a short sleep in the morning. Before the people set out on their march some one said : " Let us look around and see if we can find what has troubled our pet." They sent two couriers to the east and two to the west. The former returned, having found nothing. The latter said they had seen strange footprints, as of people who had approached the camp and then gone back far to the west. Their pursuers, they thought, had returned to their homes.

427. They had now been four days without finding water, and the children were crying with thirst. On the fifth day's march they halted at noon and held a council. " How shall we procure water?" said one. " Let us try the power of our magic wands," said another. A man of the gens who owned the wand of turquoise stuck this wand into the ground, and worked it back and forth and round and round to make a good-sized hole. Water sprang from the hole. A woman of another gens crouched down to taste it. "It is bitter water," she cried. " Let that, then, be your name and the name of your people," said those who heard her; thus did the gens of *To‘dĭ-tsíni*, Bitter Water People, receive its name.

428. When the people had cooked and eaten food and drunk their fill of the bitter water, they said : " Let us try to reach yonder moun-

tain before night." So they pushed on to a distant mountain they had beheld in the east. When they got near the mountain they saw moccasin tracks, and knew there must be some other people at hand. At one place, near the base of the mountain, they observed a cluster of cottonwood trees, and, thinking there might be a spring there, they went straight to the cottonwood. Suddenly they found themselves among a strange people who were dwelling around a spring. The strangers greeted the wanderers in a friendly manner, embraced them, and asked them whence they came. The wanderers told their story briefly, and the strangers said : " We were created at this spring and have always lived here. It is called Mai*tó*', Coyote Water (Coyote Spring), and we are the Ma*íd*ĭne' " (Coyote People). The Navahoes called them Mai*tó*'*d*ĭne'.

429. The travellers tarried four days at the Coyote Spring, during which time they talked much to their new friends, and at length persuaded the latter to join them on their eastern journey. Before they started, the Coyote People declared that their spring was the only water in the neighborhood ; that they knew of no other water within two days' journey in any direction. On the morning of the fifth day they all moved off toward the east. They travelled all day, and made a dry camp at night. The next day at noon they halted on their way, and decided to try again the power of a magic wand. This time the white shell was used by a member of the gens to whom it had been given, in the same way that the turquoise wand was used before. Water sprang up. A woman of another gens said : "It is muddy ; it may make the children sick." "Let your people then be named *Haslĭ'z*ni, Mud People," cried voices in the crowd. Thus the gens of *Haslĭ'z*, or *Haslĭ'z*ni, was named.

430. The second night after leaving Coyote Spring, darkness overtook the wanderers at a place where there was no water, and they rested there for the night. At noon on the following day all were thirsty, and the children were crying. The people halted, and proposed to try again the efficacy of a sacred wand. The wand of haliotis was used this time. When the water sprang up, a woman of the Coyote People stooped first and drank. " It is *To*'*dokónz*, alkaline (or sapid) water," she exclaimed. To her and her children the name *To*'*dokónz*i was then given, and from them the present gens of that name is descended. Its members may not marry with Mai*tó*'*d*ĭne', to whom they are related.

431. On the night after they found the alkaline water, they encamped once more at a place where no water was to be found, and on the following day great were their sufferings from thirst. At midday they rested, and begged the bearers of the black stone wand to try the power of their magic implement. A stream of fine, clear

water sprang up when the wand was stuck in the ground. They filled their vessels and all drank heartily, except a boy and a girl of the gens that bore the black stone wand. " Why do you not come and drink before the water is all gone ?" some one asked. The children made no reply, but stood and looked at the water. The girl had her arms folded under her dress. They gave then to her and to her gens the name of Bïtá'ni,[190] which signifies the arms under the dress.

432. The night after the Bïtá'ni was named, the travellers slept once more at a place where no water was to be found, and next day they were very thirsty on their journey. In the middle of the day they stopped, and the power of the red stone wand was tried. It brought forth water from the ground, as the other wands had done, and all drank till they were satisfied ; but no member of the gentes still unnamed said anything and no name was given.

433. After this they camped two nights without water. On the second noon they arrived at a spring in a canyon known to the Maídïne' and called by them *H*alkaíto', Water of the White Valley. They journeyed no farther that day, but camped by the water all night.

434. From *H*alkaíto' they travelled steadily for twenty five days, until they came to a little river near San Francisco Mountain, and west of it. During this part of the journey they found sufficient water for their needs every day. They stopped at this river five nights and five days and hunted. Here one man, and one only, — whose name was Baïnilï'ni (Looks on at a Battle), — killed a deer, a large one, which he cut into small pieces and distributed around so that every one might get a taste.

435. From the banks of this stream they came to the east side of San Francisco Mountain, to where, beside a little peak, there is a spring that has no name. Here the travellers stopped several days, and built around their camp a stone wall that still stands.

436. The puma belonged to the gens that bore the black stone wand, and that was afterwards called Ki*n*aá'ni. While the people were camped at this spring he killed a deer. The bear sometimes killed rabbits. The snake and the porcupine were of no use, but were a trouble instead, since they had to be carried along. The deer ran among the crowd and did neither good nor harm. The people lived mostly on rabbits and other small animals and the seeds of wild plants.

437. From the spring near San Francisco Mountain they travelled to Bïtá*h*otsi (Red Place on Top),[191] and from there to Tsé'zïntsïdïlya. Here they held a council about the big snake. He was of no use to them, and a great incumbrance. They turned him loose among the

rocks, and his descendants are there in great numbers to this day. At Natsïsaán (Navaho Mountain) they turned the porcupine loose, and that is why there are so many porcupines on the Navaho Mountain now.

438. They next went to the place now called Agá*l*a,¹⁹² or Agá*l*ani, Much Wool, or Hair, and were now in the land of the Ozaí (Oraibes). They camped all around the peak of Agá*l*a and went out hunting. Some who wore deer-masks for decoys, and went to get deer, succeeded in killing a great number. They dressed many skins, and the wind blew the hair from the skins up in a great pile. Seeing this, one of the *H*onagá'ni proposed that the place be called Agá*l*a, so this name was given to it.

439. From Agá*l*a the wanderers went to Tse'*h*otsóbia*z*i, Little Place of Yellow Rocks, and from there to Yótso, Big Bead. On the way they camped often, and sometimes tarried a day or two to hunt. It was now late in the autumn. At Yótso they saw moccasin tracks, evidently not fresh, and they said to one another: " Perhaps these are the footprints of the people whom we seek." Now there were diverse counsels among the immigrants. Some were in haste to reach the end of the journey, while others, as the season was late, thought it prudent to remain where they were. Thus they became divided into two parties, one of which remained at Yótso, while the other (containing parts of several gentes) continued the journey. Soon after the latter was gone, those who remained at Yótso sent two messengers, and later they sent two more, to induce the seceders to return ; but the latter were never overtaken. The couriers came to a place where the runaways had divided into two bands. From one of these the Jicarilla Apaches are supposed to have descended. The other band, it is thought, wandered far off and became part of the *D*ïné' Na*h*otlóni.¹⁹³

440. The last two messengers sent out pursued one of the fugitive bands some distance, gave up the task, and returned to Yótso. The messengers sent first pursued the other band. After a while they saw its camp-fires ; but at such a great distance that they despaired of overtaking it and turned toward the San Juan River, where they found at length the long-sought Navahoes. These two messengers were the men, of whom you have heard before, who entered the camp of Big Knee at *T*o'yĕ'tli while the dance of nats*ï*'d was going on, and announced the approach of the immigrants from the west. (See par. 143.)

441. When spring-time came, the people who had remained at Yótso set out again on their journey ; but before long some of the *T*o'dïts*í*ni got tired. They said that the children's knees were swollen, that their feet were blistered, and that they could not go

much farther. Soon after they said this they came to a place where a great lone tree stood, and here they declared : " We shall stop at this tree. After a while the people will come here and find us." They remained and became the gens of Tsïnsaka*d*ni, People of the (Lone) Tree, who are closely related to *To*'dïts*í*ni and cannot marry with the latter.

442. At Pï*n*bï*t*ó', Deer Spring, some more of the gens of *To*'dïts*í*ni halted, because, they said, their children were lame from walking and could travel no farther. Here they formed a new gens of Pï*n*bï*t*ó'*d*ïne', People of Deer Spring,[194] who are also closely related to *To*'dïts*í*ni. At this place they wanted their pet deer to leave them, but he would not go ; he remained at the spring with the people who stayed there. What finally became of him is not known.[195]

443. The main body of the immigrants kept on their way, and, soon after passing Deer Spring, arrived at Hy*l*ĕ*t*y*ï*n, where the people of *Th*á'paha had their farms. Big Knee was still alive when they came ; but he was very old and feeble, and was not respected and obeyed as in former days. When *Th*á'paha and *Ha*s*l*ï'*z*ni met, they traced some relationship between the two gentes : their names had much the same meaning ; their headdresses and accoutrements were alike ; so the *Ha*s*l*ï'*z*ni stopped with *Th*á'paha and became great friends with the latter. Yet to-day a member of one of these gentes may marry a member of the other.

444. The bear was the last of their five pets which the immigrants retained. When they were done their journey they said to him : " Our pet, you have served us well ; but we are now safe among our friends and we need your services no more. If you wish you may leave us. There are others of your kind in Ts*ú*skai (the Chusca Mountains). Go there and play with them." They turned him loose in Ts*ú*skai, and bears have been numerous there ever since.

445. Of the people from the west, there was yet one gens — that to which Estsánatlehi had given the wand of turquoise — which had no name. This nameless people did not stay long on the banks of the San Juan before they wandered off far toward the south. One day two men of the party, while hunting, came to a place called Tsé'nahapï*l*, where there were high overhanging rocks. Here they saw the fresh prints of unshod human feet. They followed these tracks but a short distance when they beheld a man watching them from a rocky pinnacle. As soon as he saw that he was observed, he crouched and disappeared. They ran quickly behind the rock on which they had seen him and again observed him, running as fast as he could. " Why do you fly from us ? " they shouted. " We mean no harm to you." Hearing this he stopped till they came up

to him.   Then they found he spoke the same language they did, and they addressed him in terms of relationship.   "Where do you live?" they asked.   "In a canyon high on the mountain," he replied.   "What do you live on?" they queried.   "We live mostly on seeds," he answered; "but sometimes we catch wood-rats, and we raise small crops."   "We shall have many things to tell one another," said the hunters; "but your home is too far for our people to reach to-day.   Tell your people to come to this spot, and we shall tell ours to come up here and meet them."   When the hunters got home they found their friends cooking rabbits and making mush of wild seeds.   When the meal was finished all climbed the mountain to the appointed place and found the strangers awaiting them. The two parties camped together that night and related to one another their histories and adventures.   The strangers said that they had been created at the place where they were all then camped only seven years previously; that they were living not far off at a place called Natanbĭ*lh*átĭn, but that they came often to their natal place to pick cactus fruit and yucca fruit.   They said they called themselves Tsé'*d*íne', or Rock People; but the nameless ones gave them the name of Tse'nahapĭ'*l*ni, Overhanging Rocks People, from the place where they met.   With this name they became a gens of the Navahoes.

446. The Tse'nahapĭ'*l*ni told their new friends that they had some corn and pumpkins cached at a distance, and they proposed to open their stores and get ready for a journey.   They knew of some Apaches to the south, whom they would all visit together.   These Apaches, they said, had some gentes of the same names as those of the Navahoes.   Then they all went to where the provisions were stored, and they made corn-cakes to use on the journey.   When they were ready they went to the south and found, at a place called Ts*ó*hanaa, the Apaches, who recognized them as friends, and treated their visitors so well that the latter concluded to remain for a while.

447. At the end of three years the Tse'nahapĭ'*l*ni went off to join the Navahoes on the San Juan.   The nameless people stayed four years longer.   About the end of that time they began to talk of leaving, and their Apache friends tried to persuade them to remain, but without avail.   When they had all their goods packed and were ready to start, an old woman was observed walking around them. She walked around the whole band, coming back to the place from which she started; then she turned towards them and said: "You came among us without a name, and you have dwelt among us, nameless, for seven years; no one knew what to call you; but you shall not leave us without a name.   I have walked around you, and I call you *H*onagá'ni (Walked-around People)." [196]

448. When the *H*onagá'ni got back to the San Juan they found that the Tse'nahapī'/ni had been long settled there and had become closely related to Tlast*s*íni, *D*ĕst*s*íni, Kǐn*l*ĭtsíni, and Tsïnad*z*ï'ni. The *H*onagá'ni in time formed close relationships with *Tha*'nĕzá'ni, Dsǐ*l*tlá'ni, *T*ó'*h*ani, and Na*h*opáni. These five gentes are now all the same as one gens, and no member of one may marry a member of another.

449. It happened about this time, while some of the *Thá*'paha were sojourning at Agá*l*a, that they sent two children, one night, to a spring to get water. The children carried out with them two wicker bottles, but returned with four. "Where did you get these other bottles?" the parents inquired. "We took them away from two little girls whom we met at the spring," answered the children. "Why did you do this, and who are the girls?" said the elders. "We do not know. They are strangers," said the little ones. The parents at once set out for the spring to find the strange children and restore the stolen bottles to them; but on their way they met the little girls coming toward the *Thá*'paha camp, and asked them who they were. The strange children replied: "We belong to a band of wanderers who are encamped on yonder mountain. They sent us two together to find water." "Then we shall give you a name," said the *Thá*'paha; "we shall call you *T*o'ba*z*naá*z*i," Two Come Together for Water. The *Thá*'paha brought the little girls to their hut and bade them be seated. "Stay with us," they said. "You are too weak and little to carry the water so far. We will send some of our young men to carry it for you." When the young men found the camp of the strangers they invited the latter to visit them. The *Thá*'paha welcomed the new-comers as friends, and told them they had already a name for them, *T*o'ba*z*naá*z*i. Under this name they became united to the Navahoes as a new gens, and they are now closely affiliated with *Thá*'paha.[197]

450. Shortly after the coming of *T*o'ba*z*naá*z*i, the Navahoes were joined by a band of Apaches, who were adopted by *Thá*'paha and not formed into a new gens. About the same time a band of Pah Utes came and were likewise adopted by *Thá*'paha. A little later some more Apaches arrived and became a part of *Thá*'paha; but, although no distinct name is now given them, their descendants are known among the *Thá*'paha as a people of different origin from the others.

451. Another party of Apaches, who came afterwards, dwelt a long time among the *T*o'*d*okó*z*i; but later they abode with the *Thá*'paha, and became closely related to the latter. They are still affiliated with *Thá*'paha, but these call them *T*o'*d*okó*z*i.

452. Some years passed before the next accession was made. This was another party of Zuñi Indians, and they were admitted into the gens of the *Thá*'paha. Soon after them came the Zuñi People, who were at last formed into a separate gens, — that of Nana*stě'zin*. This is the Navaho name for all the Zuñians, and means Black Horizontal Stripe Aliens.[198] All these people deserted the Zuñi villages on account of scarcity of food.

453. A new people, with painted faces, came from the west about the same time as those who formed the gens of Zuñi, or a little later. They are supposed to have been a part of the tribe now called Mohaves on the banks of the Colorado. They bore the name of *D*ild*z*éhi, and their descendants now form a gens of that name among the Navahoes. At first they affiliated with Nana*stě'zin*; but to-day they are better friends with *Thá*'t*s*ini than with Nana*stě'zin*.

454. A war-party, consisting of members of different gentes, was now organized among the Navahoes to attack a pueblo called *S*aíbe*hog*an, House Made of Sand. At that place they captured two girls and brought them home as slaves. There was a salt lake near their old home, and the girls belonged to a gens of Salt People there. So their numerous descendants now among the Navahoes form the gens of Á*s*ihi, or Salt. The captives were taken by members of the Tse'd*z*ïnkí'ni, hence Á*s*ihi and Tse'd*z*ïnkí'ni are now affiliated.

455. Then a war party was gotten up to attack the people of Jemez pueblo. On this raid one of the Tlast*s*íni captured a Jemez girl, but sold her to one of the Tse'd*z*ïnkí'ni. She was the progenitor of the gens of Mai*d*ěskï'*z*ni, People of Wolf Pass (*i. e.*, Jemez), which is now affiliated with Tse'd*z*ïnkí'ni.

456. After the Navahoes attacked *S*aíbe*hog*an there was a famine there, and some of the people abandoned their homes and joined the Navahoes. They said that in their pueblo there was a gens of *Thá*'paha, and hearing there was such a gens among the Navahoes they came to join it. Therefore they sought *Thá*'paha till they found it and became a part of it.

457. There came once a party of seven people from a place called Tse'yana*tó*'ni, Horizontal Water under Cliffs, to pay a short visit to the Navahoes; but from time to time they delayed their departure, and at last stayed forever with the Navahoes. They formed the gens of Tse'yana*tó*'ni, which is now extinct.

458. The people whom Estsánatlehi created from the skin under her right arm, and to whom she gave the wand of white shell, was called, after they came among the Navahoes, Ki*n*aá'ni, High Stone House People; not because they built or dwelt in such a house, but because they lived near one.[199]

459. When the Bïtá'ni were encamped at a place called *T*ó'tso, or Big Water, near the Carrizo Mountains, a man and a woman came up out of the water and joined them. From this pair is descended the gens of *T*ó'tsoni, People of the Big Water, which is affiliated with Bï*t*á'ni.

NA*TĬ*′NĔS*TH*ANI.

460. Na*tĭ*′nĕs*th*ani,[201] He Who Teaches Himself, lived, with his relations, near the mountain of Dsĭ*l*náo*tĭl*. The few people who lived there used to wander continually around the mountain, hence its name, Encircled Mountain. Na*tĭ*′nĕs*th*ani delighted in gambling, but was not successful. He lost at game, not only all his own goods, but all the goods and jewels of his relations, until there was only one article of value left — a necklace consisting of several strings of white beads. His parents and brother lived in one lodge ; his grandmother and niece lived in another, a little distance from the first. When the gambler had parted with everything except the necklace, his brother took this to the lodge of his grandmother and gave it to her, saying : "My brother has gambled away everything save this. Should he lose this at game, it is the last thing he will ever lose, for then I shall kill him."

461. Na*tĭ*′nĕs*th*ani did not spend all his time gambling; sometimes he hunted for wood-rats and rabbits in the mountains. The day the necklace was brought, in returning from his hunt, he came to the house of his grandmother and saw the necklace hanging up there. "Why is this here?" he asked. "It is put here for safekeeping," replied his niece. "Your brother values it and has asked us to take care of it. If you lose it in gambling, he has threatened to kill you. I have heard the counsels of the family about you. They are tired of you. If you lose this necklace at play, it is the last thing you will ever lose." On hearing this he only said to his niece, "I must think what I shall do," and he lay down to rest.

462. Next morning he rose early, made his breakfast of woodrats, and went out to hunt, travelling toward the east. He stopped at one place, set fall-traps for wood-rats, and slept there all night. During the night he pondered on many plans. He thought at first he would go farther east and leave his people forever ; but again he thought, "Who will hunt wood-rats for my niece when I am gone?" and he went back to her lodge and gave her all the little animals he had killed.

463. In the morning he breakfasted again on wood-rats, and said

to himself: "I shall go to-day to the south and never return." Such was his intention as he went on his way. He travelled to the south, and spent the night out again; but in the morning he changed his mind, and came back to his niece with wood-rats and rabbits and the seeds of wild plants that he had gathered. The women cooked some of the wood-rats for his supper that night. When he lay down he thought of his brother's threats, and made plans again for running away. He had not touched the beads, though he longed to take them.

464. Next morning he went to the west, hunted there all day, and camped out at night as before; but again he could not make up his mind to leave his people, though he thought much about it; so he returned to his niece with such food as he had been able to get for her, and slept in the lodge that night.

465. On the following day he went to the north and hunted. He slept little at night while camping out, for his mind was filled with sad thoughts. "My brother disowns me," he said to himself. "My parents refuse me shelter. My niece, whom I love most, barely looks at me. I shall never go back again." Yet, for all these words, when morning came he returned to the lodge.[19]

466. By this time he was very poor, and so were his grandmother and niece. His sandals, made of grass and yucca-fibre, were worn through, and the blanket made of yucca-fibre and cedar-bark, which covered his back, was ragged.[177] But the people in the other lodge were better off. They gave the grandmother and niece food at times; but always watched these closely when they came for food, lest they should carry off something to give the gambler. "Let him live," said his parents, "on wood-rats and rabbits as well as he can."

467. The night after he returned from his hunt to the north he slept little, but spent the time mostly in thinking and making plans. What these plans were you shall soon know, for the next day he began to carry them out. His thought for his niece was now the only thing that made him care to stay at home.

468. In the morning after this night of thought he asked his niece to roast for him four wood-rats; he tied these together and set out for the San Juan River. When he got to the banks of the river he examined a number of cottonwood trees until he found one that suited him. He burned this down and burned it off square at the base. He kept his fire from burning up the whole trunk by applying mud above the place to be burned. His plan was to make a hollow vessel by which he could go down the San Juan River. It was his own plan. He had never heard of such a thing before. The Navahoes had never anything better than rafts, and these were

good only to cross the river. He lay down beside the log to see where he should divide it, for he had planned to make the vessel a little longer than himself, and he burned the log across at the place selected. All this he did in one day, and then he went home, collecting rats on the way; but he told his niece nothing about the log. He slept that night in the lodge.

469. He went back, next morning, to his log on the banks of the San Juan, and spent the day making the log hollow by means of fire, beginning at the butt end. He succeeded in doing only a part of this work in one day. It took him four days to burn the hole through from one end of the log to the other and to make it wide enough to hold his body. At the end of each day's work he returned to his grandmother's lodge, and got wood-rats and rabbits on his way home.

470. The next day, after the hole was finished, was spent in making and inserting plugs. He moistened a lot of shredded cedar-bark and pounded it between stones so as to make a soft mass. He shoved a large piece of this in at the butt end and rammed it down to the tip end. In burning out the log, he had burned, where the tree branched, four holes which he did not need, and these he filled with plugs of the cedar-bark. He prepared another plug to be rammed into the butt from the inside, after he entered the log, and when this was finished he went home to his grandmother's house, collecting wood-rats from his traps as he went.

471. The next morning his niece cooked several wood-rats and ground for him a good quantity — as much as could be held in two hands — of the seeds of tlo'tsózi (*Sporobolus cryptandrus*). This meal she put in a bag of wood-rat skins sewed together. Thus provided he went back to his log. He put the provisions into the hole and then proceeded to enter, in person, to see if the log was sound and the hole big enough. He entered, head foremost, and crawled inwards until half of his chest was in the log, when he heard a voice crying, "Wu‘hu‘hu‘hú!"[26] and he came out to see who called. He looked in every direction and examined the ground for tracks, but seeing no signs of any intruder he proceeded again to enter the log. This time he got in as far as his waist, when again he heard the cry of "Wu‘hu‘hu‘hú," but louder and nearer than before. Again he came out of the log and looked around farther and more carefully than he did the first time, going in his search to the margin of the river; but he saw no one, found no tracks, and returned to his log. On the next trial he entered as far as his knees, when for the third time the cry sounded, and he crept out once more to find whence it came. He searched farther, longer, and more closely than on either of the previous occasions, but without success, and he went back to

enter the log again. On the fourth trial, when he had entered as far as his feet, he heard the cry loud and near, and he felt some one shaking the log. He crept out for the fourth time and beheld *H*ast*s*éyal*t*i, the Talking God,[73] standing over him.

472. *H*ast*s*éyal*t*i did not speak at first, but told the man by signs that he must not get into the log, that he would surely be drowned if he did, and that he must go home. Then *H*ast*s*éyal*t*i walked off a distance from the log and motioned to the Navaho to come to him. When Na*t*í'nĕs*th*ani came near the god, the latter spoke, saying : " My grandchild, why are you doing all this work ? Where do you intend to go with this log ? " The man then told the god all his sad story, and ended by saying : " I am an outcast. I wish to get far away from my people. Take pity on me. Stop me not, but let me go in this log as far as the waters of the Old Age River (San Juan) will bear me." *H*ast*s*éyal*t*i replied : " No. You must not attempt to go into that log. You will surely be drowned if you do. I shall not allow you." Four times Na*t*í'nĕs*th*ani pleaded, and four times the god denied him. Then the god said : " Have you any precious stones ? " " Yes," replied the man. " Have you white shell beads ? Have you turquoise ? " and thus the god went on asking him, one by one, if he had all the original eighteen sacred things[202] that must be offered to the gods to gain their favor. To each of his questions the man replied " Yes," although he had none of these things, and owned nothing but the rags that covered him. " It is well," said the god. " You need not enter that log to make your journey. Go home and stay there for four nights. At daylight, after the fourth night, you may expect to see me again. Have yourself and your house clean and in order for my coming. Have the floor and all around the house swept carefully. Have the ashes taken out. Wash your body and your hair with yucca suds the night before I arrive, and bid your niece to wash herself also with yucca. I shall go off, now, and tell the other divine ones about you."

473. As soon as he came home, Na*t*í'nĕs*th*ani told his niece what things he wanted (except the baskets and the sacred buckskins) ; but he did not tell her for what purpose he required them, and he asked her to steal them from their neighbors. This she did, a few things at a time, and during many visits. It took her three days to steal them all. On the evening of the third day, after they had washed themselves with the yucca suds, he told her about the baskets and the sacred buckskins which he needed. She went to the neighboring lodge and stole these articles, wrapping the baskets up in the buckskins. When she returned with her booty, he wrapped all the stolen goods up in the skins, put them away in the edge of the lodge, and lay down to rest. He was a good sleeper, and usually

slept all night ; but on this occasion he woke about midnight, and could not go to sleep again.

474. At dawn he heard, faintly, the distant " Wu‘hu‘hu‘hú " of *H*ast*s*éyal*t*i. At once he woke his grandmother, saying : " I hear a voice. The *d*íginí (holy ones, divine ones) are coming." " You fool," she replied. " Shut your mouth and go to sleep. They would never come to visit such poor people as we are," and she fell asleep again. In a little while he heard the voice a second time, louder and nearer, and again he shook his grandmother and told her he heard the voices of the gods ; but she still would not believe him, and slept again. The third time that he awoke her, when he heard the voices still more plainly, she remained awake, beginning to believe him. The fourth time the call sounded loud and clear, as if cried by one standing at the door. " Hear," he said to his grandmother. " Is that not truly the voice of a divine one ? " At last she believed him, and said in wonder : " Why should the *d*ígíni come to visit us ? "

475. *H*ast*s*éyal*t*i and *H*ast*s*é*h*og*a*n were at the door, standing on the rainbow on which they had travelled. The former made signs to the man, over the curtain which hung in the doorway, bidding him pull the curtain aside and come out. " Grandmother," said the Navaho, " *H*ast*s*éyal*t*i calls me to him." " It is well," she answered. " Do as he bids you." As he went out, bearing his bundle of sacrificial objects, he said : " I go with the divine ones, but I shall come back again to see you." The niece had a pet turkey [203] that roosted on a tree near the lodge. *H*ast*s*éyal*t*i made signs to the Navaho to take the turkey along. The Navaho said : " My niece, the gods bid me take your turkey, and I would gladly do it, for I am going among strange people, where I shall be lonely. I love the bird ; he would be company to me and remind me of my home. Yet I shall not take him against your will." " Then you may have my turkey pet," replied the niece. The old woman said to the god : " I shall be glad to have my grandchild back again. Will you let him return to us ? " *H*ast*s*éyal*t*i only nodded his head. The gods turned the rainbow around sunwise, so that its head, [204] which formerly pointed to the door of the lodge, now pointed in a new direction. *H*ast*s*éyal*t*i got on the bow first. He made the Navaho get on behind him. *H*ast*s*é*h*og*a*n got on behind the man. " Shut your eyes," commanded *H*ast*s*éyal*t*i, and the Navaho did as he was bidden.

476. In a moment *H*ast*s*éyal*t*i cried again : " Open your eyes." The Navaho obeyed and found himself far away from his home at Tsé‘*t*a*d*i, where the *d*ígíni dwelt. They led him into a house in the rock which was full of divine people. It was beautiful inside — the walls were covered with rock crystal, which gave forth a brilliant light. *H*ast*s*éyal*t*i ordered food brought for his visitor. The latter

was handed a small earthen cup only so big (a circle made by the thumb and index finger joined at the tips) filled with mush. " What a poor meal to offer a stranger ! " thought the Navaho, supposing he would finish it in one mouthful.   But he ate, and ate, and ate, and ate, from the cup and could not empty it.   When he had eaten till he was satisfied the little cup was as full as in the beginning.[205]   He handed the cup, when he was done, back to *H*ast*s*éyal*t*i, who, with one sweep of his finger, emptied it, and it remained empty.   The little cup was then filled with water and given to the guest to drink. He drank till his thirst was satisfied ; but the cup was as full when he was done as it was when he began.   He handed it again to *H*ast*s*éyal*t*i, who put it to his own lips and emptied it at a single swallow.

477. The gods opened the bundle of the Navaho and examined the contents to see if he had brought all they required, and they found he had done so.   In the mean time he filled his pipe and lighted it.   While he was smoking, the gods Nayénězg̣ani, *T*ó'ba-d*z*ĭst*s*íni, and *H*ast*s*éol*t*oi [206] arrived from *T*o'yĕ'tli and entered the house.   Nayénězg̣ani said to the visitor : " I hear that you were found crawling into a hole which you had made in a log by burning.   Why were you doing this ? "   In reply the Navaho told his whole story, as he had told it to *H*ast*s*éyal*t*i, and ended by saying : " I wished to go to *T*o'yĕ'tli, where the rivers meet, or wherever else the waters would bear me.   While I was trying to carry out this plan, my grandfather, *H*ast*s*éyal*t*i, found me and bade me not to go. For this reason only I gave my plan up and went home."   " Do you still wish to go to *T*o'yĕ'tli ? " said Nayénězg̣ani.   " Yes," said the Navaho, " I wish to go to *T*o'yĕ'tli or as far down the San Juan as I can get."   " Then you shall go," said the god.

478. Nayénězg̣ani went forth from the house and the other gods followed him.   They went to a grove of spruce, and there picked out a tree of unusual size.   They tied rainbow ropes to it, so that it might not fall with too great force and break in falling.   Nayénĕz-g̣ani and *T*o'bad*z*ĭst*s*íni cut it near the root with their great stone knives, and it fell to the north.   Crooked Lightning struck the fallen tree and went through it from butt to tip.   Straight Lightning struck it and went through it from tip to butt.   Thus the hole was bored in the log, and this was done before the branches were cut away. The hole that Crooked Lightning bored was too crooked.   Straight Lightning made it straight, but still it was too small.   Black Wind was sent into the hole, and he made it larger, but not large enough. Blue Wind, Yellow Wind, and White Wind entered the hole, each in turn, and each, as he went through, made it a little larger.   It was not until White Wind had done his work that the hole was big

enough to contain the body of a man. *Hastséyalti* supplied a bowl of food, a vessel of water, and a white cloud for bedding. They wrapped the Navaho up in the cloud and put him into the log. They plugged the ends with clouds, — a black cloud in the butt and a blue cloud in the tip, — and charged him not to touch either of these cloudy plugs. When they got him into the log some one said: " How will he get light? How will he know when it is night and when it is day?" They bored two holes in the log, one on each side of his head, and they put in each hole, to make a window, a piece of rock crystal, which they pushed in so tightly that water could not leak in around it.

479. While some of the gods were preparing the log, others were getting the pet turkey ready for his journey, but they did this unknown to the Navaho. They put about his body black cloud, he-rain, black mist, and she-rain. They put under his wings white corn, yellow corn, blue corn, corn of mixed colors, squash seed, watermelon seed, muskmelon seed, gourd seed, and beans of all colors. These were the six gods who prepared the turkey : four of the Gánaskĭdi [207] from a place called *Depéhahatil,* one *Hastséhogan* from Tse'gíhi,[165] and the *Hastséhogan* from Tsé'tadi, — the one who found the Navaho entering his cottonwood log and took him home to the house in the rocks.

480. The next thing they had to think about was how they should carry the heavy log to the river with the man inside of it. They put under the log (first) a rope of crooked lightning, (second) a rope of rainbow, (third) a rope of straight lightning, and (fourth) another rope of rainbow. They attached a sunbeam to each end of the log. All the gods except those who were engaged in preparing the turkey tried to move the log, but they could not stir it; and they sent for the six who were at work on the turkey to come to their aid. Two of the Gánaskĭdi were now stationed at each end, and two of the *Hastséhogan* in the middle. The others were stationed at other parts. The Gánaskĭdi put their wands under the log crosswise, thus, X. All lifted together, and the log was carried along. Some of them said: "If strength fail us and we let the log fall, we shall not attempt to raise it again, and the Navaho will not make his journey." As they went along some became tired and were about to let the log go, but the winds came to help them — Black Wind and Blue Wind in front, Yellow Wind and White Wind behind, and soon the log was borne to the margin of the river. As they went along, *Tó'nenĭli,*[98] the Water Sprinkler, made fun and played tricks, as he now does in the dances, to show that he was pleased with what they were doing. While the gods were at work the Navaho sang five songs, each for a different part of the work ; the significant words of the songs were these : —

First Song, " A beautiful tree they fell for me."
Second Song, " A beautiful tree they prepare for me."
Third Song, " A beautiful tree they finish for me."
Fourth Song, " A beautiful tree they carry with me."
Fifth Song, " A beautiful tree they launch with me." [283]

481. When they threw the log on the surface of the water it floated around in different directions, but would not go down stream, so the gods consulted together to determine what they should do. They covered the log first with black mist and then with black cloud. Some of the gods standing on the banks punched the log with their plumed wands, when it approached the shore or began to whirl round, and they kept this up till it got into a straight course, with its head pointed down stream, and floated on. When the gods were punching the log to get it into the current, the Navaho sang a song, the principal words of which were : —

1. " A beautiful tree, they push with me."

When the log was about to go down the stream, he sang : —

2. " A beautiful tree is about to float along with me,"

and when the log got into the current and went down, he sang : —

3. " A beautiful tree floats along with me." [284]

482. All went well till they approached a pueblo called Kĭ́ndoʇlĭz, or Blue House,[208] when two of the Kisáni, who were going to hunt eaglets, saw the log floating by, though they could not see the gods that guided its course. Wood was scarce around Blue House. When the men saw the log they said, " There floats a big tree. It would furnish us fuel for many days if we could get it. We must try to bring it to the shore." The two men ran back to the pueblo and announced that a great log was coming down the river. A number of people turned out to seize it. Most of them ran down the stream to a shallow place where they could all wade in, to await the arrival of the log, while a few went up along the bank to herald its approach. When it came to the shallow place they tried to break off branches, but failed. They tied ropes to the branches, and tried to pull it ashore ; but the log, hurried on by the current, carried the crowd with it. But the next time the log got to a shallow place the Kisáni got it stranded, and sent back to the pueblo for axes, intending to cut off branches and make the log light. When the gods saw the people coming with axes they said : " Something must be done." They sent down a great shower of rain, but the Kisáni held on to the log. They sent hail, with hailstones as big as two fists ; but still the Kisáni held on. They sent lightning to the right — the people to the left held on. They sent lightning to the left — the people to the right held on. They sent lightning in all direc-

tions four times, when, at last, the Kisáni let go and the log floated on. Now the gods laid upon the log a cloud so thick that no one could see through it; they put a rainbow lengthwise and a rainbow crosswise over it, and they caused the zigzag lightning to flash all around it. When the Kisáni saw all these things they began to fear. "The gods must guard this log," they said. "Yes," said the chief. "Go to your homes, and let the log pass on. It must be holy."

483. The log floated steadily with the stream till it came to a place where a ridge of rocks, standing nearly straight up, disturbs the current, and here the log became entangled in the rocks. But two of the Fringe-mouths [209] of the river raised it from the rocks and set it floating again. They turned the log around, one standing at each end, until they got it lying lengthwise with the current, and then they let it float away.

484. Thence it floated safely to *Tó'hodoʛliz*, where the gods on the bank observed it stopping and slowly sinking, until only a few leaves on the ends of the branches could be seen. It was the sacred people under the water who had pulled the log down this time. These were Tiéholtsodi, Tieʛín,[210] Frog, Fish, Beaver, Otter, and others. They took the Navaho out of the log and bore him down to their home under the water. The gods on the bank held a council to consider why the tree stuck. They shook it and tried to get it loose, but they could not move it. Then they called on *Tó'nenĭli*, Water Sprinkler, to help them. He had two magic water jars, *To'sadĭlyĭ'l*, the black jar, which he carried in his right hand, and *To'sadoʛlĭ'z*, the blue jar, which he carried in his left hand; with these he struck the water to the right and to the left, crying as he did so his call of "Tu'wu'wu'wú!" The water opened before him and allowed him to descend. He went around the tree, and when he came to the butt he found that the plug had been withdrawn and that the Navaho was no longer there. He called up to his friends on the bank and told them what he had found. They spread a short rainbow [211] for him to travel on, and he went to the house of the divine ones under the water. This house consisted of four chambers, one under another, like the stories of a pueblo dwelling. The first chamber, that on top, was black; the second was blue; the third yellow; the fourth white.[18] Two of the Tieʛín, or water pets with blue horns, stood at the door facing one another, and roared as *Tó'nenĭli* passed. He descended from one story to another, but found no one till he came to the last chamber, and here he saw Tiéholtsodi, the water monster; Tsal, Frog (a big rough frog); Tsa, Beaver, *Tábastĭn*, Otter, Tlo'ayuĭnlĭ'tigi (a great fish), and the captive Navaho. "I seek my grandchild. Give him to me," said *Tó'nenĭli*. "Shut your mouth and begone," said Tiéholtsodi.

"Such as you cannot come here giving orders. I fear you not, Water Sprinkler; you shall not have your grandchild." Then *Tó'-nenïli* went out again and told his friends what had happened to him, and what had been said in the house of Tiéholtsodi under the water.

485. The gods held another council. "Who shall go down and rescue our grandchild?" was the question they asked one another. While they were talking *Hastsézïni* [212] (Black God), who owns all fire, sat apart and took no part in the council. He had built a fire, while the others waited, and sat with his back to it, as was his custom. "Go tell your grandfather there what has occurred," said the others to *Tó'nenïli*. The latter went over to where Hastsézïni sat. "Why are they gathered together yonder and of what do they talk so angrily?" said the Black God. In answer, *Tó'nenïli* told of his adventures under the water and what Tiéholtsodi had said to him. *Hastsézïni* was angry when he heard all this. "I fear not the sacred people beneath the water," he said. "I shall have my grandchild." He hastened to the river, taking *Tó'nenïli* with him, for *Tó'nenïli* had the power to open the water, and these two descended into the river. When they reached the room where Tiéholtsodi sat, the Black God said, "We come together for our grandchild." "Run out there, both of you. Such as you may not enter here," said Tiéholtsodi. "I go not without my grandson. Give him to me, and I shall go," said the other. "Run out," repeated Tiéholtsodi, "I shall not release your grandchild." "I shall take my grandchild. I fear you not." "I shall not restore him to you. I heed not your words." "I never recall what I have once spoken. I have come for my grandchild, and I shall not leave without him." "I said you should not go with him, and I mean what I say. I am mighty." Thus they spoke defiantly to one another for some time. At length *Hastsézïni* said: "I shall beg no longer for my grandchild. You say you are mighty. We shall see which is the more powerful, you or I," and Tiéholtsodi answered: "Neither shall I ask your permission to keep him. I should like to see how you will take him from me." When *Hastsézïni* heard this he took from his belt his fire-stick and fire-drill.[213] He laid the stick on the ground, steadied it with both feet, and whirled the drill around, pausing four times. The first time he whirled the drill there was a little smoke; the second time there was a great smoke; the third time there was flame; the fourth time the surrounding waters all took fire. Then Tiéholtsodi cried: "Take your grandchild, but put out the flames." "Ah," said *Hastsézïni*, "you told me you were mighty. Why do you implore me now? Why do you not put out the fire yourself? Do you mean what you say this time? Do you really want

the fire quenched?" "Oh! yes," cried Tiéholtsodi. "Take your grandchild, but put out the flames. I mean what I say." At a sign from Black God, Water Sprinkler took the stoppers out of his jars and scattered water all around him four times, crying his usual "Tu'wu'wu'wú" as he did so, and the flames died out. The water in *Tó'nenïli's* jars consisted of all kinds of water — he-rain, she-rain, hail, snow, lake-water, spring-water, and water taken from the four quarters of the world. This is why it was so potent.[67]

486. When the fire was extinguished the three marched out in single file — *Tó'nenïli* in front, to divide the water, the Navaho in the middle, and *Hastsézïni* in the rear. Before they had quite reached the dry land they heard a flopping sound behind them, and, looking around, they saw T*sal*, the Frog. "Wait," said he. "I have something to tell you. We can give disease to those who enter our dwelling, and there are cigarettes, sacred to us, by means of which our spell may be taken away. The cigarette of Tiéholtsodi should be painted black; that of Tie*lïn*, blue; those of the Beaver and the Otter, yellow; that of the great fish, and that sacred to me, white." Therefore, in these days, when a Navaho is nearly drowned in the water, and has spewed the water all out, such cigarettes[12] are made to take the water sickness out of him.

487. The gods took Na*ti'*něs*th*ani back to his log. *Tó'nenïli* opened a passage for them through the river, and took the water out of the hollow in the log. The Navaho crawled into the hollow. The gods plugged the butt again, and set the log floating. It floated on and on until it came to a fall in the San Juan River, and here it stuck again. The gods had hard labor trying to get it loose. They tugged and worked, but could not move it. At length the Dsaha-*dold*z*á*, the Fringe-mouths of the water, came to help. They put the zigzag lightning which was on their bodies[209] under the butt of the log, — as if the lightning were a rope, — and soon they got the log loose and sent it floating down the river.

488. At the end of the San Juan River, surrounded by mountains, there is a whirling lake or large whirlpool called *Tó'nihilin*, or End of the Water. When the log entered here it whirled around the lake four times. The first time it went around it floated near the shore, but it gradually approached the centre as it went round again and again. From the centre it pointed itself toward the east and got near the shore; but it retreated again to the centre, pointed itself to the south, and at last stranded on the south shore of the lake. When it came to land four gods stood around it thus: *Hastsé-hogan* on the east, *Hastséyalti* on the south, one Gá*na*skï*di* on the west, and one on the north. They pried out one of the stoppers with their wands, and the Navaho came out on the land. They took

out what remained of the food they had given him, a bow of cedar with the leaves on, and two reed arrows that they had placed in the log before they launched it. This done, they plugged the log again with a black cloud.

489. Then the gods spoke to the Navaho and said : " We have taken you where you wished to go. We have brought you to the end of the river. We have done for you all that in the beginning you asked us to do, and now we shall give you a new name. Henceforth you shall be called Á*hod*íse*l*i, He Who Floats. Go sit yonder" (pointing out a place), "and turn your back to us." He went and sat as he was told, and soon they called to him and bade him go to a hill west of the lake. When he ascended it he looked around and saw the log moving back in the direction whence, he thought, he had come. He looked all around, but could see no one. The gods had disappeared, and he was all alone. He sat down to think. He felt sad and lonely. He was sorry he had come ; yet, he thought, "This is my own deed; I insisted on coming here, and had I stayed at home I might have been killed." Still the more he thought the sadder he felt, and he began to weep.

490. The mountains all around the lake were very precipitous, except on the west side. Here they were more sloping, and he began to think of crossing, when he heard faintly in the distance

Fig. 34. Trail of turkey approaching his master.

the gobbling of a turkey. He paused and listened, and soon heard the gobbling again, more distinctly and apparently nearer. In a short time he heard the sound for the third time, but louder and clearer than before. The fourth time that the gobbling was heard it seemed very loud and distinct ; and a moment later he beheld, running toward him, his pet turkey, whom he had thought he would never see again. The turkey, which had followed him all the way down the San Juan River, now approached its master from the east, as if it were coming to him at once; but when it got within arm's length of the man it retreated and went round him sunwise, approaching and retreating again at the south, the west, and the north. When it got to the east again it ran up to its master and allowed itself to be embraced. (Fig. 34 shows the way it approached its master.) "A*h*aláni, *si̇́lín* (Welcome, my pet)," said Na*t̠í*'ně*st̠h*ani, " I am sorry for you that you have followed me, I pity you; but now that you are here, I thank you for coming."

491. The man now began to think again of crossing the mountain in the west, but suddenly night came on. He had not noticed the light fading until it was too dark to begin the journey, and he felt obliged to seek a resting-place for the night. They went to a gulch near at hand where there were a few small cedar-trees. They spread out, for a bed, the dead leaves and the soft débris which they found under the trees and lay down, side by side, to sleep. The Navaho spread his bark blanket over himself, and the turkey spread one of its wings over its master, and he slept well that night.

492. Next morning they rose early and went out to hunt wood-rats. They went down a small winding valley till they came to a beautiful flat, through which ran a stream of water. "This would be a good place for a farm if I had but the seeds to plant," said the Navaho aloud. When he had spoken he observed that his turkey began to act in a very peculiar manner. It ran to the western border of the flat, circled round to the north, and then ran directly from north to south, where it rejoined its master, who had in the mean time walked around the edge of the flat from east to west. This (fig. 35) shows how they went. When they met they walked together four times around the flat, gradually approaching the centre as they walked. Here, in the centre, the man sat down and the turkey gambolled around him. " My pet," said the Navaho, "what a beautiful farm I could make here if I only had the seeds." The turkey gobbled in reply and spread out its wings.

493. Na*t̠í*'ně*st̠h*ani had supposed that when the gods were preparing the log for him they had done something to the turkey, but what they had done he knew not. Now that his pet was acting so strangely, it occurred to him that perhaps it could aid him. " My pet," he said, "can you do anything to help me make a farm here?" The turkey ran a little way to the east and shook its wings, from which four grains of white corn dropped out; then it ran to the south and shook from its wings four grains of blue corn; at the west it shook out four grains of yellow corn, and at the north four

grains of variegated corn. Then it ran up to its master from the east and shook its wings four times, each time shaking out four seeds. The first time it dropped pumpkin seeds; the second time, watermelon seeds; the third time, muskmelon seeds; the fourth time, beans. "E'yéhe, *sĭlĭn* (Thanks, my pet). I thought you had something for me," said Natĭ'nĕsthani.

494. He went away from the flat, roasted wood-rats for a meal, and when he had eaten he made two planting sticks, one of greasewood and one of tsĭntlĭ'zi [214] (*Fendleria rupicola*). He returned to the flat and began to make his farm. He dug four holes in the east

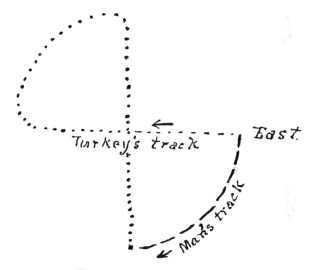

Fig. 35. Tracks of man and turkey.

with the stick of tsĭntlĭ'zi, and dropped into each hole a grain of white corn. He dug four holes in the south with his greasewood stick, and placed in each hole one grain of blue corn. He dug four holes in the west with the tsĭntlĭ'zi stick, and planted in each one grain of yellow corn. He made four holes in the north with the greasewood, and put in each one grain of variegated corn. With the implement of tsĭntlĭ'zi he planted the pumpkin seed between the white corn and the blue corn. With the implement of greasewood he planted watermelon seed between the blue corn and the yellow corn. With the stick of tsĭntlĭ'zi he planted muskmelon seeds between the yellow corn and the variegated corn. With the stick of greasewood he planted beans between the variegated corn and the white corn.[215] He looked all around to see if he had done everything properly, and he went to the west of his farm among the foothills and camped there.

495. He felt uneasy during the night, fearing that there might be some one else to claim the land, and he determined to examine the surrounding country to see if he had any neighbors. Next day he walked in a circle, sunwise, around the valley, and this he did for four consecutive days, taking a wider circle each day; but he met no people and saw no signs of human life, and he said: "It is a good place for a farm. No one claims the land before me." Each morning, before he went on his journey, he visited his farm. On the fourth morning he saw that the corn had grown half a finger-length above the ground.

496. On the fourth night, after his long day's walk around the valley, when darkness fell, he sat by his fire facing the east, and was surprised to see a faint gleam half way up the side of the mountains in the east. "Strange," he said, "I have travelled all over that ground and have seen neither man nor house nor track nor the remains of fire." Then he spoke to the turkey, saying: "Stay at home to-morrow, my pet; I must go and find out who builds that fire."

497. Next day, leaving his turkey at home, he went off to search the mountain-side, where he had seen the gleam; but he searched well and saw no signs of human life. When he came home he told all his adventures to his turkey and said: "It must have been a great glow-worm that I beheld." He got home pretty early in the day and went out to trap wood-rats, accompanied by his turkey. In the evening when he returned to his camp, he looked again, after dark, toward the eastern mountain, and saw the gleam as he had seen it the night before. He set a forked stick in the ground, got down on his hands and knees, and looked at the fire through the fork. (See par. 382.)

498. On the following morning he placed himself in the same position he was in the night before, — putting his hands and knees in the tracks then made, — and looked again over the forked stick. He found his sight directed to a spot which he had already explored well. Notwithstanding this he went there again, leaving his turkey behind, and searched wider and farther and with greater care than on previous occasions; but he still saw no traces of human life. When he returned to camp he told his turkey all that had happened to him. That night he saw the light again, and once more he sighted over the forked stick with care.

499. When morning came, he found that he had marked the same spot he had marked before; and though he had little hope he set out for the third time to find who made the distant fire. He returned after a time, only to tell his disappointment to his turkey. As usual he spent the rest of the day, accompanied by the turkey, setting traps for wood-rats and other small animals. After dark,

when he saw the distant flame again, he set a second forked stick in the ground and laid between the two forks a long, straight stick, which he aimed at the fire as he would aim an arrow. When this was done he went to sleep.

500. Next morning he noted with great care the particular spot to which the straight stick pointed, and set out to find the fire. Before he left he said to his turkey : " I go once more to seek the distant fire ; but it is the last time I shall seek it. If I find it not to-day, I shall never try again. Stay here till I return." While he spoke the turkey turned its back on him, and showed its master that it was angry. It acted like a pouting child. He went to the place on the eastern mountain to which the stick pointed, and here he found, what he had not observed before, a shelf in the rocks, which seemed to run back some distance. He climbed to the shelf and discovered there two nice huts. He thought that wealthy people must dwell in them. He felt ashamed of his ragged bark blanket, of his garment of wood-rat skins, of his worn grass sandals, of his poor bow and arrows ; so he took these off, laid them in the fork of a juniper-tree, and, retaining only his breech-cloth of wood-rat skins, his belt, tobacco pouch, and pipe, he approached one of the houses.

501. He pushed aside the curtain and saw, sitting inside, a young woman making a fine buckskin shirt which she was garnishing beautifully with fringes and shells. Ashamed of his appearance, he hung his head and advanced, looking at her under his eyebrows. " Where are the men ? " he said, and he sat on the ground. The young woman replied : " My father and mother are in the other hut." Just as the Navaho had made up his mind to go to the other house the father entered. Doubtless the Navaho had been observed while disrobing, for the old man, as he came in, brought the poor rags with him. " Why do you not take in my son-in-law's goods ? " said the old man to his daughter, as he laid the ragged bundle in a conspicuous place on top of a pile of fine fabrics. Poor Natĭ'-nĕs*th*ani hung his head again in shame and blushed, while the woman looked sideways and smiled. " Why don't you spread a skin for my son-in-law to sit on ? " said the old man to his daughter. She only smiled and looked sideways again. The old man took a finely dressed Rocky Mountain sheep-skin and a deer-skin, — skins finer than the Navaho had ever seen before, — spread them on the ground beside the woman, and said to the stranger : " Why do you not sit on the skins ? " Natĭ'nĕs*th*ani made a motion as if to rise and take the offered seat, but he sank back again in shame. Invited a second time, he arose and sat down beside the young woman on the skins.

502. The old man placed another skin beside the Navaho, sat on

it, tapped the visitor on the knee to attract his attention, and said : " I long for a smoke. Fill your pipe [216] with tobacco and let me smoke it." The Navaho answered : " I am poor. I have nothing." Four times this request was made and this reply given. On the fourth occasion the Navaho added : " I belong to the Ninokádïne' (the People up on the Earth),[217] and I have nothing." " I thought the Ninokádïne' had plenty of tobacco," said the old man. The young man now drew from his pouch, which was adorned with pictures of the sun and moon, a mixture of native wild tobacco with four other plants.[218] His pipe was made of clay, collected from a place where a wood-rat had been tearing the ground. He filled the pipe with the mixture, lighted it with the sun,[219] sucked it four times till it was well kindled, and handed it to the old man to smoke. When the latter had finished the pipe and laid it down he began to perspire violently and soon fell into a swoon. The young woman thought her father was dead or dying, and ran to the other lodge to tell her mother. The mother gave the young woman a quantity of goods and said : " Give these to my son-in-law and tell him they shall all be his if he restores your father to life." When the daughter returned to the lodge where her father lay, she said to the Navaho : " Here are goods for you. Treat my father. You must surely know what will cure him." They laid the old man out on his side, in the middle of the floor, with his head to the north and his face to the east. The Navaho had in his pouch a medicine called ké'tlo, or atsósi ké'tlo,[220] consisting of many different ingredients. Where he got the ingredients we know not ; but the medicine men now collect them around the headwaters of the San Juan. He put some of this medicine into a pipe, lighted it with the sunbeams, puffed the smoke to the earth, to the sky, to the earth, and to the sky again ; puffed it at the patient from the east, the south, the west, and the north. When this fumigation was done, the patient began to show signs of life, — his eyelids twitched, his limbs jerked, his body shook. Naťï'něsťhani directed the young woman to put some of the medicine, with water, to soak in an earthen bowl, — no other kind of bowl is now used in making this infusion, — and when it was soaked enough he rubbed it on the body of the patient.

503. " Saďáni, sïťá (My son-in-law, my nephew)," said the old man, when he came to his senses once more, " fill the pipe for me again. I like your tobacco." The Navaho refused and the old man begged again. Four times did the old man beg and thrice the young man refused him ; but when the fourth request was made the young man filled the pipe, lit it as before, and handed it to the old man. The latter smoked, knocked out the ashes, laid down the pipe, began to perspire, and fell again into a deathly swoon. As on

the previous occasion, the women were alarmed and offered the Navaho a large fee, in goods, if he would restore the smoker to life. The medicine being administered and the ceremonies being repeated, the old man became again conscious.

504. As soon as he recovered he said : " My son-in-law, give me another smoke. I have travelled far and smoked much tobacco ; but such fine tobacco as yours I never smoked before." As on the other occasions, the old man had to beg four times before his request was granted. A third time the pipe was filled ; the old man smoked and swooned ; the women gave presents to the Navaho ; the atsósi ké'tlo was administered, and the smoker came to life again.

505. But as soon as he regained his senses he pleaded for another smoke. " The smoke is bad for you," said the Navaho. " It does you harm. Why do you like my tobacco so well ? " " Ah ! it makes me feel good to the ends of my toes. It smells well and tastes well." " Since you like it so well," said the young man, " I shall give you one more pipeful." This time the old man smoked vigorously ; he drew the smoke well into his chest and kept it there a long time before blowing it out. Everything happened now as before, but in addition to the medicine used previously, the Navaho scattered the fragrant yád id ínil [221] on the hot coals and let the patient breathe its fumes. The Navaho had now four large bundles of fine goods as pay for his services. When the old man recovered for the fourth time he praised loudly the tobacco of the Navaho. He said he had never felt so happy as when smoking it. He asked the Navaho : " How would you like to try my tobacco ? " and he went to the other lodge to fetch his tobacco pouch. While he was gone the Wind People whispered into the ear of the Navaho : " His tobacco will kill you surely. It is not like your tobacco. Those who smoke it never wake again ! "

506. Presently the old man returned with a pouch that had pictures of the sun and moon on it, and with a large pipe — much larger than that of the Navaho — decorated with figures of deer, antelope, elk, and Rocky Mountain sheep.[222] The old man filled his pipe, lighted it, puffed the smoke to earth and sky, each twice, alternately, and handed the pipe to the Navaho. The young man said : " I allow no one to fill the pipe for me but myself. My customs differ from yours. You ask a stranger for a smoke. I ask no man for a smoke. I pick my own tobacco. Other people's tobacco makes me ill ; that is why I do not use it." Thus he spoke, yet the stuff he had given the old man to smoke was not the same that he used himself. The latter consisted of four kinds of tobacco : glón̨a/o, or weasel tobacco, depén̨a/o, or sheep tobacco, dsī́/ln̨a/o, or mountain tobacco, and kósnato, or cloud tobacco.[223] He had differ-

ent compartments in his pouch for his different mixtures. The old
man invited him four times to smoke; but four times the Navaho
refused, and said at last: "I have my pipe already filled with my
own tobacco. I shall smoke it. My tobacco injures no one unless
he is ill." He proceeded to smoke the pure tobacco. When he had
done smoking, he said: "See. It does me no harm. Try another
pipeful."

507. He now filled his pipe with the mixture of four kinds of real
tobacco and handed it to the old man to smoke. When the latter
had finished he said: "Your tobacco does not taste as it did before,
and I do not now feel the same effect after smoking it as I did at
first. Now it cools me; formerly it made me perspire. Why did
I fall down when I smoked it before? Tell me, have I some disease?" The Navaho answered: "Yes. It is yasi′ntsogi, something bad inside of you, that makes the tobacco affect you so.
There are four diseases that may cause this: they are the yellow
disease, the cooked-blood disease, the water-slime disease, and the
worm disease. One or more of these diseases you surely have."[224]
The old man closed his eyes and nodded his head to show that he
believed what was told him. Of course the Navaho did not believe
what he himself had said; he only told this to the old man to conceal
the fact that he had filled the pipe with poisoned tobacco.

508. While all these things were happening the Navaho had paid
no heed to how the day was passing; but now he became suddenly
aware that it was late in the afternoon and that the sun was about
to set. "I must hasten away. It is late," he said. "No, my son-
in-law; do not leave us," pleaded the old man. "Sleep here to-
night." He ordered his daughter to make a bed for the stranger.
She spread on the floor fine robes of otter-skin and beaver-skin,
beautifully ornamented. He laid down on the rugs and slept there
that night.

509. Next morning the young woman rose early and went out.
Soon after her departure the old man entered the lodge and said to
his guest: "I and my daughter were so busy yesterday with all that
you did to me, and all the cures you wrought on me, that we had no
time to cook food and eat; neither had you. She has gone now to
prepare food. Stay and eat with us." Presently the young woman
returned, bringing a dish of stewed venison and a basket filled with
mush made of wild seeds. The basket was such a one as the
Navahoes now use in their rites.[5] On the atáatlo (the part where
the coil terminates, the point of finish), the old man had, with
the knowledge of his daughter, placed poison. She presented the
basket to the stranger, with the point of finish toward him, as her
father had directed her to do, saying: "When a stranger visits us

we always expect him to eat from the part of the basket where it is finished." As he took the basket the Wind People [75] whispered to him: "Eat not from that part of the basket; death is there, but there is no death in the venison." The young man turned the basket around and began to eat from the side opposite to that which was presented to him, saying: "It is my custom to eat from the edge opposite to the point of finish." He did not eat all the mush. He tried the venison stew; but as it was made of dried meat he did not like it and ate very little of it. When he had done she took the dishes back to the other lodge. "From which side of the basket did my son-in-law eat?" asked the old man. "From the wrong side. He told me it was his custom never to eat from the side where the basket was finished," said the young woman. Her father was surprised. When a visitor came to him he always tried the poisoned tobacco first; if that failed he next tried the poisoned basket. "My husband says he wants to go home now," said the young woman. "Tell him it is not the custom for a man to go home the morning after his marriage. He should always remain four days at least," said the old man. She brought this message back to the Navaho. He remained that day and slept in the lodge at night.

510. Next morning the young woman rose early again and went to the other lodge. Soon after she was gone the old man entered and said to Natĭ′nĕsthani: "You would do well not to leave till you have eaten. My daughter is preparing food for you." In a little while, after he left, the young woman entered, bringing, as before, a dish of stewed venison and a basketful of mush, which she handed to the Navaho without making any remark. But Wind whispered: "There is poison all around the edge of the basket this time; there is none in the venison." The Navaho ate some of the stew, and when he took the basket of mush he ate only from the middle, saying: "When I eat just as the sun is about to come up, it is my custom to eat only from the middle of the basket." The sun was about to rise as he spoke. When she went back to the other lodge with the remains of the meal, her father asked: "How did he eat this morning?" She replied: "He ate the stew; but the mush he ate only from the middle of the basket." "Ahăhăhá!" said the old man, "it never took me so long, before." The Navaho remained in the lodge all that day and all night.

511. The next (third) morning things happened as before: the woman rose early, and while she was gone the old man came into the lodge, saying: "The women are cooking food for you. Don't go out till you have eaten." The reason they gave their visitor only one meal a day was that he might be so ravenous with hunger when

it came that he would not notice the poison and would eat plenty of it. When the food was brought in, the Wind People whispered to the Navaho: "Poison is mixed all through the mush, take none of it." He ate heartily of the stew, and when he was done he said to the young woman: "I may eat no mush to-day. The sun is already risen, and I have sworn that the sun shall never see me eat mush." When she went back to the other lodge her father asked: "How did my son-in-law eat this morning?" "He ate only of the stew," she said. "He would not touch the mush." "Ahăhăhá," said the old man in a suspicious tone; but he said no more. Again the Navaho stayed all day and all night.

512. On the fourth morning when the daughter went to prepare food and the old man entered the lodge, he said: "Go out somewhere to-day. Why do you not take a walk abroad every day? Is it on your wife's account that you stay at home so much, my son-in-law?" When the young woman brought in the usual venison stew and basket of mush, Wind whispered: "All the food is poisoned this morning." When she handed the food to the young man he said: "I do not eat at all to-day. It is my custom to eat no food one day in every four. This is the day that I must fast." When she took the untasted food back to the other lodge, her father inquired: "What did my son-in-law eat this morning?" and she answered: "He ate nothing." The old man was lying when he spoke; he rose when she answered him and carefully examined the food she had brought back. "Truly, nothing has been touched," he said. "This must be a strange man who eats nothing. My daughter, do you tell him anything he should not know?" "Truly, I tell him nothing," she replied.

513. When the young woman came back again from her father's lodge, the Navaho said to her: "I have a hut and a farm and a pet not far from here; I must go home to-day and see them." "It is well," she said. "You may go." He began to dress for the journey by putting on his old sandals. She brought him a pair of fine new moccasins, beautifully embroidered, and urged him to put them on; but he refused them, saying: "I may put them on some other time. I shall wear my old sandals to-day."

514. When Naŭ'nĕsťhani got back to his farm he found the tracks of his turkey all around, but the turkey itself he could not see. It was evident from the tracks that it had visited the farm and gone back to the hut again. The Navaho made four circuits around the hut — each circuit wider than the preceding — to see whither the tracks led. On the fourth circuit he found they led to the base of a mountain which stood north of the hut. "I shall find my pet somewhere around the mountain," thought the Navaho. The tracks had

the appearance of being four days old, and from this he concluded that the turkey had left the same day he had. It took him four days, travelling sunwise and going spirally up the mountain, to reach the summit, where he found many turkey tracks, but still no turkey. He fancied his pet might have descended the mountain again, so he went below and examined the ground carefully, but found no descending tracks. He returned to the summit and, looking more closely than at first, discovered where the bird had flown away from a point on the eastern edge of the summit and gone apparently toward the east.

515. The Navaho sat down, sad and lonely, and wept. "Dear pet," he said, "would that I had taken you with me that day when I set out on my journey. Had I done so I should not have lost you. Dear pet, you were the black cloud ; you were the black mist ; you were the beautiful he-rain ;[225] you were the beautiful she-rain ;[137] you were the beautiful lightning ; you were the beautiful rainbow ; you were the beautiful white corn ; you were the beautiful blue corn ; you were the beautiful yellow corn ; you were the beautiful corn of all colors ; you were the beautiful bean. Though lost to me, you shall be of use to men, upon the earth, in the days to come — they shall use your feathers and your beard in their rites." The Navaho never saw his pet again ; it had flown to the east, and from it we think the tame turkeys of the white men are descended. But all the useful and beautiful things he saw in his pet are still to be seen in the turkey. It has the colors of all the different kinds of corn in its feathers. The black of the black mist and the black cloud are there. The flash of the lightning and the gleam of the rainbow are seen on its plumes when it walks in the sun. The rain is in its beard ; the bean it carries on its forehead.

516. He dried his tears, descended the mountain, and sought his old hut, which was only a poor shelter of brush, and then he went to visit his farm. He found his corn with ears already formed and all the other plants well advanced toward maturity.[226] He pulled one ear from a stalk of each one of the four different kinds of corn, and, wrapping the ears in his mantle of wood-rat skins, went off to see his wife. She saw him coming, met him at the door, and relieved him of his weapons and bundle. "What is this?" she said, pointing to the bundle after she had laid it down. He opened it. She started back in amazement. She had never seen corn before. He laid the ears down side by side in a row with their points to the east, and said : "This is what we call na*tán*, corn. This (pointing to the first ear — the most northerly of the row) is white corn ; this (pointing to the next) is blue corn ; this (pointing to the third) is yellow corn, and this (pointing to the fourth) is corn of all colors."[227]

"And what do your people do with it?" she asked. "We eat it," he replied. "How do you prepare it to eat?" she inquired. He said: "We have four ways when it is green like this. We put it, husk and all, in hot coals to roast. We take off the husk and roast it in hot ashes. We boil it whole in hot water. We cut off the grains and mix it with water to make mush."

517. She wrapped the four ears in a bundle and carried them to the other lodge to show them to her parents. Both were astonished and alarmed. The old man rose and shaded his eyes with his open hand to look at them. They asked her questions about the corn, such as she had asked her husband, and she answered them as he had answered her. She cooked the four ears of corn, each one in a different way, according to the methods her husband described. They increased in cooking so that they made food enough to furnish a hearty meal for all. The old people, who were greatly pleased, said the mush smelled like fawn-cheese.[228] "Where does my son-in-law get this fine stuff? Ask him. I wish to know, it is so delicious. Does he not want some himself?" said the old man to his daughter. She brought a large dish of the corn to her husband in the other lodge, and they ate it together. The Navaho had no fear of poison this time, for the food did not belong to the old man.

518. At night when they were alone together she asked him where he got the corn. "I found it," he said. "Did you dig it out of the ground?" she asked. "No. I picked it up," was his answer. Not believing him, she continued to question him until at last he told her: "These things I plant and they grow where I plant them. Do you wish to see my field?" "Yes, if my father will let me," the woman replied.

519. Next morning she told her father what she had found out on the previous night and asked his advice. He said he would like to have her go with Naťínĕ*st*ʰani to see what the farm looked like and to find out what kind of leaves the plant had that such food grew on. When she came back from her father's lodge she brought with her pemmican made of venison and a basket of mush. The Wind People whispered to him that he need not fear the food to-day, so he ate heartily of it. When the breakfast was over, the Navaho said: "Dress yourself for the journey, and as soon as you are ready I shall take you to my farm." She dressed herself for travel and went to the lodge of her parents, where she said: "I go with my husband now." "It is well," they said; "go with him."

520. The Navaho and his wife set out together. When they came to a little hill from which they could first see the field, they beheld the sun shining on it; yet the rain was falling on it at the same

time, and above it was a dark cloud spanned by a rainbow. When they reached the field they walked four times around it sunwise, and as they went he described things in the field to his wife. "This is my white corn, this is my blue corn, this is my yellow corn, and this is my corn of all colors. These we call squashes, these we call melons, and these we call beans," he said, pointing to the various plants. The bluebirds and the yellowbirds were singing in the corn after the rain, and all was beautiful. She was pleased and astonished and she asked many questions, — how the seeds were planted, how the food was prepared and eaten, — and he answered all her questions. "These on the ground are melons ; they are not ripe yet. When they are ripe we eat them raw," he explained. When they had circled four times around the field they went in among the plants. Then he showed her the pollen and explained its sacred uses.[11] He told her how the corn matured ; how his people husked it and stored it for winter use, how they shelled, ground, and prepared it, and how they preserved some to sow in the spring. " Now, let us pluck an ear of each kind of corn and go home," he said. When she plucked the corn she also gathered three of the leaves and put them into the same bundle with the corn ; but as they walked home the leaves increased in number, and when she got to the house and untied the bundle she found not only three, but many leaves in it.

521. He explained to her how to make the dish now known to the Navahoes as *dǐtlógi klesán,*[230] and told her to make this of the white corn. He instructed her how to prepare corn as *dǐtlógǐn tsǐdǐkói,*[231] and told her to make this of the blue corn. He showed her how to prepare corn in the form of *tłábǐtsa,*[232] or three-ears, and bade her make this of the yellow corn. He told her to roast, in the husk, the ear of many colors. She took the corn to the other lodge and prepared it as she had been directed. In cooking, it all increased greatly in amount, so that they all had a big meal out of four ears.

522. The old people questioned their daughter about the farm — what it looked like, what grew there. They asked her many questions. She told them of all she had seen and heard : of her distant view of the beautiful farm under the rain, under the black cloud, under the rainbow ; of her near view of it — the great leaves, the white blossoms of the bean, the yellow blossoms of the squash, the tassel of the corn, the silk of the corn, the pollen of the corn, and all the other beautiful things she saw there. When she had done the old man said : " I thank you, my daughter, for bringing me such a son-in-law. I have travelled far, but I have never seen such things as those you tell of. I thought I was rich, but my son-in-law is

richer. In future cook these things with care, in the way my son-in-law shows you."

523. The old man then went to see his son-in-law and said: "I thank you for the fine food you have brought us, and I am glad to hear you have such a beautiful farm. You know how to raise and cook corn; but do you know how to make and cook the pemmican [229] of the deer?" "I know nothing about it," said the Navaho. (The one knew nothing of venison; the other knew nothing of corn.) "How does it taste to you?" asked the old man. "I like the taste of it and I thank you for what you have given me," replied the Navaho. "Your wife, then, will have something to tell you." When he got back to the other lodge he said: "My son-in-law has been kind to us; he has shown you his farm and taught you how to prepare his food. My daughter, now we must show him our farm." She brought to her husband a large portion of the cooked corn.

524. When night came and they were alone together she asked him to tell her his name. "I have no name," he replied. Three times he answered her thus. When she asked for the fourth time he said: "Why do you wish to know my name? I have two names. I am Naṯi'něsṯḥani, He Who Teaches Himself, and I am Áḥodíseḷi, He Who Has Floated. Now that I have told you my name you must tell me your father's name." "He is called Píniltani, Deer Raiser. I am Píniltani-bitsí, Deer Raiser's Daughter, and my mother is Píniltani-baád, She Deer Raiser," the young woman answered.

525. In the morning after this conversation they had a breakfast of mush and venison; but Naṯi'něsṯḥani received no warning from the Wind People and feared not to eat. When the meal was over, the young woman said to her husband: "My father has told me that, as you have shown me your farm, I may now show you his farm. If you wish to go there, you must first bathe your body in yucca-suds and then rinse off in pure water." After he had taken his bath as directed he picked up his old sandals and was about to put them on when she stopped him, saying: "No. You wore your own clothes when you went to your own farm. Now you must wear our clothes when you come to our farm." She gave him embroidered moccasins; fringed buckskin leggings; a buckskin shirt, dyed yellow, beautifully embroidered with porcupine quills, and fringed with stripes of otter-skin; and a headdress adorned with artificial ears called Tṡáhaḍolkohi — they wore such in the old days, and there are men still living who have seen them worn.

526. Dressed in these fine garments he set out with his wife and they travelled toward the southeast. As they were passing the other hut she bade him wait outside while she went in to procure a

wand of turquoise. They went but a short distance (about three hundred yards) [233] when they came, on the top of a small hill, to a large, smooth stone, adorned with turquoise, sticking in the ground like a stopple in a water-jar. She touched this rock stopple with her wand in four different directions — east, south, west, north — and it sprang up out of the ground. She touched it in an upward direction, and it lay over on its side, revealing a hole which led to a flight of four stone steps.

527. She entered the hole and beckoned to him to follow. When they descended the steps they found themselves in a square apartment with four doors of rock crystal, one on each side. There was a rainbow over each door. With her wand she struck the eastern door and it flew open, disclosing a vast and beautiful country, like this world, but more beautiful. How vast it was the Navaho knew not, for he could not see the end of it. They passed through the door. The land was filled with deer and covered with beautiful flowers. The air was filled with the odor of pollen and the odor of fragrant blossoms. Birds of the most beautiful plumage were flying in the air, perching on the flowers, and building nests in the antlers of the deer. In the distance a light shower of rain was falling, and rainbows shone in every direction. "This, then, is the farm of my father-in-law which you promised to show me," said the Navaho. "It is beautiful; but in truth it is no farm, for I see nothing planted here." She took him into three other apartments. They were all as beautiful as the first, but they contained different animals. In the apartment to the south there were antelope ; in that to the west, Rocky Mountain sheep ; in that to the north, elk.

528. When they closed the last door and came out to the central apartment they found Deer Raiser there. "Has my son-in-law been in all the rooms and seen all the game ?" he asked. "I have seen all," said Natĭ'nĕsthani. "Do you see two sacrificial cigarettes of the deer above the rainbow over the eastern door?" "I see them now," responded the Navaho, "but I did not notice them when I entered." The old man then showed him, over the door in the south, two cigarettes of the antelope; over the door in the west, two cigarettes of the Rocky Mountain sheep ; over the door in the north, the single white cigarette of *Hastséyalti* [234] (the elk had no cigarette), and at the bottom of the steps by which they had entered, two cigarettes of the fawn. "Look well at these cigarettes," said the old man, "and remember how they are painted, for such we now sacrifice in our ceremonies." "Are you pleased ?" "Do you admire what you have seen ?" "What do you think of it all ?" Such were the questions the old man asked, and the Navaho made answer: "I thank you. I am glad that I have seen your farm and your pets. Such things I never saw before."

529. "Now, my daughter," said Deer Raiser, "catch a deer for my son-in-law, that we may have fresh meat." She opened the eastern door, entered, and caught a big buck by the foot (just as we catch sheep in these days). She pulled it out. The Navaho walked in front ; the young woman, dragging the buck, came after him, and the old man came last of all, closing the doors and putting in the stopple as he came. They brought the buck home, tied its legs together with short rainbows, cut its throat with a stone arrow point, and skinned it as we now skin deer.

530. Now Deer Raiser began again to plot the death of his son-in-law. He found he could not poison him, so he determined to try another plan. In a neighboring canyon, to which there was but one entrance, he kept four fierce pet bears. He determined to invite his son-in-law out to hunt with him, and get him killed by these bears. The rest of that day the Navaho remained at home with his wife, while the old man took the hoofs of the slain deer and made with them a lot of tracks leading into the canyon of the bears.

531. On the following morning, while the young woman was cooking in the other lodge, Deer Raiser came in where the Navaho sat and said : "My son-in-law, four of my pet deer have escaped from the farm. I have tracked them to a canyon near by, which has only one entrance. As soon as you have eaten I want you to help me to hunt them. You will stand at the entrance of the canyon while I go in to drive the deer toward you, and you can kill them as they come out. No," said the old man after pausing for a while and pretending to think, "you must go into the canyon, my son-in-law, while I stay at the entrance and kill the deer. That will be better." When about to start on his hunt, the Wind People whispered to the Navaho : "Do not enter the canyon."

532. The two men walked along the steep side of the valley, following the tracks until they came to the high rugged cliffs that marked the entrance to the canyon. "When my deer escape, here is where they usually come," said Deer Raiser. A little stream of water ran out of the canyon, and here the old man had raised a dam to make a pool. When they reached the pool he said : "Here I shall stop to shoot the deer. Go you in and drive them out for me." "No, I fear the deer will pass me," said Naȟ'nĕsťhani. Four times these words were said by both. At last the old man, seeing that his companion was obstinate, said : "Stay here, then, but do not let the deer escape you, and do not climb the hillsides around for fear the deer should see you," and he went himself into the canyon. In spite of all the warnings he had received, Naȟ'nĕsťhani climbed a rocky eminence where he could watch and be out of danger. After waiting a while in silence he heard a distant cry like

that of a wolf,[235] woo-oo-oo-oo, and became aware that something was moving toward him through the brush. He soon descried four bears walking down the canyon in single file, about thirty paces apart, alternately a female and a male. The old man had probably told them there was some one for them to kill, for they advanced with hair bristling, snouts up, and teeth showing. When he saw them coming he said, "I am Nayénĕzgani. I am *H*astséyal*t*i. I am *S*a*s*nalkáhi. I am a god of bears," and he mentioned the names of other potent gods. As the bears were passing their hidden enemy he drew arrow after arrow to the head and slew them all, one by one. He killed them as they walked along a ledge of rock, and their bodies tumbled down on the other side of the ledge, where they were hidden from view. Soon the voice of the old man was heard in the distance crying: "Oh, my pets! Oh, T*s*ananaí! Oh, T*s*ĕ′sko*d*i! (for the bears had names).[236] Save a piece for me! Save a piece for me!" And a little later he came in sight, running and panting. He did not see his son-in-law till he was right beside him. He showed at once that he was surprised and angry, but he quickly tried to make it appear that he was angry from another cause. "I should have been here. You have let them run by," he cried in angry tones. "Oh, no," said the Navaho, "I have not let them run by. I have killed them. Look over the ledge and you will see them." The old man looked as he was told, and was struck dumb with astonishment and sorrow. He sat down in silence, with his head hanging between his knees, and gazed at the bodies of his dead pets. He did not even thank his son-in-law.[237]

533. Why did Deer Raiser seek the life of his son-in-law? Now Na*t*ĭ′nĕst*h*ani knew, and now you shall know. The old man was a *d*ĭné‘yiani, or man-eater, and a wizard. He wanted the flesh of the Navaho to eat, and he wanted parts of the dead body to use in the rites of witchcraft. But there was yet another reason; he was jealous of the Navaho, for those who practise witchcraft practise also incest.

534. "Why did you shoot them?" said the old man at last; "the deer went out before them. Why did you not shoot the deer? Now you may skin the bears." "You never drove deer to me," said the Navaho. "These are what you drove to me. When a companion in the hunt drives anything to me I kill it, no matter what it is. You have talked much to me about hunting with you. Now I have killed game and you must skin it." "Help me, then, to skin it," said Deer Raiser. "No. I never skin the game I kill myself.[238] You must do the skinning. I killed for you," said the Navaho. "If you will not help me," said the old man, "go back to the house and tell my daughter to come and assist me to skin the bears. Go back by the way we came when we trailed the deer."

535. Naíí'něs*th*ani set off as the Deer Raiser had directed him. As soon as he was out of sight the old man rushed for the house by a short cut. Reaching home, he hastily dressed himself in the skin of a great serpent, went to the trail which his son-in-law was to take, and lay in ambush behind a log at a place where the path led through a narrow defile. As the Navaho approached the log the Wind People told him : "Your father-in-law awaits you behind the log." The Navaho peeped over the log before he got too near, and saw Deer Raiser in his snake-skin suit, swaying uneasily back and forth, poising himself as if preparing to spring. When he saw the young man looking in his direction he crouched low. "What are you doing there?" called the Navaho (in a way which let Deer Raiser know he was recognized),[239] and he drew an arrow on the old man. "Stop! stop!" cried the latter. "I only came here to meet you and hurry you up." "Why do you not come from behind, if that is so? Why do you come from before me and hide beside my path?" said the Navaho, and he passed on his way and went to his wife's house.

536. When Naíí'něs*th*ani reached the house he told his wife that he had killed four animals for his father-in-law, but he did not tell her what kind of animals they were, and he told her that her father sent for her mother to help skin the animals and cut up the meat. The daughter delivered the message to her mother, and the latter went out to the canyon to help her husband. When Deer Raiser saw his wife coming he was furious. "It was my daughter I sent for, not you," he roared. "What sort of a man is he who cannot carry my word straight, who cannot do as he is told? I bade him tell my daughter, not you, to come to me." Between them they skinned and dressed the bears and carried them, one at a time, to his house. He sent to his son-in-law to know if he wanted some meat, and the Navaho replied that he did not eat bear meat. When he heard this, Deer Raiser was again furious, and said : "What manner of a man is this who won't eat meat? (He did not say what kind of meat.) When we offer him food he says he does not want to eat it. He never does what he is told to do. We cook food for him and he refuses it. What can we do to please him? What food will satisfy him?"

537. The next morning after the bears were killed, the young woman went out as usual, and the old man entered during her absence. He said to Naíí'něs*th*ani: "I wish you to go out with me to-day and help me to fight my enemies. There are enemies of mine, not far from here, whom I sometimes meet in battle." "I will go with you," said the Navaho. "I have long been hoping that some one would say something like this to me."

538. They went from the lodge toward a mountain which was edged on two sides by steep cliffs, which no man could climb. On the top of the mountain the old man said there was a round hole or valley in which his enemies dwelled. He stationed his son-in-law on one side of this round valley where no cliffs were, and he went to the opposite side to drive the enemy, as he said. He promised to join the Navaho when the enemy started. Deer Raiser went around the mountain and cried four times in imitation of a wolf. Then, instead of coming to his comrade's help, he ran around the base of the hill and got behind his son-in-law. Soon after the old man made his cry, the Navaho saw twelve great ferocious bears coming toward him over the crest of the hill. They were of the kind called *saʃnalkáhi*, or tracking bears, such as scent and track a man, and follow till they kill him. They were of all the sacred colors, — white, blue, yellow, black, and spotted. They came toward the Navaho, but he was well armed and prepared to meet them. He fought with them the hardest fight he ever fought ; but at length he killed them all, and suffered no harm himself.[240]

539. In the mean time the old man ran off in the direction of his home, sure that his son-in-law was killed. He said : "I think we shall hear no more of Natĭ'nĕsthani. I think we shall hear no more of Áhodĭseli. Hereafter it will be Natĭ'nĕsthanini (the dead Natĭ'-nĕsthani). Hereafter it will be Áhodĭselini (the dead Áhodĭseli).[241] He can't come back out of the tracking bears' mouths." After killing the bears, the Navaho found the old man's trail and followed it. Presently he came to Deer Raiser, who was sitting on a knoll. The old man could not conceal his astonishment at seeing the Navaho still alive. "When we went out to this battle," said the young man, "we promised not to desert one another. Why did you run away from me?" The Deer Raiser answered : "I am sorry I could not find you. I did not see where you were, so I came on this way. What did you do where I left you? Did you kill any of the bears?" "Yes, I killed all of them," said Natĭ'nĕsthani. "I am glad you killed all and came away with your own life, my dear son-in-law," said the old cheat.

540. They started to walk home together, but night fell when they reached a rocky ridge on the way ; here they picked out a nice spot of ground to sleep on, built a shelter of brushwood, and made a fire. Before they went to rest the old man said : "This is a bad place to camp. It is called Kedĭdĭ'lyena'a' (Ridge of the Burnt Moccasins)." As they lay down to sleep, one on either side of the fire, each took off his moccasins and put them under his head. The old man said : "Take good care of your moccasins, my son-in-law. Place them securely." "Why does he say these things?"

asked the Navaho to himself. As he lay awake, thinking of the warning of the old man, he heard the latter snoring. He rose softly, took away the old man's moccasins, put his own in their place, and lay down to sleep with Deer Raiser's moccasins under his head. Later in the night the old man got up, pulled the moccasins from under the young man's head, and buried them in the hot embers. He was anxious to get home next morning before his son-in-law.

541. At dawn the old man aroused his companion with "It is time we were on our road." The young man woke, rubbed his eyes, yawned, and pretended to look for his moccasins. After searching a while he asked: "Where are my moccasins? Have I lost them?" "Huh!" said Deer Raiser. "You did not listen to what I told you last night. I said that this was the Ridge of the Burned Moccasins." In the mean time, on the other side of the fire, the old man was putting on his companion's moccasins, not noticing that they were not his own. "Look. You are putting on my moccasins instead of your own. Give me my moccasins," said the Navaho, reaching across the fire. He took them out of his companion's hands, sat down and put them on. "Now we must hurry back," he said. "I can't see what made you burn your moccasins, but I cannot wait for you. I am going now." [242]

542. Before the young man left, his father-in-law gave him a message. "I cannot travel as fast as you on my bare feet. When you go home, tell my daughter to come out with a pair of moccasins and some food, and meet me on the trail." When the Navaho got home he said to his wife : "I camped with your father last night, and he burned his moccasins. He is limping home barefoot. He bids his wife to come out and meet him with moccasins and food." The daughter delivered the message to her mother, and the latter went out to meet her husband with moccasins, food, and a brand of burning cedar-bark. When the old man met her he was angry. "Why have you come? Why has not my daughter come?" he asked. "Your son-in-law said that I should come," the old woman replied. "Oh, what a fool my son-in-law is," cried Deer Raiser. "He never can remember what he is told to say." He ate his food, put on his moccasins, and hurried home with his wife.

543. When Deer Raiser visited his son-in-law on the following morning he said : "I warn you never to stray alone to the east of the lodge in which you dwell. There is a dangerous place there." The old man went home, and the Navaho pondered all day over what his father-in-law had said, and during the night he made up his mind to do just what the old man had told him not to do.

544. When Naťí'nĕsťhani had eaten in the morning he dressed himself for a journey, left the lodge, and travelled straight to the east.

He came to a steep white ridge ;[243] when he had climbed this about
half way, he observed approaching him a man of low stature. His
coat, which fitted him skin-tight, was white on the chest and insides of
the arms, while it was brown elsewhere, like the skin of a deer. He
wore on his head a deer-mask, with horns, such as deer-hunters use.
He carried a turquoise wand, a black bow with sinew on the back,
and two arrows with featherings of eagle-tail. He was one of the
Tsĭdas*t*óid*′*ĭne‘.[244] When the men met, the stranger, who had a pale
face,[245] looked out from under his mask and said : " Whence come
you, my grandchild ? " " I come, my grandfather, from a place near
here. I come from the house of Pĭnĭl*t*ani," the Navaho answered.
" My grandchild, I have heard of you. Do you know how my cigarette is made ? " said the man with the deer-mask. " No, my grandfather, I never heard of your cigarette," was the reply. " There is
a cigarette [12] for me, my grandson," said the stranger. " It is painted
white, with a black spot on it, and is so long (second joint of middle finger). It should be laid in the fork of a piñon-tree. I am
now walking out, and am going in the direction whence you came.
There are people living behind the ridge you are climbing. You
should visit them, and hear what they will have to tell you."

545. The Navaho climbed the ridge ; and as he began to descend
it on the other side, he observed below him two conical tents, such
as the Indians of the plains use. The tents were white below and
yellow above, representing the dawn and the evening twilight. As
he approached the tents he observed that two games of nán*z*o*z* were
being played, — one beside each tent, — and a number of people
were gathered, watching the games. As he advanced toward the
crowd a man came forward to meet him, saying : " Go to the lodge in
the south. There are many people there." He went to the lodge
in the south, as he was bidden. A woman of bright complexion,
fairer than the Navahoes usually are, the wife of the owner of the
lodge, came out and invited him to enter.

546. When Na*t*ĭ′nĕs*t*ani entered the lodge he found its owner
seated in the middle. The latter was a man past middle age, but
not very old. He was dressed in a beautiful suit of buckskin embroidered with porcupine quills. He pointed to a place by his side,
and said to the Navaho : " Sit here, my grandchild." When the
Navaho was seated his host said : " Whence do you come? The
people who live up on the earth are never seen here." " I come
from the house of Pĭnĭl*t*ani," the young man answered. " Oh ! Do
you ? " questioned the host. " And do you know that Deer Raiser
is a great villain ; that he kills his guests ; that he talks softly, and
pretends friendship, and lures people to stay with him until he can
quietly kill them ? Has he never spoken thus softly to you ? How

long have you been staying with him?" "I have dwelt with him for many days," Naťǐ'něs*th*ani answered. "Ah!" said his host. "Many of our young men have gone over there to woo his daughter; but they have never returned. Some are killed on the first day; others on the second day; others on the third day; others on the fourth; but no one ever lives beyond the fourth day. No one has ever lived there as long as you have." "He seems to be such a man as you describe him," said Naťǐ'něs*th*ani. "He has been trying to kill me ever since I have been with him." "You must be a wise man to have escaped him so long; your prayer must be potent; your charm must be strong,"[246] declared the host. "No, truly, I know no good prayer; I possess no charm," the Navaho replied, and then he went on to tell how he came into that country, and all that happened to him, till he came to the house of Deer Raiser. "He is rich, but he is no good. That daughter of his is also his wife, and that is why he wants to poison her suitors," said the owner of the lodge, and then he described four ways in which Pǐn*ǐlt*ani killed his guests. The Navaho remained silent. He knew all the ways of the Deer Raiser, but he pretended not to know. Then the host went on: "The house of Deer Raiser is a place of danger. You will surely be killed if you stay there. I am sorry you are in such bad company, for you seem to be a good man." "You speak of Deer Raiser as a great man; but he cannot be so great as you think he is. Four times have I killed him with smoke, and four times have I brought him to life again," said the Navaho, and then he related all his adventures since he had been with Pǐn*ǐlt*ani.

547. The host thanked him for having slain the bears, and went out to call the players and all the crowd that stood around them to come to his tent. They came, for he was their chief, and soon the tent was crowded. Then he spoke to the assembly, and told them the story of the Navaho. There was great rejoicing when they heard it. They thanked Naťǐ'něs*th*ani for what he had done. One said that Deer Raiser had killed his brother; another said he had killed his son; another said the bears had slain his nephew, and thus they spoke of their many woes.

548. The people were of five kinds, or gentes: the Puma People, the Blue Fox People, the Yellow Fox People, the Wolf People, and the Lynx People, and the host was chief of all.

549. The chief ordered one of his daughters to prepare food for the visitor. She brought in deer pemmican. The Navaho ate, and when he was done he said: "I am now ready to go, my grandfather." "Wait a while," said the chief. "I have some medicine to give you. It is an antidote for Deer Raiser's poison." He gave his visitor two kinds of medicine; one was an object the size of the

last two joints of the little finger, made of the gall of birds of prey,
— all birds that catch with their claws ; the other was a small quantity (as much as one might grasp with the tips of all the fingers of
one hand) of a substance composed of material vomited by each of
the five animals that were the totems of this people. "Now have
no fear," said the chief. "The bears are slain, and you have here
medicines that will kill the wizard's poison. They are potent against
witchcraft." [247]

550. When the Navaho went back to the house where his wife
was, she said : "My father has been here inquiring for you. When
I told him you had gone to the east he was very angry, and said that
he told you not to go there." Soon the old man entered and said
fiercely : "Why have you gone to the east? I told you not to go
there. I told you it was a bad place." The young man made no
reply, but acted as if he had seen and heard nothing while he was
gone, and in a little while Deer Raiser calmed down and acted as if
he wished to be at peace again with his son-in-law ; but before he
left he warned him not to go to the south. Natĭ́nĕsthani pondered
on the words of his father-in-law that night, and made up his mind
to again disobey him when morning came.

551. Next day, when he had eaten, he dressed himself for a journey and walked toward the south. He came, in time, to a blue
ridge, and when he was ascending it he met a little man, much like
the one he had met the day before, but he had a bluish face. Instead of being dressed to look like a deer, he was dressed to look
like an antelope ; he wore an antelope hunting-mask with horns, he
carried a wand of haliotis, and a bow made of a wood called tsĕ́lkáni,
with no sinew on the back, and he had arrows trimmed with the tail
feathers of the red-tailed buzzard.[248] Like the little man of the east,
he was also one of the Tsïdas*t*ói People. He told the Navaho how
to make the cigarette that belonged to him, to make it the length of
the middle joint of the little finger, to paint it blue, spot it with yellow, and deposit it in the fork of a cedar-tree. The little man told
the Navaho to go on over the ridge till he came to two lodges and
to listen there to what the people would tell him. He went and
found two lodges, and people playing nán*z*o*z*, and had all things
happen to him nearly the same as happened to him in the east.
When he returned home he had again an angry talk from his father-
in-law, and was warned not to go to the west ; but again he determined to pay no heed to the warning.

552. When he went to the west, next day, he found a yellow ridge
to cross. The little man whom he met had a yellowish face ; he
was armed and dressed the same as the little man of the east, except
that he had no horns on his deer-mask, for he represented a doe.

He described to the Navaho how to make a cigarette sacred to himself, which was to be painted yellow, spotted with blue, and deposited in a piñon-tree, like the cigarette of the east. Other events happened much as on the two previous days.

553. On the fourth of these forbidden journeys the Navaho went to the north. The ridge which he had to cross was black. The little man whom he met was armed and dressed like the man in the south, but he had no horns on his mask. His face was very dark. The cigarette which he described was to be painted black and spotted with white; it was to be the same length as the cigarette of the south, and disposed of in the same way.

554. When he got home from his fourth journey, his father-in-law came into the lodge and reviled him once more with angry words; but this time the Navaho did not remain silent. He told the old man where he had been, what people he had met, what stories he had heard, and all that he knew of him. He told him, too, that he had learned of cigarettes, and medicines, and charms, and rites to protect him against a wizard's power. "You have killed others," said Naɟï′něs*th*ani, "you have tried to kill me. I knew it all the time, but said nothing. Now I know all of your wickedness." "All that you say is true," said the old man; "but I shall seek your life no more, and I shall give up all my evil ways. While you were abroad on your journeys you learned of powerful sacrifices, and rites, and medicines. All that I ask is that you will treat me with these." His son-in-law did as he was desired, and in doing so performed the first atsósi *h*atál.[249]

555. After treating his father-in-law, Naɟï′něs*th*ani returned to his people, taught them all he had learned while he was gone, and thus established the rite of atsósi *h*atál among the Navahoes. Then he went back to the whirling lake of *T*ó'nihili*n*, and he dwells there still.

THE GREAT SHELL OF KĬNTYÉL.

556. Kĭntyél,[72] Broad House, and Kĭ'ndoŧlĭz, Blue House,[208] are two pueblo houses in the Chaco Canyon. They are ruins now ; but in the days when Kĭ*n*íki lived on earth many people dwelt there. Not far from the ruins is a high cliff called Tse'dezá', or Standing Rock. Near these places the rite of yói *hatál*,[250] or the bead chant,

Fig. 36. Ruin in the Chaco Canyon, probably Kĭntyél (after Bickford).

was first practised by the Navahoes, and this is the tale of how it first became known to man : —

557. Two young men, one from Kĭntyél and one from Kĭ'ndoŧlĭz, went out one day to hunt deer. About sunset, as they were return-ing to Kĭ'ndoŧlĭz, weary and unsuccessful, they observed a war-eagle soaring overhead, and they stopped to watch his flight. He

moved slowly away, growing smaller and smaller to their gaze until at length he dwindled to a black speck, almost invisible; and while they strained their sight to get a last look he seemed to them to descend on the top of Standing Rock. In order to mark the spot where they last saw him they cut a forked stick, stuck it in the ground fork upward, and arranged it so that when they should look over it again, crouching in a certain position, their sight would be guided to the spot. They left the stick standing and went home to Kĭ′ndoᴧlĭz.[251]

558. In those days eagles were very scarce in the land; it was a wonder to see one; so when the young men got home and told the story of their day's adventures, it became the subject of much conversation and counsel, and at length the people determined to send four men, in the morning, to take sight over the forked stick, in order to find out where the eagle lived.

559. Next morning early the four men designated went to the forked stick and sighted over it, and all came to the conclusion that the eagle lived on the point of Tse‘dezá‘. They went at once to the rock, climbed to the summit, and saw the eagle and its young in a cleft on the face of the precipice below them. They remained on the summit all day and watched the nest.

560. At night they went home and told what they had seen. They had observed two young eagles of different ages in the nest. Of the four men who went on the search, two were from Kĭntyél and two were from Kĭ′ndoᴧlĭz, therefore people from the two pueblos met in counsel in an estufa, and there it was decided that Kĭ′ndoᴧlĭz should have the elder of the two eaglets and that Kĭntyél should have the younger.

561. The only way to reach the nest was to lower a man to it with a rope; yet directly above the nest was an overhanging ledge which the man, descending, would be obliged to pass. It was a dangerous undertaking, and no one could be found to volunteer for it. Living near the pueblos was a miserable Navaho beggar who subsisted on such food as he could pick up. When the sweepings of the rooms and the ashes from the fireplaces were thrown out on the kitchen heap, he searched eagerly through them and was happy if he could find a few grains of corn or a piece of paper bread. He was called Nahodĭtáhe, or He Who Picks Up (like a bird). They concluded to induce this man to make the dangerous descent.

562. They returned to the pueblo and sent for the poor Navaho to come to the estufa. When he came they bade him be seated, placed before him a large basket of paper bread, bowls of boiled corn and meat, with all sorts of their best food, and told him to eat his fill. He ate as he had never eaten before, and after a long time

he told his hosts that he was satisfied. "You shall eat," said they, "of such abundance all your life, and never more have to scrape for grains of corn among the dirt, if you will do as we desire." Then they told him of their plan for catching the young eagles, and asked him if he were willing to be put in a basket and lowered to the nest with a rope. He pondered and was silent. They asked him again and again until they had asked him four times, while he still sat in meditation. At last he answered: "I lead but a poor life at best. Existence is not sweet to a man who always hungers. It would be pleasant to eat such food for the rest of my days, and some time or other I must die. I shall do as you wish."

563. On the following morning they gave him another good meal; they made a great, strong carrying-basket with four corners at the top; they tied a strong string to each corner, and, collecting a large party, they set out for the rock of Tse'dezá'.

564. When the party arrived at the top of the rock they tied a long, stout rope to the four strings on the basket. They instructed the Navaho to take the eaglets out of the nest and drop them to the bottom of the cliff. The Navaho then entered the basket and was lowered over the edge of the precipice. They let the rope out slowly till they thought they had lowered him far enough and then they stopped; but as he had not yet reached the nest he called out to them to lower him farther. They did so, and as soon as he was on a level with the nest he called to the people above to stop.

565. He was just about to grasp the eaglets and throw them down when Wind whispered to him: "These people of the Pueblos are not your friends. They desire not to feed you with their good food as long as you live. If you throw these young eagles down, as they bid you, they will never pull you up again. Get into the eagles' nest and stay there." When he heard this, he called to those above: "Swing the basket so that it may come nearer to the cliff. I cannot reach the nest unless you do." So they caused the basket to swing back and forth. When it touched the cliff he held fast to the rock and scrambled into the nest, leaving the empty basket swinging in the air.

566. The Pueblos saw the empty basket swinging and waited, expecting to see the Navaho get back into it again. But when they had waited a good while and found he did not return they began to call to him as if he were a dear relation of theirs. "My son," said the old men, "throw down those little eagles." "My elder brother! My younger brother!" the young men shouted, "throw down those little eagles." They kept up their clamor until nearly sunset; but they never moved the will of the Navaho. He sat in the cleft and never answered them, and when the sun set they ceased calling and went home.

567. In the cleft or cave, around the nest, four dead animals lay; to the east there was a fawn; to the south a hare; to the west the young of a Rocky Mountain sheep, and to the north a prairie-dog. From time to time, when the eaglets felt hungry, they would leave the nest and eat of the meat; but the Navaho did not touch it.

568. Early next day the Pueblo people returned and gathered in a great crowd at the foot of the cliff. They stayed there all day repeating their entreaties and promises, calling the Navaho by endearing terms, and displaying all kinds of tempting food to his gaze; but he heeded them not and spoke not.

569. They came early again on the third day, but they came in anger. They no longer called him by friendly names; they no longer made fair promises to him; but, instead, they shot fire-arrows at the eyry in hopes they would burn the Navaho out or set fire to the nest and compel him to throw it and the eaglets down. But he remained watchful and active, and whenever a fire-arrow entered the cave he seized it quickly and threw it out. Then they abused him and reviled him, and called him bad names until sunset, when again they went home.

570. They came again on the fourth day and acted as they had done on the previous day; but they did not succeed in making the Navaho throw down the little eagles. He spoke to the birds, saying: "Can you not help me?" They rose in the nest, shook their wings, and threw out many little feathers, which fell on the people below. The Navaho thought the birds must be scattering disease on his enemies. When the latter left at sunset they said: "Now we shall leave you where you are, to die of hunger and thirst." He was then altogether three nights and nearly four days in the cave. For two days the Pueblos had coaxed and flattered him; for two days they had cursed and reviled him, and at the end of the fourth day they went home and left him in the cave to die.

571. When his tormentors were gone he sat in the cave hungry and thirsty, weak and despairing, till the night fell. Soon after dark he heard a great rushing sound which approached from one side of the entrance to the cave, roared a moment in front, and then grew faint in the distance at the other side. Thus four times the sound came and went, growing louder each time it passed, and at length the male Eagle lit on the eyry. Soon the sounds were repeated, and the female bird, the mother of the eaglets, alighted. Turning at once toward the Navaho, she said: "Greeting, my child! Thanks, my child! You have not thrown down your younger brother, *Doniki.*" [285] The male Eagle repeated the same words. They addressed the Navaho by the name of *Doniki,* but afterwards they named him Ki*n*níki, after the chief of all the Eagles in the sky. He only replied to the Eagles: "I am hungry. I am thirsty."

572. The male Eagle opened his sash and took out a small white cotton cloth which contained a little corn meal, and he took out a small bowl of white shell no bigger than the palm of the hand. When the Indian saw this he said: "Give me water first, for I am famishing with thirst." "No," replied the Eagle; "eat first and then you shall have something to drink." The Eagle then drew forth from among his tail feathers a small plant called el*t*indʐakas,[252] which has many joints and grows near streams. The joints were all filled with water. The Eagle mixed a little of the water with some of the meal in the shell and handed the mixture to the Navaho. The latter ate and ate, until he was satisfied, but he could not diminish in the least the contents of the shell vessel. When he was done eating there was as much in the cup as there was when he began. He handed it back to the Eagle, the latter emptied it with one sweep of his finger, and it remained empty. Then the Eagle put the jointed plant to the Navaho's lips as if it were a wicker bottle, and the Indian drank his fill.

573. On the previous nights, while lying in the cave, the Navaho had slept between the eaglets in the nest to keep himself warm and shelter himself from the wind, and this plan had been of some help to him; but on this night the great Eagles slept one on each side of him, and he felt as warm as if he had slept among robes of fur. Before the Eagles lay down to sleep each took off his robe of plumes, which formed a single garment, opening in front, and revealed a form like that of a human being.

574. The Navaho slept well that night and did not waken till he heard a voice calling from the top of the cliff: "Where are you? The day has dawned. It is growing late. Why are you not abroad already?" At the sound of this voice the Eagles woke too and put on their robes of plumage. Presently a great number of birds were seen flying before the opening of the cave and others were heard calling to one another on the rock overhead. There were many kinds of Eagles and Hawks in the throng. Some of all the large birds of prey were there. Those on top of the rock sang: —

> Ki*n*nakíye, there he sits.
> When they fly up,
> We shall see him.
> He will flap his wings.[286]

575. One of the Eagles brought a dress of eagle plumes and was about to put it on the Navaho when the others interfered, and they had a long argument as to whether they should dress him in the garment of the Eagles or not; but at length they all flew away without giving him the dress. When they returned they had

thought of another plan for taking him out of the cave. Laying him on his face, they put a streak of crooked lightning under his feet, a sunbeam under his knees, a piece of straight lightning under his chest, another under his outstretched hands, and a rainbow under his forehead.

576. An Eagle then seized each end of these six supports, — making twelve Eagles in all, — and they flew with the Navaho and the eaglets away from the eyry. They circled round twice with their burden before they reached the level of the top of the cliff. They circled round twice more ascending, and then flew toward the south, still going upwards. When they got above the top of Tsótsíl (Mt. Taylor), they circled four times more, until they almost touched the sky. Then they began to flag and breathed hard, and they cried out: "We are weary. We can fly no farther." The voice of one, unseen to the Navaho, cried from above: "Let go your burden." The Eagles released their hold on the supports, and the Navaho felt himself descending swiftly toward the earth. But he had not fallen far when he felt himself seized around the waist and chest, he felt something twining itself around his body, and a moment later he beheld the heads of two Arrow-snakes [253] looking at him over his shoulders. The Arrow-snakes bore him swiftly upwards, up through the sky-hole, and landed him safely on the surface of the upper world above the sky.

577. When he looked around him he observed four pueblo dwellings, or towns: a white pueblo in the east, a blue pueblo in the south, a yellow pueblo in the west, and a black pueblo in the north. Wolf was the chief of the eastern pueblo, Blue Fox of the southern, Puma of the western, and Big Snake of the northern. The Navaho was left at liberty to go where he chose, but Wind whispered into his ear and said: "Visit, if you wish, all the pueblos except that of the north. Chicken Hawk [254] and other bad characters dwell there."

578. Next he observed that a war party was preparing, and soon after his arrival the warriors went forth. What enemies they sought he could not learn. He entered several of the houses, was well treated wherever he went, and given an abundance of paper bread and other good food to eat. He saw that in their homes the Eagles were just like ordinary people down on the lower world. As soon as they entered their pueblos they took off their feather suits, hung these up on pegs and poles, and went around in white suits which they wore underneath their feathers when in flight. He visited all the pueblos except the black one in the north. In the evening the warriors returned. They were received with loud wailing and with tears, for many who went out in the morning did not return at night. They had been slain in battle.

579. In a few days another war party was organized, and this time the Navaho determined to go with it. When the warriors started on the trail he followed them. "Whither are you going?" they asked. "I wish to be one of your party," he replied. They laughed at him and said: "You are a fool to think you can go to war against such dreadful enemies as those that we fight. We can move as fast as the wind, yet our enemies can move faster. If they are able to overcome us, what chance have you, poor man, for your life?" Hearing this, he remained behind, but they had not travelled far when he hurried after them. When he overtook them, which he soon did, they spoke to him angrily, told him more earnestly than before how helpless he was, and how great his danger, and bade him return to the villages. Again he halted; but as soon as they were out of sight he began to run after them, and he came up with them at the place where they had encamped for the night. Here they gave him of their food, and again they scolded him, and sought to dissuade him from accompanying them.

580. In the morning, when the warriors resumed their march, he remained behind on the camping-ground, as if he intended to return; but as soon as they were out of sight he proceeded again to follow them. He had not travelled far when he saw smoke coming up out of the ground, and approaching the smoke he found a smoke-hole, out of which stuck an old ladder, yellow with smoke, such as we see in the pueblo dwellings to-day. He looked down through the hole and beheld, in a subterranean chamber beneath, a strange-looking old woman with a big mouth. Her teeth were not set in her head evenly and regularly, like those of an Indian; they protruded from her mouth, were set at a distance from one another, and were curved like the claws of a bear. She was Nastsé Estsán, the Spider Woman. She invited him into her house, and he passed down the ladder.

581. When he got inside, the Spider Woman showed him four large wooden hoops, — one in the east colored black, one in the south colored blue, one in the west colored yellow, and one in the north white and sparkling. Attached to each hoop were a number of decayed, ragged feathers. "These feathers," said she, "were once beautiful plumes, but now they are old and dirty. I want some new plumes to adorn my hoops, and you can get them for me. Many of the Eagles will be killed in the battle to which you are going, and when they die you can pluck out the plumes and bring them to me. Have no fear of the enemies. Would you know who they are that the Eagles go to fight? They are only the bumblebees and the tumble-weeds." [256] She gave him a long black cane and said: "With this you can gather the tumble-weeds into a pile, and then you can

set them on fire. Spit the juice of tsĭldĭlgĭ'si [257] at the bees and they cannot sting you. But before you burn up the tumble-weeds gather some of the seeds, and when you have killed the bees take some of their nests. You will need these things when you return to the earth." When Spider Woman had done speaking the Navaho left to pursue his journey.

582. He travelled on, and soon came up with the warriors where they were hiding behind a little hill and preparing for battle. Some were putting on their plumes; others were painting and adorning themselves. From time to time one of their number would creep cautiously to the top of the hill and peep over; then he would run back and whisper: " There are the enemies. They await us." The Navaho went to the top of the hill and peered over; but he could see no enemy whatever. He saw only a dry, sandy flat, covered in one place with sunflowers, and in another place with dead weeds; for it was now late in the autumn in the world above.

583. Soon the Eagles were all ready for the fray. They raised their war-cry, and charged over the hill into the sandy plain. The Navaho remained behind the hill, peeping over to see what would occur. As the warriors approached the plain a whirlwind arose; [258] a great number of tumble-weeds ascended with the wind and surged around madly through the air; and, at the same time, from among the sunflowers a cloud of bumblebees arose. The Eagles charged through the ranks of their enemies, and when they had passed to the other side they turned around and charged back again. Some spread their wings and soared aloft to attack the tumble-weeds that had gone up with the whirlwind. From time to time the Navaho noticed the dark body of an Eagle falling down through the air. When the combat had continued some time, the Navaho noticed a few of the Eagles running toward the hill where he lay watching. In a moment some more came running toward him, and soon after the whole party of Eagles, all that was left of it, rushed past him, in a disorderly retreat, in the direction whence they had come, leaving many slain on the field. Then the wind fell; the tumble-weeds lay quiet again on the sand, and the bumblebees disappeared among the sunflowers.

584. When all was quiet, the Navaho walked down to the sandy flat, and, having gathered some of the seeds and tied them up in a corner of his shirt, he collected the tumble-weeds into a pile, using his black wand. Then he took out his fire-drill, started a flame, and burnt up the whole pile. He gathered some tsĭldĭlgĭ'si, as the Spider Woman had told him, chewed it, and went in among the sunflowers. Here the bees gathered around him in a great swarm, and sought to sting him; but he spat the juice of the tsĭldĭlgĭ'si at them and

stunned with it all that he struck. Soon the most of them lay helpless on the ground, and the others fled in fear. He went around
with his black wand and killed all that he could find. He dug into
the ground and got out some of their nests and honey; he took a
couple of the young bees and tied their feet together, and all these
things he put into the corner of his blanket. When the bees were
conquered he did not forget the wishes of his friend, the Spider
Woman ; he went around among the dead eagles, and plucked as
many plumes as he could grasp in both hands.

585. He set out on his return journey, and soon got back to the
house of Spider Woman. He gave her the plumes and she said :
"Thank you, my grandchild, you have brought me the plumes that
I have long wanted to adorn my walls, and you have done a great
service to your friends, the Eagles, because you have slain their enemies." When she had spoken he set out again on his journey.

586. He slept that night on the trail, and next morning he got
back to the towns of the Eagles. As he approached he heard from
afar the cries of the mourners, and when he entered the place the
people gathered around him and said: "We have lost many of our
kinsmen, and we are wailing for them ; but we have been also
mourning for you, for those who returned told us you had been
killed in the fight."

587. He made no reply, but took from his blanket the two young
bumblebees and swung them around his head. All the people were
terrified and ran, and they did not stop running till they got safely
behind their houses. In a little while they got over their fear, came
slowly from behind their houses, and crowded around the Navaho
again. A second time he swung the bees around his head, and a
second time the people ran away in terror ; but this time they only
went as far as the front walls of their houses, and soon they returned
again to the Navaho. The third time that he swung the bees
around his head they were still less frightened, ran but half way to
their houses, and returned very soon. The fourth time that he
swung the bees they only stepped back a step or two. When their
courage came back to them, he laid the two bees on the ground ;
he took out the seeds of the tumble-weeds and laid them on the
ground beside the bees, and then he said to the Eagle People: "My
friends, here are the children of your enemies ; when you see these
you may know that I have slain your enemies." There was great
rejoicing among the people when they heard this, and this one said :
"It is well. They have slain my brother," and that one said : "It is
well. They have slain my father," and another said : "It is well.
They have slain my sons." Then Great Wolf, chief of the white
pueblo, said : "I have two beautiful maiden daughters whom I shall

give to you." Then Fox, chief of the blue pueblo in the south, promised him two more maidens, and the chiefs of the other pueblos promised him two each, so that eight beautiful maidens were promised to him in marriage.

588. The chief of the white pueblo now conducted the Navaho to his house and into a large and beautiful apartment, the finest the poor Indian had ever seen. It had a smooth wall, nicely coated with white earth, a large fireplace, mealing-stones, beautiful pots and water-jars, and all the conveniences and furniture of a beautiful pueblo home. And the chief said to him : " *Sad́ani*, my son-in-law, this house is yours."

589. The principal men from all the pueblos now came to visit him, and thanked him for the great service he had done for them. Then his maidens from the yellow house came in bringing corn meal ; the maidens from the black house entered bringing soapweed, and the maidens of the white house, where he was staying, came bearing a large bowl of white shell. A suds of the soap-weed was prepared in the shell bowl. The maidens of the white house washed his head with the suds ; the maidens of the black house washed his limbs and feet, and those of the yellow house dried him with corn meal. When the bath was finished the maidens went out ; but they returned at dark, accompanied this time by the maidens of the blue house. Each of the eight maidens carried a large bowl of food, and each bowl contained food of a different kind. They laid the eight bowls down before the Navaho, and he ate of all till he was satisfied. Then they brought in beautiful robes and blankets, and spread them on the floor for his bed.

590. Next morning the Navaho went over to the sky-hole, taking with him the young bees and the seeds of the tumble-weeds. To the former he said : "Go down to the land of the Navahoes and multiply there. My people will make use of you in the days to come ; but if you ever cause them sorrow and trouble, as you have caused the people of this land, I shall again destroy you." As he spoke, he flung them down to the earth. Then taking the seeds of the tumble-weeds in his hands, he spoke to them as he had spoken to the bees, and threw them down through the sky-hole. The honey of the bees and the seeds of the tumble-weeds are now used in the rites of yói *hat́al*, or the bead chant.

591. The Navaho remained in the pueblos of the Eagle People twenty-four days, during which time he was taught the songs, prayers, ceremonies, and sacrifices of the Eagles, the same as those now known to us in the rite of yói *hat́al*;[259] and when he had learned all, the people told him it was time for him to return to the earth, whence he had come.

592. They put on him a robe of eagle plumage, such as they wore themselves, and led him to the sky-hole. They said to him: "When you came up from the lower world you were heavy and had to be carried by others. Henceforth you will be light and can move through the air with your own power." He spread his wings to show that he was ready; the Eagles blew a powerful breath behind him; he went down through the sky-hole, and was wafted down on his outstretched wings until he lit on the summit of Tsótsĭ*l*.

593. He went back to his own relations among the Navahoes; but when he went back everything about their lodge smelt ill; its odors were intolerable to him, and he left it and sat outside.[260] They built for him then a medicine-lodge where he might sit by himself. They bathed his younger brother, clothed him in new raiment, and sent him, too, into the lodge, to learn what his elder brother could tell him. The brothers spent twelve days in the lodge together, during which the elder brother told his story and instructed the younger in all the rites and songs learned among the Eagles.

594. After this he went to visit the pueblo of Kĭntyél, whose inmates had before contemplated such treachery to him; but they did not recognize him. He now looked sleek and well fed. He was beautifully dressed and comely in his person, for the Eagles had moulded, in beauty, his face and form. The pueblo people never thought that this was the poor beggar whom they had left to die in the eagles' nest. He noticed that there were many sore and lame in the pueblo. A new disease, they told him, had broken out among them. This was the disease which they had caught from the feathers of the eaglets when they were attacking the nest. "I have a brother," said the Navaho, "who is a potent shaman. He knows a rite that will cure this disease." The people of the pueblo consulted together and concluded to employ his brother to perform the ceremony over their suffering ones.

595. The Navaho said that he must be one of the atsá*'l*ei,[261] or first dancers, and that in order to perform the rite properly he must be dressed in a very particular way. He must, he said, have strings of fine beads — shell and turquoise — sufficient to cover his legs and forearms completely, enough to go around his neck, so that he could not bend his head back, and great strings to pass over the shoulder and under the arm on each side. He must have the largest shell basin to be found in either pueblo to hang on his back, and the one next in size to hang on his chest. He must have their longest and best strings of turquoise to hang to his ears. The Wind told him that the greatest shell basin they had was so large that if he tried to embrace it around the edge, his finger-tips would scarcely

meet on the opposite side, and that this shell he must insist on having. The next largest shell, Wind told him, was but little smaller.[262]

596. Three days after this conference, people began to come in from different pueblos in the Chaco Canyon and from pueblos on the banks of the San Juan, — all these pueblos are now in ruins, — and soon a great multitude had assembled. Meantime, too, they collected shells and beads from the various pueblos in order to dress the atsá'*l*ei as he desired. They brought him some great shell basins and told him these were what he wanted for the dance; but he measured them with his arms as Wind had told him, and, finding that his hands joined easily when he embraced the shells, he discarded them. They brought him larger and larger shells, and tried to persuade him that such were their largest; but he tried and rejected all. On the last day, with reluctance, they brought him the great shell of Kĭntyél and the great shell of Kĭ'n*d*ot*l*ĭ*z*. He clasped the first in his arms; his fingers did not meet on the opposite side. He clasped the second in his arms, and the tips of his fingers just met. "These," said he, "are the shells I must wear when I dance."

597. Four days before that on which the last dance was to occur, the pueblo people sent out messengers to the neighboring camps

Fig. 37. Circle of branches of the rite of the mountain chant, after ceremony is over.

of Navahoes, to invite the latter to witness the exhibition of the last night and to participate in it with some of their alíli (dances or dramas). One of the messengers went to the Chelly Canyon and there he got Gá*n*askĭ*d*i, with his son and daughter, to come and perform a dance. The other messengers started for the Navaho camp at the foot of Tsótsĭ*l* on the south (near where Cobero is now). On his way he met an akáni̇nïli, or messenger, coming from Tsótsi̇*l* to invite the people of the Chaco Canyon to a great Navaho ceremony. (You have heard all about the meeting of these messengers in the legend of the mountain chant. I shall not now repeat it.) [263] The messengers exchanged bows and quivers as a sign they had met one another, and the messenger from K̓intyél returned to his people without being able to get the Navahoes to attend. This is the reason that, on the last night of the great ceremony of yói *halál*, there are but few different dances or shows.

598. On the evening of the last day they built a great circle of branches, such as the Navahoes build now for the rites of the mountain chant (fig. 37), and a great number of people crowded into the inclosure. They lighted the fires and dressed the atsá'*l*ei in all their fine beads and shells just as he desired them to dress him. They put the great shell of K̓intyél on his back, and the great shell of K̓i̇'n*do*l̄i̇z on his chest, and another fine shell on his forehead. Then the Navaho began to dance, and his brother, the medicine-man, began to sing, and this was the song he sang : —

> The white-corn plant's great ear sticks up.
> Stay down and eat.
>
> The blue-corn plant's great ear sticks up.
> Stay down and eat.
>
> The yellow-corn plant's great ear sticks up.
> Stay down and eat.
>
> The black-corn plant's great ear sticks up.
> Stay down and eat.
>
> All-colored corn's great ear sticks up.
> Stay down and eat.
>
> The round-eared corn's great ear sticks up.
> Stay down and eat.[287]

599. This seemed a strange song to the pueblo people, and they all wondered what it could mean ; but they soon found out what it meant, for they observed that the dancing Navaho was slowly rising from the ground. First his head and then his shoulders appeared above the heads of the crowd ; next his chest and waist ; but it was not until his whole body had risen above the level of their heads that they began to realize the loss that threatened them. He was rising toward the sky with the great shell of K̓intyél, and all the wealth of many pueblos in shell-beads and turquoise on his body. Then they screamed wildly to him and called him by all sorts of dear names — father, brother, son — to come down again, but the

more they called the higher he rose. When his feet had risen above them they observed that a streak of white lightning passed under his feet like a rope, and hung from a dark cloud that gathered above. It was the gods that were lifting him ; for thus, the legends say, the gods lift mortals to the sky. When the pueblos found that no persuasions could induce the Navaho to return, some called for ropes that they might seize him and pull him down ; but he was soon beyond the reach of their longest rope. Then a shout was raised for arrows that they might shoot him ; but before the arrows could come he was lost to sight in the black cloud and was never more seen on earth.

NOTES.

NOTES.

1. How and when the name Navajo (pronounced Nă'vă-ho) originated has not been discovered. It is only known that this name was given by the Spaniards while they still claimed the Navaho land. The name is generally supposed to be derived from navaja, which means a clasp-knife, or razor, and to have been applied because the Navaho warriors carried great stone knives in former days. It has been suggested that the name comes from navájo, a pool or small lake. The Navahoes call themselves *Dïné'* or *Dïné*, which means simply, men, people. This word in the various forms, Dénè, Tinnéh, Tunné, etc., is used as a tribal designation for many branches of the Athapascan stock.

2. The Carrizo Mountains consist of an isolated mountain mass, about 12 miles in its greatest diameter, situated in the northeast corner of Arizona. It is called by the Navahoes Dsĭ*l*náodsĭ*l*, which means mountain surrounded by mountains; such is the appearance of the landscape viewed from the highest point, Pastora Peak, 9,420 feet high.

3. The San Juan River, a branch of the Colorado of the West, flows in a westerly direction through the northern portion of the Navaho Reservation, and forms in part its northern boundary. It is the most important river in the Navaho country. It has two names in the Navaho language : one is Sá*n*bĭ*t*o' (Water of Old Age, or Old Age River), said to be given because the stream is white with foam and looks like the hair of an old man; the other is *T*o'baká (Male Water), given because it is turbulent and strong in contrast to the placid Rio Grande, which the Navahoes call *T*o'baád, or Female Water. (See note 137.) Perhaps the river has other names.

4. *T*u-ĭn-t*s*á is derived from *t*o' or *t*u (water) and ĭnt*s*á or ĭnt*s*á (abundant, scattered widely). The name is spelled Tuincha, Tuintcha, and Tunicha on our maps. The Tuincha Mountains are situated partly in New Mexico and partly in Arizona, about 30 miles from the northern boundary of both Territories. They form the middle portion of a range of which the Chusca and Lukachokai Mountains form the rest. The portion known as *T*uĭnt*s*á is about 12 miles long. The highest point is 9,575 feet above sea-level. The top of the range, which is rather level and plateau-like, is well covered with timber, mostly spruce and pine, and abounds in small lakes and ponds; hence the name *T*uĭnt*s*á.

5. The basket illustrated in fig. 16 is made of twigs of aromatic sumac (*Rhus aromatica*, var. *trilobata*). It is 13' in diameter and 3⅜' deep. In forming the helical coil, the fabricator must always put the butt end of the twig toward the centre of the basket and the tip end toward the periphery, in accordance with the ceremonial laws governing the disposition of butts and tips (see notes 12 and 319). The sole decoration is a band, red in the middle with black zigzag edges. This band is intersected at one point by a narrow line of uncolored wood. This line has probably no relation to the "line of life" in ancient and modern pueblo pottery. It is put there to assist in the orientation of the basket at night, in the dim light of the medicine-lodge. In making the basket, the butt of the first twig is placed in the centre; the tip of the last twig, in the helix, must be in the same radial line, which is marked by the uncolored line crossing the ornamental band.

This line must lie due east and west on certain ceremonial occasions, as for instance when the basket, inverted, is used as a drum during the last five nights of the night chant. The margin of this, as of other Navaho baskets, is finished in a diagonally woven or plaited pattern, and there is a legend, which the author has related in a former paper,[321] accounting for the origin of this form of margin. If the margin is worn through or torn, the basket is unfit for sacred use. The basket is one of the perquisites of the shaman when the rites are done ; but he, in turn, must give it away, and must be careful never to eat out of it. Notwithstanding its sacred uses, food may be served in it. Fig. 25 represents a basket of this kind used as a receptacle for sacrificial sticks and cigarettes. In this case the termination of the helix must be in the east, and the sacrifices sacred to the east must be in the eastern quarter of the basket.

Fig. 17 shows the other form of sacred basket. It is also made of aromatic sumac, and is used in the rites to hold sacred meal. The crosses are said to represent clouds, and the zigzag lines to indicate lightning.

6. The ceremonies of " House Dedication " are described at some length by Mr. A. M. Stephen in his excellent paper on " The Navajo," [329] and he gives a free translation of a prayer and a song belonging to these rites.

7. A-na-yé, or a-ná-ye, is composed of two words, aná and yéi or ye. Aná, sometimes contracted to na, signifies a member of an alien tribe, — one not speaking a language similar to the Navaho, — and is often synonymous with enemy. Ye (see par. 78) may be defined as genius or god. The anáye were the offspring of women conceived during the separation of the sexes in the fourth world.

8. Ti-é-hol-tso-di is a water god, or water monster, a god of terrestrial waters, — not a rain god. He seems akin to the Unktehi of the Dakotas. He is said to dwell in the great water of the east, *i. e.*, the Atlantic Ocean. Although commonly spoken of as one, there is little doubt that the Navahoes believe in many of the Tiéholtsodi. Probably every constant stream or spring has its own water god, (See note 152.) A picture of this god is said to be made in a dry-painting of the rite of *hozóni hatál*, but the author has not seen it. Tiéholtsodi is described as having a fine fur, and being otherwise much like an otter in appearance, but having horns like a buffalo. (See pars. 140, 187, 484, 485.)

9. Tsús-kai or Tsó-is-kai is the name given by the Navahoes to a prominent conical hill rising 8,800 feet above sea-level, in northwestern New Mexico, about twenty-six miles north of Defiance Station on the Atlantic and Pacific Railroad. It is called Chusca Knoll, Chusca Peak, and Choiskai Peak by geographers. It rises abruptly four hundred feet or more above the level of the neighboring ridge. is visible at a great distance from the south (but not from the north), and forms a prominent landmark. The Navahoes limit the name Tsúskai to this knoll, but the Mexicans, and following them the Americans, apply the name in different forms (Chusca Mountains, Sierra de Chusca, Chuska, Chuskai, Tchuskai, etc.) to the whole mountain mass from which the knoll rises. The name, not accurately translated, contains the words for spruce (tso) and white (kai).

10. The bath forms an important part of the Navaho rites, being administered on many occasions, and it is often mentioned in the tales. It usually consists of a suds made in a water-tight wicker basket by soaking the root of some species of yucca (see note 88) in water ; the root of *Yucca baccata* being usually preferred, as it seems richest in saponine. After the application of the suds, the subject is commmonly rinsed off with plain water and dried by rubbing on corn meal. In different ceremonies different observances are connected with the bath. In the myth of " The Mountain Chant," [314] pp. 389, 390, a bath is described as part of the ceremony of the deer-hunt. It is given, no doubt, in preparing for the hunt, for practical as well as religious reasons. It is important that the hunter should divest himself as much as possible of his personal odor when he goes to kill game.

11. Pollen (Navaho, *thadítín*) is obtained, for sacred uses, from various plants, but Indian corn is the chief source of supply. The pollen is carried in small buckskin bags, which also usually contain small sacred stones, such as rock crystal and pyrophyllite, or small animal fetiches. The administration or sacrifice of pollen is a part of all rites witnessed, and almost always follows or accompanies prayer. It is used in different ways on different occasions ; but the commonest way is to take a small pinch from the bag, apply a portion of it to the tongue and a portion to the crown of the head. For some purposes, the shaman collects a quantity of pollen, puts it in a large bag, immerses in it some live bird, insect, or other animal, and then allows the prisoner to escape. This is supposed to add extra virtue to the pollen. In one kind called i'yidĕzná a bluebird, a yellowbird, and a grasshopper are put in the pollen together. In note 49 we have a mythic account of pollen put on the young of the sea monster and then preserved. Pollen which has been applied to a ceremonial dry-painting is preserved for future uses. Pollen in which a live striped lizard has been placed is used to favor eutocia. The term *thadítín* is applied to various things having the appearance of an impalpable powder, such as the misty hues of the horizon in the morning and evening, due in Arizona more frequently to dust in the air than to moisture. Captain Bourke, in " The Medicine-men of the Apache," [295] chapter ii., describes many modes of using pollen which exist also among the Navahoes.

12. The following are a few additional observances with regard to kethawns : —

In cutting the reed used for a series of cigarettes, they cut off a piece first from the end nearest the root, and they continue to cut off as many pieces as may be necessary from butt to point. The pieces, according as they are cut, are notched near the butt (with a stone knife), so that the relations of the two extremities of the piece may not be forgotten. All through the painting of the cigarettes, and the various manipulations that follow, the butt end must be the nearer to the operator, and the tip end the farther away from him. Since the cigarette-maker sits in the west of the medicine-lodge facing the east, the cigarettes, while there, must lie east and west, with the tips to the east. If a number of cigarettes are made for one act of sacrifice, the first piece cut off is marked with one notch near the base, the second piece with two notches, the third piece with three notches, the fourth piece with four notches, all near the butt ends. This is done in order that they may always be distinguished from one another, and their order of precedence from butt to tip may not be disregarded. When they are taken up to be painted, to have the sacred feathers of the bluebird and yellowbird inserted into them, to be filled with tobacco, to be sealed with moistened pollen, or to be symbolically lighted with the rock crystal, the piece that came from nearest the butt (the senior cigarette, let us call it) is taken first, that nearest the tip last. When they are collected to be placed in the patient's hands, when they are applied to his or her person, and finally when they are taken out and sacrificed, this order of precedence is always observed. The order of precedence in position, when sacrifices are laid out in a straight row, is from north to south ; the senior sacrifice is in the northern extremity of the row, the junior or inferior in the southern extremity. When they are laid out in a circle, the order is from east back to east by the way of the south, west, and north. The gods to whom the sacrifices are made have commonly also an order of precedence, and when such is the case the senior sacrifice is dedicated to the higher god, the junior sacrifice to the lower god. When it is required that other articles, such as feathers, beads, powdered vegetable and mineral substances, be sacrificed with the cigarettes, all these things are placed in corn-husks. To do this, the husks are laid down on a clean cloth with their tips to the east; the cigarettes are laid in them one by one, each in a separate husk, with their tip ends to the east; and the sacred feathers are added to the bundle with their tips also to the east. When dry pollen is sprinkled on the cigarette, it is sprinkled from butt to tip. When moist pollen is daubed on the side of the cigarette, it is daubed from butt to tip. (From " A Study in Butts and Tips.")[819] The hollow internode of the reed only is used. The part containing the solid node is discarded and is split up, so that when thrown away the gods may not mistake it for a true cigarette and suffer disappointment. All the débris of manufacture is carefully collected and deposited to the north of the medicine-lodge. The tobacco of commerce must not be employed. A plug of feathers, referred to above, is shoved into the tube from tip to butt (with an owl's feather) to keep the tobacco from falling out at the butt. The moistened pollen keeps the tobacco in at the tip end. The rules for measuring kethawns are very elaborate. One or more finger-joints; the span; the width of the outstretched hand, from tip of thumb to tip of little finger; the width of three finger-tips or of four finger-tips joined, — are a few of the measurements. Each kethawn has its established size. This system of sacrifice is common among the pueblo tribes of the Southwest, and traces of it have been found elsewhere. Fig. 23 represents a thing called ke*t*án yal*t*í, or talking kethawn (described in " The Mountain Chant,"[814] p. 452), consisting of a male stick painted black and a female stick painted blue. Fig. 24 shows a kethawn used in the ceremony of the night chant; a dozen such are made for one occasion, but male and female are not distinguished. Fig. 25 depicts a set of fifty-two kethawns, used also in the night chant : of these the four in the centre are cigarettes lying on meal ; the forty-eight surrounding the meal are sticks of wood. Those in the east are made of mountain mahogany, those in the south of *Forestiera neo-mexicana*, those in the west of juniper, and those in the north of cherry. A more elaborate description of them must be reserved for a future work.

13. " Sacred buckskin " is a term employed by the author, for convenience, to designate those deerskins specially prepared for use in making masks and for other purposes in the Navaho rites. The following are some of the particulars concerning their preparation; perhaps there are others which the author has not learned: The deer which is to furnish the skin must not be shot, or otherwise wounded. It is surrounded by men on foot or horseback, and caused to run around until it falls exhausted ; then a bag containing pollen is put over its mouth and nostrils, and held there till the deer is smothered. The dead animal is laid on its back. Lines are marked with pollen, from the centre outwards along the median line of the body and the insides of the limbs. Incisions are made with a stone knife along the pollen lines, from within outwards, until the skin is opened; the flaying may then be completed with a steel knife. When the skin is removed it is laid to the east of the carcass, head to the east, and hairy side down. The fibulæ and ulnæ are cut out and put in the skin in the places where they belong, — *i. e.*, each ulna in the skin of its appropriate fore-leg, each fibula in the skin of its appropriate hind-leg. The hide may then be rolled up and carried off. Both ulnæ are used as scrapers of the skin. If masks are to be made of the skin, the fibulæ are used as awls, — the right fibula in sewing the right sides of the masks, the left fibula in sewing the left sides of the masks. Other rules (very numerous) for making the masks will not be mentioned in this place. Fibulæ and ulnæ other than those belonging to the deer that furnished the skin must not be used on the latter.

14. This mask, made of leaves of *Yucca baccata*, from which the thick dorsal portions have been torn away, is used in the rite of the night chant. The observances connected with the culling of the leaves, the manufacture of the mask, and the destruction of the same after use, are too numerous to be detailed here. The author never succeeded in getting such a mask to keep (the obligation on the shaman to tear it up when it has served its purpose seemed imperative), but he

was allowed to take two photographs of it, one before the fringe of spruce twigs was applied, the other when the mask was finished, as shown in fig. 26.

15. The following account taken from " The Prayer of a Navajo Shaman," [315] and repeated here at the request of Mr. Newell, shows how definitely fixed was the limit of this part of the tale in the mind of the narrator: —

" In none of my interviews with him (*Hatá*/i Nĕz) had he shown any impatience with my demands for explanations as we progressed, or with interruptions in our work. He lingered long over his meals, lighted many cigarettes and smoked them leisurely, got tired early in the evening, and was always willing to go to bed as early as I would let him. When, however, he came to relate the creation myth, all this was changed. He arrived early; he remained late; he hastened through his meals; he showed evidence of worry at all delays and interruptions, and frequently begged me to postpone minor explanations. On being urged to explain this change of spirit he said that we were travelling in the land of the dead, in a place of evil and potent ghosts, just so long as he continued to relate those parts of the myth which recount the adventures of his ancestors in the nether world, and that we were in danger so long as our minds remained there; but that when we came to that part of the tale where the people ascend to this — the fifth and last world — we need no longer feel uneasy and could then take our time. His subsequent actions proved that he had given an honest explanation.

" It was near sunset one afternoon, and an hour or more before his supper time, that he concluded his account of the subterranean wanderings of the Navajos and brought them safely through the " Place of Emergence," in the San Juan Mountains, to the surface of this world. Then he ceased to speak, rolled a cigarette, said he was tired, that he would not be able to tell me any more that night, and left me.

" After his departure I learned that he had announced to some of his friends during the day that he would have to pray at night to counteract the evil effects of his journey through the lower world. After his supper he retired to the apartment among the old adobe huts at Defiance in which he had been assigned room to sleep. I soon followed, and, having waited in the adjoining passage half an hour or more, I heard the voice of the old man rising in the monotonous tones of formulated prayer. Knowing that the rules of the shaman forbade the interruption of any prayer or song, I abruptly entered the room and sat down on the floor near the supplicant."

(Thus the prayer in question became known to the author.)

15*a*. " Tune us the sitar neither low nor high." — *The Light of Asia.*

16. *Hatá*/, in Navaho, means a sacred song, a hymn or chant, — not a trivial song: hence the names of their great ceremonies contain this word, as dsĭ/yĭ´dze *hatá*/ (the mountain chant); klédzi *hatá*/ (the night chant), etc. The man who conducts a ceremony is called *hatá*/i (chanter or singer). As equivalents for this word the author uses the terms shaman, priest, medicine-man, and chanter. One who treats disease by drugs is called azé-elĭ´ni, or medicine-maker.

17. No antecedent. We are first told to whom " they " refers in paragraph 139.

18. In symbolizing by color the four cardinal points, the Navahoes have two principal systems, as follows: —

	East.	South.	West.	North.
First System	White.	Blue.	Yellow.	Black.
Second System . . .	Black.	Blue.	Yellow.	White.

Both systems are the same, except that the colors black and white change places. The reasons for this change have not been satisfactorily determined. In general, it seems that when speaking of places over ground — lucky and happy places — the first system is employed; while, when places underground — usually places of danger — are described, the second system is used. But there are many apparent exceptions to the latter rule. In one version of the Origin Legend (Version B) the colors are arranged according to the second system both in the lower and upper worlds. In the version of the same legend here published the first system is given for all places in the lower worlds, except in the house of Tiéholtsodi under the waters (par. 178), where the east room is described as dàrk and the room in the north as being of all colors. Yet the Indian who gave this version (*Hatáli* Nĕz), in his Prayer of the Rendition (note 315), applies the second system to all regions traversed below the surface of the earth by the gods who come to rescue the lost soul. Although he does not say that the black chamber is in the east, he shows it corresponds with the east by mentioning it first. *Hatáli* Natlói, in the "Story of Na*tl*'nĕs*th*ani," follows the first system in all cases except when describing the house of Tiéholtsodi under the water, where the first chamber is represented as black and the last as white. Although in this case the rooms may be regarded as placed one above another, the black being mentioned first shows that it is intended to correspond with the east. In all cases, in naming the points of the compass, or anything which symbolizes them, or in placing objects which pertain to them (note 227), the east comes first, the south second, the west third, the north fourth. The sunwise circuit is always followed. If the zenith and nadir are mentioned, the former comes fifth and the latter sixth in order. The north is sometimes symbolized by "all colors," *i. e.*, white, blue, yellow, and black mixed (note 22), and sometimes by red. In the myth of dsĭ*l*/yĭ'dze *hatál* [314] (the story of Dsĭ'*l*yi' Neyáni) five homes of holy people underground are described, in all of which the second system is used. See, also, note 111, where the second system is applied to the house of the sun. In the story of the "Great Shell of Kĭntyél" at the home of the Spider Woman underground, in the sky world, the east is represented by black and the north by white. (See par. 581 and note 40.)

19. There are but three streams and but nine villages or localities mentioned, while twelve winged tribes are named. Probably three are supposed to have lived in the north where no stream ran, or there may have been a fourth river in the Navaho paradise, whose name is for some reason suppressed.

References to the sacred number four are introduced with tiresome pertinacity into all Navaho legends.

20. Version B.—In the first world three dwelt, viz.: First Man, First Woman, and Coyote.

21. The swallow to which reference is made here is the cliff swallow, — *Petrochelidon lunifrons.*

22. The colors given to the lower worlds in this legend — red for the first, blue for the second, yellow for the third, and mixed for the fourth — are not in the line of ordinary Navaho symbolism (note 18), but they agree very closely with some Moki symbolism, as described by Victor Mindeleff in his "Study of Pueblo Architecture," [324] p. 129. The colors there mentioned, if placed in order according to the Navaho system (note 18), would stand thus: red (east), blue (south), yellow (west), white (north). Mixed colors sometimes take the place of the north or last in Navaho symbolism. Possibly Moki elements have entered into this version of the Navaho legend. (See par. 91.)

23. Version B.—In the second world, when First Man, First Woman, and Coyote ascended, they found those who afterwards carried the sun and moon, and, beyond the bounds of the earth, he of the darkness in the east, he of the blue-

ness in the south, he of the yellowness in the west, and he of the whiteness in the north (perhaps the same as White Body, Blue Body, etc., of the fourth world in the present version. See par. 160). Sun and First Woman were the transgressors who caused the exodus.

24. Version B.—When the five individuals mentioned in note 23 came from the second world, they found the "people of the mountains" already occupying the third world.

25. Version B.—The people were chased from the third world to the fourth world by a deluge and took refuge in a reed, as afterwards related of the flight from the fourth world.

26. In the Navaho tales, when the yéi (genii, gods) come to visit men, they always announce their approach by calling four times. The first call is faint, far, and scarcely audible. Each succeeding call is louder and more distinct. The last call sounds loud and near, and in a moment after it is heard the god makes his appearance. These particulars concerning the gods' approach are occasionally briefly referred to; but usually the story-teller repeats them at great length with a modulated voice, and he pantomimically represents the recipient of the visit, starting and straining his attention to discern the distant sounds.

Nearly every god has his own special call. A few have none. Imperfect attempts have been made in this work to represent some of these calls by spelling them; but this method represents the original no better than "Bob White" represents the call of a quail. Some of the cries have been recorded by the writer on phonographic cylinders, but even these records are very imperfect. In the ceremonies of the Navahoes, the masked representatives of the gods repeat these calls. The calls of *H* astséyal*t*i and *H*asts*é*ho*g*an are those most frequently referred to in the tales. (Pars. 287, 378, 471, etc.)

27. Yellow corn belongs to the female, white corn to the male. This rule is observed in all Navaho ceremonies, and is mentioned in many Navaho myths. (Pars. 164, 291, 379; note 107, etc.)

28. An ear of corn used for sacred purposes must be completely covered with full grains, or at least must have been originally so covered. One having abortive grains at the top is not used. For some purposes, as in preparing the implements used in initiating females in the rite of kléd*z*i *h*atá*l*, not only must the ear of corn be fully covered by grains, but it must be tipped by an arrangement of four grains. Such an ear of corn is called *t*ohono*t*i'ni.

29. The Navaho word nátli or nŭ'tle is here translated hermaphrodite, because the context shows that reference is made to anomalous creatures. But the word is usually employed to designate that class of men, known perhaps in all wild Indian tribes, who dress as women, and perform the duties usually allotted to women in Indian camps. Such persons are called berdaches (English, bardash) by the French Canadians. By the Americans they are called hermaphrodites (commonly mispronounced "morphodites"), and are generally supposed to be such.

30. These so-called hermaphrodites (note 29) are, among all Indian tribes that the author has observed, more skilful in performing women's work than the women themselves. The Navahoes, in this legend, credit them with the invention of arts practised by women. The best weaver in the Navaho tribe, for many years, was a nátli.

31. Masks made from the skins of deer-heads and antelope-heads, with or without antlers, have been used by various Indian tribes, in hunting, to deceive the animals and allow the hunters to approach them. There are several references to such masks in the Navaho tales, as in the story of Na*t*í'nĕs*t*/ani (par. 544) and in the myth of "The Mountain Chant," page 391.[314] In the latter story, rites connected with the deer mask are described.

32. The quarrel between First Man and First Woman came to pass in this way: When she had finished her meal she wiped her hands in her dress and said: "E'yéhe ṣi-tṣoḍ" (Thanks, my vagina). "What is that you say?" asked First Man. "E'yéhe ṣi-tṣoḍ," she repeated. "Why do you speak thus?" he queried; "Was it not I who killed the deer whose flesh you have eaten? Why do you not thank me? Was it tṣoḍ that killed the deer?" "Yes," she replied; "if it were not for that, you would not have killed the deer. If it were not for that, you lazy men would do nothing. It is that which does all the work." "Then, perhaps, you women think you can live without the men," he said. "Certainly we can. It is we women who till the fields and gather food: we can live on the produce of our fields, and the seeds and fruits we collect. We have no need of you men." Thus they argued. First Man became more and more angry with each reply that his wife made, until at length, in wrath, he jumped across the fire.

33. During the separation of the sexes, both the men and the women were guilty of shameful practices, which the story-tellers very particularly describe. Through the transgressions of the women the anáye, alien gods or monsters, who afterwards nearly annihilated the human race, came into existence; but no evil consequences followed the transgressions of the men. Thus, as usual, a moral lesson is conveyed to the women, but none to the men.

34, 35. Notes 34 and 35 are omitted.

36. Version A. — Water in the east, black; south, blue; west, yellow; north, white. In the ceremony of *hozóni hatál* a picture representing Tiéholtsodi and the four waters is said to be made.

37. Version A says that the nodes were woven by the spider, and that different animals dwelt in the different internodes. Version B says that the great reed took more than one day to grow to the sky; that it grew by day and rested by night; that the hollow internodes now seen in the reed show where it grew by day, and the solid nodes show where it rested by night. Some say four reeds were planted to form one, others that one reed only was planted.

38. Version B. — The Turkey was the last to take refuge in the reed, therefore he was at the bottom. When the waters rose high enough to wet the Turkey he gobbled, and all knew that danger was near. Often did the waves wash the end of his tail; and it is for this reason that the tips of turkeys' tail-feathers are, to this day, lighter than the rest of the plumage.

39. Version A. — First Man and First Woman called on all the digging animals (I'ndatṣidi ḍáltso) to help. These were: Bear, Wolf, Coyote, Lynx, and Badger. First, Bear dug till he was tired; then Coyote took his place, and so on. When badger was digging, water began to drip down from above: then they knew they had struck the waters of the upper world, and sent Locust up. Locust made a sort of shaft in the soft mud, such as locusts make to this day.

40. Version A says there were four cranes; Version B, that there were four swans. Both versions say that the bird of the east was black, that of the south blue, that of the west yellow, and that of the north white. (See note 18.)

41. Two versions, A and B, have it that the bird passed the arrows through from mouth to vent, and *vice versa*, but all make the Locust pass his arrows through his thorax. Another version relates that two of the birds said: "You can have the land if you let us strike you in the forehead with an axe." Locust consented. They missed their aim and cut off his cheeks, which accounts for his narrow face now. Version A relates that the arrows were plumed with eagle-feathers.

42. Version A. — The Locust, before transfixing himself with the arrows, shoved his vitals down into his abdomen; then he changed his mind and shoved them high into his chest. That accounts for his big chest now.

43. A small lake situated somewhere in the San Juan Mountains is said to be the place through which the people came from the fourth world to this world. It is surrounded, the Indians tell, by precipitous cliffs, and has a small island near its centre, from the top of which something rises that looks like the top of a ladder. Beyond the bounding cliffs there are four mountain peaks, — one to the east, one to the south, one to the west, and one to the north of the lake, — which are frequently referred to in the songs and myths of the Navahoes. These Indians fear to visit the shores of this lake, but they climb the surrounding mountains and view its waters from a distance. The place is called *Ha*-dẓi-naí, or Ni-*ho*-yos-tsá-tse, which names may be freely translated Place of Emergence, or Land Where They Came Up. The San Juan Mountains abound in little lakes. Which one of these is considered by the Navahoes as their Place of Emergence is not known, and it is probable that it could only be determined by making a pilgrimage thither with a party of Navahoes who knew the place. Mr. Whitman Cross, of the United States Geological Survey, who has made extensive explorations in the San Juan Mountains, relates that Trout Lake is regarded by the Indians as a sacred lake; that they will not camp near it, and call it a name which is rendered Spirit Lake. This sheet of water is designated as San Miguel Lake on the maps of Hayden's Survey. It lies near the line of the Rio Grande Southern Railroad, at the head of the South Fork of San Miguel River. It has no island. A small lake, which accords more in appearance with the Navahoes' description of their sacred lake, is Island Lake. This has a small, rocky island in the middle. It is situated on a branch of the South Fork of Mineral Creek, three miles southeast of Ophir, Colorado, at an altitude of 12,450 feet. Prof. A. H. Thompson has suggested that Silver Lake, about five miles southeasterly from Silverton, Colorado, may be the Place of Emergence. This lake is 11,600 feet above sea-level, and is surrounded by four high mountain peaks, but it has no island.

44. Version A. — Gá*n*askĭ*d*i struck the cliffs with his wand. " Gong ê' " it sounded, and broke the cliffs open. Version B. — He of the darkness of the east cut the cliffs with his knife shaped like a horn.

45. Version A. — They prayed to the four Winds, — the black Wind of the east, the blue Wind of the south, the yellow Wind of the west, and the white Wind of the north, — and they sang a wind-song which is still sung in the rite of *hoz*óni *ha*tál. Version B. — They prayed to the four Winds.

46. The Kisáni, being builders of stone houses, set up a stone wall; the others, representing the Navahoes, set up a shelter of brushwood, as is the custom of the Navahoes now.

47. Tsĭ-*dĭ'l*, or tsĭn-*dĭ'l* is a game played by the Navaho women. The principal implements of the game are three sticks, which are thrown violently, ends down, on a flat stone, around which the gamblers sit. The sticks rebound so well that they would fly far away, were not a blanket stretched overhead to throw them back to the players. A number of small stones, placed in the form of a square, are used as counters; these are not moved, but sticks, whose positions are changed according to the fortunes of the game, are placed between them. The rules of the game have not been recorded. The other games were: *d*ilkó*n*, played with two sticks, each the length of an arm; atsá, played with forked sticks and a ring; and aspĭ'n.

48. Version A. — Coyote and *H*ast*s*é*z*ĭni were partners in the theft of the young of Tiéholtsodi. When Coyote saw the water rising, he pointed with his protruded lips (as Indians often do) to the water, and glanced significantly at his accomplice. First Man observed the glance, had his suspicions aroused, and began to search.

49. Other variants of the story of the restoration of Tiéholtsodi's young speak

of sacrifices and peace offerings in keeping with the Indian custom. Version A. — They got a haliotis shell of enormous size, so large that a man's encircling arm could barely surround it. Into this they put other shells and many precious stones. They sprinkled pollen on the young and took some of it off again, for it had been rendered more holy by contact with the bodies of the young sea monsters. Then they put these also into the shell and laid all on the horns of Tiéholtsodi; at once he disappeared under the earth and the waters went down after him. The pollen taken from the young was distributed among the people, and brought them rain and game and much good fortune. Version B. — "At once they threw them (the young) down to their father, and with them a sacrifice of the treasures of the sea, — their shell ornaments. In an instant the waters began to rush down through the hole and away from the lower worlds."

50. Some give the name of the hermaphrodite who died as Natliyil*h*át*s*e, and say that "she" is now the chief of devils in the lower world, — perhaps the same as the Woman Chief referred to in the "Prayer of a Navaho Shaman." [315] Version B says that the first to die was the wife of a great chief. (See note 68.)

51. Version A describes the making of the sacred mountains thus: Soon after the arrival of the people in the fifth world (after the first sudatory had been built and the first corn planted), some one said: "It would be well if we had in this world such mountains as we had in the world below." "I have brought them with me," said First Man. He did not mean to say he had brought the whole of the mountains with him, but only a little earth from each, with which to start new mountains here. The people laid down four sacred buckskins [18] and two sacred baskets [5] for him to make his mountains on, for there were six sacred mountains in the lower world, just as there are six in this, and they were named the same there as they now are here. The mountain in the east, Tsïsnadzï'ni, he made of clay from the mountain of the east below, mixed with white shell. The mountain of the south, Tsótsï*l*, he made of earth from below mixed with turquoise. The mountain of the west he made of earth mixed with haliotis or abalone shell. The mountain of the north he made of earth mixed with cannel coal. [158] Dsï*l*náo*tï*l he made of earth from the similar mountain in the lower world, mixed with goods of all kinds (yú*d*i al*th*asaí). T*s*olíhi he made of earth from below, mixed with shells and precious stones of all kinds (ïnklï'z al*th*asaí). While they were still on the buckskins and baskets, ten songs were sung which now belong to the rites of *h*ozóni *h*atál. The burdens of these songs are as follows: —

    1st. Long ago he thought of it.
    2d. Long ago he spoke of it.
    3d. A chief among mountains he brought up with him.
    4th. A chief among mountains he has made.
    5th. A chief among mountains is rising.
    6th. A chief among mountains is beginning to stand.
    7th. A chief among mountains stands up.
    8th. A cigarette for a chief among mountains we make.
    9th. A chief among mountains smokes.
    10th. A chief among mountains is satisfied.

When the people came up from the lower world they were under twelve chiefs, but only six of them joined in the singing these songs, and to-day six men sing them. When the mountains were made, the god of each of the four quarters of the world carried one away and placed it where it now stands. The other two were left in the middle of the world and are there still. A pair of gods were then put to live in each mountain, as follows: East, Dawn Boy and Dawn Girl, called also White Shell Boy and White Shell Girl; south, Turquoise Boy and Turquoise Girl; west, Twilight Boy and Haliotis Girl; north, Darkness (or Cannel Coal)

Boy and Darkness Girl: at Dsĭ*l*náo*t*i*l*, All-goods (Yú*d*i-al*th*asaí) Boy and All-goods Girl; at T*s*olíhi, All-jewels (Ĭnklĭ′z-al*th*asaí) Boy and All-jewels Girl.

Version B speaks of the making of only four mountains, and very briefly of this.

52. Tsĭs-na-d*z*ĭ′n-i is the name of the sacred mountain which the Navahoes regard as bounding their country on the east. It probably means Dark Horizontal Belt. The mountain is somewhere near the pueblo of Jemez, in Bernalillo County, New Mexico. It is probably Pelado Peak, 11,260 feet high, 20 miles N. N. E. of the pueblo. White shell and various other objects of white — the color of the east — belong to the mountain.

53. Tse‘-gá-*d*ĭ-na-*t*ĭ-ni A-*s*i-ké (Rock Crystal Boy) and Tse‘-gá-*d*ĭ-na-*t*ĭ-ni A-*t*é*t* (Rock Crystal Girl) are the deities of Tsĭsnad*z*ĭ′ni. They were brought up from the lower world as small images of stone; but as soon as they were put in the mountain they came to life.

54. Tsó-tsĭ*l*, or Tsó‘-dsĭ*l*, from tso, great, and dsĭ*l*, a mountain, is the Navaho name of a peak 11,389 feet high in Valencia County, New Mexico. Its summit is over twelve miles distant, in a direct line, east by north, from McCarty's Station on the Atlantic and Pacific Railroad. It is called by the Mexicans San Mateo, and was on September 18, 1849, named Mt. Taylor, "in honor of the President of the United States," by Lieut. J. H. Simpson, U. S. Army.[328] On the maps of the United States Geological Survey, the whole mountain mass is marked "San Mateo Mountains," and the name "Mount Taylor" is reserved for the highest peak. This is one of the sacred mountains of the Navahoes, and is regarded by them as bounding their country on the south, although at the present day some of the tribe live south of the mountain. They say that San Mateo is the mountain of the south and San Francisco is the mountain of the west, yet the two peaks are nearly in the same latitude. One version of the Origin Legend (Version B) makes San Mateo the mountain of the east, but all other versions differ from this. Blue being the color of the south, turquoise and other blue things, as named in the myth, belong to this mountain. As blue also symbolizes the female, she-rain belongs to San Mateo. Plate III. is from a photograph taken somewhere in the neighborhood of Chavez Station, about thirty-five miles in a westerly direction from the summit of the mountain.

55. *D*ot-lĭ′-*z*i *L*á-i Na-yo-á-*l*i A-*s*i-ké, Boy Who Carries One Torquoise; Na-*t*á *L*á-i Na-yo-á-*l*i A*t*é*t*, Girl Who Carries One (Grain of) Corn.

56. *D*o-kos-lí*d* or *D*o-ko-os-lĭ′*d*, is the Navaho name of San Francisco Mountain, one of the most prominent landmarks in Arizona. The summit of this peak is distant in a direct line about twelve miles nearly north from the town of Flagstaff, on the Atlantic and Pacific Railroad, in Yavapai County, Arizona. The precise meaning of the Indian name has not been ascertained, but the name seems to contain, modified, the words *t*o‘ and kos, the former meaning water and the latter cloud. It is the sacred mountain of the Navahoes, which they regard as bounding their land on the west. The color of the west, yellow, and the various things, mostly yellow, which symbolize the west, as mentioned in the myth, are sacred to it. Haliotis shell, although highly iridescent, is regarded by the Navahoes as yellow, and hence is the shell sacred to the mountain. In Navaho sacred songs, the peak is called, figuratively, The Wand of Haliotis. Plate II. is from a photograph taken on the south side of the mountain, at a point close to the railroad, two or three miles east of Flagstaff.

57. The name Na-*t*á*l*-kai A-*s*i-ké (White Corn Boy) is from na*t*á*n* (corn), *l*a*k*aí (white), and a*s*iké or ĭské (boy). The name Na*t*á*l*tsoi A*t*é*t* (Yellow Corn Girl), comes from na*t*á*n* (corn), *l*ĭtsói (yellow), and a*t*é*t* (girl). In paragraph 291 mention is made of the creation of a White Corn Boy and a Yellow Corn Girl.

It is not certain whether these are the same as the deities of *D*okoslí*d*, but it is probable the Navahoes believe in more than one divine pair with these names.

58. *D*epĕ'ntsa, the Navaho name for the San Juan Mountains in southwestern Colorado, is derived from two words, — *d*epé (the Rocky Mountain sheep) and intsá (scattered all over, widely distributed). These mountains are said to bound the Navaho land on the north. Somewhere among them lies Ní*h*oyostsátse, the Place of Emergence (note 43). Black being the color of the north, various black things, such as pászïni (cannel coal),[158] blackbirds, etc., belong to these mountains. There are many peaks in this range from 10,000 to 14,000 feet high.

59. *T*ha-*d*ï-tín *A*-si-ké (Pollen Boy), A-nil-*t*á-ni A-*t*é*t* (Grasshopper Girl). In paragraphs 290, 291, these are referred to again. In a dry-painting of *k*lédzi *h*a*t*á*l*, Grasshopper Girl is depicted in corn pollen.

60. Dsï*l*-ná-o-*t*í*l* seems to mean a mountain encircled with blood, but the Navahoes declare that such is not the meaning. They say it means the mountain that has been encircled by people travelling around it, and that, when Estsánatlehi and her people lived there they moved their camp to various places around the base of the mountain. Of course this is all mythical. Had the author ever seen this mountain, he might conjecture the significance of the name; but he does not even know its location. The name of the Carrizo Mountains, Dsï*l*náodsï*l*, meaning Mountain Surrounded with Mountains, is nearly the same; but when the writer visited the Carrizo Mountains in 1892 he was assured by the Indians that the sacred hill was not there. Dsï*l*náo*t*í*l* is rendered in this work Encircled Mountain, which is only an approximate translation. It is altogether a matter of conjecture why goods of all kinds — yúdi al*th*asaí (see note 61) — are thought to belong to this mountain.

61. Yú-*d*i Nai-dï-sï's-i A-si-ké, Boy who Produces Goods, or causes the increase of goods; Yú-*d*i Nai-di-sï's-i A-*t*é*t* (Girl Who Produces Goods). Yó*d*i or yú*d*i is here translated "goods." It originally referred to furs, skins, textile fabrics, and such things as Indians bartered among themselves, except food and jewels. The term is now applied to nearly all the merchandise to be found in a trader's store.

62. *Ts*o-lí-hi, or *Ts*o-lí*n*-i, is one of the seven sacred mountains of the Navaho country. Its location has not been determined, neither has the meaning of its name. Perhaps the name is derived from ts*ó*, the spruce (*Pseudotsuga taxifolia*). We can only conjecture what relation the mountain may have to jewels.

63. *Ts*oz-gá-*l*i, a large yellow bird, species undetermined.

64. Ïn-klï'z Nai-di-sï's-i A-si-ké (Boy Who Produces Jewels); Ïn-klï'z Nai-dï-sï's-i A*t*é*t* (Girl who Produces Jewels). Ïnklï'z means something hard and brittle. It is here translated "jewels" for want of a better term. It is not usually applied to finished jewels, but to the materials out of which the Navaho jewels are made, such as shells, turquoise in the rough, cannel coal, and other stones, many of which are of little value to us, but are considered precious by the Navahoes.

65. A-kï-*d*a-nas-*t*á-ni, signifying One-round-thing-sitting-on-top-of-another, is the Navaho name of an eminence called on our maps Hosta Butte, which is situated in Bernalillo County, New Mexico, 14 miles N. N. E. of Chavez Station on the Atlantic and Pacific Railroad. This butte or mesa has an altitude of 8,837 feet. Being surrounded by hills much lower, it is a prominent landmark.

66. Tse'-*h*a-*d*á-*k*o-ni-ge, or mirage-stone, is so called because it is thought in some way to look like a mirage. The writer has seen pieces of this in the pollen bags of the medicine-men, but never could procure a piece of it. They offered to exchange for another piece, but would not sell. A stone (Chinese idol) which they pronounced similar was analyzed by the chemists of the United States Geological Survey in Washington, and found to be silicate of magnesia, probably pyro-

phyllite. Such, perhaps, is the mirage-stone. The author offered the Chinese idol to one of the shamans in exchange for his mirage-stone; but, having heard that the stone image represented a Chinese god, the shaman feared to make the trade.

67. *Tó‘-la*-nas-tsi is a mixture of all kinds of water, *i. e.*, spring water, snow water, hail water, and water from the four quarters of the world. Such water *Tó‘nenïli* is supposed to have carried in his jars. Water used to-day in some of the Navaho rites approximates this mixture as closely as possible.

68. The subject of the dead belonging to the Sun and the Moon is explained at length in the version of Náltsos Nigéhani (Version B) thus: " On the fifth day (after the people came up to the surface of this world) the sun climbed as usual to the zenith and (then) stopped. The day grew hot and all longed for the night to come, but the sun moved not. Then the wise Coyote said: 'The sun stops because he has not been paid for his work; he demands a human life for every day that he labors; he will not move again till some one dies.' At length a woman, the wife of a great chief, ceased to breathe and grew cold, and while they all drew around in wonder, the sun was observed to move again, and he travelled down the sky and passed behind the western mountains. . . . That night the moon stopped in the zenith, as the sun had done during the day; and the Coyote told the people that the moon also demanded pay and would not move until it was given. He had scarcely spoken when the man who had seen the departed woman in the nether world died, and the moon, satisfied, journeyed to the west. Thus it is that some one must die every night, or the moon would not move across the sky. But the separation of the tribes occurred immediately after this, and now the moon takes his pay from among the alien races, while the sun demands the life of a Navaho as his fee for passing every day over the earth."

69. Many of the Indians tell that the world was originally small and was increased in size. The following is the version of Náltsos Nigéhani (B): " The mountains that bounded the world were not so far apart then as they are now; hence the world was smaller, and when the sun went over the earth he came nearer to the surface than he does now. So the first day the sun went on his journey it was intolerably hot; the people were almost burned to death, and they prayed to the four winds that each one would pull his mountain away from the centre of the earth, and thus widen the borders of the world. It was done as they desired, and the seas that bounded the land receded before the mountains. But on the second day, although the weather was milder, it was still too hot, and again were the mountains and seas removed. All this occurred again on the third day; but on the fourth day they found the weather pleasant, and they prayed no more for the earth to be changed."

70. The story of the making of the stars is told in essentially the same way by many story-tellers. It is surprising that *Hatáli* Něz totally omitted it. The following is the tale as told by Náltsos Nigéhani: " Now First Man and First Woman thought it would be better if the sky had more lights, for there were times when the moon did not shine at night. So they gathered a number of fragments of sparkling mica of which to make stars, and First Man proceeded to lay out a plan of the heavens, on the ground. He put a little fragment in the north, where he wished to have the star that would never move, and he placed near it seven great pieces, which are the seven stars we behold in the north now. He put a great bright one in the south, another in the east, and a third in the west, and then went on to plan various constellations, when along came Coyote, who, seeing that three pieces were red, exclaimed, ' These shall be my stars, and I will place them where I think best; ' so he put them in situations corresponding to places that three great red stars

now occupy among the celestial lights. Before First Man got through with his work, Coyote became impatient, and, saying, 'Oh! they will do as they are,' he hastily gathered the fragments of mica, threw them upwards, and blew a strong breath after them. Instantly they stuck to the sky. Those to which locations had been assigned adhered in their proper places; but the others were scattered at random and in formless clusters over the firmament." See "A Part of the Navajo's Mythology," pp. 7, 8.[306]

71. The following are some of the destroyers who sprang from this blood : —

Tse'nagáhi, Travelling Stone.

Tsĭn*d*il*h*á*s*itso, Great Wood That Bites.

Bĭts*ó*ziyeada'a'i,

Sá*n*ĭsd*z*o*l*, Old Age Lying Down.

Tse'tla*h*ó*d*ĭ*l*yĭ*l*, Black Under Cliffs.

Tse'tla*h*ó*d*o*l*lĭ'z, Blue Under Cliffs.

Tsé'tla*h*a*l*tsó, Yellow Under Cliffs.

Tsé'tla*h*a*l*kaí, White Under Cliffs.

Tse'tla*h*ó*d*itsos, Sparkling Under Cliffs.

T*s*a*d*i*d*a*h*a*l*tá*l*i, Devouring Antelope.

Yeitso*l*apáhi, Brown Yéitso.

*L*okáadikĭ*s*i, Slashing Reeds.

"You see colors under the rocks, at the bottoms of the cliffs, and when you approach them some invisible enemy kills you. These are the same as the Tse'-tlayal*t*í', or Those Who Talk Under the Cliffs." Thus said Ha*tál*i Nĕz when questioned.

72. Kĭntyél or Kĭntyê'li. — This name (from kin, a stone or adobe house, a pueblo house, and tyel, broad) means simply Broad Pueblo, — one covering much ground. It is applied to àt least two ruined pueblos in the Navaho country. One of these — the Pueblo Grande of the Mexicans, situated "twenty-two or twenty-three miles north of Navaho Springs," a station on the Atlantic and Pacific Railroad, in Arizona — is well described and depicted by Mr. Victor Mindeleff in his "Study of Pueblo Architecture."[325] The other — the Kĭntyél to which reference is made in this story — is in the Chaco Canyon, in New Mexico. With its name spelled "Kintail," and rendered "the Navajo name for ruin," it is mentioned by Mr. F. T. Bickford,[293] and one of his pictures, probably representing Kĭntyél, is here reproduced (fig. 36). In the *Journal of American Folk-Lore*, April–June, 1889, the author says: "I have reason to believe that this pueblo is identical with that seen and described in 1849 by Lieut. J. H. Simpson, U. S. A., under the name of Pueblo Chettro Kettle."

73. The name *H*as-tsé-yal-*t*i, spelled according to the alphabet of the Bureau of Ethnology "Qastcéyalçi" may be translated Talking God, or Talking Elder of the Gods. *H*asts*é*yal*t*i is otherwise called Yébĭt*s*ai, or the Maternal Grandfather of the Gods. He is a chief or leader among several groups of local divinities who are said to dwell at Kĭninaékai, in the Chelly Canyon, at Tsĕ'nit*s*e, Tsé'hĭhi, and at various other sacred places. Although called a talking god, the man who personates him in the rites never speaks while in character, but utters a peculiar whoop and makes signs. In the myths, however, the god is represented as speaking, usually after he has whooped and made signs. (Par. 472.) He is a beneficent character, always ready to help man and rescue him from peril. He is sometimes spoken of and prayed to as if there were but one, but the myths show that the Navahoes believe in many gods of this name, and in some prayers it is distinctly specified which one is meant by naming his home in connection with him. In plate I. he is shown, as represented in the dry-paintings, carrying a tobacco bag made of the skin of Abert's squirrel (*Sciurus aberti*). In the picture the black

tips of toes, nose, and ears, and the reddish (chestnut) spot on the back of the squirrel, are carefully indicated. The dry-painting shows the more important characters of the mask worn by the personator, — the eagle-plumes at the back, the owl-feathers at the base of the plume-ornament, and the peculiar symbols at mouth and eyes, — but it does not show the cornstalk symbol over the nose. Fig. 27, taken from a photograph, shows the mask trimmed with its collar of fresh spruce boughs, as it appears when used in the dance of naak*h*aí on the last night of the ceremony of klédzi *h*atál. The personator of *H*ast*s*éyal*t*i has his whole person clothed, while the representatives of other gods go nearly naked. The proper covering for his back is a number of finely dressed deerskins, one over another, tied together in front by the skins of the legs; but of late years the masquerader often appears in an ordinary calico shirt. The symbol surrounding each of the holes for the eyes and mouth is this ⌐⌐. It is said to represent the storm cloud hanging above, and the mist rising from below to meet it. Thus cloud and mist often appear in the mountains of the Navaho land during the rainy season. *H*ast*s*éyal*t*i or the Yébĭt*s*ai is the principal character in the great rite of klédzi *h*atál, or the night chant. Our people, who often go to witness the public performance of the last night in this rite, call it the Yébĭt*s*ai (Yáybichy) dance. The songs and prayers in which *H*ast*s*éyal*t*i is mentioned are numerous. For the points in which fig. 2, plate I., agree with fig. 1, plate I., see note 74.

74. *H*as-t*s*é-*h*o-*g*an, spelled with alphabet of Bureau of Ethnology, Qastcéqogan, may be freely translated House God. *H*ast*s*é*h*ogan is one of the leading personages in each of the local groups of the yéi, or divine beings, who dwell in caves and old cliff-dwellings. He is commonly spoken of as if there were but one; but an examination of the myths shows that the Navahoes believe in many of these gods. Those of Tse'gíhi, T*s*é'ni*h*ogan, T*s*é'nit*s*e, Kininaékai, and the sacred mountains are the ones most commonly worshipped. In most myths he appears as second in authority to *H*ast*s*éyal*t*i, the Talking God, but occasionally he is represented as equal or even superior to the latter. He is a farm god as well as a house god. To him are attributed the farm-songs sung during the night chant (see note 322), and many other songs. He is a beneficent character and a friend to man. There are many songs and prayers in his honor. In the rite of klédzi *h*atál, or the night chant, he is represented in the dance by a man wearing a collar of spruce, a blue mask decorated with eagle-plumes and moccasins, with shirt and leggings, which should be (but of late years are not always) of buckskin. He is depicted in the dry-paintings thus (see plate I., fig. 1): He wears a black shirt ornamented with four star-like ornaments embroidered in porcupine quills, and having a fancy fringe of porcupine quills at the bottom; white buckskin leggings; colored garters; quill-embroidered moccasins, tied on with white strings; long ear-pendants of turquoise and coral; bracelets of the same; an otter-skin (hanging below the right ear), from which depend six buckskin strings with colored porcupine quills wrapped around them; a cap-like (male) mask painted blue, fringed with red hair, and adorned with eagle-plumes and owl-feathers. He carries a staff (gĭ*s*) painted black (with the charcoal of four sacred plants), streaked transversely with white, and adorned with a single cluster of turkey tail-feathers arranged as a whorl, and two eagle plumes, which, like the plumes on the head, are tipped with small, downy eagle-feathers. The yellow stripe at the chin indicates a similar stripe on the mask actually worn, and symbolizes the yellow light of evening (na*h*otsóí). The neck of this as well as the other divine figures is painted blue, and crossed with four stripes in red. Some say that this indicates the larynx with its cartilaginous rings; others say that it represents the collar of spruce-twigs; others are uncertain of its meaning. If it does not represent the spruce collars, it represents nothing in the costume of

the maquerader, which, in other respects, except the quill embroideries, agrees closely with the picture. *H*ast*s*éyal*t*i is also a dawn god, *H*ast*s*é*h*og*a*n a god of evening.

75. In the Navaho tales, men frequently receive friendly warnings or advice from wind gods who whisper into their ears. Some story-tellers — as in the version of the origin myth here given — speak of one wind god only, whom they call simply Nĭ′lt*s*i (Wind); while others — as in the story of Na*tĭ*′nes*t*hani — speak of Nĭ′lt*s*i-*d*iné‘ (Wind People) and Nĭl*ts*iá*z*i-*d*iné‘ (Little Wind People) as the friendly prompters.

76. The game of nán*z*o*z*, as played by the Navahoes, is much the same as the game of chungkee played by the Mandans, described and depicted by Catlin in his " North American Indians," [296] vol. i., page 132, plate 59. A hoop is rolled along the ground and long poles are thrown after it. The Mandan pole was made of a single piece of wood. The pole of the Navahoes is made of two pieces, usually alder, each a natural fathom long; the pieces overlap and are bound together by a long branching strap of hide called *t*hágib*ĭ*ke, or turkey-claw.

77. These shells may not be altogether mythical. Possibly they are the same as those described in the story of " The Great Shell of Kĭntyél " given in this book.

78. Vague descriptions only of Bé-ko-t*s*ĭ-*d*i so far have been obtained. He is not represented by any masked characters in the ceremonies, or by any picture in the dry-paintings. No description of his appearance has been recorded, except that he looks like an old man. There is a myth concerning him of which a brief epitome has been recorded. There are four songs of sequence connected with this myth. If a Navaho wants a fine horse, he thinks he may get it by singing the second and third of these songs and praying to Békot*s*ĭ*d*i. In his prayer he specifies the color and appearance of the horse desired. Some say that Békot*s*ĭ*d*i made all the animals whose creation is not otherwise accounted for in the myths. Others say that he and the Sun made the animals together. Others, again, limit his creation work to the larger game animals and the modern domestic animals. In this paragraph (228) it is said he is the god who carries the moon, while in paragraph 199 it is said the moon-bearer is Kléhanoai. Perhaps these are two names for one character. Some say he is the same as the God of the Americans.

79. Bayeta, Spanish for baize. The variety of baize which finds its way into the Navaho country is dyed some shade of crimson, and has a very long nap. It is supposed to be made in England especially for the Spanish-American trade, for each original bale bears a gaudy colored label with an inscription in Spanish. It takes the place in the Southwest of the scarlet strouding which used to form such an important article in the trade of our northern tribes. The bright red figures in the finer Navaho blankets, fifteen years or more ago, were all made of threads of ravelled bayeta.

80. The coyote, or prairie-wolf (*Canis latrans*), would seem to be regarded by the Navahoes as the type, or standard for comparison, among the wild *Canidæ* of the Southwest. The coyote is called mai; the great wolf, maítso, which means great coyote; and the kit fox (*Vulpes velox*) is called mai*d*o*tlĭ*′*z*, which means blue or gray coyote.

81. Some versions say there were twelve brothers and one sister in this divine family, making thirteen in all. In this version the narrator tells how another brother was created by Estsánatlehi to make up for the loss of *L*éyaneyani, who left the brotherhood. (Par. 417.) Although called *D*iné‘ Naki*dát*a, or the Twelve People, these brothers are evidently divinities. True, they once died ; but they came to life again and are now immortal. They are gifted with superhuman powers.

82. The sweat-house of the Navahoes (par. 25, fig. 15) is usually not more than

Fig. 38. Natural bridge, near Fort Defiance, Arizona.

three feet high. Diaphoresis is produced on the principle of the Turkish (not the Russian) bath. While the Indians of the North pour water on the hot stones and give a steam bath, the Navahoes simply place stones, heated in a fire out-side, on the floor of the sweat-house, cover the entrance with blankets, and thus raise a high heat that produces violent perspiration. When the occupant comes out, if the bath is not ceremonial, he rolls himself in the sand, and, when his skin is thus dried, he brushes the sand away. He usually returns then to the sweat-house, and may repeat the operation several times in a single afternoon. If the sweat is ceremonial, the bath of yucca suds usually follows (see note 10), and the subject is dried with corn meal.

83. One version relates that, before they entered the sudatory, Coyote proposed they should produce emesis by tickling their throats, — a common practice among the Navahoes. He placed a large piece of pine bark before each, as a dish, and bade Yélapahi keep his eyes shut till he was told to open them. That day Coyote had fared poorly. He had found nothing to eat but a few bugs and worms, while Yélapahi had dined heartily on fat venison. When the emesis was over, Coyote exchanged the bark dishes and said to Yélapahi: " Open your eyes and see what bad things you have had in your stomach. These are the things that make you sick." The giant opened his eyes and beheld on the bark a lot of bugs and worms. " It is true, my friend, what you tell me," he said. " How did I get such vile things into me? No wonder I could not run fast." Coyote then told the giant to go before him into the sudatory, and when the giant had turned his back the hungry Coyote promptly devoured the contents of the other dish of bark.

84. The word *tóhe* (Englished thóhay), which may be interpreted stand, stick, or stay, is, in various rites, shouted in an authoritative tone when it is desired that some object shall obey the will of the conjurer. Thus in the dance of the standing arcs, as practised in the rite of the mountain chant, when an arc is placed on the head of a performer, and it is intended that it should stand without

apparent means of support, the cry "*tó*he" is frequently repeated. (See "The Mountain Chant," [314] p. 437.)

85. The statement that the hair of the gods, both friendly and alien, is yellow, is made in other tales also. The hair of the ceremonial masks is reddish or yellowish. (See plates IV. and VII.) The hair of the gods is represented by red in the dry-pictures. Dull tints of red are often called yellow by the Navahoes. Various conjectures may be made to account for these facts.

86. The bridge of rainbow, as well as the trail of rainbow, is frequently introduced into Navaho tales. The Navaho land abounds in deep chasms and canyons, and the divine ones, in their wanderings, are said to bridge the canyons by producing rainbows. In the myth of "The Mountain Chant," p. 399 (note 314), the god *H*ast*s*éyal*t*i is represented as making a rainbow bridge for the hero to walk

Fig. 39. Yucca baccata.

on. The hero steps on the bow, but sinks in it because the bow is soft; then the god blows a breath that hardens the bow, and the man walks on it with ease. A natural bridge near Fort Defiance, Arizona, is thought by the Navahoes to have been originally one of the rainbow bridges of *H*ast*s*éyal*t*i. (See fig. 38.)

87. The spiders of Arizona are largely of the classes that live in the ground, including trap-door spiders, tarantulas, etc.

88. This legend and nearly all the legends of the Navaho make frequent allusions to yucca. Four kinds are mentioned: *t*st, ts*á*si or *h*as*k*án. *Yucca baccata*

(Torrey); 2d, tsasitsóz, or slender yucca, *Yucca glauca* (Nuttall), *Yucca angusti-folia* (Pursh); 3d, yébĭtsasi, or yucca of the gods, probably *Yucca radiosa* (Tre-lease), *Yucca elata* (Engelmann); 4th, tsasibĭté, or horned yucca, which seems to be but a stunted form or dwarf variety of *Yucca baccata*, never seen in bloom or in fruit by the author. Tsási is used as a generic name. All kinds are employed in the rites, sometimes indifferently; at other times only a certain species may be used. Thus in the sacred game of kĕsĭtsé,[176] the counters are made of the leaves of *Y. glauca;* in the initiation into the mystery of the Yébĭtsai, the candi-date is flogged with the leaf of *Y. baccata.* Fig. 26 represents a mask used in the rites of klédzi *hatál,* which must be made only of the leaves of *Y. baccata,* culled with many singular observances. All these yuccas have saponine in their roots (which are known as *t*álawu*s* or foam), and all are used for cleansing purposes. All have, in their leaves, long tough fibres which are utilized for all the purposes to which such fibres may be applied. One species only, *Yucca baccata,* has an edible fruit. This is called *h*askán (from *h*o*s,* thorny, and kan, sweet), a name sometimes ap-plied to the whole plant. The fruit is eaten raw and made into a tough, dense jelly, both by the Navaho and Pueblo Indians. The first and sec-ond kinds grow abundantly in the Navaho coun-try; the third and fourth kinds are rarer. Fig. 40 represents a drumstick used in the rites of klédzi *hatál,* which must be made only of four leaves of *Yucca baccata.* The intricate observ-ances connected with the manufacture, use, de-struction, and sacrifice of this drumstick have already been described by the author.[321]

89. The cane cactus is *Opuntia arborescens* (Engelm.).

90. T*s*iké *Sas* Nátlehi means literally Young Woman Who Changes to a Bear, or Maid Who Becomes a Bear. To judge from this tale, it might be thought that there was but one such character in the Navaho mythology and that she had died. But it appears from other legends and from ritu-als that the Navahoes believe in several such maidens, some of whom exist to this day. The hill of T*s*ú*s*kai (note 9) is said in the myth of dsĭ*l*/yĭ'dze *hatál* to be the home of several of the T*s*iké *Sas* Nátlehi now. It would seem from the songs of dsĭ*l*/yĭ'dze *hatál* that the Maid Who Becomes a

Fig. 40.   Drumstick made of Yucca leaves.

Bear of later days is not considered as malevolent as the first of her kind. Her succor is sought by the sick.

91. See par. 26. From the language of this story, the conclusion may be drawn that death is not the only thing that renders a house haunted or evil but that, if great misfortune has entered there, it is also to be avoided.

92. This remark must refer only to the particular group whose story is traced. According to the legend, other bands of *D*ĭné‘, who had escaped the fury of the alien gods, existed at this time, and when they afterwards joined the Navahoes

they were known as *dïné'* *dï*gíni (holy or mystic people). (See pars. 385 and 387.)

93. The gods, and such men as they favor, are represented in the tales as making rapid and easy journeys on rainbows, sunbeams, and streaks of lightning. Such miraculous paths are called *etï'n dï*gíni, or holy trails. They are also represented as using sunbeams like rafts to float through the air.

94. Compare this account with the creation of First Man and First Woman. (Pars. 162–164.)

95. Es-tsá-na-tle-hi (par. 72) is never represented in the rites by a masquerader, and never depicted in the sand-paintings, as far as the author has been able to learn. Other versions of the legend account for her creation in other ways. Version A.—First Man and First Woman stayed at Dsïlnáo*tï*l and camped in various places around the mountain. One day a black cloud descended on the mountain of T*s*olíhi, and remained there four days. First Man said: "Surely something has happened from this; let some one go over there and see." First Woman went. She approached the mountain from the east, and wound four times around it in ascending it. On the top she found a female infant, who was the daughter of the Earth Mother (Naestsán, the Woman Horizontal) and the Sky Father (Yá*dï*ly*ï*l, the Upper Darkness). She picked up the child, who till that moment had been silent; but as soon as she was lifted she began to cry, and never ceased crying until she got home to Dsï*l*náo*tï*l. Salt Woman said she wanted the child. It is thought the sun fed the infant on pollen, for there was no one to nurse it. In twelve days she grew to be a big girl, and in eighteen days she became a woman, and they held the nubile ceremony over her. Twelve songs belong to this ceremony. Version B only says that First Woman found the infant lying on the ground and took it home to rear it. (See "Some Deities and Demons of the Navajos," [313] pp. 844, 846.)

96. Yo*l*-kaí Es-tsán signifies White Shell Woman. Yo*l*kaí is derived by syncope from yo (a bead, or the shell from which a bead is made) and *l*akaí (white). Estsán means woman. As far as known, she is not represented by a character in any of the ceremonies, and not depicted in the dry-paintings.

97. Note omitted.

98. *T*ó'-ne-nï-li or *T*ó-ne-nï-li, Water Sprinkler, is an important character in Navaho mythology. He is a rain-god. In the dry-paintings of the Navaho rites he is shown as wearing a blue mask bordered with red, and trimmed on top with life-feathers. Sometimes he is represented carrying a water-pot. In the rite of klé*dz*i *l*a*tá*l, during the public dance of the last night, he is represented by a masked man who enacts the part of a clown. While other masked men are dancing, this clown performs various antics according to his caprice. He walks along the line of dancers, gets in their way, dances out of order and out of time, peers foolishly at different persons, or sits on the ground, his hands clasped across his knees, his body rocking to and fro. At times he joins regularly in the dance; toward the close of a figure, and when the others have retired, pretending he is unaware of their departure, he remains, going through his steps. Then, feigning to suddenly discover the absence of the dancers, he follows them on a full run. Sometimes he carries a fox-skin, drops it on the ground, walks away as if unconscious of his loss; then, pretending to become aware of his loss, he turns around and acts as if searching anxiously for the skin, which lies plainly in sight. He screens his eyes with his hand and crouches low to look. Then, pretending to find the skin, he jumps on it and beats it as if it were a live animal that he seeks to kill. Next he shoulders and carries it as if it were a heavy burden. With such antics the personator of *T*ó'nenïli assists in varying the monotony of the long night's performance. Though shown as a fool in the rites, he is not so shown in the myths.

99. They manipulated the abdominal parietes, in the belief that by so doing they would insure a favorable presentation. This is the custom among the Navahoes to-day.

100. Among the Navahoes, medicine-men act as accoucheurs.

101. Other versions make Estsánatlehi the mother of both War Gods, and give a less imaginative account of their conception. Version A. — The maiden Estsánatlehi went out to get wood. She collected a bundle, tied it with a rope, and when she knelt down to lift it she felt a foot pressed upon her back ; she looked up and saw no one. Three times more kneeling, she felt the pressure of the foot. When she looked up for the fourth time, she saw a man. "Where do you live ? " he asked. " Near by," she replied, pointing to her home. " On yonder mountain," he said, " you will find four yuccas, each of a different kind, cut on the north side to mark them. Dig the roots of these yuccas and make yourself a bath. Get meal of *l*ohono*s*í'ni corn (note 28), yellow from your mother, white from your father (note 27). Then build yourself a brush shelter away from your hut and sleep there four nights." She went home and told all this to her foster parents. They followed all the directions of the mysterious visitor, for they knew he was the Sun. During three nights nothing happened in the brush shelter that she knew of. On the morning after the fourth night she was awakened from her sleep by the sound of departing footsteps, and, looking in the direction that she heard them, she saw the sun rising. Four days after this (or twelve days, as some say) Nayénĕzgani was born. Four days later she went to cleanse herself at a spring, and there she conceived of the water, and in four days more *T*o'badz*i*sts*i*ni, the second War God, was born to her. Version B. — The Sun (or bearer of the sun) met her in the woods and designated a trysting place. Here First Man built a corral of branches. Sun visited her, in the form of an ordinary man, in the corral, four nights in succession. Four days after the last visit she gave birth to twins, who were Nayénĕzgani and *T*o'badz*i*sts*i*ni. (See " A Part of the Navajos' Mythology," [306] pp. 9, 10.)

102. Version A thus describes the baby basket of the elder brother : The child was wrapped in black cloud. A rainbow was used for the hood of the basket and studded with stars. The back of the frame was a parhelion, with the bright spot at its bottom shining at the lowest point. Zigzag lightning was laid on each side and straight lightning down the middle in front. N*i*ltsát*l*ol (sunbeams shining on a distant rainstorm) formed the fringe in front where Indians now put strips of buckskin. The carrying-straps were sunbeams.

103. The mountain mahogany of New Mexico and Arizona is the *Cercocarpus parvifolius*, Nutt. It is called by the Navahoes Tsé'estagi, which means hard as stone.

104. Round cactus, one or more species of *Mammilaria*. Sitting cactus, *Cereus phœniceus*, and perhaps other species of *Cereus*.

105. Yé-i-tso (from yéi, a god or genius, and tso, great) was the greatest and fiercest of the anáye, or alien gods. (Par. 80, note 7.) All descriptions of him are substantially the same. (See pars. 323, 325, 326.) According to the accounts of *H*a*t*á*l*i Nĕz and Torlino, his father was a stone ; yet in par. 320 and in Version B the sun is represented as saying that Yéitso is his child. Perhaps they mean he is the child of the sun in a metaphysical sense.

106. This part of the myth alludes to the trap-door spiders, or tarantulæ of the Southwest, that dwell in carefully prepared nests in the ground.

107. By life-feather or breath-feather (hy*i*ná b*i*lts*ó*s) is meant a feather taken from a live bird, especially one taken from a live eagle. Such feathers are supposed to preserve life and possess other magic powers. They are used in all the rites. In order to secure a supply of these feathers, the Pueblo Indians catch

eaglets and rear them in captivity (see pars. 560 *et seq.*); but the Navahoes, like
the wild tribes of the north, catch full-grown eagles in traps, and pluck them while
alive. This method of catching eagles has been described by the author in his
"Ethnography and Philology of the Hidatsa Indians." [805]

108. Pollen being an emblem of peace, this is equivalent to saying, "Put your
feet down in peace," etc.

109. Version A in describing the adventure with Spider Woman adds: There
were only four rungs to the ladder. She had many seats in her house. The elder
brother sat on a seat of obsidian; the younger, on a seat of turquoise. She
offered them food of four kinds to eat; they only accepted one kind. When they
had eaten, a small image of obsidian came out from an apartment in the east and
stood on a serrated platform, or platform of serrate knives. The elder brother
stood on the platform beside the image. Spider Woman blew a strong breath
four times on the image in the direction of the youth, and the latter became thus
endowed with the hard nature of the obsidian, which was to further preserve him
in his future trials. From the south room came a turquoise image, and stood on
a serrated platform. The younger brother stood beside this. Spider Woman
blew on the turquoise image toward him, and he thus acquired the hard nature of
the blue stone. To-day in the rites of *hozóni hatál* they have a prayer concerning these incidents beginning, "Now I stand on pés*d*olgas." (See note 264.)

110. In describing the journey of the War Gods to the house of the Sun, version
A adds something. At *Tó*'sa*t*o or Hot Spring (Ojo Gallina, near San Rafael), the
brothers have an adventure with Tiéholtsodi, the water monster, who threatens
them and is appeased with prayer. They encounter Old Age People, who treat
them kindly, but bid them not follow the trail that leads to the house of Old Age.
They come to *H*ayo*l*ká*l*, Daylight, which rises like a great range of mountains
in front of them. (Songs.) They fear they will have to cross this, but Daylight
rises from the ground and lets them pass under. . . . They come to Tsa*l*yé*l*, Darkness. Wind whispers into their ears what songs to sing. They sing these songs
and Tsa*l*yé*l* rises and lets them pass under. They come to water, which they
walk over. On the other side they meet their sister, the daughter of the Sun, who
dwells in the house of the Sun. She speaks not, but turns silently around, and
they follow her to the house.

111. According to version A, there were four sentinels of each kind, and they
lay in the passageway or entrance to the house. A curtain hung in front of each
group of four. In each group the first sentinel was black, the second blue, the
third yellow, the fourth white. The brothers sang songs to the guardians and
sprinkled pollen on them.

112. Version A gives the names of these two young men as Black Thunder and
Blue Thunder.

113. The teller of the version has omitted to mention that the brothers, when
they entered the house, declared that they came to seek their father, but other
story-tellers do not fail to tell this.

114. Four articles of armor were given to each, and six different kinds of
weapons were given to them. The articles of armor were: pe*s*ké (knife moccasins), pe*s*ïstlé' (knife leggings), pe*s*ê' (knife shirt), and pe*s*tsá (knife hat). The
word "pe*s*," in the above names for armor, is here translated knife. The term
was originally applied to flint knives, and to the flakes from which flint knives
were made. After the introduction of European tools, the meaning was extended
to include iron knives, and now it is applied to any object of iron, and, with quali-
fying suffixes, to all kinds of metal. Thus copper is pe*s*ïtsí, or red metal, and
silver, pe*s*lakaí, or white metal. Many of the Navahoes now think that the mythic
armor of their gods was of iron. Such the author believed it to be in the earlier

years of his investigation among the Navahoes, and he was inclined to believe that they borrowed the idea of armored heroes from the Spanish invaders of the sixteenth century. Later studies have led him to conclude that the conception of armored heroes was not borrowed from the whites, and that the armor was supposed to be made of stone flakes such as were employed in making knives in the prehistoric days. The Mokis believe that their gods and heroes wore armor of flint.

115. The weapons were these: —
atsīniklī'ska (chain-lightning arrows)
ḫatsīlkī'ska or ḫadīlkī'ska (sheet-lightning arrows)
saʻbitlólka (sunbeam arrows)
natsilī'ʇka (rainbow arrows)
peshál (stone knife-club)
ḫatsoilḫál, which some say was a thunderbolt, and others say was a great stone knife, with a blade as broad as the hand. Some say that only one stone knife was given, which was for Nayénĕzgạni, and that only two thunderbolts were given, both of which were for Toʻbadzīstsíni. The man who now personates Nayénĕzgạni in the rites carries a stone knife of unusual size (plate IV.); and he who personates Toʻbadzīstsíni carries in each hand a wooden cylinder (one black and one red) to represent a thunderbolt. (Plate VII.)

116. Version A adds that when they were thus equipped they were dressed exactly like their brothers Black Thunder and Blue Thunder, who dwelt in the house of the Sun.

117. The man who told this tale explained that there were sixteen poles in the east and sixteen in the west to join earth and sky. Others say there were thirty-two poles on each side. The Navahoes explain the annual progress of the sun by saying that at the winter solstice he climbs on the pole farthest south in rising; that as the season advances he climbs on poles farther and farther north, until at the summer solstice he climbs the pole farthest north; that then he retraces his way, climbing different poles until he reaches the south again. He is supposed to spend about an equal number of days at each pole.

118. Many versions relate that the bearer of the sun rode a horse, or other pet animal. The Navaho word here employed is *lin*, which means any domesticated or pet animal, but now, especially, a horse. Version A says the animal he rode was made of turquoise and larger than a horse. Such versions have great difficulty in getting the horse up to the sky. Version A makes the sky dip down and touch the earth to let the horse ascend. Of course the horse is a modern addition to the tale. They never saw horses until the sixteenth century, and previous to that time it is not known that any animal was ridden on the western continent. Version B merely says that the Sun "put on his robe of cloud, and, taking one of his sons under each arm, he rose into the heavens."

119. Version B says they all ate a meal on their journey to the sky-hole. Version A says that they ate for food, at the sky-hole, before the brothers descended, a mixture of five kinds of pollen, viz.: pollen of white corn, pollen of yellow corn, pollen of dawn, pollen of evening twilight, and pollen of the sun.[11] These were mixed with *tóʻlanastsi*, all kinds of water.[67]

120. *Tóʻ-sa-to* or Warm Spring is at the village of San Rafael, Valencia County, New Mexico. It is about three miles in a southerly direction from Grant's, on the Atlantic and Pacific Railroad, five miles from the base and eighteen miles from the summit of Mount Taylor, in a southwesterly direction from the latter. The lake referred to in the myth lies about two miles southeast of the spring.

121. According to Version A, the monsters or anáye were all conceived in the fifth world and born of one woman (a granddaughter of First Woman), who

travelled much and rarely stayed at home. According to Version B, the monsters were sent by First Woman, who became offended with man.

122. Version A gives, in addition to Tsótsi*l*, the names of the other three hills over which Yéitso appeared. These were: in the east, Sa'akéa'; in the south, Dsi*l*sits*í* (Red Mountain); in the west, Tse'*l*painá*l*i (Brown Rock Hanging Down).

123. Version A. — " Hragh ! " said he, with a sigh of satisfaction (pantomimically expressed), " I have finished that."

124. Yinike*t*óko ! No etymology has been discovered for this expression. It is believed to be the equivalent of the " Fee Fa Fum ! " of the giants in our nursery tales.

125. Version B. — This bolt rent his armor.

126. It is common in this and all other versions to show that evil turns to good (see pars. 338, 345, 349, *et al.*), and that the demons dead become useful to man in other forms. How the armor of Yéitso became useful to man, the narrator here forgot to state ; but it may be conjectured that he should have said that it furnished flint flakes for knives and arrow-heads.

127. Other versions state, more particularly, that, in accordance with the Indian custom, these names were given when the brothers returned to their home, and the ceremony of rejoicing (the " scalp-dance ") was held for their first victory. Nayénĕzgạni is derived from na, or ana (alien or enemy: see note 7); yéi, ye or ge (a genius or god ; hence anáye, an alien god or giant : see par. 80) ; nĕzgá' (to kill with a blow or blows, as in killing with a club) ; and the suffix ni (person). The name means, therefore, Slayer of the Alien Gods, or Slayer of Giants. As the sounds of g and y before e are interchangeable in the Navaho language, the name is heard pronounced both Nayénĕzgạni and Nagénĕzgạni, — about as often one way as the other. In previous essays the author has spelled it in the latter way ; but in this work he gives preference to the former, since it is more in harmony with his spelling of other names containing the word " ye " or " yéi." (See par. 78.) *T*o'-ba-dz*í*s-ts*í*-ni is derived from *t*o' (water), ba (for him), dz*í*sts*í*n (born), and the suffix ni. The name therefore means, literally, Born for the Water ; but the expression badz*í*sts*í*n (born for him) denotes the relation of father and child, — not of a mother and child, — so that a free translation of the nam*e* is Child of the Water. The second name of this god, Na*í*d*í*k*í*si, is rarely used.

128. About 40 miles to the northeast of the top of Mt. San Mateo there is a dark, high volcanic hill called by the Mexicans *El Cabezon*, or The Great Head. This is the object which, according to the Navaho story-tellers, was the head of Yéitso. Around the base of San Mateo, chiefly toward the east and north, there are several more high volcanic peaks, of less prominence than *El Cabezon*, which are said to have been the heads of other giants who were slain in a great storm raised by the War Gods. (See pars. 358, 359.) Plate V. shows six of these volcanic hills. The high truncated cone in the distance (17 miles from the point of view) is *El Cabezon*. Captain Clarence E. Dutton, U. S. A., treats of the geologic character of these cones in his work on Mount Taylor.[299] Plate V. is taken from the same photograph as his plate XXI. In Lieut. Simpson's report,[328] p. 73, this hill is described under the name *Cerro de la Cabeza*, and a picture of it is given in plate 17 of said report. It is called " Cabezon Pk." on the accompanying map.

129. To the south and west of the San Mateo Mountains there is a great plain of lava rock of geologically recent origin, which fills the valley and presents plainly the appearance of having once been flowing. The rock is dark and has much resemblance to coagulated blood. This is the material which, the Navahoes think, was once the blood of Yéitso. In some places it looks as if the blood were suddenly arrested, forming high cliffs ; here the war god is supposed to have

stopped the flow with his knife. Plate VI. shows this lava in the valley of the Rio San José, from a photograph supplied by the United States Geological Survey.

130. Version A adds some particulars to the account of the return of the brothers to their home, after their encounter with Yéitso. They first went to Azíhi, the place at which they descended when they came from the sky, and then to Kainipéhi. On their way home they sang twenty songs — the Ni*d*o*t*átsogisïn — which are sung to-day in the rites of *h*ozóni *h*atál. Near Dsï*l*náo*t*í*l*, just at daybreak, they met *H*ast*s*éyal*t*i and *H*ast*s*é*h*ogan, who embraced them, addressed them as grand-children, sang two songs, now belonging to the rites, and conducted the young heroes to their home.

131. *T*é-el-gĕ*t*, *T*ê-el-gĕ'-*t*i and *D*ĕl-g*ĕt* are various pronunciations of the name of this monster. In the songs he is sometimes called Bï-*t*é-ĕl-gĕ-*t*i, which is merely prefixing the personal pronoun " his " to the name. The exact etymology has not been determined. The name has some reference to his horns ; tê, or *t*e, meaning horns, and bi*t*é, his horns, in Navaho. All descriptions of this anáye are much alike. His father, it is said, was an antelope horn.

132. *Arabis holböllii* (Hornemann), a-ze-*l*a-*d*ï*l*-*t*é-he, " scattered " or " lone medicine." The plants grow single and at a distance from one another, not in beds or clusters. (See " Navajo Names for Plants," [312] p. 770.)

133. Version A relates that they sang, while at work on these kethawns, six songs, which, under the name of Atsós Bigï'n, or Feather Songs, are sung now in the rite of *h*ozóni *h*atál.

134. Version A says that the horns of *T*éelgĕ*t* were like those of an antelope, and that Nayénĕzg̣ani cut off the short branch of one as an additional trophy.

135. Tse'nä'-ha-le. These mythic creatures, which in a previous paper, " A Part of the Navajos' Mythology," [306] the author calls harpies, from their analogy to the harpies of Greek mythology, are believed in by many tribes of the Southwest. According to *H*a*t*á*l*i Nĕz they were the offspring of a bunch of eagle plumes.

136. Tsé'-bï-*t*a-i, or Winged Rock, is a high, sharp pinnacle of dark volcanic rock, rising from a wide plain in the northwestern part of New Mexico, about 12 miles from the western boundary of the Territory, and about 20 miles from the northern boundary. The Navahoes liken it to a bird, and hence the name of Winged Rock, or more literally Rock, Its Wings. The whites think it resembles a ship with sails set, and call it Ship Rock. Its bird-like appearance has probably suggested to the Navahoes the idea of making it the mythic home of the bird-like Tse'nä'hale.

137. There are many instances in Navaho language and legend where, when two things somewhat resemble each other, but one is the coarser, the stronger, or the more violent, it is spoken of as male, or associated with the male ; while the finer, weaker, or more gentle is spoken of as female, or associated with the female. Thus the turbulent San Juan River is called, by the Navaho, *T*o·baká, or Male Water ; while the placid Rio Grande is known as *T*o·baád, or Female Water. A shower accompanied by thunder and lightning is called nïltsabaká, or male rain ; a shower without electrical display is called nïltsabaád, or female rain. In the myth of Na*t*ï'nĕs*t*hani the mountain mahogany is said to be used for the male sacrificial cigarette, and the cliff rose for the female. These two shrubs are much alike, particularly when in fruit and decked with long plumose styles, but the former (the " male ") is the larger and coarser shrub. In the myth of Dsï*l*yi· Neyáni another instance may be found where mountain mahogany is associated with the male, and the cliff rose with the female. Again, in the myth of Na*t*ï'nĕs*t*hani a male cigarette is described as made of the coarse sunflower, while its associated female is said to be made of the allied but more slender *Verbesina*. Instances of

this character might be multiplied indefinitely. On this principle the north is associated with the male, and the south with the female, for two reasons: 1st, cold, violent winds blow from the north, while gentle, warm breezes blow from the south; 2d, the land north of the Navaho country is more rough and mountainous than the land in the south. In the former rise the great peaks of Colorado, while in the latter the hills are not steep and none rise to the limit of eternal snow. A symbolism probably antecedent to this has assigned black as the color of the north and blue as the color of the south; so, in turn, black symbolizes the male and blue the female among the Navaho. (From " A Vigil of the Gods.")[328]

138. Version A. — The young birds were the color of a blue heron, but had bills like eagles. Their eyes were as big as a circle made by the thumbs and middle fingers of both hands. Nayénĕzgani threw the birds first to the bottom of the cliff and there metamorphosed them.

139. The etymology of the word Tsĕ'-dă-ni (Englished, chedany) has not been determined. It is an expression denoting impatience and contempt.

140. On being asked for the cause of this sound, the narrator gave an explanation which indicated that the " Hottentot apron " exists among American Indians. The author has had previous evidence corroborative of this.

141. Version B here adds: " Giving up her feathers for lost, she turned her attention to giving names to the different kinds of birds as they flew out, — names which they bear to this day among the Navajos, — until her basket was empty."

142. Tseʻ-*ta*-*ho*-ts*ĭ*l-*tá*ʻ-*l*i is said to mean He (Who) Kicks (People) Down the Cliff. Some pronounce the name Tseʻ-*ta*-yĭ-ts*i*l-*tá*ʻ-*l*i.

143. In versions A and B, the hero simply cuts the hair of the monster and allows the latter to fall down the cliff.

144. Na-tsĭs-a-án is the Navaho Mountain, an elevation 10,416 feet high, ten miles south of the junction of the Colorado and San Juan rivers, in the State of Utah.

145. Thus does the Navaho story-teller weakly endeavor to score a point against his hereditary enemy, the Pah Ute. But it is poor revenge, for the Pah Ute is said to have usually proved more than a match for the Navaho in battle. In Version A, the young are transformed into Rocky Mountain sheep; in Version B, they are changed into birds of prey.

146. This is the place at which the Bĭnáye A*h*áni were born, as told in par. 203. The other monsters mentioned in Part II. were not found by Nayénĕzgani at the places where they were said to be born.

147. Other versions make mention, in different places, of a Salt Woman, or goddess of salt, Á*s*ihi Est*s*án; but the version of *H*atá*l*i Nĕz does not allude to her. Version A states that she supplied the bag of salt which Nayénĕzgani carried on his expedition.

148. Ts*ĭ*-d*ĭ*l-*t*ó-i means shooting or exploding bird. The name comes, perhaps, from some peculiarity of this bird, which gives warning of the approach of an enemy.

149. *H*o*s*-t*ó*-*d*i is probably an onomatopoetic name for a bird. It is said to be sleepy in the daytime and to come out at night.

150. Version B says that scalps were the trophies.

151. In all versions of this legend, but two hero gods or war gods are prominently mentioned, viz., Nayénĕzgani and *T*oʻbadzĭsts*í*ni; but in these songs four names are given. This is to satisfy the Indian reverence for the number four, and the dependent poetic requirement which often constrains the Navaho poet to put four stanzas in a song. *L*éyaneyani, or Reared Beneath the Earth (par. 286), is an obscure hero whose only deed of valor, according to this version of the legend, was the killing of his witch sister (par. 281). The deeds of Tsówenatlehi, or the

Changing Grandchild, are not known to the writer. Some say that *Léyaneyani* and Tsówenatlehi are only other names for Nayénĕzgạni and *To*ʻbadsʻĭstsʻíni; but the best authorities in the tribe think otherwise. One version of this legend says that Estsánatlehi hid her children under the ground when Yéitso came seeking to devour them. This may have given rise to the idea that one of these children was called, also, Reared Beneath the Earth.

152. The following are the names of places where pieces were knocked off the stone: —

Bĭs*d*á, Edge of Bank.

*To*ʻkohokádi, Ground Level with Water. (Here Nayénĕzgạni chased the stone four times in a circle; the chips he knocked off are there yet.)

Daatsĭʻn*d*aheo*l*, Floating Corn-cob.

Nita*ti*ʼs, Cottonwood below Ground.

*Sa*sdĕstsáʻ, Gaping Bear.

Béikĭ*th*atyêl, Broad Lake.

Nánzozilin, Make Nanzoz Sticks.

Akĭ'*dd*ahalkaí, Something White on Top (of something else).

Anádsĭ*l*, Enemy Mountain.

*Sá*sbĭʻtoʻ, Bear Spring (Fort Wingate).

Tseʻtyêlĭskĭ'*d*, Broad Rock Hill.

*Ts*adi*h*ábĭtĭn, Antelope Trail Ascending.

Kĭnhitsói, Much Sumac.

*Ts*úskai (Chusca Knoll).

*L*estsí*d*elkai, Streaks of White Ashes.

Dsĭ*l*náodsĭ*l*, Mountain Surrounded by Mountains (Carrizo Mountains.).

*T*isnáspas, Circle of Cottonwood.

The above, it is said, are all places where constant springs of water (rare in the Navaho land) are to be found. Some are known to be such. This gives rise to the idea expressed in note 8. There is little doubt that the Navahoes believe in many of the Tiéholtsodi. Probably every constant spring or watercourse has its water god.

153. Version A adds an account of a wicked woman who dwelt at Kĭ'n*do*t*l*ĭz and slew her suitors. Nayénĕzgạni kills her. It also adds an account of vicious swallows who cut people with their wings. Version B omits the encounter with *Sa*snalkáhi and Tséʻnagahi.

154. Possibly this refers to Pueblo legends.

155. Version B, which gives only a very meagre account of this destructive storm, mentions only one talisman, but says that songs were sung and dances performed over this.

156. Such pillars as the myth refers to are common all over the Navaho land.

157. Version A makes Nayénĕzgạni say here: " I have been to niʻĭn*d*ahazlágo (the end of the earth); to *to*ʻĭn*d*ahazlágo (the end of the waters); to yaĭn*d*ahazlágo (the end of the sky); and to dsĭ*l*ĭn*d*ahazlágo (the end of the mountains), and I have found none that were not my friends."

158. Pás-sĭn-i is the name given by the Navahoes to the hard mineral substance which they use to make black beads, and other sacrifices to the gods of the north. Specimens of this substance have been examined by Prof. F. W. Clark of the United States Geological Survey, who pronounces it to be a fine bituminous coal of about the quality of cannel coal; so it is, for convenience, called cannel coal in this work. It is scarce in the Navaho land and is valued by the Indians.

159. This refers to large fossil bones found in many parts of Arizona and New Mexico.

160. *Ha*-*d*á-*h*o-ni-ge-*d*ĭ-neʻ (Mirage People), *Ha*-*d*á-*h*o-nes-*t*id-*d*ĭ-neʻ (Ground-

heat People). *Hadáhonestid* is translated ground-heat, for want of a more convenient term. It refers to the waving appearance given to objects in hot weather, observed so frequently in the arid region, and due to varying refraction near the surface of the ground.

161. The ceremony at Tsïnlí (Chinlee Valley) was to celebrate the nubility of Estsánatlehi. Although already a mother, she was such miraculously, and not until this time did she show signs of nubility. Such a ceremony is performed for every Navaho maiden now. The ceremony at San Francisco Mountain occurred four days after that at Tsïnlí. It is now the custom among the Navahoes to hold a second ceremony over a maiden four days after the first. On the second ceremony with Estsánatlehi they laid her on top of the mountain with her head to the west, because she was to go to the west to dwell there. They manipulated her body and stretched out her limbs. Thus she bade the people do, in future, to all Navaho maidens, and thus the Navahoes do now, in the ceremony of the fourth day, when they try to mould the body of the maiden to look like the perfect form of Estsánatlehi. Version A makes the nubile ceremony occur before the child was born.

162. Dsïl-líí-zïʻn, or Dsïllízïʻni (Black Mountain), is an extensive mesa in Apache County, Arizona. The pass to which the myth refers is believed to be that named, by the United States Geological Survey, Marsh Pass, which is about 60 miles north of the Moki villages. The name of the mesa is spelled " Zilh-le-jïni " on the accompanying map.

163. To'-yĕ't-li (Meeting Waters) is the junction of two important rivers somewhere in the valley of the San Juan River, in Colorado or Utah. The precise location has not been determined. It is a locality often mentioned in the Navaho myths. (See par. 477.)

164. The following appeared in the "American Naturalist" for February, 1887 : —

" In the interesting account entitled ' Some Deities and Demons of the Navajos,' by Dr. W. Matthews, in the October issue of the " Naturalist" (note 306), he mentions the fact that the warriors offered their sacrifices at the sacred shrine of Thoyetli, in the San Juan Valley. He says that the Navajos have a tradition that the gods of war, or sacred brothers, still dwell at Thoyetli, and their reflection is sometimes seen on the San Juan River. Dr. Matthews is certain the last part is due to some natural phenomenon. The following account seems to furnish a complete explanation of this part of the myth. Several years ago a clergyman, while travelling in the San Juan Valley, noticed a curious phenomenon while gazing down upon the San Juan River as it flowed through a deep canyon. Mists began to arise, and soon he saw the shadows of himself and companions reflected near the surface of the river, and surrounded by a circular rainbow, the ' Circle of Ulloa.' They jumped, moved away, and performed a number of exercises, to be certain that the figures were their reflections, and the figures responded. There was but slight color in the rainbow. Similar reflections have no doubt caused the superstitious Indians to consider these reflections as those of their deities." — G. A. Brennan, Roseland, Cook County, Illinois, January 12, 1887.

165. Tse'-gí-hi is the name of some canyon, abounding in cliff-dwellings, north of the San Juan River, in Colorado or Utah. The author knows of it only from description. It is probably the McElmo or the Mancos Canyon. It is supposed by the Navahoes to have been a favorite home of the yéi or gods, and the ruined cliff-houses are supposed to have been inhabited by the divine ones. The cliff ruins in the Chelly Canyon, Arizona, are also supposed to have been homes of the gods; in fact, the gods are still thought to dwell there unseen. Chelly is but a Spanish orthography of the Navaho name Tsé'gi, Tséyi or Tséyi. When a Navaho would say "in the Chelly Canyon," he says Tséyigi. The resemblance

of this expression to Tse'gíhi (g and y being interchangeable) led the author at first to confound the two places. Careful inquiry showed that different localities were meant. Both names have much the same meaning (Among the Cliffs, or Among the Rocks).

166. The expression used by the story-teller was, "seven times old age has killed." This would be freely translated by most Navaho-speaking whites as "seven ages of old men." The length of the age of an old man as a period of time is variously estimated by the Navahoes. Some say it is a definite cycle of 102 years, — the same number as the counters used in the game of kesitsé (note 176); others say it is "threescore years and ten;" while others, again, declare it to be an indefinite period marked by the death of some very old man in the tribe. This Indian estimate would give, for the existence of the nuclear gens of the Navaho nation, a period of from five hundred to seven hundred years. In his excellent paper on the "Early Navajo and Apache," [301] Mr. F. W. Hodge arrives at a much later date for the creation or first mention of the Tse'dzínkí'ni by computing the dates given in this legend, and collating the same with the known dates of Spanish-American history. He shows that many of the dates given in this story are approximately correct. While the Tse'dzínkí'ni is, legendarily, the nuclear gens of the Navahoes, it does not follow, even from the legend, that it is the oldest gens; for the *d*íné' *d*igíni, or holy people (see note 92), are supposed to have existed before it was created.

167. Tse'-dzín-kí'n-i is derived from tse' (rock), dzín (black, dark), and kin (a straight-walled house, a stone or adobe house, not a Navaho hut or *hog*án). Tse' is here rendered "cliffs," because the house or houses in question are described as situated in dark cliffs. Like nearly all other Navaho gentile names, it seems to be of local origin.

168. The rock formations of Arizona and New Mexico are often so fantastic that such a condition as that here described might easily occur.

169. The author has expressed the opinion elsewhere [31b] that we need not suppose from this passage that the story-teller wishes to commiserate the Tse'tláni on the inferiority of their diet; he may merely intend to show that his gens had not the same taboo as the elder gentes. The modern Navahoes do not eat ducks or snakes. Taboo is perhaps again alluded to in par. 394, where it is said that the *Th*á'paha ate ducks and fish. The Navahoes do not eat fish, and fear fish in many ways. A white woman, for mischief, emptied over a young Navaho man a pan of water in which fish had been soaked. He changed all his clothes and purified himself by bathing. Navahoes have been known to refuse candies that were shaped like fish.

170. A common method of killing deer and antelope in the old days was this: They were driven on to some high, steep-sided, jutting mesa, whose connection with the neighboring plateau was narrow and easily guarded. Here their retreat was cut off, and they were chased until constrained to jump over the precipice.

171. The name *To*'-*d*o-kón-*z*i is derived from two words, — *to*' (water) and *d*okónz (here translated saline). The latter word is used to denote a distinct but not an unpleasant taste. It has synonyms in other Indian languages, but not in English. It is known only from explanation that the water in question had a pleasant saline taste.

172. The arrow-case of those days is a matter of tradition only. The Indians say it looked something like a modern shawl-strap.

173. In the name of this gens we have possibly another evidence of a former existence of totemism among some of the Navaho gentes. *H*askán*h*atso may mean that many people of the Yucca gens lived in the land, and not that many yuccas grew there.

174. From the description given of this tree, which, the Indians say, still stands, it seems to be a big birch-tree.

175. Tsĭn-a-dzĭ′-ni is derived by double syncopation from tsĭn (wood), na (horizontal), dzĭn (dark or black), and the suffix ni. The word for black, dzĭn, in compounds is often pronounced zĭn. There is a place called Tsĭ′nadzĭn somewhere in Arizona, but the author has not located it.

176. Kĕ-sĭ-tsé, or kesitsé, from ke (moccasins), and sitsé (side by side, in a row), is a game played only during the winter months, at night and inside of a lodge. A multitude of songs, and a myth of a contest between animals who hunt by day and those who hunt by night, pertain to the game. Eight moccasins are buried in the ground (except about an inch of their tops), and they are filled with earth or sand. They are placed side by side, a few inches apart, in two rows, — one row on each side of the fire. A chip, marked black on one side (to represent night), is tossed up to see which side should begin first. The people of the lucky side hold up a screen to conceal their operations, and hide a small stone in the sand in one of the moccasins. When the screen is lowered, one of the opponents strikes the moccasins with a stick, and guesses which one contains the stone. If he guesses correctly, his side takes the stone to hide and the losers give him some counters. If he does not guess correctly, the first players retain the stone and receive a certain number of counters. (See note 88.) A better account of this game, with an epitome of the myth and several of the songs, has already been published.[116]

177. There are many allusions in the Navaho tales to the clothing of this people before the introduction of sheep (which came through the Spanish invaders), and before they cultivated the art of weaving, which they probably learned from the Pueblo tribes, although they are now better weavers than the Pueblos. The Navahoes represent themselves as miserably clad in the old days (par. 466), and they tell that many of their arts were learned from other tribes. (Par. 393.)

178. Allusion is here made to the material used by Indians on the backs of bows, for bow-strings, as sewing-thread, and for many other purposes, which is erroneously called "sinew" by ethnographers and travellers. It is not sinew in the anatomical or histological sense of the word. It is yellow fibrous tissue taken from the dorsal region, probably the aponeurosis of the trapezius.

179. The Navaho country abounds in small caves and rock-shelters, some of which have been walled up by these Indians and used as store-houses (but not as dwellings, for reasons elsewhere given, par. 26). Such store-houses are in use at this day.

180. The legends represent the Navahoes not only as poorly clad and poorly fed in the old days, but as possessing few arts. Here and elsewhere in the legends it is stated that various useful arts became known to the tribe through members of other tribes adopted by the Navahoes.

181. Another version states that when the Western immigrants were travelling along the western base of the Lukachokai Mountains, some wanted to ascend the Tse‘ĭnlín valley; but one woman said, " No: let us keep along the base of the mountain." From this they named her Base of Mountain, and her descendants bear that name now. This explanation is less likely than that in par. 393.

182. This statement should be accepted only with some allowance for the fact that it was made by one who was of the gens of *T*há‘paha.

183. Punishments for adultery were various and severe among many Indian tribes in former days. Early travellers mention amputation of the nose and other mutilations, and it appears that capital punishment for this crime was not uncommon. If there is any punishment for adultery among the Navahoes to-day, more severe than a light whipping, which is rarely given, the author has never heard of it. The position of the Navaho woman is such that grievous punishments would

not be tolerated. In the days of Góntso even, it would seem they were scarcely less protected than now, for then the husband, although a potent chief, did not dare to punish his wives — so the legend intimates — until he had received the consent of their relatives.

184. For the performance of these nine-days' ceremonies the Navahoes now build temporary medicine-lodges, which they use, as a rule, for one occasion only. Rarely is a ceremony performed twice in the same place, and there is no set day, as indicated by any phase of any particular lunation, for the beginning of any great ceremony. Many ceremonies may be performed only during the cold months, but otherwise the time for performance is not defined. There is a tradition that their customs were different when they lived in a compact settlement on the banks of the San Juan River (before they became shepherds and scattered over the land); that they then had permanent medicine-lodges, and exact dates for the performance of some ceremonies. In paragraph 411 we hear of a ceremony which lasted all winter.

185. For a description of this ceremony see " The Mountain Chant: a Navaho Ceremony," [314] by the author. It is an important healing ceremony of nine days' duration. The rites, until the last night, are held in the medicine-lodge and are secret. Just after sunset on the last day, a great round corral, or circle of evergreen branches, is constructed, called i/násdzĭn, or the dark circle of branches. This is about forty paces in diameter, about eight feet high, with an opening in the east about ten feet wide. From about eight P. M. on the last night of the ceremony until dawn next morning, a number of dances, dramatic shows, medicine rites, and tricks of legerdemain are performed in this corral, in the presence of a large group of spectators, — several hundred men, women, and children. No one is refused admittance. Fig. 37 shows the dark circle of branches as it appears at sunrise when the rites are over, and, in addition to the original opening in the east, three other openings have been made in the circle. Fig. 30 shows the alíl (rite, show, or ceremony) of nahikáï, which takes place on this occasion, and it is designed largely for the entertainment and mystification of the spectators. The performers march around (and very close to) the great central fire, which emits an intense heat. Their skin would probably be scorched if it were not heavily daubed with white earth. Each actor carries a short wand, at the tip of which is a ball of eagle-down. This ball he must burn off in the fire, and then, by a simple sleight-of-hand trick, seem to restore the ball again to the end of his wand. When this is accomplished, he rushes out of the corral, trumpeting like a sand-hill crane. In " The Mountain Chant " this is called a dance, but the movements of the actors are not in time to music. Nahikáï signifies " it becomes white again," and refers to the reappearance of the eagle-down. The show is very picturesque, and must be mystifying to simple minds.

186. Tse'-zĭn-di-aí signifies Black Rock Standing (like a wall). It might mean an artificial wall of black rock ; but as the result of careful inquiry it has been learned that the name refers to a locality where exists the formation known to geologists as trap-dyke. It cannot be averred that it is applied to all trap-dyke.

187. Slaves were numerous among the Navahoes, and slavery was openly recognized by them until 1883, when the just and energetic agent, Mr. D. M. Riordan, did much to abolish it. Yet as late as 1893, when the writer was last in the Navaho country, he found evidence that the institution still existed, though very occultly, and to a more limited extent than formerly.

188. Some translate *H*áltso as Yellow Valley, and give a different myth to account for the name. As most Navaho gentile names are undoubtedly of local origin, there may be a tendency to make all gentile names accord with the general rule.

189. The word here translated pet (*lin*) means also a domestic animal and a personal fetich. (See par. 63.)

190. Although this name, Bĭ-*tá*'-ni, seems so much like that of Bĭtáni that one might think they were but variants of the same word, they are undoubtedly distinct names and must not be confounded.

191. This is believed to be the notable landmark called by the whites Sunset Peak, which is about ten miles east of San Francisco Peak, in Yavapai County, Arizona. Sunset Peak is covered with dark forests nearly to its summit. The top is of brilliant red rock capped by a paler stratum, and it has the appearance, at all hours of the day, of being lighted by the setting sun.

192. This locality is in Apache County, Arizona, about sixty miles from the eastern boundary and twelve miles from the northern boundary of the Territory. A sharp volcanic peak, 6,825 feet high above sea-level, which marks the place from afar, is called "Agathla Needle" on the maps of the United States Geological Survey, and on the accompanying map, which was compiled from the government maps by Mr. Frank Tweedy of the Geological Survey.

193. The Navahoes are aware that in lands far to the north there are kindred tribes which speak languages much like their own. They have traditions that long ago some of their number travelled in search of these tribes and found them. These distant kinsmen are called by the Navaho Dĭné' Na*h*otlóni, or Navahoes in Another Place.

194. A version has been recorded which says that, on the march, one woman loitered behind at Deer Spring for a while, as if loath to leave; that for this reason they called her Deer Spring, and that her descendants became the gens of that name. The same version accounts in a similar manner for the names given at the magic fountains. The women did not call out the names of the springs, but they loitered at them.

195. The story of the Deer Spring People affords, perhaps, the best evidence in favor of the former existence of totemism to be found in the legend. Assuming that the immigrants from the west had once totemic names, we may explain this story by saying that it was people of the Deer gens who stayed behind and gave their name to the spring where they remained; that in the course of time they became known as People of the Deer Spring; and that, as they still retain their old name in a changed form, the story-teller is constrained to say that the fate of the deer is not known. Perhaps the name of the Mai*tó*'*d*'ĭne' (par. 428) may be explained in somewhat the same way. (See "The Gentile System of the Navajo Indians," p. 107.[818])

196. The more proper interpretation of *H*o-na-gá'-ni seems to be People of the Walking Place, from *h*o (locative), nága (to walk), and ni (people). It is not unreasonable to suppose that, like nearly all other Navaho gentile names, this name has a local meaning, and that the story here told to account for its origin is altogether mythical.

197. This episode indicates that kindness and pity are sentiments not unknown to the Navahoes, and that (though there are many thieves) there are honest men and women among them.

198. Na-na*s*-tě'-*zin*, the Navaho name for the Zuñi Indians, is said to be derived from aná (an alien or an enemy), nas*te* (a horizontal stripe), and *z*ĭn (black). Some say it refers to the way the Zuñians cut their hair, — "bang" it, — straight across the forehead; others say it is the name of a locality.

199. Ki*n*-a-á'-ni, or Ki*n*-ya-á'-ni, means People of the High Pueblo House, — the high wall of stone or adobe. The name ki*n*aá' might with propriety be applied to any one of hundreds of ruins in the Navaho country, but the only one to which the name is known to be given is a massive ruin six or seven stories high

in Bernalillo County, New Mexico, about seventeen miles in a northerly direction from Chaves Station, on the Atlantic and Pacific Railroad. This ruin consists of unusually large fragments of stone, and looks more like a ruined European castle than other old Indian dwellings. It seems too far east and south, and too far away from the settlements on the San Juan, where the western immigrants finished their journey, to be the place, as some say it is, from which the gens of Kinaá'ni derived its name. The high stone wall which the immigrants passed en route, mentioned in par. 435 in connection with the gens of Kinaá'ni, may be the place to which the legend originally ascribed the origin of the name. There are many pueblo remains around San Francisco Mountain. The name is written " Kin-ya-a-ni " on the accompanying map.

200. Plate I., fig. 1, shows a yébaad, or female yéi or goddess, as she is usually represented in the dry-paintings. The following objects are here indicated: (1) A square mask or domino, which covers the face only (see fig. 28), is painted blue, margined below with yellow (to represent the yellow evening light), and elsewhere with lines of red and black (for hair above, for ears at the sides), and has downy eagle-feathers on top, tied on with white strings; (2) a robe of white, extending from the armpits to near the knees, adorned with red and blue to represent sun-beams, and fringed beautifully at the bottom; (3) white leggings secured with colored garters (such as Indians weave); (4) embroidered moccasins; (5) an orna-mental sash; (6) a wand of spruce-twigs in each hand (sometimes she is shown with spruce in one hand and a seed-basket in the other); (7) jewels — ear-pendants, bracelets, and necklaces — of turquoise and coral; (8) long strips of fox-skin orna-mented at the ends, which hang from wrists and elbows. (For explanation of blue neck, see note 74.) In the dance of the nahikáï, there are properly six yébaad in masquerade; but sometimes they have to get along with a less number, owing to the difficulty in finding suitable persons enough to fill the part. The actors are usually low-sized men and boys, who must contrast in appearance with those who enact the part of males. Each yébaad actor wears no clothing except moccasins and a skirt, which is held on with a silver-studded belt; his body and limbs are painted white; his hair is unbound and hangs over his shoulders; he wears the square female mask and he carries in each hand a bundle of spruce twigs, which is so secured, by means of strings, that he cannot carelessly let it fall. Occasion-ally females are found to dance in this character: these have their bodies fully clothed in ordinary woman's attire; but they wear the masks and carry the wands just as the young men do. While the male gods, in plate I., except Dsahadoldzá, are represented with white arms, the female is depicted with yellow arms. This symbolism is explained in note 27.

201. The exact etymology of the word Na-tí'n-ĕs-tha-ni has not been deter-mined. The idea it conveys is: He who teaches himself, he who discovers for himself, or he who thinks out a problem for himself. We find the verb in the expression nasíniťin, which means, " Teach me how to do it." Here the second and third syllables are pronouns. Although the hero has his name changed after a while, the story-teller usually continues to call him Natí'nĕsthani to the end of the story. Often he speaks of him as the man or the Navaho.

202. The eighteen articles here referred to are as follows: 1, white shell; 2, tur-quoise; 3, haliotis shell; 4, pászini or cannel coal; 5, red stone; 6, feathers of the yellow warbler; 7, feathers of the bluebird; 8, feathers of the eagle; 9, feathers of the turkey; 10, beard of the turkey; 11, cotton string; 12, i'yidĕzná; [11] 13, white shell basket; 14, turquoise basket; 15, haliotis basket; 16, pászini basket; 17, rock crystal basket; 18, sacred buckskin. (See note 13.) These were the sacred articles which the gods were said to require in the myths of klédzi hatál and atsósidze hatál. In the myths of the former rite they are mentioned over and

over again, to the weariness of the hearer. They are all used to-day in the rites mentioned, except the five baskets. Now ordinary sacred baskets (note 5, par. 28) are used ; the jeweled baskets are legendary only.

203. The knowledge of domestic or pet turkeys is not new to the Navahoes. The Pueblo Indians of the Southwest have kept them for centuries. The Navahoes declare that in former years they kept pet turkeys themselves; but this seems doubtful, considering their mode of life. A conservative Navaho will not now eat turkey flesh, although he will not hesitate to shoot a wild turkey to sell it to a white man.

204. In the Navaho dry-paintings the rainbow is usually depicted with a head at one end and legs and feet at the other. The head is represented with a square mask to show that it is a goddess. It is apotheosized. (See fig. 29.) In one of the dry-paintings of the mountain chant the rainbow is depicted without limbs or head, but terminating at one end with five eagle-plumes, at the other end with five magpie-plumes, and decorated near its middle with plumes of the bluebird and the red-shafted woodpecker. (See " The Mountain Chant," p. 450.[814])

205. This magic cup figures in many other Navaho myths. (See paragraph 572.)

206. *H*as-ts*é*-ol-*t*o-i means the Shooting *H*ast*s*é (par. 78), or Shooting Deity. As the personator of this character always wears a female mask (fig. 28), it would seem that this divinity of the chase, like the Roman Diana, is a goddess. The personator (a man) carries a quiver of puma skin, a bow, and two arrows. The latter are made of reed, are headless, and are feathered with the tail and wing feathers of the red-tailed buzzard (*Buteo borealis*), tied on with fibrous tissue. The tips of the arrows are covered with moistened white earth and moistened pollen. Each arrow is at least two spans and a hand's-breadth long ; but it must be cut off three finger-widths beyond a node, and to accomplish this it may be made a little longer than the above dimensions. There are very particular rules about applying the feathers. The man who personates *H*asts*é*ol*t*oi, in a rite of succor in the ceremony of the night chant, follows the personators of the War Gods. While the patient stands on a buffalo robe in front of the medicine-lodge, the actor waves with the right hand one arrow at him, giving a peculiar call ; then, changing the arrows from one hand to another, he waves the other arrow at the patient. This is done east, south, west, and north. The actor repeats these motions around the lodge ; all then enter the lodge ; there the patient says a prayer, and, with many formalities, presents a cigarette to the personator (after he has prayed and sacrificed to the War Gods). The three masqueraders then go to the west of the lodge to deposit their sacrifices (that of *H*asts*é*ol*t*oi is put under a weed, — *Gutierrezia euthamiæ*, if possible). When this is done, they take off their masks, don ordinary blankets, — brought out by an accomplice, — hide the masks under their blankets, and return to the lodge in the guise of ordinary Indians. Some speak as if there were but one *H*asts*é*ol*t*oi, and say she is the wife of Nay*é*n*ĕ*zg*ạ*ni. Others speak as if there were one at every place where the y*é*i have homes.

207. The G*á*n-as-k*ĭ*-*d*i are a numerous race of divinities. Their chief home is at a place called *D*ep*é*ha*h*a*t*íl (Tries to Shoot Sheep), near Tse'g*í*hi, north of the San Juan ; but they may appear anywhere, and, according to the myths, are often found in company with the y*é*i and other gods. They belong to the Mountain Sheep People, and often appear to man in the form of Rocky Mountain sheep. In the myths of the night chant it is said that they captured the prophet of the rites, took him to their home, and taught him many of the mysteries of the night chant. In the treatment accompanying these, the tendo-achillis of a mountain sheep is applied to an aching limb to relieve pain ; the horn is pressed to an

aching head to relieve headache; and water from the sheep's eye is used for sore eyes. The Gánaskĭdᵢ are gods of plenty and harvest gods. A masquerader, representing one of these, sometimes appears in an act of succor about sundown on the last day of the night chant, following representatives of *H*astséyal*t*i and Dsaha*d*oldzá. He wears the ordinary blue mask of a yébaka with the fringe of hair removed. He carries a crown or headdress made of a basket from which the bottom has been cut, so that it may fit on the head. The basket crown is adorned with artificial horns; it is painted on the lower surface black, with a zigzag streak to represent lightning playing on the face of a black cloud; it is painted red on the upper surface (not shown in picture), to indicate the sunlight on the other side of the cloud; and it is decorated with radiating feathers, from the tail of the red-shafted woodpecker (*Colaptes mexicanus*), to represent the rays of the sun streaming out at the edge of the cloud. The god is crowned with the storm-cloud. The horns on the crown are made of the skin of the Rocky Mountain sheep (sewed with yucca fibre); they are stuffed with hair of the same, or with black wool; they are painted part black and part blue, with white markings; and they are tipped with eagle-feathers tied on with white string. On his back the actor carries a long bag of buckskin, which is empty, but is kept distended by means of a light frame made of the twigs of aromatic sumac, so as to appear full; it is decorated at the back with eagle-plumes, and sometimes also with the plumes of the red-shafted woodpecker; it is painted on the sides with short parallel white lines (12 or 16), and at the back with long lines of four colors. This bag represents a bag of black cloud, filled with produce of the fields, which the god is said to carry. The cloudy bag is so heavy, they say, that the god is obliged to lean on a staff, bend his back, and walk as one bearing a burden; so the personator does the same. The staff, or gĭs, which the latter carries, is made of cherry (new for each occasion); it is as long as from the middle of the left breast to the tip of the outstretched right hand; it is painted black with the charcoal of four sacred plants; it bears a zigzag stripe in white to represent lightning, and it is trimmed with many turkey-feathers in two whorls, and one eagle-feather. These properties and adornments are conventionally represented in the dry-paintings. (See plate I., fig. 5.) The red powder thinly sprinkled over the eagle-plumes at the back represents pollen. The cloud bag is tied on the god, says the myth, with rainbows. The yellow horizontal line at the chin in the picture represents a yellow line on the mask which symbolizes the evening twilight. The actor wears a collar of fox-skin (indicated by mark under right ear) and ordinary clothing. The elaborate ceremony of succor will not be described here. Gánaskĭdᵢ means Humpback. The name is sometimes given Ná*n*askĭdᵢ.

208. The only Kĭ′n*d*olᵢz, or Kĭ′n*d*o*t*lᵢz (Blue House), the writer knows of is a ruined pueblo of that name in the Chaco Canyon; but this can hardly be the Blue House referred to in the myth. There is probably another ruin of this name on the banks of the San Juan.

209. The Dsaha*d*oldzá, or Fringe-mouths, are a class of divine beings of whom little information has been gained. They are represented in the rite of klé*dz*i *h*atál by sand-paintings, and by masqueraders decked and masked as shown in the pictures. There are two kinds, — Fringe-mouths of the land and Fringe-mouths of the water (plate I., fig. 3), or *T*-astlátsi Dsaha*d*oldzá; the latter are the class referred to in this story. The zigzag lines on their bodies shown in the pictures represent the crooked lightning, which they used as ropes to lift the log. On the mask (shown in the dry-painting) the mouth is surrounded by white radiating lines; hence the name Fringe-mouths. The actor who represents the Fringe-mouths of the land has one half of his body and one half of his mask painted black, the other half red. He who represents the Fringe-mouths of the water

has his body painted half blue and half yellow, as shown in plate I., fig. 3. Both wear a similar mask and a similar crown or headdress. The crown consists of a basket from which the bottom has been cut, so that it may fit on the head; the lower surface is painted black, to represent a dark cloud, and is streaked with white to represent lightning; the upper surface (not shown in the painting) is colored red, to represent the sunlight of the back of the cloud; and feathers of the red-shafted woodpecker are attached to the edge, to represent sunbeams. So far, this crown is like that worn by Gánaskïdi (note 207). Ascending from the basket crown is a tripod of twigs of aromatic sumac, painted white; between the limbs of the tripod finely combed red wool is laid, and a downy eagle-feather tips each stick. The actor carries in his left hand a bow adorned with three eagle-plumes and two tufts of turkey feathers, and in his right hand a white gourd rattle, sometimes decorated with two whorls of feathers. His torso, arms, and legs are naked, but painted. He wears a shirt around his loins, and rich necklaces and ear pendants. All these things are plainly indicated in the dry-paintings. The fox-skin collar which he wears is vaguely shown by an appendage at the right ear. The angles of the white lightning on the chest and limbs of the actor are not as numerous as in the paintings.

210. Tie*lín* are ferocious pets that belong to Tiéholtsodi, the water monster, and guard the door of his dwelling. They are said to have blue horns.

211. Na-tsi-lï′*t* a-kó-di (short rainbow), the fragmentary or incomplete rainbow.

212. *H*as-tsé-z*ï*n-i signifies Black *H*astsé, or Black God. There are several of them (dwelling at Tsení′*hod*ī*l*yī*l*, near Tse′gíhi), but the description will be given in the singular. He is a reserved, exclusive individual. The yéi at other places do not visit him whenever they wish. He owns all fire; he was the first who made fire, and he is the inventor of the fire-drill. It is only on rare occasions that he is represented by a masquerader at a ceremony. When it is arranged to give a night chant without the public dance of the last night (and this seldom occurs), Black God appears in a scene of succor [206] on the evening of the ninth day in company with three other gods, — Nayénězgạni, *T*o′badzïstsíni, and *H*astséol*t*oi. It is said that the personator is dressed in black clothes; wears a black mask, with white marks and red hair on it, and a collar of fox-skin; and that he carries a fire-drill and a bundle of cedar-bark. The author has never seen *H*astsézïni represented either in a dry-painting or in masquerade, and he has therefore never witnessed the scene or ceremony of succor referred to. This ceremony, which is very elaborate, has been described to the author by the medicine-men. The actor has to be well paid for his tedious services, which occupy the whole day from sunrise to sunset, though the act of succor lasts but a few minutes.

213. The fire-drill is very little used by the Navahoes at the present time, — matches and flint-and-steel having taken its place; but it is frequently mentioned in the myths and is employed in the ceremonies. Of the many aboriginal fire-drills, described and depicted by Dr. Walter Hough in his excellent paper on "Fire-making Apparatus," [302] that of the Navahoes is the rudest. It looks like a thing that had been made to order.

214. Tsïn-tlï′-zi signifies hard, brittle wood.

215. It is probable that the various peculiar acts described in this paragraph have reference to agricultural rites still practised, or recently practised, by the Navahoes, but the writer has never witnessed such rites.

216. The Navahoes now universally smoke cigarettes, but they say that in ancient days they smoked pipes made of terra-cotta. Fragments of such pipes are often picked up in New Mexico and Arizona. The cliff-dwellers also had pipes, and these articles are still ceremonially used by the Mokis. The Navahoes

now invariably, in ceremonies, sacrifice tobacco in the form of cigarettes. But cigarettes are not new to the Southwest: they are found in ancient caves and other long-neglected places in New Mexico and Arizona.

217. Ni-no-ká-*d̓*-ne' (People up on the Earth) may mean people living up on the mountains, in contradistinction to those dwelling in canyons and valleys; but other tribes use a term of similar meaning to distinguish the whole Indian race from the whites or other races, and it is probable that it is used in this sense here and in other Navaho myths. The people whom Na*t̓*'něs*t̓h*ani now meets are probably supposed to be supernatural, and not Indians.

218. The plants mixed with the tobacco were these: tsohodzïlaï', *s*ilátso (my thumb), a poisonous weed, azébini', and azétloi. It has not been determined what plants these are; but the Navaho names are placed on record as possibly assisting in future identification.

219. In the Navaho ceremonies, when sacred cigarettes are finished, and before they are deposited as offerings to the gods, they are symbolically lighted with sunbeams. (See par. 94.) The statement made here, that the hero lighted his pipe with the sun, refers probably to this symbolic lighting.

220. Kĕ'tlo is a name given to any medicine used externally, *i. e.*, rubbed on the body. Atsósi kĕ'tlo means the liniment or wash of the atsósi *hatál*, or feather ceremony. It is also called atsósi azé (feather medicine), and atsósi ts*ï*l (feather herbs).

221. Yá-*d̓*-*d̓*-ni*l*, the incense of the Navaho priests, is a very composite substance. In certain parts of the healing ceremonies it is scattered on hot coals, which are placed before the patient, and the latter inhales actively the dense white fumes that arise. These fumes, which fill with their odor the whole medicine-lodge, are pungent, aromatic, and rather agreeable, although the mixture is said to contain feathers. The author has obtained a formula for yá*d̓*id̓ini*l*, but has not identified the plants that chiefly compose it.

222. These are the animals he raises and controls, as told in par. 527.

223. The Navahoes say they are acquainted with four kinds of wild tobacco, and use them in their rites. Of these the author has seen and identified but two. These are *Nicotiana attenuata*, which is the ds*ï*'*l*na*t*o, or mountain tobacco; and *Nicotiana palmeri*, which is the *d*epéna*t*o, or sheep tobacco. *N. attenuata* grows widely but not abundantly in the mountains of New Mexico and Arizona. *N. palmeri* is rare; the writer has seen it growing only in one spot in the Chelly Canyon. It has not been learned what species are called weasel tobacco and cloud tobacco; but one or more of the three species, *N. rustica*, *N. quadrivalvis*, and *N. trigonophylla*, are probably known to the Navahoes.

224. The description of these diseases given by the narrator of this tale is as follows: "Patients having these diseases are weak, stagger, and lose appetite; then they go to a sweat-house and take an emetic. If they have *l*ï'tso, or the yellow disease, they vomit something yellow (bile?). If they have *t*ï*l*-*l*itá, or cooked blood disease, they vomit something like cooked blood. Those having the yellows have often yellow eyes and yellow skin. *Th*a*t*lï'*t*, or slime disease, comes from drinking foul water full of green slime or little fish (tadpoles?). T*s*os, worms, usually come from eating worms, which you sometimes do without knowing it; but ts*ï*'lgo, tapeworm, comes from eating parched corn." Probably the last notion arises from the slight resemblance of the joints of *Tænia solium* to grains of corn. This little chapter in pathology from Ha*t*á*l*i Natlói is hardly in accordance with the prevalent theory that savages regard all disease as of demoniac origin.

225. The adjective yaz*ó*ni, or ya*s*óni, here used, which is translated " beautiful," means more than this: it means both good (or useful) and beautiful. It contains

elements of the words ya*tí*ʻ, good, and of ïn*z*óni, nï*z*óni, and *h*o*z*óni, which signify beautiful.

226. According to the Navaho myths and songs, the corn and other products in the gardens of the yéi or divine ones grow and mature in a very short time. The rapid growth of the crops in Na*tí*ʻnĕs*th*ani's farm is supposed to result from the divine origin of the seed.

227. The order in which Na*tí*ʻnĕs*th*ani lays down the ears of corn is the order in which sacrificial cigarettes, kethawns, and other sacred objects, when colored, are laid down in a straight row. The white, being the color of the east, has pre-cedence of all and is laid down first. The blue, the color of the south, comes next, for when we move sunwise (the sacred ceremonial circuit of the Navahoes) south follows immediately after east. Yellow, the color of the west, on the same principle, comes third; and black (in this case mixed) comes fourth. Mixed is properly the coloring of the upper region, and usually follows after black; but it sometimes takes the place of black. These apparently superfluous particulars of laying down the corn have a ceremonial or religious significance. In placing sacred objects ceremonially in a straight row, the operator proceeds southward from his starting-point, for this approximates the sunwise circuit, and he makes the tip ends point east.

228. Pí*n*-i-a*z* bï-tsó (fawn-his-cheese), or fawn-cheese, is a substance found in the abdomen of the fawn. A similar substance is found in other young mammals. They say it looks like curds, or cottage cheese, and that it is pleasant to the taste. They eat it raw. The author has not determined by observation what this sub-stance is. Dr. C. Hart Merriam, of the Department of Agriculture, suggests that it is the partly digested milk in the stomach of the fawn, and this is probably the case.

229. The dish offered to Na*tí*ʻnĕs*th*ani is called by the Navahoes at*s*ó*n*, which is here translated "pemmican." It consists of dried venison pounded on a stone and fried in grease.

230. To make *d*ï-tló-gi kle-sán, cut the grain off the ear, grind it to a pulp on a metate, spread out the embers, lay a number of green corn leaves on them, place the pulp on the leaves, put other leaves on top of the pulp, rake hot embers over all, and leave it to bake.

231. *D*ï-tló-gï*n* *ts*ï-dï-kó-i is made of a pulp of green corn ground on a metate, like *d*ïtlógi klesán. The pulp is encased in husks, which are folded at the ends, and is then placed between leaves and hot coals to bake.

232. *Th*á-bï-t*s*a (three-ears) is made also of pulp of green corn. This is placed in folded cones made of husks; three cones being made of one complete husk, whose leaves are not removed from their stem. It looks like three ears fastened together, whence the name. It is boiled in water.

233. The story-teller said: "about as far as from here to Jake's house," — a distance which the writer estimated at 300 yards.

234. Over the east door, one cigarette, that for the male, was made of moun-tain mahogany (tsé‘es*t*agi, *Cercocarpus parvifolius*), perforated, painted blue, and marked with four symbols of deer-tracks in yellow; the other cigarette, that for the female, was made of cliff rose (awétsal, *Cowania mexicana*), painted yellow and marked with four symbols of deer-tracks in blue. Over the south door the cigaret*ṭ*e for the male was made of sunflower (ïn*d*ïgíli), painted yellow and dotted with four symbols of antelope-tracks in blue; the cigarette for the female was made of "strong-smelling sunflower" (ïn*d*ïgíli nïlt*s*óni, *Verbesina enceloides*), painted white and dotted with four symbols of antelope-tracks in black. Over the west door, the cigarettes were of the same material as those in the east; but one was painted black with symbols of deer-tracks in blue, and the other was

painted blue with symbols of deer-tracks in black. At the bottom of the steps, one of the cigarettes was painted black and dotted with four symbols of fawn-tracks in yellow; the other was painted yellow and dotted with four symbols of fawn-tracks in black. The above was written from the description of the narrator. The writer has never seen such cigarettes; but they are said to be employed in some Navaho ceremonies at the present time. In this series of cigarettes the colors are not in the usual order,[18] but there may be a special symbolism for these animals, or the variation may arise because they are the cigarettes of a wizard and therefore unholy.

235. When driving game to a party in ambush, the Navahoes often imitate the cry of the wolf. In this myth the old man is supposed to give the cry, not to drive the bears, but to make Naťí'něsťhani believe that deer are being driven.

236. The name Tsa-na-naí is derived from tsan, which means dung. Tsĕ'-sko-ďi means Spread-foot. The narrator said the other bears had names, but he could not remember them.

237. "He did not even thank his son-in-law" is an instance of sarcasm.

238. The bear is a sacred animal with the Navahoes; for this reason the hero did not skin the bears or eat their flesh. The old man, being a wizard, might do both.

239. Há-la-dzï-ni? means "What are you doing?" but it is a jocose expression, used only among intimate relations, or relations by marriage. In employing this interrogatory the Navaho gave the old man to understand that he was recognized.

240. This episode of the twelve bears is the weakest and least artistic in the tale. Moreover, it details a fifth device on the part of Deer Raiser to kill his son-in-law. Under ordinary circumstances we should expect but four devices. It seems an interpolation, by some story-teller less ingenious than he who composed the rest of the tale, introduced to get the men out together once more, so that, on their way home, the incident of the burnt moccasins might occur. The latter incident has been previously recorded by the writer in another connection. (See note 242.)

241. Among the Navahoes, when a person dies, the suffix ni, or ini, is added to his (or her) name, and thus he is mentioned ever afterwards.

242. Before the story of Naťí'něsťhani was obtained, the writer had already recorded this tale of the burnt moccasins in a version of the Origin Legend. In the latter connection it is introduced as one of the Coyote tales. The mischievous Coyote is made to try this trick on his father-in-law; but the latter, warned by the Wind, foils the Coyote.

243. The ridge which he crosses in the east and also those which he crosses later in the south, west, and north are colored according to the regular order of Navaho symbolism.

244. The narrator described the bird called tsï-das-tó-i thus: When a man passes by where this bird is sitting, the latter does not fly off, but sits and looks at the man, moving its head in every direction. It is about the size of a screech-owl.

245. It must not be supposed that in this and the following paragraph, when pale-faced people are mentioned, any allusion is made to Caucasians. The reference is merely symbolic. White is the color of the east in Navaho symbolism: hence these people in the east are represented as having pale faces. For similar reasons the man in the south (par. 551) is said to have a blue face, the man in the west (par. 552) a yellow face, and the man in the north (par. 553) a dark face. (See note 18.)

246. Bï-za (his treasure), something he specially values; hence his charm, his amulet, his personal fetich, his magic weapon, something that one carries to mysteriously protect himself. Even the divinities are thought to possess such

charms. The songs often mention some property of a god which they say is " Bĭ′za-yedĭgĭ′ngo " (The treasure which makes him holy or sacred). (See par. 367 and note 280.)

247. These medicines are still in use among the Navahoes. The medicine made of gall consists mostly of gall of eagles. If a witch has scattered evil medicine on you, use this. If there are certain kinds of food that disagree with you, and you still wish to eat them, use the vomit medicine. Hunters obtain the materials when they go out hunting. All the totemic animals named (puma, blue fox, yellow fox, wolf, and lynx, see par. 548) vomit when they eat too much. So said the narrator.

248. *Buteo borealis.* The tail is described as red ("bright chestnut red," Coues) by our ornithologists; but the Navahoes consider it yellow, and call the bird atsé-*l*ĭtsói, or yellow-tail.

249. A-tsó-**si-**dƶe *ha-tál*, or a-tsó-si *ha-tál*, means feather chant or feather ceremony. The following particulars concerning the ceremony were given by the narrator of the story. Dry-paintings are made on the floor of the medicine-lodge much like those of the klédƶi *hatál*, and others are made representing different animals. It is still occasionally celebrated, but not often, and there are only four priests of the rite living. It lasts nine days, and it has more stories, songs, and acts than any other Navaho ceremony. A deer dance was part of the rite in the old days, but it is not practised now. The rite is good for many things, but especially for deer disease. If you sleep on a dry, undressed deer-skin or foul one, or if a deer sneezes at you or makes any other marked demonstration at you, you are in danger of getting the deer disease.

250. Yó-i *ha-tál*, or yói-dƶe *ha-tál* (bead chant), is a nine days' ceremony, which is becoming obsolete. The author has been informed that there is only one priest of the rite remaining; that he learned it from his father, but that he does not know as much about it as his father did.

251. The device of setting up forked sticks to assist in locating fires seen by night and in remembering the position of distant objects is often mentioned in the Navaho tales. (See pars. 382 and 497.)

252. *Equisetum hiemale*, and perhaps other species of *Equisetum*, or horse-tail.

253. ["Klĭ́s-ka′, the arrow-snake, is a long slender snake that moves with great velocity, — so great that, coming to the edge of a cliff when racing, he flies for some distance through the air before reaching the ground again. The Navahoes believe he could soar if he wanted to. He is red and blue on the belly, striped on the back, six feet long or longer. Sometimes moves like a measuring-worm."] From the above description Dr. H. C. Yarrow, formerly curator of reptiles in the Smithsonian Institution, is of the opinion that the arrow-snake is *Bascanium flagelliforme.*

254. *Accipiter cooperii*, called gíni by the Navahoes.

255. Compare with description of Spider Woman and her home in paragraph 306. It would seem that the Navahoes believe in more than one Spider Woman. (May be they believe in one for each world.) In paragraph 581 we have an instance of black being assigned to the east and white to the north. (See note 18.)

256. There are several plants in New Mexico and Arizona which become tumble-weeds in the autumn, but the particular weed referred to here is the *Amarantus albus*. It is called tlo*t*áhi nagĭ′si, or rolling tlo*t*áhi, by the Navahoes. Tlo*t*áhi is a name applied in common to several species of the *Amarantaceæ* and allied *Chenopodiaceæ*. (See "Navaho Names for Plants." [312]) The seeds of plants of these families formerly constituted an important part of the diet of the Navahoes, and they still eat them to some extent.

257. Tsĭ́l-*d*ĭl-gĭ́-si is said to mean frightened-weed, scare-weed, or hiding-weed,

and to be so named because snakes, lizards, and other animals hide in its dense foliage when frightened. It is a yellow-flowered composite, *Gutierrezia euthamiæ* (T. and G.), which grows in great abundance in Arizona and New Mexico. It is used extensively in the Navaho ceremonies in preparing and depositing sacrifices, etc.

258. Whirlwinds of no great violence are exceedingly common throughout the arid region. One seldom looks at an extensive landscape without seeing one or more columns of whirling dust arising.

259. In the full myth of yói *hatál*, as told by a priest of the rite, a complete account of the ceremonies, songs, and sacrifices taught to the Navaho would here be given; but in this account, told by an outsider, the ritual portion is omitted.

260. In the myth of the "Mountain Chant," [314] p. 410, it is stated, as in this tale, that the wanderer returning to his old home finds the odors of the place intolerable to him. Such incidents occur in other Navaho myths.

261. In the rite of the klédʐi *hatál*, or the night chant, the first four masked characters, who come out to dance in the public performance of the last night, are called atsá'ʃei. From this story it would seem that a similar character or characters belong to the yói *hatál*.

262. These great shells are perhaps not altogether mythical. Similar shells are mentioned in the Origin Legend (pars. 211, 213, 226), in connection with the same pueblos. Shells of such size, conveyed from the coast to the Chaco Canyon, a distance of 300 miles or more, before the introduction of the horse, would have been of inestimable value among the Indians.

263. In the myth recorded in "The Mountain Chant: a Navaho Ceremony," [314] p. 413, there is an account of a journey given by a courier who went to summon some distant bands to join in a ceremony. From this account the following passage is taken: "I . . . went to the north. On my way I met another messenger, who was travelling from a distant camp to this one to call you all to a dance in a circle of branches of a different kind from ours. When he learned my errand he tried to prevail on me to return hither and put off our dance until another day, so that we might attend their ceremony, and that they might in turn attend ours; but I refused, saying our people were in haste to complete their dance. Then we exchanged bows and quivers, as a sign to our people that we had met, and that what we would tell on our return was the truth. You observe the bow and quiver I have now are not those with which I left this morning. We parted, and I kept on my way toward the north." In par. 597 of "The Great Shell of Kíntyél" reference is made to the same identical meeting of couriers. It is interesting to observe how one legend is made to corroborate the other, — each belonging to a different rite.

264. Pésdolgas is here translated serrate knife. A saw is called benitsíhi, but in describing it the adjective dolgás is used for serrate. The pésdolgas is mentioned often in song and story. It is said to be no longer in use. Descriptions indicate that it was somewhat like the many-bladed obsidian weapon of the ancient Mexicans.

265. The cliff-ruin known as the White House, in the Chelly Canyon, Arizona, has been often pictured and described. It is called by the Navahoes Kin-i-na-é-kai, which signifies Stone House of the White Horizontal Streak (the upper story is painted white). The name White House is a free translation of this. The Navaho legends abound in references to it, and represent it as once inhabited by divinities. (See par. 78 and fig. 22.)

266. *Hát-das-tsí-si* is a divinity who is not depicted in the dry-paintings, and whose representative the author has not seen. He appears rarely in the ceremonies and is thus described: The actor wears an ordinary Navaho costume, and

an ordinary yébaka mask adorned with owl-feathers, but not with eagle-plumes. He carries on his back an entire yucca plant with the leaves hanging down, and a large ring, two spans in diameter, made of yucca leaves (to show that he is a great gambler at nán*z*o*z*). He carries a whip of yucca leaves, and goes around among the assembled crowd to treat the ailing. If a man has lumbago he bends over before the actor and presents his back to be flagellated; if he has headache he presents his head. When the actor has whipped the ailing one, he turns away from him and utters a low sound (like the lowing of a cow). When he can find no more people to whip, he returns to the medicine-lodge and takes off his mask. The cigarette (which the author has in his possession) appropriate to this god is painted black, and bears rude figures of the yucca ring and the yucca plant. It is buried east of the lodge beside a growing yucca. Ten songs are sung when the cigarette is being made, and a prayer is repeated when the work is done. The yucca which the actor carries must have a large part of its root-stock over ground. It is kicked out of the ground, — neither pulled nor cut. The principal home of the divinity is at Tsasitsozsaká*d* (*Yucca Glauca, Standing*), near the Chelly Canyon.

267. The following is a list of the twenty-one divinities represented by masks in the ceremony of the klé*dz*i *hatál*: —

MALE.

1. *H*ast*s*éyal*t*i.	8. *H*ast*s*é*h*ogan.
2. Gá*n*askí*d*i.	9. *H*át*d*ast*s*ïsi.[266]
3. *T*ó'ne*n*ïli.	10. *H*ast*s*él*t*si.[271]
4. Nayé*n*ĕzga̧ni.	11. T*s*óhanoai.
5. *T*o'bad*z*ïst*s*íni.	12. Kléhanoai, or Tléhanoai.
6. Dsaha*d*old*z*á.	13. *H*ast*s*ébaka.
7. *H*ast*s*é*z*ïni.	

Each, for the first seven, wears a different mask. The last six wear masks of one pattern, that of yébaka. (See plate I., fig. 1.)

FEMALE.

14. *H*ast*s*éol*t*oi.	15 to 21. *H*ast*s*ébaad, or goddesses.

All the female characters wear masks of one kind. (See fig. 28 and plate I., fig. 3.)

268. The language of the Eleventh Census is quoted here, although it differs slightly from the official report of the count of 1869, made by the acting agent, Capt. Frank T. Bennett, U. S. A. Captain Bennett says the count was made on two separate days, October 2d and 18th, and gives the number of Indians actually counted at 8,181. (Report of Commission of Indian Affairs for 1869, p. 237.[298])

269. Plate IV. represents a man dressed to personate Nayé*n*ĕzga̧ni, or Slayer of the Alien Gods, as he appears in an act of succor in the ceremony of the night chant, on the afternoon of the ninth day, in company with two other masqueraders (*T*o'bad*z*ïst*s*íni [270] and *H*ast*s*éol*t*oi [206]). The personator has his body painted black with charcoal of four sacred plants, and his hands painted white. He wears a black mask which has a fringe of yellow or reddish hair across the crown and an ornament of turkey's and eagle's feathers on top. Five parallel lines with five angles in each, to represent lightning, are painted on one cheek of the mask (sometimes the right, sometimes the left). Small, diamond-shaped holes are cut in the mask for eyes and mouth, and to the edge of each hole a small white shell is attached. On his body there are drawn in white clay the figures of eight bows ; six are drawn as shown in the picture and two more are drawn over the

shoulder-blades. All these bows are shown as complete (or strung) except those on the left leg and left side of the back, which are represented open or unstrung, as shown in the plate and fig. 41. The symbol at the left leg is made first, that on the left shoulder last of all. All the component lines of the symbol are drawn from above downward; fig. 41 shows the order in which they must be drawn. The symbols must all turn in one direction. The personator wears a collar of fox-skin, a number of rich necklaces of shell, turquoise and coral, a fine skirt or sash around his loins (usually scarlet baize, *bayeta*, but velvet or any rich material will do), a belt decorated with silver, and ordinary moccasins. He carries in his right hand a great stone knife, with which, in the scene of succor, he makes motions at the patient and at the medicine-lodge to draw out the disease. The patient prays to him, and gives him a cigarette painted black and decorated with the bow-symbols in white. This cigarette is preferably deposited under a

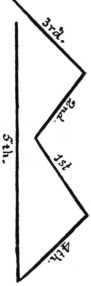

Fig. 41. Diagram
of the bow-symbol
on the left leg of the
personator of Na-
yénĕzgani.

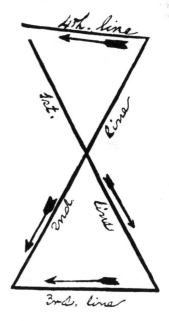

Fig. 42. Diagram of queue-sym-
bol on the left leg of the personator
of *To‘badzĭstsíni.*

piñon-tree. A dry-painting of this god has never been seen by the author, and he has been told that none is ever made.

270. Plate VII. represents the personator of the War God, *To‘badzĭstsíni*, or Child of the Water, as he appears in the act of succor described in notes 206 and 269. His body and limbs are painted with a native red ochre; his hands are smeared with white earth; and eight symbols are drawn in his body in white, — two on the chest, two on the arms, two on the legs, and two on the back, partly over the shoulder-blades. As with the bow-symbols of Nayénĕzgani (note 269), two of the symbols are left open or unfinished, — that on the left leg (painted first) and that over the left shoulder-blade (painted last), to indicate (some say) that the labors of the god are not yet done. Fig. 42 shows the order and direction in which each component line of the symbol must be drawn. The symbols repre-

sent a queue, such as the Navahoes now wear (fig. 31). Some say these figures represent the queue of the god's mother, others say they represent the scalps of conquered enemies; the latter is a more probable explanation. The personator wears a mask painted also with red ochre (all except a small triangular space over the face, which is colored black and bordered with white); and it is decorated both in front and behind with a number of queue-symbols (the number is never the same in two masks, but is always a multiple of four). The mask has a fringe of red or yellow hair, and a cockade of turkey-tail and a downy eagle-feather. The holes for the eyes and mouth are diamond-shaped, and have white shells attached to them. The actor carries in his left hand a small round cylinder of cedar-wood painted red, and in his right a cylinder of piñon painted black. With these, in the scene of succor, he makes motions at the patient and at the lodge. Like his companion, the personator of Nayénĕzgani, he wears a collar of fox-skin (*Vulpes velox*); rich necklaces of shell, turquoise, and coral; a skirt or sash of *bayeta*, or some other rich material; a belt adorned with plaques of silver; and ordinary moccasins. The sacrificial cigarette which he receives is painted red, marked with the queue-symbols, and deposited under a cedar-tree. No dry-painting of To'badzı́stsı́ni has been seen by the author, and he has been assured that none is made.

271. The name *H*as-tsél-tsi (Red God) is derived from *H*astsé (God, see par. 78) and *l*ı́tsí (red). The Red God, it is said, is never depicted in dry-paintings. The author has never seen the character in masquerade; it seldom appears, — only on the rare occasions when there is no dance of the naak*h*aí on the last night of the night chant. He seems to be a god of racing. The following account of him is from verbal description: Red God is one of the yéi, and dwells wherever other yéi dwell (hence there are many). His representative never appears in an act of succor and never helps the patient. A fast runner is chosen to play the part. He goes round among the assembled Indians and challenges men, by signs and inarticulate cries, to race with him. If he wins, he whips the loser with two wands of yucca leaves (culled with special observances) which he carries. If he loses, the winner must not whip him. If the loser begs him to whip softly he whips hard, and *vice versa*. His body is painted red and has queue-symbols drawn on it, like those of To'badzı́stsı́ni (plate VII.). His mask, which is a domino and not a cap, is painted red and marked with circles and curves in white. His cigarette is prepared on the fourth day, but it is not given to him to sacrifice; it is placed by other hands. Song and prayer accompany the preparation and sacrifice of the cigarette. The latter is painted red, and decorated in white with queue-symbols, either two or four; if four, two are closed or complete, and two open or incomplete. (Note 270.)

NAVAHO MUSIC.

BY PROF. JOHN COMFORT FILLMORE.

272. The twenty-eight songs which I have transcribed from phonographic records made by Dr. Washington Matthews have very great scientific interest and value, inasmuch as they throw much light on the problem of the form spontaneously assumed by natural folk-songs. Primitive man, expressing his emotions, especially strongly excited feeling, in song, without any rules or theories, must, of course, move spontaneously along the lines of least resistance. This is the law under which folk-melodies must necessarily be shaped. The farther back we can get toward absolutely primitive expression of emotion in song, the more valuable is our material for scientific purposes; because we can be certain that it is both spontaneous and original, unaffected by contact with civilized music and by

any and all theories. In such music we may study the operation of natural psychical laws correlated with physical laws, working freely and coming to spontaneous expression through the vocal apparatus.

These Navaho songs are especially valuable because they carry us well back toward the beginnings of music-making. One only needs to hear them sung, or listen to them in the admirable phonographic records of Dr. Matthews, to be convinced of this from the very quality of tone in which they are sung. In all of them the sounds resemble howling more than singing, yet they are unmistakably musical in two very important particulars: (1) In their strongly marked rhythm; (2) In the unquestionably harmonic relations of the successive tones. I shall deal with them, therefore, under the two heads of RHYTHM and HARMONIC MELODY.

1. RHYTHM. — Mr. Richard Wallascheck, the distinguished author of "Primitive Music," has lately called attention to the importance of sonant rhythm. Not only does the rhythmic impulse precede the other musical elements, but the superiority of sonant rhythm is such as to serve as an incitement to tone-production. Rhythm tends to set the voice going; and of course vocal sounds, which constitute the first music, do not become music until they are rhythmically ordered. They tend to become so ordered by a natural law of pulsation which need not be discussed here. The regularly recurring pulsations, which specially show themselves in all prolonged emissions of vocal sounds, tend also to form themselves in metrical groups; speaking broadly, these metrical groups are usually twos or threes, or simple multiples of twos or threes. This is so, for the most part, in savage folk-music, in our most advanced culture-music, and in all the development which comes between. The metrical grouping into fives or sevens is comparatively rare; but I have found it more frequently by far in savage folk-music than in our music of civilization.

The most striking characteristic of the metrical grouping of tones in the Navaho songs here given is the freedom with which the singer changes from one elementary metre to the other; *i. e.* from twos to threes and *vice versa*. So in the compound metres: two twos and three twos, or two threes and three threes, are intermingled with the utmost freedom, so that few of them can be marked in the notation with a single-time signature. Or, if they are, there is almost sure to be an exceptional measure or two here and there which varies from the fundamental metrical type. Thus, the first song on cylinder No. 38 has metrical groupings of three threes and of two threes; *i. e.* ⅜ and ⅜ time. The two songs on cylinder No. 41 have three twos and two twos, treating the eighth note as a unit; or, better, ¾ and ⅜ metre, mingled at the pleasure of the singer. Nearly all the songs vary the metre in this way. The one on cylinder No. 62 has an exceptionally rich variety of metrical arrangement; while the second one, on cylinder No. 38, is exceptionally simple and monotonous in metre and rhythm. A few of them, like No. 25, recorded on cylinder No. 143, are singularly irregular. This song would seem to be based on a grouping of simple twos (¾ time, equal to ⁴⁄₈) as its fundamental metrical conception; yet a great many measures contain only three eighth notes, and some contain five or even six. The song numbered 28, on cylinder No. 144, has a ⅜ metre as its foundation, but varied by ¾, equal to ⁴⁄₈. In respect of metrical grouping, these Navaho songs do not differ in any essential characteristic from the songs of the Omahas, the Kwakiutls, the Pawnees, the Otoes, the Sioux, and other aboriginal folk-music, nor from that of other nations and races, including our own. The complexity of metrical arrangement has been carried much farther by some other tribes, notably the Omahas and the Kwakiutls, than by the Navahoes, so far as appears from the present collection of songs. There is no record here of an accompanying drum-beat, so that, if the combinations of dissimilar rhythms which are so common in the two above-named tribes exist among the Navahoes, they are yet to be recorded and transcribed.

2. HARMONIC MELODY. — These songs seem to be a real connecting link between excited shouting and excited singing. In *quality* of tone they are shouts
or howls. In *pitch-relations* they are *unmistakably harmonic*. Some of them
manifest this characteristic most strikingly. For example, the two songs on
cylinder No. 41 contain *all* the tones which compose the chord of C major, *and
no others*. The second one on cylinder No. 38 has the tones D and F sharp and
no others, except in the little preliminary flourish at the beginning, and here there
is only a passing E, which fills up the gap between the two chord-tones. D is
evidently the key-note, and the whole melody is made up of the Tonic chord incomplete. The first song on the same cylinder is similarly made up of the incomplete
Tonic chord in C minor ; only the opening phrase has the incomplete chord of E
flat, the relative major. Cylinder No. 49 has nothing but the Tonic chord in C
major, and the chord is complete. No. 61 has the complete chord of B flat minor
and nothing else. No. 62 is made up mainly of the chord of F major complete.
It has two by-tones occasionally used, G and D, the former belonging to the
Dominant and the other to both the Sub-dominant and Relative minor chords.
Song No. 9 on cylinder No. 100 has the incomplete chord of D sharp minor, with
G sharp, the Sub-dominant in the key, as an occasional by-tone. The last tone
of each period, the lowest tone of the song, sounds in the phonograph as if the
singer could not reach it easily, and the pitch is rather uncertain. It was probably meant for G sharp ; but a personal interview with the singer would be necessary to settle the point conclusively. Song No. 10, on the same cylinder, has the
complete Tonic chord in D sharp minor and nothing else except the tone C sharp,
which is here *not* a melodic by-tone, but a *harmonic tone, a minor seventh added
to the Tonic chord.* This is curiously analogous to some of the melodies I heard
in the Dahomey village at the World's Fair, and also to some of the melodies of
our own Southern negroes. Song No. 11, on the same cylinder, has the same
characteristics as No. 9. Nos. 12 and 13, on cylinder No. 135, contain the complete chord of D flat and nothing else. The two songs on cylinder No. 138 contain the complete chord of C major and nothing else, except at the beginning,
where A, the relative minor tone, comes in, in the opening phrase. As a rule,
whatever by-tones there are in these songs are used in the preliminary phrase or
flourish of the song, and then the singer settles down steadily to the line of the
Tonic chord. The two songs recorded on No. 139 have the complete major
chord of B flat, with G, the relative minor, as a by-tone. The two songs on No.
143 are in C sharp minor and embody the Tonic chord, with F sharp, the Sub-
dominant, as a by-tone. Only the first of the two begins with the tone B, which does
not occur again. Song No. 27, on cylinder No. 144, embodies only the complete
chord of C sharp minor. No. 28 has the same chord, with F sharp as a by-tone.
The two songs on No. 145 are in D minor and are made up mainly of the Tonic
chord. The by-tones used are G and B flat, which make up two thirds of the
Sub-dominant chord, and C, which belongs to the relative major. No. 32, on
cylinder No. 146, has more of diatonic melody. It is in G major, and embodies
the chord of the Tonic with by-tones belonging to both the Dominant and Sub-
dominant chords, one from each chord. No. 33, on the same cylinder, is less
melodious, but has the same harmonic elements. Cylinder 147 has two songs in
D major which embody the Tonic chord complete, with slight use of a single by-
tone, B, the relative minor. The same is true of song No. 36, on cylinder No.
148. Song No. 37, on the same cylinder, has the major chord of C and nothing
else.

There are two striking facts in all this : (1) When these Navahoes make music
spontaneously, — make *melodies* by singing tones in rhythmically ordered succession, — there is always a tone which forces itself on our consciousness as a key-

note, or Tonic, and this tone, together with the tones which make up its chord (whether major or minor), invariably predominates overwhelmingly; (2) Whenever by-tones are employed, they invariably belong to the chords which stand in the nearest relation to the Tonic.

I do not care at present to go into any speculations as to why this is so. No matter now what may be the influence of sonant rhythm; what may be the relations of the psychical, physiological, and physical elements; how sound is related to music; how men come to the conception of a minor Tonic when only the major chord is given in the physical constitution of tone. All these questions I wish to waive at this time and only to insist on this one fact, viz.: That, so far as these Navaho songs are concerned, *the line of least resistance is always a harmonic line.* If we find the same true of all other folk-melodies, I can see no possible escape from the conclusion that *harmonic perception is the formative principle in folk-melody.* This perception may be sub-conscious, if you please; the savage never heard a chord sung or played as a simultaneous combination of tones in his life; he has no notion whatever of the harmonic relations of tones. But it is not an accident that he sings, or shouts, or howls, straight along the line of a chord, and never departs from it except now and then to touch on some of the nearest related chord-tones, using them mainly as passing-tones to fill up the gap between the tones of his Tonic chord. Such things do not happen by accident, but by law.

That these Navahoes do precisely this thing, no listener can doubt who knows a chord when he hears it. But the same thing is true of all the folk-music I have ever studied. Hundreds of Omaha, Kwakiutl, Otoe, Pawnee, Sioux, Winnebago, Iroquois, Mexican Indian, Zuñi, Australian, African, Malay, Chinese, Japanese, Hindoo, Arab, Turkish, and European folk-songs which I have carefully studied, taking down many of them from the lips of the native singers, all tell the same story. They are all built on simple harmonic lines, all imply harmony, are all equally intelligible to peoples the most diverse in race, and consequently owe their origin and shaping to the same underlying formative principles.

Mr. Wallascheck has called attention to the fact that the rhythmic impulse precedes the musical tones, and also to the part played by sonant rhythm in setting tone-production going. The rhythmic impulse is doubtless the fundamental one in the *origination* of music. But when the tone-production is once started by the rhythmic impulse, *it takes a direction in accordance with the laws of harmonic perception.* I was long ago forced to this conclusion in my study of the Omaha music; and these Navaho songs furnish the most striking corroboration of it. How else can we possibly account for the fact that so many of these songs contain absolutely nothing but chord tones? How can we escape the conclusion that the line of least resistance is a harmonic line? Is it not plain that, in the light of this principle, every phenomenon of folk-music becomes clear and intelligible? Is there any other hypothesis which will account for the most striking characteristics of folk-music? Every student must answer these questions for himself. But I, for my part, am wholly unable to resist the conviction that *the harmonic sense is the shaping, formative principle in folk-melody.*

[In the numbers of *The Land of Sunshine* (Los Angeles, Cal.), for October and November, 1896, under the title of "Songs of the Navajos," the poetry and music of this tribe have already been discussed by Professor Fillmore and the author. All the music which follows (see pp. 258, 279–290), except that of the "Dove Song," was written by Professor Fillmore.]

273. DOVE SONG.

(See par. 50.)   Music by CHRISTIAN BARTHELMESS.
Slow.

Wos wos nai-*d*i - la   a   a, Wos wos nai-*d*i - lo   o   o,

Wos wos nai - *d*i - la   a a, Tsi - nol - ka - *z*i nai-*d*i - la   a a,

Ke - *l*ĭ - tsi - tsi nai - *d*i - la   a   a, Wos wos nai-*d*i - lo   o   o.

TEXTS AND INTERLINEAR TRANSLATIONS.

274. ASSEVERATION OF TORLINO (IN PART).

Naestsán   bayántsĭn.
Earth (Woman Horizontal), for it I am ashamed.

Yá*d*ĭ/yĭ*l*   bayántsĭn.
Sky (dark above), for it I am ashamed.

*H*ayolká*l*   bayántsĭn.
    Dawn,   for it I am ashamed.

Na*h*otsói   bayántsĭn.
Evening (Land of Horizontal for it I am ashamed.
       Yellow),

Na*h*odo*tl*ĭ′*z*i   bayántsĭn.
Blue sky (Land or Place of   for it I am ashamed.
    Horizontal Blue),

Tsa*l*yé*l* bayántsĭn.

Darkness, for it I am ashamed.

Tsóhanoai   bayántsĭn.
    Sun,   for it I am ashamed.

*S*i sĭzíni beya*s*tĭ′yi   bayántsĭn.
In me it stands, with me it talks, for it I am ashamed.

275. BEGINNING OF ORIGIN LEGEND.

To‘bĭ*l*haskĭ′*d*igi   *h*aá*d*ze *l*akaígo ta*ʻ*ĭ′nd*ĭl*to;   tsin dzi*l*ínla tsĭ′ni.
Water with Hill Central in to the east   white   up rose;   day they thought it they say.

*S*ada*á*dze do*tl*ĭ′*z*go ta*ʻ*ĭ′nd*i*lto;   táb*ĭ*tsin   ĭndzĭ*l*té   tsĭ′ni. Iná*d*ze
To the south   blue   up rose;   still their day they went around they say. To the west

*l*ĭtsógo ta*ʻ*ĭ′nd*ĭl*to;   inin*á*la   á‘le   tsĭ′ni. Akógo ná*h*okosdze *d*ĭ*l*yĭ′*l*go
  yellow   up rose;   evening always it showed they say. Then   to the north   dark

ta*ʻ*ĭ′nd*ĭl*to; akógo *d*az*ĭ*ntsá *d*á*d*zĭ*l*kos tsĭ′ni.
     up rose;   then   they lay down   they slept   they say.

To‘bĭ*l*haskĭ′*d*i   to‘altsá*h*azlin;   *h*aá*d*ze *l*a ilín, sada*á*go *l*a ilín,   *l*a
Water with Hill Central   water flowed from in to the east one flowed, at the south one flowed, one
                         different directions;

inádze ilín tsɨ́'ni. *H*aádze ilínigi ban ké*h*odzɨ́ti; sadaádze ĕltó';
to the west flowed they say. To the east where it flowed its border place where to the south also;
they dwelt;

inádze ĕltó' ban ké*h*odzɨ́ti tsɨ́'ni.
to the west also its border place where they say.
they dwelt

*H*aádze *T*an *h*olgé; sadaádze Naho*d*oóla *h*olgé; inádze
To the east Corn a place called; to the south Naho*d*oóla a place called; to the west

Lókatsosaká*d* *h*olgé. *H*aádze Ăsa*l*ái *h*olgé; sadaádze *T*o'*h*ádzɨ́tɨ́l
Reed Great Standing a place called. To the east Pot One a place called; to the south Water They Come
for Often

*h*olgé; inádze Dsɨ́*l/l*ɨ́tsíbe*h*ogan *h*olgé. *H*aádze *L*éya*h*ogan
a place called; to the west Mountain Red Made of a place called. To the east Earth under House
House

*h*olgé; sadaádze *T*sɨ́ltsɨ́'nt*h*a *h*olgé; inádze Tse'*l*ɨ́tsíbe*h*oga*n*
a place called; to the south Aromatic Sumac a place called; to the west Rock Red Made of House
among

*h*olgé.
a place called.

*H*olatsí Dɨ́lyɨ́'*l*e ké*h*ati ɨ́nté. *H*olatsí Lɨ́tsí ké*h*ati ɨ́nté. *T*anɨ́laí
Ants Dark lived there. Ants Red lived there. Dragon-flies

ké*h*ati ɨ́nté. *T*saltsá ké*h*ati ɨ́nté. Woɨ́ntlɨ́'zi ké*h*ati ɨ́nté. Tse'yoá*l*i
lived there. (Yellow beetles) lived there. Beetles (?) hard lived there. Stone carriers
(beetles)

ké*h*ati ɨ́nté. Kɨ́n*l*ɨ́'zɨ́n ké*h*ati ɨ́nté. Maitsán ké*h*ati ɨ́nté. Andɨ́'ta *T*sápani
lived there. Bugs black lived there. Coyote-dung lived there. Besides Bats
(beetles) (beetles)

ké*h*ati ɨ́nté. *T*otsó' ké*h*ati ɨ́nté. Wonɨ́stsíd i ké*h*ati ɨ́nté. Wonɨ́stsíd i Kaí
lived there. (White-faced lived there. Locusts lived there. Locusts White
beetles)

ké*h*ati ɨ́nté. Naki*d*á*t*ago dɨ́né' aísi *d*ez*d*él.
lived there. Twelve people these started (in life).

*H*aádze hahóse *t*o'sɨ́gɨ́'n tsɨ́'ni; sadaádze *t*o'sɨ́gɨ́'n tsɨ́'ni; inádze *t*o'sɨ́gɨ́'n
To the east extended ocean they say; to the south ocean they say; to the west ocean

tsɨ́'ni; ná*h*okosdze *t*o'sɨ́gɨ́'n tsɨ́'ni. *H*aádze *t*o'sɨ́gɨ́'n bígi Tié*h*oltsodi
they say; to the north ocean they say. To the east ocean within Tié*h*oltsodi

si*t*ín tsɨ́'ni. Na*t*áni ɨ́nlíngo; *h*anan*t*áï tsɨ́'ni. Sadaádze *t*o'sɨ́gɨ́'n bígi
lay they say. Chief he was; Chief of the people they say. To the south ocean within

*T*haltláhale si*t*ín tsɨ́'ni. Na*t*áni ɨ́nlin'go; *h*anan*t*áï tsɨ́'ni. Inádze
Blue Heron lay they say. Chief he was; chief of the people they say. To the west

*t*o'sɨ́gɨ́'n bígi *T*sa*l* si*t*ín tsɨ́'ni. Na*t*áni ɨ́nlíngo; *h*anan*t*áï tsɨ́'ni.
ocean within Frog lay they say. Chief he was; chief of the people they say.

Ná*h*okosdze *t*o'sɨ́gɨ́'n bígi Idnɨ́'dsɨ́*l*kai si*t*ín tsɨ́'ni; *h*anan*t*áï tsɨ́'ni.
To the north ocean within Thunder Mountain lay they say; chief of the they say.
White people

*T*ígi itégo *h*azágo kédaћatsitigo; ĕ'hyi*d*elnago a*h*á*d*azɨ́'lge tsɨ́'ni.
In this way they quarrelled around where they with one another they committed they say.
lived; adultery

Ĕ'hyi*d*elnago estsáni altsan *t*atsɨ́kɨ́d tsɨ́'ni. Yúwe tsé*h*alni tsɨ́'ni.
With one another women several committed crime they say. To banish it they failed they say.

Tié*h*oltsodi *h*aádze "*H*a*t*égola *d*o*l*é*l*a? Hwehéya *h*o*l*dá'o*d*aka'*l*a." Sadaádze
Tié*h*oltsodi to the east "In what way shall we act? Their land the place they dislike." To the south

*T*haltláhale *h*alní tsɨ́'ni. Inádze "Ka*t* si *d*okoné ke*h*adzi*t*í*d*ole*l*,"
Blue Heron spoke to them they say. To the west "Now I (say) not here shall they dwell,"

*T*sa*l* ћatsí. Na*t*áni ɨ́nlɨ́'ni, ћatsí tsɨ́'ni. Ná*h*okosdze Idnɨ́'dsɨ́*l*kai
Frog he said. Chief he was, he said they say. To the north Thunder Mountain White

"*T*a'ka*d*á' *h*á*d*zeta *d*ahíz*d*ɨ́nolidi" tsɨ́'ni.
"Quickly elsewhere they must depart" they say.

*H*aádze Tiéholtsodi a*h*ána*d*a*zd*eyago alkinat*s*idz*é* *t*o*h*atsí tsĭ'ni.
To the east   Tiéholtsodi   when again they   among themselves   nothing he said   they say.
             committed adultery   again fought

*S*ada*á*dz*e* *Th*altláhale *t*a*t*o*h*anantsí*d*a tsĭ'ni. I*n*ádze Tsa*l* na*t*áni
To the south   Blue Heron   again said nothing to them   they say.   To the west   Frog   chief

*Ĭ*nlĭ*n*éni *t*a*t*o*h*anantsí*d*a tsĭ'ni. *N*á*h*okosdz*e* I*d*nĭ'ds*ĭ*ĺkai *t*a*t*o*h*anantsí*d*a
he formerly   again said nothing to   they say.   To the north   Thunder Mountain   again said nothing
was   them   White   to them

tsĭ'ni. *T*ó*b*ĭ*lt*a*h*o*z*on*d*a*l*a tsĭ'ni.
they say.   Not with pleasant ways, one   they say.

*T*i*n* naikálago *t*akoná*h*otsa tsĭ'ni. *S*ada*á*dz*e* ké*h*odz*ĭ*tini *t*akonátsi*d*za
Four   again ends of   again the same   they say.   To the south   the dwellers   did the same again
       nights   happened

tsĭ'ni; kinat*s*idz*é* tsĭ'ni. *H*aádz*e* *l*a estsánigo *l*a *d*ĭnégo yahatsaá*z*
they say;   again they fought   they say.   To the east   one   woman   one   man   tried to enter two
                                        together

*Ĭ*nté; ts*éh*o*d*ĭnĕltsa, tsĭ'ni. *S*ada*á*dz*e* *Th*altláhale si*t*ínedz*e* yahanát*s*ata*z*
there;   they were driven   they say.   To the south   Blue Heron   to where he lay   again they tried to enter
                                                  two together

*Ĭ*nté; tsená*h*o*d*ĭnĕltsa tsĭ'ni. I*n*ádze Tsa*l* na*t*áni ĭnlĭ'nedz*e* yahanát*s*ata*z*
there;   again they were   they say.   To the west   Frog   chief   to where he was   again they tried to enter
      driven out   two together

*Ĭ*nté; tsená*h*o*d*ĭnĕltsa tsĭ'ni. *N*á*h*okosdz*e* ts*ĕ*ná*h*o*d*ĭnĕltsa. "*T*óta ní'yi*l*a.
there;   again they were   they say.   To the north   again they were   " Not   one of you.
      driven out.   driven out.

Dainoká' *h*á*d*zeta," ho'*d*oní tsĭ'ni. An*d*ĭ'*t*a aibĭtlé Na*h*o*d*oóla
Keep on going   elsewhere,"   thus he spoke   they say.   Besides   the same night   Nahodoóla

ba*ĭ'n*da*d*zitigo iská' *t*a*t*oas*t*etsá*d*a tsĭ'ni. Na'*d*éyayilkágo Tiéholtsodi
they discussed it   the end of the night   they did not decide   they say.   After dawn   Tiéholtsodi

*h*ayál*t*i tsĭ'ni. "*T*o*d*a*d*otsá*d*a tsĭní'yitsi*n*yasti *h*á*d*is *t*a*d*idotsí*l*;
began to talk   they say.   " You pay no attention   all I said to you   anywhere   you will disobey;

ní'yila' *h*á*d*ze*t*a *t*anelída; ko*n*é *t*ó*t*a ti' ni *d*asakádgi ka*t* *t*ó*t*a; "
all of you   elsewhere   must go;   here   not   this   earth   upon stand in   now   not; "

*h*o*d*oní tsĭ'ni.
thus he said   they say.

Estsánigo *t*in iskágo basa*h*atsilágo tsĭ'ni. *T*ín iská' apĭ'nigo
Among the women   four   ends of nights,   they talked about it   they say.   Four   ends of   in the morning
                                   till   nights

náz*d*itse *Ĭ*nté tsĭ'ni, haádze *h*atísi *l*akáigo *t*aigánil tsĭ'ni; an*d*ĭ'*t*a
as they were rising   there   they say,   to the east   something   white   it appeared   they say;   besides

*s*ada*á*dz*e* ĕ*l*tó' *t*aigánil tsĭ'ni; naako*n*é i*n*ádze ĕ*l*tó' *t*aigánil tsĭ'ni;
to the south   also   it appeared   they say;   again here   to the west   also   it appeared   they say;

an*d*ĭ'*t*a ná*h*okosdz*e* ĕ*l*tó' *t*aigánil tsĭ'ni. Ds*ĭ*l ahyéna'a' ná*h*alĭni
besides   to the north   also   it appeared   they say.   Mountains   rising up around   like

sil*ĭ*n tsĭ'ni; *t*a*t*ob*ĭ*tá'hazani. *T*o'ahyéntsil tsĭ'ni; *t*o'tob*ĭ't*yĭó,
it stretched   they say;   without opening.   Water all around   they say;   water not to be crossed,

ta*t*ó*d*ĭzaatego ahyé*ĭ*ntsĭlin tsĭ'ni. *T*áako taha*d*ĭl*t*él tsĭ'ni.
not to be climbed   flowed all around   they say.   At once   they started   they say.

Ahyé*ĭ*l*t*égo nihizi*ĭ*l*t*é tsĭ'ni; yabi*ĭ*l*t*é tsĭ'ni. D*ĭ*lkógo. *T*áa*d*o
They went around in   thus they went   they say;   they went to the sky   they say.   It was smooth.   Thence
circles

*t*an *Ĭ*nda*z*déti tsĭ'ni; *t*o' *Ĭ'n*da*d*ĭ*ĭ*tlaye*n*gi; *t*o' *t*oaho*t*é*h*i*d*a tsĭ'ni.
down   they looked   they say;   water   where it had risen;   water   nothing else there   they say.

Nité ko*n*dé *l*a *h*a*z*no*l*án tsĭ'ni; tsi *d*o*t*l*ĭ'z* *l*éi; *h*atsotsí
There   from here   one   stuck out   they say;   head   blue   it had;   he called to them

tsĭ'ni; "Kó*n*ne," tsĭnĕ, "*h*aádzego a*h*ótsa*l*a" tsĭ'ni. Akó*n*ne
they say;   " In here,"   he said,   " to the eastward   a hole "   they say.   In here

ooĭ*l*té tsĭ'ni ; bĭnaká' ĭ*l*té tsĭ'ni ba*g*ánd*z*e *h*asté tsĭ'ni.
they went they say ; through it they went they say ; to the upper surface they came out they say.
entering

*Do*tlĭ'*z*eni *H*asts*ó*sid*ï*ne' a*t*i'*n*la tsĭ'ni. *H*asts*ó*sid*ï*ne' *k*éha*t*il tsĭ'ni.
The blue one Swallow People belonged to they say. Swallow People lived there they say.

*H*o*g*ánin *t*og*ó*lgo naznĭ'l, tsĭ'ni ; *h*áho*s*i' yilá' tsĭ'ni. Bĭla*th*ád*z*e
The houses rough (lumpy) scattered they say ; a great many were placed they say. Toward their tops
around,

*d*ahats*ó*zgo ; á*d*e yaha*d*áhaztsa' tsĭ'ni. Háho*s*i' *d*íné altsí
they tapered ; from that gave entrance an they say. A great many people colleeted
opening

ko*t*gá tsĭ'ni. *H*áa*l*ahazlí*n* tsĭ'ni.
together they say. They crowded together they say.

276. SONG OF ESTSÁNATLEHI.

Aieneyá.
(No meaning.)
Eó eá aiá ahèea aía eeeaía ainá.
(A meaningless prelude twice repeated.)

I.

1. Yéinaĕzg̣ani sa' niyĭ'nigi, yeyeyéna.
Nayénĕzg̣ani for me he brings, (meaningless.)
2. K*ạ*t Bĭtéelgĕti sa' niyĭ'nigi, yeyeyéna.
Now *T*éelgĕt for me he brings, (meaningless.)
3. Tsĭ'*d*a *l*a bĭd*z*ái sa' niyĭ'nigi, yeyeyéna.
Truly one his lung for me he brings, (meaningless.)
4. *D*ĭné' nahostlĭ'*d*i. *S*a' niyĭ'nigi, yeyeyéna.
People are restored, for me he brings, (meaningless.)
Haía aína aiyéya aína.
(Meaningless refrain after each stanza.)

II.

1. K*ạ*t *T*o'bad*z*ĭstsíni sa' niyĭ'nigi, yeyeyéna.
Now *T*o'bad*z*istsíni for me he brings, (meaningless.)
2. Tsĕninaholĭ'si sa' niyĭ'nigi, yeyeyéna.
Tse'náhale for me he brings, (meaningless.)
3. Tsĭ'*d*a *l*a bĭtái, sa' niyĭ'nigi, yeyeyéna.
Truly one his wing, for me he brings, (meaningless.)
4. *D*ĭné' nahostlĭ'*d*i. *S*a' niyĭ'nigi, yeyeyéna.
People are restored. For me he brings, (meaningless.)

III.

1. K*ạ*t *L*éyaneyani sa' niyĭ'nigi, yeyeyéna.
Now *L*éyaneyani for me he brings, (meaningless.)
2. Tse'*ta*hotsĭltá'*l*i sa' niyĭ'nigi, yeyeyéna.
Tse'*ta*hotsĭltá'*l*i for me he brings, (meaningless.)
3. Tsĭ'*d*a bĭtlapĭ'*l*e sa' niyĭ'nigi, yeyeyéna.
Truly his side-lock for me he brings, (meaningless.)
4. *D*ĭné' nahostlĭ'*d*i. *S*a' niyĭ'nigi, yeyeyéna.
People are restored. For me he brings, (meaningless.)

IV.

1. K*ạ*t Tsówenatlehi sa' niyĭ'nigi, yeyeyéna.
Now Tsówenatlehi for me he brings, (meaningless.)
2. Bĭnáye T*s*agáni sa' niyĭ'nigi, yeyeyéna.
Bĭnáye A*h*áni for me he brings, (meaningless.)

3. Tsĭ′*d*a *l*a bĭnái *s*a‘ niyĭ′nigi, yeyeyéna.

Truly   one his eye for me he brings, (meaningless.)

4. *D*ĭné‘ nahostlĭ′*d*i. *S*a‘ niyĭ′nigi, yeyeyéna.

People   are restored.   For me   he brings, (meaningless.)

In line I, stanza I., Nayénĕzgạni is changed to Yéinaĕzgạni, and in line I, stanza IV., Bĭnáye A*h*áni is changed to Bĭnáye T*s*agáni. Nahostlĭ′*d*i in the last line of each stanza is rendered here "restored," but the more exact meaning is, not that the original people are called back to life, but that others are given in plạçe of them. This verb is used if a man steals a horse and gives another horse as restitution for the one he stole.

277. SONG OF NAYÉNĚZGẠNI (NAYÉNĚZGẠNI BĬGĬ′N).

I.

Atsé Estsán Nayénĕzgạni yil*h*aholnĭ′*z*,

Atsé   Estsán   Nayénĕzgạni began to tell her of,

Bĭ*t*éelgĕ*t*i yil*h*aholnĭ′*z*,

*T*éelgĕt   began to tell her of,

Nayé holó*d*e yil*h*aholnĭ′*z*.

Anáye from where they are began to tell her of.

II.

Estsánatlehi *T*o‘bad*z*ĭst*s*íni yil*h*aholnĭ′*z*,

Estsánatlehi   *T*o‘bad*z*ĭst*s*íni began to tell her of,

Tse‘nahalé*s*i yil*h*aholnĭ′*z*,

Tsé‘nahale began to tell her of,

Nayé holó*d*e yil*h*aholnĭ′*z*.

Anáye from where they are began to tell her of.

III.

Atsé Estsán *L*éyaneyani yil*h*aholnĭ′z,

Atsé   Estsán   *L*éyaneyani began to tell her of,

Tse‘*ta*hots*ĭ*ltá‘*l*i yil*h*aholnĭ′z,

Tse‘*ta*hotsĭltá‘*l*i began to tell her of,

Nayé holó*d*e yil*h*aholnĭ′z.

Anáye from where they are began to tell her of.

IV.

Estsánatlehi Tsówenatlehi yil*h*aholnĭ′*z*,

Estsánatlehi   Tsówenatlehi began to tell her of,

Bĭnáye T*s*agáni yil*h*aholnĭ′*z*,

Bĭnáye   A*h*áni began to tell her of,

Nayé holó*d*e yil*h*aholnĭ′*z*.

Anáye from where they are began to tell her of.

Prelude, refrain, and meaningless syllables are omitted from this text.

278. SONG OF NAYÉNĚZGẠNI.

I.

Kạ*t* Nayénĕzgạni koanígo *d*ĭgíni,

Now Slayer of the Alien Gods thus he says a holy one,

Kạ*t* T*s*óhanoai koanígo,

Now   The Sun   thus he says,

*D*ĭgĭ′n yiká‘ sĭzíni koanígo.

Holy   thereon he stands thus he says.

II.

Kạ*t* *T*o‘badẓĭstsíni koanígo *d*ĭgíni,
Now Child of the Water thus he says a holy one,
Kạ*t* Kléhanoai koanígo,
Now   The Moon   thus he says,
*D*ĭgĭ′n yiká‘   *h*olési   koanígo.
Holy   thereon he goes forth thus he says.

III.

Kạ*t* *L*éyaneyani   koanígo *d*ĭgíni,
Now Reared under the Earth thus he says a holy one,
Kạ*t* Tsóhanoai koanígo,
Now   The Sun   thus he says,
*D*ĭgĭ′n yiká‘   sĭzíni   koanígo.
Holy   thereon he stands thus he says.

IV.

Kạ*t*   Tsówenatlehi   koanígo *d*ĭgíni,
Now Changing Grandchild thus he says a holy one,
Kạt Kléhanoai koanígo,
Now   The Moon   thus he says,
*D*ĭgĭ′n yika‘   *h*olési   koanígo.
Holy   thereon he goes forth thus he says.

Meaningless parts omitted.   Koanígo is from kónigo, which is the prose form.

279.   SONG OF NAYÉNĔZGẠNI.

I.

Kạ*t*   Yénaezgạni   *l*a *d*ĭsĭtsáya.
Now Slayer of the Alien Gods one I hear him.
(Nayénĕzgani)
Ya benikás*d*e *l*a *d*ĭsĭtsáya.
Sky through from one I hear him.
Bíniye tsíye   *t*ĭ′snĭsa*d*   lée.
His voice sounds in every direction (no meaning).
Bíniye tsíye   *d*ígini   lée.
His voice sounds holy, divine (no meaning).

II.

Kạ*t* *T*o‘badẓĭstsíni *l*a *d*ĭsĭtsáya.
Now Child of the Water one I hear him.
*T*o‘ benikás*d*e   *l*a *d*ĭsĭtsáya.
Water through from one   I hear him.
Bíniye tsíye   *t*ĭ′snĭsa*d*   lée.
His voice sounds in every direction (no meaning).
Bíniye tsíye *d*ígini   lée.
His voice sounds divine (no meaning).

III.

Kạ*t*   *L*éyaneyani   *l*a *d*ĭsĭtsáya.
Now Reared under the Ground one I hear him.
Ni‘ benikás*d*e *l*a *d*ĭsĭtsáya.
Earth through from one I hear him.

Bíniye tsíye *tí*'snĭsa*d* lée.
His voice sounds in every direction (no meaning).
Bíniye tsíye *d*ígini lée.
His voice sounds divine (no meaning).

IV.

Ka*t* Tsówenatlehi *l*a *d*ĭsĭtsáya.
Now Changing Grandchild one I hear him.
Kos benikás*d*e *l*a *d*ĭsĭtsáya.
Clouds through from one I hear him.
Bíniye tsíye *tí*'snĭsa*d* lée.
His voice sounds in every direction (no meaning).
Bíniye tsíye *d*ígini lée.
His voice sounds divine (no meaning).

Nayénĕzga̧ni changed to Yénaezga̧ni; bĭné (his voice) changed to bíniye; *d*ígĭ'n changed to *d*ígini, for poetic reasons. Preludes and refrains omitted.

280. A SONG OF NAYÉNĔZGA̧NI.

I.

Ka*t* Nayénĕzga̧ni na*h*aníya,
Now Slayer of the Alien Gods he arrives,
Pe*s* *d*ĭ*l*yĭ'*l*i be*h*ogán*l*a ás*d*e na*h*aníya,
Knives dark a house made of from he arrives,
Pe*s* *d*ĭ*l*yĭ'*l*i *d*a'honíhe ás*d*e na*h*aníya.
Knives dark dangle high from he arrives.
Nizáza *d*ĭnĭgíni, síka tóta.
Your treasures you holy one, for my sake not.

II.

Ka̧*t* *T*o'badzĭstsíni na*h*aníya,
Now Child of the Water he arrives,
Pe*s* *d*olgási be*h*ogán*l*a ás*d*e na*h*aníya,
Knives serrate a house made of from he arrives,
Pe*s* *d*olgási *d*a'honíhe ás*d*e na*h*aníya.
Knives serrate dangle high from he arrives.
Nizáza *d*ĭnĭgíni, síka tóta.
Your treasures you holy one, for my sake not.

III.

Ka̧*t* *L*éyaneyani na*h*aníya,
Now Reared under the Earth he arrives,
Pe*s* al*th*asaí be*h*ogán*l*a ás*d*e na*h*aníya,
Knives of all kinds a house made of from he arrives,
Pe*s* al*th*asaí *d*a'honíhe ás*d*e na*h*aníya.
Knives of all kinds dangle high from he arrives.
Nizáza *d*ĭnĭgíni, síka tóta.
Your treasures you holy one, for my sake not.

IV.

Ka̧*t* Tsówenatlehi na*h*aníya,
Now Changing Grandchild he arrives,
Pe*s* *l*ĭtsói be*h*ogán*l*a ás*d*e na*h*aníya,
Knives yellow a house made of from he arrives,

Pe*s* *l*ĭtsói *d*a'honíhe ásde na*h*aníya.
Knives yellow dangle high from he arrives.

Ni*z*áza *d*ĭnĭgíni, *s*íka *t*óta.
Your treasures you holy one, for my sake not.

In endeavoring to explain the meaning of this song, the singer related that
Nayénězga̜ni said to his mother, " You are the divine one, not I." She replied,
" No, you are the divine one." They were exchanging compliments. Then he
said, " Not for my sake, but for yours, were these treasures (weapons, etc.) given
by the Sun. They are yours." For the meaning of bĭzá (his treasure), see note
246. Ni*z*á or nĭ′*z*a means your treasure; the last syllable is here repeated perhaps as a poetic plural. The houses of knives are said to be the different chambers in the house of the Sun. Meaningless syllables are omitted in this text.

281. SONG OF THE SUN.

I.

Ka̜*t* Nayénězga̜ni *s*ĭ*d*eyáïye,
Now Slayer of the Alien Gods I come (or approach) with,

Pe*s* *d*ĭlyĭ′*l*i be*h*ogán*d*e *s*ĭ*d*eyáïye,
Knives dark from house made of I come with,

Pe*s* *d*ĭlyĭ′*l*i *d*a'honí*d*e *s*ĭ*d*eyáïye,
Knives dark from where they dangle high I come with,

*S*a' alíli *s*ĭ*d*eyáïye, aní*h*oyele anieyáhi ainé.
For me an implement I come with, to you dreadful (no meaning).
of the rites

II.

Ka̜*t* *T*o'badzĭsts*í*ni *s*ĭ*d*eyáïye,
Now Child of the Water I come with,

Pe*s* *d*olgási [264] be*h*ogán*d*e *s*ĭ*d*eyáïe,
Knives serrate from house made of I come with,

Pe*s* *d*olgási *d*a'honí*d*e *s*ĭ*d*eyáïye,
Knives serrate from where they dangle high I come with,

*S*a' alíli *s*ĭ*d*eyáïye, aní*d*ĭgĭnle aineyáhi ainé.
For me an implement I come with, to you sacred (no meaning).
of the rites (divine, holy)

III.

Ka̜*t* *L*éyaneyani *s*ĭ*d*eyáïye,
Now Reared Beneath the Earth, I come with,

Pe*s* al*th*asaí be*h*ogán*d*e *s*ĭ*d*eyáïye,
Knives of all kinds from house made of I come with,

Pe*s* al*th*asaí *d*a'honí*d*e *s*ĭ*d*eyáïye,
Knives of all kinds from where they dangle high I come with,

*S*a' alíli *s*ĭ*d*eyáïye, aní*h*oyéle, aineyáhi ainé.
For me an implement I come with, to you dreadful, (no meaning).
of the rites

IV.

Ka̜*t* Tsówenatlehi *s*ĭ*d*eyáïye,
Now Changing Grandchild I come with,

Pe*s* *l*ĭtsói be*h*ogán*d*e *s*ĭ*d*eyáïye,
Knives yellow from house made of I come with,

Pe*s* *l*ĭtsói *d*a'honí*d*e *s*ĭ*d*eyáïye,
Knives yellow from where they dangle high I come with,

*S*a' alíli *s*ĭ*d*eyáïye, aní*d*ĭgĭnle aineyáhi ainé.
For me an implement I come with, to you sacred (no meaning.)
of the rites

Alíl or alíli means a show, dance, or other single exhibition of the rites (see fig. 30). It also means a wand or other sacred implement used in the rites. It is thought that the colored hoops for raising a storm, described in par. 355, are the alíli referred to in this song.

282. SONG OF THE SUN.

I.

Sïní‘ eé deyá aá, deyá aá,
My mind approaches, approaches,

Tsínhanoai eé deyá aá,
The Sun God approaches,

Ni‘nïnéla‘ eé deyá aá,
Border of the Earth approaches,

Estsánatlesi bigáni yúnidze deyá aá,
Estsánatlehi her house toward the hearth approaches,

Sána nagái eé deyá aá,
In old age walking approaches,

Bïké hozóni eé deyá aá.
His trail beautiful approaches.

Sïní‘ eé deyá aá, deyá aá.
My mind approaches, approaches.

II.

Sïní‘ eé deyá aá, deyá aá,
My mind approaches, approaches,

Kléhanoai eé deyá aá,
The Moon God approaches,

Ni‘nïnéla‘ eé deyá aá,
Border of the Earth approaches,

Yolkaí Estsán bigáni yúnidze deyá aá,
Yolkaí Estsán her house toward the hearth approaches,

Sána nagái eé deyá aá,
In old age walking approaches,

Bïké hozóni eé deyá aá.
His trail beautiful approaches.

Sïní‘ eé deyá aá deyá aá.
My mind approaches, approaches.

Yúni, here translated hearth, is a certain part of the floor of the Navaho lodge. Yúnidze means in the direction of the yúni.

The expressions Sána nagái and Bïké hozóni appear in many songs and prayers, and are always thus united. Their literal translation is as given above; but they are equivalent to saying, " Long life and happiness; " as part of a prayer, they are a supplication for a long and happy life. Hozóni means, primarily, terrestrially beautiful; but it means also happy, happily, or, in a certain sense, good.

Estsánatlehi is often called, in song, Estsánatlesi, and Tsóhanoai is often called (apparently with greater propriety) Tsínhanoai. Sïní‘=Sï'ni.

The syllables not translated are meaningless.

283. SIGNIFICANT WORDS OF SONGS OF THE LOG, FIRST SET.

First Song : — Tsïn nïzóni sa‘ nil'nitha.
(log, stick) Tree beautiful for me they fell.

Second Song : — Tsĭn nĭzóni sa'   haídile.
Tree beautiful for me   they prepare or trim.

Third Song : — Tsĭn nĭzóni sa'   haiyĭdíla'.
Tree beautiful for me they have prepared.

Fourth Song : — Tsĭn nĭzóni sĭlá' yidĭtí'yi'.
Tree beautiful with me they carry.

Fifth Song : — Tsĭn nĭzóni sĭlá' tháiyiyitin.
Tree beautiful with me they put in the water.

The word for beautiful is usually pronounced ĭnzóni, not nĭzóni as above.

284. SIGNIFICANT WORDS OF SONGS OF THE LOG, SECOND SET.

First Song : — Tsĭn nĭzóni sĭlá' neyĭlgó'.
Tree beautiful with me they push.

Second Song : — Tsĭn nĭzóni sĭlá' yidisél.
Tree beautiful with me   floats.

Third Song : — Tsĭn nĭzóni sĭlá' yiyilól.
Tree beautiful with me moves floating.

285. WORDS OF THE EAGLE.

Aḥaláni siáz! E'yéhe siáz ! Nĭtsĭ'li ta toadainĭnĭ'lda, Donikí.
Greeting, my child!   Thanks, my child! Your younger down you did not throw,   Donikí.
brother

286. SONG OF THE EAGLES. — A SONG OF THE BEAD CHANT.

I.

Aóoóo aiá-hená an an anaié anaié.
(Meaningless prelude.)

Kinnakíye yéye saaíyista an an,
Kinnakíye   there he sits,

Hayáaaá   yéye saaíyista an an,
When he rises,   there he sits,

Yiltsá   aá yéye saaíyista an an,
We shall see,   there he sits,

Talpíl   aá yéye saaíyista an an.
He will flap,   there he sits.

Aiadoséye aiadoséye an an an oḥaneyé.
(Meaningless refrain.)

Kinnakíye = Kinníki.   The vocables not translated have no meaning now.

287. SONG OF THE ASCENSION.

I.

Aió éo éo éo he, éo óo éo éo he.
(Meaningless prelude.)

1. Tsĭ'natan alkaí eé eé,
Plant of corn white,

2. Bidági   tso ínyan eé.
Its ear sticks great to eat.
up in

3. Nan*t*á a*n*á*n* to*s*é to*s*é.
Stay down.
To*s*é eyé eyé.

II.

(Repeat prelude as in stanza I.)

1. T*s*ï′na*tan* *d*otl′ï′*z* eé eé,
Plant of corn   blue,
2. Bidági   tso í*n*ya*n* eé.
Its ear sticks great to eat.
up in
3. Nan*t*á a*n*á*n* to*s*é to*s*é.
Stay down.

(Repeat refrain as in stanza I.)

III.

(Repeat prelude.)

1. T*s*ï′na*tan* a*l*tsói eé eé,
Plant of corn yellow,
2. Bidági   tso í*n*ya*n* eé.
Its ear sticks great to eat.
up in
3. Nan*t*á a*n*á*n* to*s*é to*s*é.
Stay down.

(Repeat refrain.)

IV.

(Repeat prelude.)

1. T*s*ï′na*t*aa *z*ï′ni eé eé,
Plant of corn black,
2. Bidági   tso í*n*ya*n* eé.
Its ear sticks great to eat.
up in
3. Nan*t*á a*n*á*n* to*s*é to*s*é.
Stay down.

(Repeat refrain.)

V.

(Repeat prelude.)

1. T*s*ï′na*t*   al*th*asaí eé eé,
Plant of corn all kinds
or colors,
2. Bidági   tso í*n*ya*n* eé.
Its ear sticks great to eat.
up in
3. Nan*t*á a*n*á*n* to*s*é to*s*é.
Stay down.

(Repeat refrain.)

VI.

(Repeat prelude.)

1. T*s*ï′na*tan* *d*ïtsól eé eé,
Plant of corn   round
(nubbin),

2. Bidági   tso *irvan* eé.
Its ear sticks gr.nt tc eat.
up in

3. Nan*t*á a*n*án to*s*é to*s*é.
Stay down.

(Repeat refrain.

Great changes are made in some of the words in this song for prosodic reasons.
T*s*ĭ'na*t*an, t*s*ĭ'na*t*aa, and t*s*ĭ'na*t* (1st lines) are all from t*s*ĭ*l* (plant) and na*t*án (corn),
Bi*d*ági (2d lines) is from bidí (its ear), iá' (it sticks up), and gi (in). A*l*kaí (line 1,
stanza I.) = *l*akaí. A*l*tsói (line 1, stanza III.) = *l*ĭtsói.

288. PRAYER OF FIRST DANCERS FROM THE CEREMONY OF THE NIGHT CHANT.

1. Tse'gíhigi,
Tse'gíhi in

2. *H*ayo*l* ká*l*   be*h*ogángi,
Dawn   made of house in,

3. Na*h*otsói   be*h*ogángi,
Evening twilight made of house in,

4. Kós*d*ĭ/yĭ*l*   be*h*ogángi,
Cloud dark   made of house in,

5. Nĭltsabaká   be*h*ogángi,
Rain male   made of house in,

6. Á'*d*ĭ/yĭ*l*   be*h*ogángi,
Mist dark   made of house in,

7. Nĭltsabaád   be*h*ogángi,
Rain female   made of house in,

8. *Th*ad'itín   be*h*ogángi,
Pollen   made of house in,

9. Anĭl*t*áni   be*h*ogángi,
Grasshoppers made of house in,

10. Á'*d*ĭ/yĭ*l* *d*ad'ĭnlági,
Mist dark   at the door,

11. Natsílĭ*t*   bĭkedzé*t*in,
Rainbow   his trail the road,

12. Atsĭniklĭ'*s*i   yíki *d*asizíni,
Zigzag lightning on it high stands,

13. Nĭltsabaká yíki *d*asizíni,
Rain male   on it high stands,

14. *H*ast*s*ébaka,
Deity male,

15. Kós*d*ĭ/yĭ*l*   nĭkégo   na*h*aíniya'.
Cloud dark   your moccasins come to us.

16. Kós*d*ĭ/yĭ*l* nĭsklégo na*h*aíniya'.
Cloud dark   your leggings come to us.

17. Kós*d*ĭ/yĭ*l* niégo   na*h*aíniya'.
Cloud dark   your shirt   come to us.

18. Kós*d*ĭ/yĭ*l* nĭtságo   na*h*aíniya'.
Cloud dark   your headdress come to us.

19. Kós*d*ĭ/yĭ*l* bininĭnlágo na*h*aíniya'.
Cloud dark   your mind en- come to us.
veloping

20. Nĭkĭ'd*z*e i*d*ní'*d*ĭ/yĭ*l* *d*ahi*t*ágo na*h*aíniya'.
You above thunder dark high flying come to us.

21. Kosistsín   bikégo *d*ahi*r*ago na*h*aíniya'.
Cloud having a shape   at feet   high flying   come to us.

22. Íntseká*d*o   kós*d*í/yí*l* beat*s*a*d*asyélgo *d*ahi*t*ágo na*h*aíniya'.
Your head over   cloud dark   made of far darkness   high flying   come to us.

23. Íntseká*d*o   ní*l*tsabaká beat*s*a*d*asyélgo *d*ahi*t*ago na*h*aíniya'.
Your head over   rain male   made of far darkness   high flying   come to us.

24. Íntseká*d*o   á'*d*í/yí*l* beat*s*a*d*asyélgo *d*ahi*t*ago na*h*aíniya'.
Your head over   mist dark   made of far darkness   high flying   come to us.

25. Íntseká*d*o   ní*l*tsabaád beat*s*a*d*asyélgo *d*ahi*t*ágo nahaíniya'.
Your head over   rain female   made of far darkness   high flying   come to us.

26. Íntseká*d*o   atsïniklï'*s*i *h*a*d*a*h*atï'lgo *d*ahi*t*ago na*h*aíniya'.
Your head over   zigzag lightning   high out flung   high flying   come to us.

27. Íntseká*d*o   natsílï*t* a*d*ahazlágo *d*ahi*t*ágo na*h*aíniya'.
Your head over   rainbow   high hanging   high flying   come to us.

28. Nï*t*a'la*th*á'*d*o   kós*d*í/yí*l* beat*s*adasyélgo *d*ahi*t*ágo na*h*aíniya'.
Your wings on ends of   cloud dark   made of far darkness   high flying   come to us.

29. Nï*t*a'la*th*á'*d*o   ní*l*tsabaká beat*s*a*d*asyélgo *d*ahi*t*ágo na*h*aíniya'.
Your wings on ends of   rain male   made of far darkness   high flying   come to us.

30. Nï*t*a'la*th*á'*d*o   á'*d* í/yí*l* beat*s*a*d*asyélgo *d*ahi*t*ágo na*h*aíniya'.
Your wings on ends of   mist dark   made of far darkness   high flying   come to us.

31. Nï*t*a'la*th*á'*d*o   ní*l*tsabaád beat*s*a*d*asyélgo *d*ahi*t*ágo na*h*aíniya'.
Your wings on ends of   rain female   made of far darkness   high flying   come to us.

32. Nï*t*a'la*th*á'*d*o   atsïniklï'*s*i *h*a*d*a*h*atï'lgo *d*ahi*t*ágo na*h*aíniya'.
Your wings on ends of   zigzag lightning   high out flung   high flying   come to us.

33. Nï*t*a'la*th*á'*d*o   natsílï*t* a*d*ahazlágo *d*ahi*t*ágo na*h*aíniya'.
Your wings on ends of   rainbow   high hanging   high flying   come to us.

34. Kós*d*í/yí*l*, ní*l*tsabaká, á'*d*í/yí*l*, ní*l*tsabaád   bi*l* benatsi*d*asyélgo na*h*aíniya'.
Cloud dark,   rain male,   mist dark,   rain female   with it made of near darkness   come to us.

35. Ni'gi*d*asyél   na*h*aíniya'.
On the earth darkness   come to us.

36. Aíbe   na*t*átso nï*t*a*d*eé*l* biági tálawu*s* yi*l*to'lín   e*s*ï'nosïn.
With the same great corn   floating over   at bottom   foam   with water flowing   that I wish.

37. Nigél   i*s*lá'.
Your sacrifice I have made.

38. Na*d*é   hilá'.
For you smoke I have prepared.

39. *S*ïké   saá*d* ïtli*l*.
My feet for me restore (as they were).

40. *S*ïtsá*t* saá*d* ïtli*l*.
My legs for me restore.

41. *S*ïtsís saá*d* ïtli*l*.
My body for me restore.

42. *S*ï'ni   saá*d* ïtli*l*.
My mind for me restore.

43. *S*ïné   saá*d* ïtli*l*.
My voice for me restore.

44. Á*d* ïstsi*n*   nalíl   saá*d* i*l*e*l*.
This day   your spell for me take out.

45. Á*d* ïstsi*n*   nalíl   *s*aanï'nla'.
This day   your spell for me remove (take away).

46. *S*ïtsád*z*e   *t*ahï'*n*d* ïnla'.
Away from me you have taken it.

47. Nïzágo   sïtsa'   nénla'.
Far off   from me it is taken.

48. Nïzágo   nastlí*n*.
Far off   you have done it.

49. *Hozógo*   na*ded*estál.
Happily (in a   I recover.
way of beauty)

50. *Hozógo*   *sï*táha*d*ïnokél.
Happily   my interior becomes cool.

51. *Hozógo*   *sï*ná   naho*d*otlél.
Happily   my eyes, I regain (the power of).

52. *Hozógo*   *sï*tsé   *d*ïnokél.
Happily   my head becomes cool.

53. *Hozógo*   *sï*ts*át*   naho*d*otlél.
Happily   my limbs   I regain.

54. *Hozógo*   na*ded*ĕstsíl.
Happily   again I hear.

55. *Hozógo*   sáha*dad*oltó‘.
Happily   for me it is taken off.

56. *Hozógo*   na*sád*o.
Happily   I walk.

57. *Toso*ho*dod*elnígo   na*sád*o.
Impervious to pain   I walk.

58. *Sï*táhago sólago   na*sád*o.
My interior   light   I walk.

59. *S*aná‘   nï*slí*ngo   na*sád*o.
My feelings   lively   I walk.

60. *Hozógo*   kós*d*ïlyïl   *s*enahotlé*d*o.
Happily (in   clouds dark I desire (in abundance).
terrestrial beauty)

61. *Hozógo*   á‘*d*ïlyïl   *s*enahotlé*d*o.
Happily   mists dark   I desire.

62. *Hozógo*   *sed*aahuiltyído   *s*enahotlé*d*o.
Happily   passing showers   I desire.

63. *Hozógo*   nanisé   *s*enahotlé*d*o.
Happily   plants of all kinds   I desire.

64. *Hozógo*   *th*a*d*itín   *s*enahotlé*d*o.
Happily   pollen   I desire.

65. *Hozógo*   *d*a*t*ó‘   *s*enahotlé*d*o.
Happily   dew   I desire.

66. *Hozógo*   na*tál*kai   ya*s*óni   ni‘*d*ahazlágo   ni‘yilokaí.
Happily   corn white good beautiful to the end of the earth may (it) come with you.

67. *Hozógo*   na*tál*tsoi   ya*s*óni   ni‘*d*ahazlágo   ni‘yilokaí.
Happily   corn yellow good beautiful to the end of the earth may come with you.

68. *Hozógo*   na*tad*o*t*lï‘zi   ya*s*óni   ni‘*d*ahazlágo   ni‘yilokaí.
Happily   corn blue   good beautiful to the end of the earth may come with you.

69. *Hozógo*   na*t*aal*th*asaí   ya*s*óni   ni‘*d*ahazlágo   ni‘yilokaí.
Happily   corn of all kinds good beautiful to the end of the earth may come with you.

70. *Hozógo*   nanisé   ya*s*óni   ni‘*d*ahazlágo   ni‘yilokaí.
Happily   plants of all kinds good beautiful to the end of the earth may come with you.

71. *Hozógo*   yú*d*i   al*th*asaí   ya*s*óni   ni‘*d*ahazlágo   ni‘yilokaí.
Happily   goods of all kinds good beautiful to the end of the earth may come with you.

72. *Hozógo*   ïnklï‘z   al*th*asaí   ya*s*óni   ni‘*d*ahazlágo   ni‘yilokaí.
Happily   jewels of all kinds good beautiful to the end of the earth may come with you.

73. *Tí*be   ni‘yitsï‘*d*e   *h*ozógo   ni‘yilokaí.
With these before you   happily may come with you.

74. *Tí*be   ni‘yiké*d*e   *h*ozógo   ni‘yilokaí.
With these behind you   happily may come with you.

75. *Tí*be   ni‘yiyági   *h*ozógo   ni‘yilokaí.
With these below you   happily may come with you.

76. *T*íbe   ni'yikígi *h*oz*ó*go   ni'yilokaí.
With these above you   happily   may come with you.

77. *T*íbe   ni'yinagi*d*áltso *h*oz*ó*go   ni'yilokaí.
With these   all around you   happily   may come with you.

78. *T*ibikégo *h*oz*ó*go   naho*d*ol*á*l.
In this way   happily   you accomplish your tasks.

79. *H*oz*ó*go na*s*túwi*n* *t*a'n*ï*shyí*t*ïnoli*l*.
Happily   old men   they will look at you.

80. *H*oz*ó*go   sáni   *t*a'n*ï*shyí*t*ïnoli*l*.
Happily   old women they will look at you.

81. *H*oz*ó*go tsïlké   *t*a'n*ï*shyí*t* ïnoli*l*.
Happily   young men   they will look at you.

82. *H*oz*ó*go   ts*ï*ké   *t*a'n*ï*shyí*t* ïnoli*l*.
Happily   young women they will look at you.

83. *H*oz*ó*go a*s*iké *t*a'n*ï*shyí*t*ïnoli*l*.
Happily   boys   they will look at you.

84. *H*oz*ó*go a*t*é*t*e *t*a'n*ï*shyí*t*ïnoli*l*.
Happily   girls   they will look at you.

85. *H*oz*ó*go alt*s*íni *t*a'n*ï*shyí*t* ïnoli*l*.
Happily   children they will look at you.

86. *H*oz*ó*go ïntani*t*aí' *t*a'n*ï*shyí*t* ïnoli*l*.
Happily   chiefs   they will look at you.

87. *H*oz*ó*go   *t*ai*d*ol*t*á'   *t*a'n*ï*shyí*t*ïnoli*l*.
Happily   scattering in different   they will look at you.
directions

88. *H*oz*ó*go ni*t*ail*t*é   *t*a'n*ï*shyí*t*ïnoli*l*.
Happily   getting home   they will look at you.

89. *H*oz*ó*go *t*ha*d*it*í*n*k*e e*t*íngo ni*t*ail*t*é*d*e.
Happily   pollen trail   on road   they get home.

90. *H*oz*ó*go nin*á**d*ahidoka.
Happily   may they all get back.

91. *H*oz*ó*go   na*s*á*d*o.
Happily (or in beauty)   I walk.

92. *S*íts*ï*'d*z*e   *h*oz*ó*go na*s*á*d*o.
Me before toward happily   I walk.

93. *S*ïké*d*e   *h*oz*ó*go na*s*á*d*o.
Me behind from   happily   I walk.

94. *S*iyági   *h*oz*ó*go na*s*á*d*o.
Me below in   happily   I walk.

95. *S*ïk*ï*'d*z*e   *h*oz*ó*go na*s*á*d*o.
Me above toward happily   I walk.

96. *S*ïná   *d*áltso *h*oz*ó*go na*s*á*d*o.
Me around   all   happily   I walk.

97. *H*oz*ó*na   *h*astlé,
In happiness (or   it is finished (or done),
beauty) again

98. *H*oz*ó*na   *h*astlé,
In beauty again it is finished,

99. *H*oz*ó*na   *h*astlé,
In beauty again it is finished,

100. *H*oz*ó*na   *h*astlé.
In beauty again   it is finished.

1. In Tsegíhi (oh you who dwell!)
2. In the house made of the dawn,
3. In the house made of the evening twilight,
4. In the house made of the dark cloud,
5. In the house made of the he-rain,
6. In the house made of the dark mist,
7. In the house made of the she-rain,
8. In the house made of pollen,
9. In the house made of grasshoppers,
10. Where the dark mist curtains the doorway,
11. The path to which is on the rainbow,
12. Where the zigzag lightning stands high on top,
13. Where the he-rain stands high on top,
14. Oh, male divinity!
15. With your moccasins of dark cloud, come to us.
16. With your leggings of dark cloud, come to us.
17. With your shirt of dark cloud, come to us.
18. With your headdress of dark cloud, come to us.
19. With your mind enveloped in dark cloud, come to us.
20. With the dark thunder above you, come to us soaring.
21. With the shapen cloud at your feet, come to us soaring.
22. With the far darkness made of the dark cloud over your head, come to us soaring.
23. With the far darkness made of the he-rain over your head, come to us soaring.
24. With the far darkness made of the dark mist over your head, come to us soaring.
25. With the far darkness made of the she-rain over your head, come to us soaring.
26. With the zigzag lightning flung out on high over your head, come to us soaring.
27. With the rainbow hanging high over your head, come to us soaring.
28. With the far darkness made of the dark cloud on the ends of your wings, come to us soaring.
29. With the far darkness made of the he-rain on the ends of your wings, come to us soaring.
30. With the far darkness made of the dark mist on the ends of your wings, come to us soaring.
31. With the far darkness made of the she-rain on the ends of your wings, come to us soaring.
32. With the zigzag lightning flung out on high on the ends of your wings, come to us soaring.
33. With the rainbow hanging high on the ends of your wings, come to us soaring.
34. With the near darkness made of the dark cloud, of the he-rain, of the dark mist, and of the she-rain, come to us.
35. With the darkness on the earth, come to us.
36. With these I wish the foam floating on the flowing water over the roots of the great corn.
37. I have made your sacrifice.
38. I have prepared a smoke for you.

39. My feet restore for me.
40. My limbs restore for me.
41. My body restore for me.
42. My mind restore for me.
43. My voice restore for me.
44. To-day, take out your spell for me.
45. To-day, take away your spell for me.
46. Away from me you have taken it.
47. Far off from me it is taken.
48. Far off you have done it.
49. Happily I recover.
50. Happily my interior becomes cool.
51. Happily my eyes regain their power.
52. Happily my head becomes cool.
53. Happily my limbs regain their power.
54. Happily I hear again.
55. Happily for me (the spell) is taken off.
56. Happily I walk.
57. Impervious to pain, I walk.
58. Feeling light within, I walk.
59. With lively feelings, I walk.
60. Happily (or in beauty) abundant dark clouds I desire.
61. Happily abundant dark mists I desire.
62. Happily abundant passing showers I desire.
63. Happily an abundance of vegetation I desire.
64. Happily an abundance of pollen I desire.
65. Happily abundant dew I desire.
66. Happily may fair white corn, to the ends of the earth, come with you.
67. Happily may fair yellow corn, to the ends of the earth, come with you.
68. Happily may fair blue corn, to the ends of the earth, come with you.
69. Happily may fair corn of all kinds, to the ends of the earth, come with you.
70. Happily may fair plants of all kinds, to the ends of the earth, come with you.
71. Happily may fair goods of all kinds, to the ends of the earth, come with you.
72. Happily may fair jewels of all kinds, to the ends of the earth, come with you.
73. With these before you, happily may they come with you.
74. With these behind you, happily may they come with you.
75. With these below you, happily may they come with you.
76. With these above you, happily may they come with you.
77. With these all around you, happily may they come with you.
78. Thus happily you accomplish your tasks.
79. Happily the old men will regard you.
80. Happily the old women will regard you.
81. Happily the young men will regard you.
82. Happily the young women will regard you.
83. Happily the boys will regard you.
84. Happily the girls will regard you.
85. Happily the children will regard you.
86. Happily the chiefs will regard you.
87. Happily, as they scatter in different directions, they will regard you.

88. Happily, as they approach their homes, they will regard you.
89. Happily may their roads home be on the trail of pollen (peace).
90. Happily may they all get back.
91. In beauty (happily) I walk.
92. With beauty before me, I walk.
93. With beauty behind me, I walk.
94. With beauty below me, I walk.
95. With beauty above me, I walk.
96. With beauty all around me, I walk.
97. It is finished (again) in beauty,
98. It is finished in beauty,
99. It is finished in beauty,
100. It is finished in beauty.

REMARKS ON THE PRAYER.

This prayer is addressed to a mythic thunder-bird, hence the reference to wings; but the bird is spoken of as a male divinity, and is supposed to dwell with other yéi at Tse‘gíhi. The prayer is said at the beginning of work, on the last night of the klédżi *hatál*. The shaman speaks it, verse by verse, as it is here recorded, and one of the atsá‘*l*ei or first dancers, repeats it, verse by verse, after him.

The word *hozó* means, primarily, terrestrial beauty. Its derivative *hozógo* means in a beautiful earthly manner. *Hozóni* means beautiful on the earth, locally beautiful (*I*nzóni refers to the beauty of objects and persons); *Hozóna* signifies *again* beautiful. But the meanings of these words, and others of similar derivation, have been extended to mean happy, happiness, in a happy or joyful manner, etc. In a free translation they must be rendered by various English words.

The four final verses have been previously recorded by the author as *hozóni haslé* (Qojòni qaslè), but he now regards the form *hozóna hastlé* as more correct.[289] This expression, repeated twice or four times, according to circumstances, ends all Navaho prayers, yet recorded. It is analogous to the Christian Amen.

289. In a few instances, in this work, a Navaho word may be found spelled or accentuated with slight differences in different places. It must not be inferred from this that one form is correct and the other not. As usage varies in the languages of the most cultured races, so does it vary (only in greater degree) in the languages of the unlettered. A word was often heard differently pronounced and was therefore differently recorded by the author. An effort has been made to decide on a single standard of form and always to give preference to this; but, in a few cases, variations may have been overlooked. Words sometimes undergo great changes when they become parts of compound words. Where the form of a word in this work varies from that presented in previous works by the author the variation may be accounted for, in some cases by the difference in the alphabets used, and in others by the changes of opinion which have come to him in time, as the result of a more extended experience or a more advanced study of the language.

290. Note 290 is omitted.

BIBLIOGRAPHIC NOTES.

BY FREDERICK WEBB HODGE.

For the convenience of the reader, a list of the principal works referred to in this book, and of all papers on the subject of the Navahoes written by the author, is here given.

291.

BACKUS, E. An account of the Navajoes of New Mexico. (In Schoolcraft, Information respecting the history, condition and prospects of the Indian tribes of the United States, part IV. pp. 209–215, Philadelphia, 1854.)

292.

BANCROFT, HUBERT HOWE. The native races of the Pacific states of North America, vol. III., New York, 1875.

293.

BICKFORD, F. T. Prehistoric cave-dwellings. (In Century Illustrated Monthly Magazine, New York, vol. XL. No. 6, pp. 896–911, October, 1890.)

294.

BOURKE, JOHN GREGORY. Snake Dance of the Moquis of Arizona, New York, 1884.

295.

—— The Medicine-men of the Apache. (In ninth annual report of the Bureau of Ethnology, pp. 443–595, Washington, 1892.)

296.

CATLIN, GEORGE. Letters and notes on the manners, customs, and condition of the North American Indians, etc., two vols., London, 1841.

297.

CENSUS. Report on Indians taxed and Indians not taxed in the United States (except Alaska) at the eleventh census : 1890, Washington, 1894.

298.

COMMISSIONER OF INDIAN AFFAIRS. Report of, to the Secretary of the Interior,

for the year 1867, Washington, 1868. The same for 1870, Washington, 1870.

299.

DUTTON, CLARENCE E. Mount Taylor and the Zuñi plateau. (In sixth annual report of the U. S. Geological Survey, pp. 105–198, Washington, 1886.)

300.

EATON, J. H. Description of the true state and character of the New Mexican tribes. (In Schoolcraft, Indian Tribes, part IV. pp. 216–221, Philadelphia, 1854.)

301.

HODGE, FREDERICK WEBB. The early Navajo and Apache. (In American Anthropologist, vol. VIII. No. 3, pp. 223–240, Washington, July, 1895.)

302.

HOUGH, WALTER. Fire-making apparatus in the United States National Museum. (In report of National Museum 1887–88. pp. 531–587, Washington, 1890.)

303.

LETHERMAN, JONA. Sketch of the Navajo tribe of Indians, territory of New Mexico. (In Smithsonian report for 1855, pp. 283–297, Washington, 1856.)

304.

MASON, OTIS TUFTON. Cradles of the American Aborigines. (In report of National Museum 1886–87, pp. 161–235, Washington, 1889.)

305.

MATTHEWS, WASHINGTON. Ethnography and philology of the Hidatsa Indians. (Department of the Interior, United

States Geological and Geographical Survey, miscellaneous publications No. 7, Washington, 1877.)

306.

—— A part of the Navajo's mythology. (In American Antiquarian, vol. v. No. 3, pp. 207–224, Chicago, April, 1883.)

307.

—— Navajo Silversmiths. (In second annual report of the Bureau of Ethnology, pp. 169–178, Washington, 1883.)

308.

—— A night with the Navajos. By Zay Elini. (In Forest and Stream, vol. XXIII. pp. 282–283, New York, Nov. 6, 1884.)

309.

—— Navajo weavers. (In third annual report of the Bureau of Ethnology, pp. 371–391, Washington, 1884.)

310.

—— The origin of the Utes. A Navajo myth. (In American Antiquarian, vol. VII. No. 5, pp. 271–274, Chicago, September, 1885.)

311.

—— Mythic dry-paintings of the Navajos. (In American Naturalist, vol. XIX. No. 10, pp. 931–939, Philadelphia, October, 1885.)

312.

—— Navajo names for plants. (In American Naturalist, vol. XX. pp. 767–777, Philadelphia, September, 1886.)

313.

—— Some deities and demons of the Navajos. (In American Naturalist, vol. XX. pp. 841–850, Philadelphia, October, 1886.)

314.

—— The mountain chant : a Navajo ceremony. (In fifth annual report of the Bureau of Ethnology, pp. 379–467, Washington, 1887.)

315.

—— The prayer of a Navajo shaman. (In American Anthropologist, vol. I. No. 2, pp. 149–170, Washington, April, 1888.)

316.

—— Navajo gambling songs. (In American Anthropologist, vol. II. No. 1, pp. 1–19, Washington, January, 1889.)

317.

—— Noqoïlpi, the gambler : a Navajo myth. (In Journal of American Folk-Lore, vol. II. No. ii. pp. 89–94, Boston and New York, April–June, 1889.)

318.

—— The gentile system of the Navajo Indians. (In Journal of American Folk-Lore, vol. III. No. ix. pp. 89–110, Boston and New York, April–June, 1890.)

319.

—— A study in butts and tips. (In American Anthropologist, vol. v. No. 4, pp. 345–350, Washington, October, 1892.)

320.

—— Some illustrations of the connection between myth and ceremony. (In Memoirs of the International Congress of Anthropology, pp. 246–251, Chicago, 1894.)

321.

—— The basket drum. (In American Anthropologist, vol. VII. No. 2, pp. 202–208, Washington, April, 1894.)

322.

—— Songs of sequence of the Navajos. (In Journal of American Folk-Lore, vol. VII. No. xxvi. pp. 185–194, Boston and New York, July–September, 1894.)

323.

—— A vigil of the gods — a Navajo ceremony. (In American Anthropologist, vol. IX. No. 2, pp. 50–57, Washington, February, 1896.)

324.

MINDELEFF, VICTOR. A study of pueblo architecture : Tusayan and Cibola. (In eighth annual report of the Bureau of Ethnology, pp. 3–228, Washington, 1891.)

325.

MORGAN, LEWIS HENRY. Ancient Society or researches in the lines of human progress from savagery, through barbarism to civilization, New York, 1877.

326.

POWERS, STEPHEN. Tribes of California. (Contributions to North American Ethnology, vol. III., Washington, 1877.)

327.
SCHOOLCRAFT, HENRY ROWE. Information respecting the history, condition and prospects of the Indian tribes of the United States, part IV. Philadelphia, 1854.

328.
SIMPSON, JAMES H. Report of an expedition into the Navajo country in 1849. (In senate ex. doc. 64, 31st cong., 1st sess.. Washington, 1850.)

329.
STEPHEN, A. M. The Navajo. (In American Anthropologist, vol. VI. No. 4, pp. 345–362, Washington, October, 1893.)

MELODIES[1]

Recorded on the phonograph by WASHINGTON MATTHEWS, *and noted from the cylinders by* JOHN C. FILLMORE.

[1] See Note 272.

No. 1.

SONG OF THE APPROACH OF THE WAR GODS.

No. 2.

SONG OF THE WAR GODS.

Melodies.

No. 3.

TWELFTH YIKAÍGĬN OR DAYLIGHT SONG.

No. 4.

A SONG OF THE NAAKHAÍ,

OR DANCE OF THE LAST NIGHT OF THE NIGHT CHANT.

he   e *hoch!*   he   e *hoch!*   he   e *hoch!*

he   e, he   e *hoch!*

Melodies.

No. 5.

A SONG OF THE NAAKHAÍ.

Composed by THOMAS TORLINO.

No. 6.

SEVENTH SONG IN THE FARM OF *HASTSÉHOGAN.*

Melodies.

No. 7.

TENTH AND ELEVENTH SONGS IN THE FARM OF
HASTSÉHOGAN.

I.

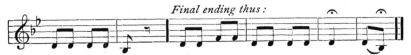

No. 8.

FIFTEENTH SONG IN THE FARM OF *HASTSÉHOGAN.*

This song offers some very curious metrical problems.

No. 9.

TWENTY-SECOND SONG IN THE FARM OF *HASTSÉHOGAN.*

Andante.

Slide.

No. 10.

TWENTY-THIRD SONG IN THE FARM OF *HASTSÉHOGAN*.

This Indian howls so that it is much more difficult than usual to be sure of the pitch-relations. Also it is hard to tell, in many places, whether he means a double or a triple rhythm.

Melodies.

No. 11.

TWENTY-FIFTH SONG IN THE FARM OF HAST*SÉHO*GAN.

INDEX.

INDEX.

ABLUTIONS, 69, 73, 83, 212.
Accouchement, 106, 231.
Adultery, 64, 66, 67.
Adultery, punishment for, 143, 144, 240.
Ągá*l*a (district), 154, 157, 242.
A*h*od'ïse*l*i, see Na*t*ïnĕs*t*hani.
Akánïnïli, messenger, 207.
Akï*d*anas*t*áni (sacred mountain), Hosta Butte, N. Mex., 79, 222.
Alphabet, 54.
Alviso, Jesus, 39.
Amarantaceæ, 250.
Amulets, or talismans, 249, 250.
Anáye, alien gods, cannibals, monsters, 37, 81, 91, 123, 126, 212.
Anáye, blood of, produces monsters, 81, 234.
Anáye, born of women, 218.
Anáye, changed to stone, 119.
Anáye, destroyed by storm, 129.
Anáye, outwitted, 92, 119.
Ant Peoples, 53.
Antelope farm, 185, 248.
Antidotes, 192, 193.
Apaches, 18, 32, 145, 146, 156, 157.
Apaches, Jicarilla, 154.
Arabis holböllii, 235.
Archaisms, 25.
Armor, 113, 116, 232, 233, 234.
Arrow-case, ancient, 140, 239.
Arrows, 18, 142, 218.
Arrow-snakes, 200, 250.
Ascension, of Na*t*ïnĕs*t*hani, 194.
Atsá'lei, first dancers, 205, 251.
Ą*s*ihi, Salt People (gens), 30, 158.
Ą*s*ihi Estsán (Salt Woman), 236.
A*t*áhyïtsoi, home of Léyaneyani, 103.
Athapascan, or Dèné, 9, 211.
Atsá (game), 219.
Atsé Estsán (goddess), 126.
Atsósi *h*a*t*á*l*, rite of, 194.
Atsósidze *h*a*t*á*l*, feather ceremony, 53, 194, 250.

Baby-case, 12, 231.
Badger, creation of, 71, 76.
Ball, game of, 86.
Barthelmess, Christian, 258.
Baskets, 18, 19, 178, 210, 211.
Bat, 84, 126.
Bat Woman, 120.
Baths, ceremonial, 184, 204, 211, 212, 226, 227.
Bead chant, see yóidze *h*a*t*á*l*.
Bean, 183.
Bear, sacred animal, 186, 249.

Bear-maiden, 99, 100.
Bear that Pursues (anáye), 124.
Bears, pet names of, 187, 249.
Beaver, 168.
Beetle Peoples, 63.
Beggar, 196.
Begging, 22.
Békot*s*i*d*i, moon-bearer, god of Americans, 86, 226.
Béla*h*a*t*ïni, prophet, 53.
Berdache, see Hermaphrodites.
Bickford, F. T., 195, 223.
Big Snake (pueblo chief), 200.
Bike*h*alzï'n, home of *T*èelgĕt, 117.
Bïnáye Aháni (anáye), 108, 113, 123, 124, 236.
Bird monsters, see Tse'nă'hale.
Bï*t*á*h*ot*s*i, Sunset Peak, 153, 242.
Bï*t*áni, Brow of Mountain People (gens), 30, 242.
Bï*t*á'ni, Folded Arms People (gens), 30, 148, 150, 153, 159, 242.
Bïtsís *D*o*t*lï'z, Blue Body (god), 68, 73, 78.
Bïtsís *L*akaí, White Body (god), 68, 73, 104, 216.
Bïtsís *L*ïtsói, Yellow Body (god), 68.
Bïtsís *L*ïzï'n, Black Body (god), 68.
Blackbird, 79.
Black Mountain, Arizona, see Dsï*l*lïzï'n.
Black Thunder (sun-youth), 111, 232, 233.
Black under the Rock (anáye), 126.
Blankets, 21, 141.
Blankets, sacred, 136.
Blue Fox (pueblo chief), 200.
Blue Fox People, 192.
Blue Heron (chief in first world), 63, 64.
Blue Sky People, 104.
Blue Thunder, 111, 232, 233.
Blue under the Rock (anáye), 126.
Blue Water (lake near *T*ó'*s*ato), 114.
Bluebird, 28, 79.
Blushing, 175.
Borrowing of rites, 41.
Bourke, J. G., 32, 212, 294.
Breath of gods, magical, 129, 228.
Breath or wind, spirit of life, 69, 78.
Bow of Darkness, 86.
Bows, 18, 142.
Bow-symbol, 253.
Boy Who Produces Goods, 79, 222.
Brennan, G. A., 238.
Buckskin, sacred, 46, 69, 214, 220, etc.
Bumblebees, war with eagles, 201–204.
Bundle, magical, 97.
Buteo borealis, 250.

Vision of the war gods, 127.
Vomiting, 227.

Wallascheck, Richard, 255, 257.
Wands, magic, 150–153, 221.
War Gods, see Nayénézgani and *To*ʻbadz̆ïs-tsíni.
War gods, apparitions of, 238.
Water bottle, invention of, 70.
Water, causes conception, 105.
Water, four kinds of, 80, 218, 223.
Water god, burned, 170.
Water god, see Tiéholtsodi.
Water made to spring up, 151.
Water of Old Age, see San Juan River.
Water People, sacred, 169.
Water, sacred, 222.
Water Sprinkler, see *To*ʻnenïli.
Waters, house under the, 73.
Weapons, divine, 113, 132, 233.
Weasels, 74.
Weaving, 19.
Western immigrants, so called, see *Diné*ʻ Na*h*otlóni.
White Corn, symbolism of, 217.
White Corn Boy, 79, 105.
White House, home of yéi, Chelly Canyon, 36, 251.
White Mountain Thunder (god), 64.
White people (not Caucasians), 249.
White shell beads, 163.
White Shell Woman, see Yo*l*kaí Estsán.
White under the Rock (anáye), 126.
Whirlwinds, 101, 202, 251.
Wind, gives life, 69.
Wind, see Nïl'tsi.
Wind, trail of, on finger-tips, 69.
Wind People, 177, 179, 184.
Winds, four, 165, 166, 219.
Witchcraft and witches, 40, 70, 187, 220, 249.
Witches, chieftainess of, see Estsán Natán.

Wolf, 77, 87, 200.
Wolf People, 192.
Woman Who Rejuvenates Herself, see Estsánatlehi.
Women, social position of, 10, 240.
Woodpeckers, red-shafted, 245.
Wood-rats, 160–162.
World, edge of, 65, 80, 113.
World, how enlarged, 223.
Worlds, five, 65–76.

Yá*d*ï*l*yï*l*, Sky Father (god), 230.
Ya*z*oni, beautiful, good, 247.
Yébaad, female yéi, 37, 243.
Yébaka, male yéi, 252.
Yébïtsai, maternal grandfather, name of *H*astséyal*t*i, 224.
Yéi, gods, 35–38, 93, 106, 217, 231, 234, 254.
Yéi, in klédz̆i *h*a*t*á*l*, list of, 252.
Yéitso (anáye), 108, 113, 114–116, 231, 234.
Yé*l*apahi (anáye), 91–94, 226.
Yellow Corn Girl, 79, 105, 136.
Yellow Fox People, 192.
Yellow Light People, 104.
Yellow under the Rock (anáye), 126.
Yellow Warbler, 79.
Yói *h*a*t*á*l*, 53, 195, 250.
Yóidz̆e *h*a*t*á*l*, bead chant, 53, 250, 267.
Yo*l*kaí Estsán, White Shell Woman (goddess), 34, 105, 135, 230, 231, etc.
Young Woman Who Rattles, see Tsiké Nazïʼli.
Yucca, 102, 103, 125, 212, 228, 229.
Yucca-fibre, 101.
Yucca People (gens), 30, 140, 239.
Yucca suds, 163, 184, 227.
Yú*d*i (goods), 222.

Zenith and nadir, 216.
Zoölatry, 38.
Zuñi, 2, 10, 22, 36, 145, 158, 242.

A NOTE ON ORTHOGRAPHY

Robert W. Young

The early travelers and military officers who recorded lists of Navajo words in the course of brief contacts were hard put to identify the unaccustomed sounds of the language and to devise an alphabet with which to represent them graphically. The resultant orthographies employed the letters of the English alphabet, with their English sound values, for the transcription of Navajo words—an approach that produced approximations of the type "nah tahnh" for naadą́ą́' (corn), and "ee ee ahngo" for 'i'íí'ą́ago (in the evening). Nor were words elicited through interpreters always accurately translated: English "paddle" emerged as teezh bee hahalkaadí (shovel) in the Eaton word list; and J. H. Beadle's attempt to inquire regarding the Navajo word for God produced "Whaillahay" as the translation he recorded in the account of his visit, in 1871, to the Navajo Country. His language research was concluded before he learned that "Whaillahay" was not the word for the Deity but rather a simple disclaimer—whaillahay is quite obviously hólahéi (damfino—I don't know)!

However, as interest grew in the languages of the Western Tribes scholars recognized the need to identify speech sounds accurately and record them in consistent form. In 1877 John Wesley Powell, the first Director of the Bureau of American Ethnology published his *Introduction to the Study of Indian Languages,* in which this need was stressed. His contemporary, Dr. Washington Matthews, attempted to follow the advice laid down by Powell, and the alphabet employed by Matthews is essentially one proposed by Powell. Matthews's orthography and a sample of text he recorded in the 1880s are reproduced below:

THE ORTHOGRAPHY

The characters used in this work, in spelling Navajo words, are given below, with the value assigned to each character.

Vowels

a has the sound of English a in father.

ă has the sound of English a in hat.

ą has the sound of English a in what.

e has the sound of English e in they. In some connections it varies to the sound of English e in their.

ĕ has the sound of English e in then.

i has the sound of English i in marine.

ĭ has the sound of English i in tin.

o has the sound of English o in bone.

u has the sound of English u in rude.

ai unmarked, or accented on the i (aí), is a diphthong having the sound of English i in bind. When it is accented on the a (ái), or has a diaeresis (aï), it is pronounced as two vowels.

ow has the sound of English ow in how. It is heard mostly in meaningless syllables.

A vowel followed by an inverted comma (') is aspirated, or pronounced with a peculiar force which cannot be well represented by adding the letter h.

Consonants

b has the sound of English b in bat.

d has the sound of English d in day.

d represents a strongly aspirated dental sonant. It is often interchanged with d

g has the sound of English g in go, or, in some connections, the sound of English g in gay.

g has a sound unknown in English. It is the velar g, like the Arabic ghain, or the Dakota g.

h has the sound of English h in hat.

h has the sound of German ch in machen. It is sometimes interchanged with h.

k has usually the sound of English k in koran; but sometimes the sound of English k in king.

l has the sound of English l in lay.

l has a sound unknown in English. It the side rather than with the tip of the with l.

m has the sound of English m in man

n has the sound of English n in name

n has the effect of French n in *bon*. It

s has the sound of English s in sand.

s has the sound of English sh in shad

t has the sound of English t in tan.

t represents a strongly aspirated de with t.

w has the sound of English w in war

y has the sound of English y in yarn

z has the sound of English z in zone

z has the sound of English z in azur

c, f, j, p, q, v, and x are not used. Th represented by ts; that of English j in j

MATTHEWS 1880s	MODERN STANDARD
b/p	b
*ts	ch/chx
*ts	ch'
d/t	d
tl/gl	dl
ds/ts	dz
g	g
*g	gh
*h/*h*/hy	h/x
hw	hw
*dz	j
ʿ	'
k/kh	k
-	kw
k	k'
l	l
*l	ł
m	m
n	n
s	s
z	z
*s	sh
*z	zh
*t/*t*	t
	t'
tl/kl	tł